THE
COMPLEAT
CALHOON

THE COMPLEAT CALHOON

TALES FROM THE TOWER

The Fiction?

WEED, WOMEN AND SONG

The Fact?

FENDER TUCKER

Introduced by Norbert Tudwallow

RAMBLE HOUSE

I remember:

Maxine Tucker
Donald Tucker
Michael Tucker
Geno Jaramillo
Kathy Delaney
David Logan
Bill Smith
Charles Davidson

ISBN 13: 978-1-60543-061-4

ISBN 10: 1-60543-061-7

THE COMPLEAT CALHOON

CONTENTS

TALES FROM THE TOWER

WEED, WOMEN AND SONG

INTRODUCTION

NYELLO.

Norbert Tudwallow here, your curator of affairs at the LOADSTAR Conservatory of the Snooty Arts. I've been privileged to know Fender Tucker for most of his 60 years, following his Huck Finn childhood in the backwoods of New Mexico in the 50s; to his John Lennon adolescence as guitar picker in Colorado; through his Jack Nicholson adulthood as publishing mogul at LOADSTAR in Louisiana, and on to his Timothy Leary old age at Ramble House, as he virtually travels throughout the world spreading his contrarian philosophy to world leaders and back-alley derelicts alike.

Fender was born in 1947, the third of four sons, to Donald and Maxine Tucker of Thibodaux LA. The family moved to Farmington NM in 1950 where young Fender (who was then known as "Tommy") received a liberal education and a conservative number of at least a dozen slaps from the Ursuline nuns who ruled St. Thomas Catholic School with thumbs of iron. He survived eight years of stultifying rote learning from the Baltimore Catechism then managed to endure four more years of Mrs. Grundyism at the local high school. He was only arrested once in his early years, for being drunk and disorderly as he exited the El Vasito Bar after a night of too much champagne. One of his earliest attempts at literature is found as the first story in our collection: *The Mojo Funk Caper.* It was a collaboration written in study hall with his friend, Geno Jaramillo, and inspired by their favorite hard-boiled detective of the time, Richard S. Prather's Shell Scott. Unfortunately, the last half of the story, which describes the Mojo Workout and leads to the violent flashforward that opens the story, is missing. The reader is left hanging at Aunt Jemima's Prophylactic Factory.

Our young author, who had adopted the name "Fender" in the 9th grade because he "had to have something to scratch into the desktops in study hall" made a cursory stab at college in the mid 60s, but mainly he bummed around, dodging the inevitable draft. In March of 1967, he succumbed to his irresistible foe and entered the U.S. Army. Several of his adventures are related in memoirs found in the mostly true second half of this book, *WEED, WOMEN AND SONG,* which ends with the lyrics[1] of the songs he wrote. The first half is some thinly disguised fiction called *TALES FROM THE TOWER.*

Fender resumed playing guitar in sleazy bars as soon as he got out of the Army, spending most of the years 1970-1987 in Durango CO and Las Cruces NM. He managed to lead a lazy, devil-may-care life during these years, making pitiful money and yet at the same time, indulging his every whim. He also managed to get arrested again; this time for growing illegal weeds in his back yard. It was 1971 and he had a beard. That was enough probable cause in those days for a deputy sheriff to be suspicious enough to climb over Fender's fence to "seize 19 marijuana plants, ranging from 1 inch to six inches in height." On the day the major bust was plastered on the front page of the *Farmington Daily Times,* the headline was "NIXON URGES WAR ON DRUGS". Fender was always proud of his being the war's first local casualty and has never ceased gloating over his eventual victory over Tricky Dick, who died in ignominy while Fender has thrived in blissful intoxication, more than a few times figuratively dancing in glee on the former despot's grave.

In 1986 an Albuquerque murder trial was held in the Las Cruces courthouse because of the pre-trial publicity upstate. Fender was on a true crime book kick at the time and thought it would be a great opportunity to see American justice in action and—in keeping with the grandest American traditions—maybe pick up a few bucks by writing the true crime novel of the murder. *LUCKY JOHN* is the result of the month he dedicated to the trial. He pooped out at the article-length stage and never sent it to any publisher. It was such a senseless, sleazy crime he felt bad about reminding people of it, anyway.

Instead, in 1987, as he was tiring of the late nights, sore backs, and dwindling groupies of the country & western music scene, he applied for and got the job of Managing Editor at LOADSTAR, a Commodore computer disk magazine in Shreveport LA.

He had been interested in computers ever since the early 80s, when his brother John pointed out that they were no longer tools

---

[1] All of the 60 or so songs he wrote and recorded are on the CD (in MP3 format) that accompanies this volume. If you didn't get a CD with the book, e-mail fender@ramblehouse.com and ask him for one.

of the corporate gargantua, but actually little puzzle machines. So he had bought a Timex Sinclair 1000, then a VIC-20, and finally a Commodore 64 which occupied most of his time away from the bar. In 1983, inspired by Umberto Eco's medieval mystery, *THE NAME OF THE ROSE*, he programmed a computer adventure game called *MURDER IN THE MONASTERY*. A decade or so later, at LOADSTAR, he novelized the computer game into a long short story, somehow handling the fact that the game had two different solutions—chosen at random by the computer. He entered the story in the LOADSTAR ProseQuest '97 Contest where it abjectly lost, even though he was one of the judges.

The history of LOADSTAR during the Tucker regime is as colorful and purple as his prose, and we all hope that someday someone will chronicle it for posterity.[2] Many of the rest of the stories in this collection come from the halcyon days at the LOADSTAR Tower, the behemoth of a building which casts its ghastly shadow over the pitiful shantytown known as Shreveport. *APPOINTMENT IN SAVANNAH* was also written for a Prose-Quest Contest, and shows just how obsessed he was with his new language, BASIC. He had been dreaming in BASIC ever since the early 80s but it wasn't till the mid 90s that he began to realize how the syntax of BASIC had permeated his thinking and philosophy. All of his thoughts were variants of "IF I do this, THEN this will happen." He figured it was just as logical as whatever other people used for their thought processes.

HE ALSO SERVES was his entry into the ProseQuest '99 Contest and while it appears to be in the same mold as other dystopian novels as Orwell's *1984* and any number of Philip K. Dick books, he insists that the futuristic tale is actually a sustained exercise in wishful thinking. The story cries out for embellishing into a real SF novel but so far he has resisted getting the gumption to do it.

As a contrarian, Fender fought against the proliferation of computers and the ubiquity of the Internet. Fruitlessly, he's quick to add. He has a fear of the chaotic anarchy of the whole concept of "chat rooms" and seldom strays from his web site, the companies that make his books (Create Space, Lightning Source and Lulu),

---

[2] In 2002 Fender collected all 199 issues of LOADSTAR magazine, converted them into .d64 and .d81 files, and placed them on one CD called appropriately, LOADSTAR COMPLEAT. He sells it on eBay and his web site.

Lulu), and eBay where he hawks the Ramble House wares. Perhaps his bias against the idea of real-time communication online is
due to his first experience with it, back in 1989, which he describes in *THE VULVEENA SAGA*. Years later, he's embarrassed
by the way he covertly insulted and baited his friends online by
taking on the persona of the ball-breaking queen of femspite, Vulveena, but back in 1989, in those innocent days, he considered
logging on in disguise as a completely obvious thing to do. He
assumed that everybody logged on as someone else all the time.

In December of 2001, he edited his last issue of LOADSTAR
and with that, his creative juices apparently dried up—for a while.
He became the Grand Exalted Mojo of Ramble House, a minis-
cule publishing house specializing in reprinting the complete
works of Harry Stephen Keeler and other forgotten authors.
Thanks to his pal Jim Weiler's inventing the no-budget publishing
process, he's managed to bring more than 250 titles back into
print, including almost every novel Harry Stephen Keeler ever
wrote. The official beacon for reviving Harry Stephen Keeler, an
excellent group called the HSK Society, publishes a monthly
newsletter called The Keeler News and has an annual "Imitate
Keeler" contest. Fender's 2001 pastiche, *THE MAN WITH THE
PLASTIC SKULL*, and his 2002 entry, *THE ELEVEN AM-
BIGUPHONES OF FARTHALOMEW SPLIB, A STARKEY FISH
STORY* in 2003, as well as 2005's *CATCH-XXII*, continue the
stories in this collection.

Fender once again was slapped senseless by the Muse in mid-
2005 when he decided to write a series of short stories about the
larger-than-life people who pioneered the oil bidness in northwestern New Mexico back in the 50s. He began with three of
them, *JICARILLA MUD, THE GLOWING GREEN GAMBIT* and
ANGELUS OF DOOM, all of which play havoc with our common
understanding of history. The three stories were packaged as *THE
TOTAH TRILOGY* and actually had a small splash at the Farmington Public Library in 2006. There was even a haunting love theme
for each of the stories on an accompanying CD.

In May of 2007 Fender had a heart attack, soon after returning
from an annual trip to Sacramento to visit with his daughter's
family, especially the mighty Kyle, his grandson who is destined
to carry on the contrary genes that run rampant in the Tucker family. While in California he had had a dream about a western setting that had a surprise visit from a very modern-seeming person-

age. Then, as he lay in ICU, connected to noisy machines via tubes and with absolutely nothing to do but think, he worked out the details of the plot and after returning home from the hospital wrote *THE BEST REVENGE.*

A few days later, inspired by his ICU feat, he dashed out *THE MARTINGALE ARMS,* a little gambling story that had been rattling around in his brain ever since he read about the "doubling down" betting strategy.

The penultimate fiction of *THE COMPLEAT CALHOON* is a mini-mystery called *THE NAKED TROCAR* which was inspired by actual homicidal happenings in the Farmington area in the 80s. He had wanted to write about some of his favorite scenic locations like Shiprock, Harper's Hill, Chokecherry Canyon and Fat Man's Misery, and the murder—about which he had some inside information—was too interesting for him to pass up. He couldn't figure out how to involve the Miley Gang in the story so he used a semifictional "Knees Calhoon" as a slugabed detective/guitar picker. So far he's not written or recorded a haunting love theme for the story but the mortuary setting almost begs for one.

But there were still a few choice spots in the Farmington area that Fender wanted to commemorate: the theaters where he worked as marquee changer, and the bars where he learned his musical chops. And he also wanted to immortalize his friendship with Geno Jaramillo. So in early 2008 he rattled off *SIEGE ON MAIN STREET,* which wraps up his Farmington travelogue. Again, he changed a few of the names—to protect the guilty—and left some real names intact. At least the bar scenes are fairly accurate: the bands are real and Joe DiMaggio's brother did have a two-week comic gig at the Office Bar, but it was in 1972, not 1965.

All in all, the town of Farmington was even more fun back then than Fender makes it seem in his "memoir fictions".

The second half of the book comes from his memoirs, *WEED, WOMEN AND SONG.* This is a collection of sexual, military and legal reminiscences that indicate that even though he only spent three years of his life in the army, most of the wild things he did happened during those years. Of course, 1967, 1968 and 1969 were memorable years for everyone at that time.

In addition to the memoirs, the lyrics to each of the 60 or so songs Knees wrote during his musician years (mainly 1970 — 1987) are listed and annotated. A CD of MP3 files of all of the songs—plus a lot more—is included at the end of the book. Have fun listening to the recordings Knees made on his home studio and try not to smile at their abject lack of commercial potential. Nothing shows off Knees' contrarianism more than the cynical lyrics and slightly off-kilter music on the CD. At least, he's willing to be held solely responsible for all of the screeching guitarwork and caterwauling vocals.

Finally, this new collection of the compleat Calhooniana contains another sort of memoir, based on the inscription that Fender's friend Geno Jaramillo wrote in his 1965 high school yearbook. Geno had listed 34 experiences he and Fender had shared between 1957 and 1965 and I helped annotate them. The two lads were young and full of piss and vinegar when these things happened and I think I managed to make all of the scatology moderately palatable. The annotation is called *THE JARAMILLO INSCRIPTION.*

Nowadays Knees occasionally thinks about writing a memoir to add to *WEED, WOMEN AND SONG,* or writes an Keeler-related article for the *Keeler News,* but in general he has lost his intellectual creativity. His irrational exuberance and undeserved confidence gone, he now prefers making books with his hands to making them with his brain.

It may be both our loss and our gain. Read on and decide for yourself.

Norbert Tudwallow, November 16, 2002
Updated May 2011

TALES FROM THE TOWER

THE MOJO FUNK CAPER

by Geno Jaramillo and Knees Calhoon (1964)

Chapter One—Night on Beaverbrick Mountain

"AAAIIIYYYEEEEEE!" The shrill scream echoed off the raised battle-axe into the hot August night as Willie's cruel lips twisted into a maniacal sneer at cad's pitiful attempt to warn the rest of the revelers at the Mojo Workout of the impending doom. Fender caught Willie's eye with a quick movement of his little finger that signaled, "Go ahead, bro, the shrimp deserves it." Willie nodded his mute assent and brought the battle-axe down in an ever-widening arc that promised to end in the close proximity of cad's groin. The Workout had indeed begun.

Chapter Two—Incident on Route 66

CAD SHIFTED his weight slightly to ease the discomfort of the two-piece pool cue that was threatening the integrity of his scrotum as he lay sprawled across the back seat of the 65 Jaguar. Adding to his unease was the assortment of Beatle boots, beer cans, church keys, leather whips, cane-swords and other jet-set paraphernalia that lay across his arthritic body. From the front seat of the speeding vehicle came the low murmuring of Fender and Willie as they discussed the logistics of the upcoming Mojo Workout the FWC[3] club was throwing that evening at their hide-away retreat underlooking Beaverbrick Mountain.

cad extended his turkey-like neck and looked back down the highway to get his bearings. He started to squawk a word of innate camaraderie to his buddies in the front seat but was startled to see a urine-colored Cadillac convertible gaining on the Jag. "Who has the nerve to try and pass the FWC's?" he thought nervously as he lifted himself out from under a velveteen bidet-

---

[3] The (F)ender (W)illie (C)ad Club

cover. His mouth gaped in unabashed amazement as the Caddy overtook the trio and, cutting sharply into their lane, sped on down the highway.

"What the—" spat Willie, with his usual aplomb, and with a glance at Fender, riding shotgun, stomped on the accelerator. The impetus of the instant acceleration drove cad back into the business end of a dildo-shaped epee causing an enchilada-flavored gust of fetidity to eructate from his gullet.

"Let me have 'im!" cad implored as the supercharged Jag approached the offensive Caddy from the left rear.

"You bet!" seethed Fender as his long, lithe digits wrapped themselves around cad's gas-bloated midsection. cad managed a bleat of joyful despair as he realized what his role in the upcoming vengeance would be. Quickly he doffed his pantaloons as Fender held him outside the car, rear end facing the surprised visage that stared back from the Caddy alongside them. Looking over his shoulder cad had just enough time to see a pair of white, bushy eyebrows jump in profound dread before he felt Fender's fingers inexorably tighten around his pyloric valve.

First came the pain. Then the nausea. Then some more pain quickly followed by acute vertigo. Then the pain again and finally the disgust. cad vaguely remembered hearing a pitiful moan from the man in the Caddy and the unmistakable growl of a Cadillac running off the road as he slowly came to his senses in the back seat of the Jag.

A warm feeling of camaraderie crept over cad as he listened to his buddies in the front seat continue to discuss the preparations for the Mojo Workout. "I can't believe anyone would dare try to pass the FWC's," he managed to muse before his consciousness crapped out.

Chapter Three—Interlude at the Carwash

SHELL SCOTT CURSED to himself in harmony with the attendants as his yellow Caddy convertible went through the car-wash for the fourth time. If he hadn't had high-speed electric windows he'd be clinically blind now, he thought. His detective skills had enabled him to get the license number of the Jaguar just before the effluvia hit the fan and with various plans for revenge flitting through his mind he paid for his car-wash and sped down the highway.

"Okay, you mothers in the silver Jag," Scott fumed, "first I find you—then I maim you."

After a call on his car-phone to a friend in the police records department the white-haired private detective headed towards the mansion of a Dr. A. Dipshux.

Chapter Four—Shootout at Dipshux Manor

WILLIE EASED the Jag to a stop outside a picturesque Victorian edifice and he and Fender, after an elaborate code-knock on the hand-carved door, entered the building. The shingle above the door read "Dr. Antoine Dipshux, World's Foremost Authority on the Mating Habits of Homosexual Aardvarks".

In the back seat, cad opened a crusty eye to get his bearings as he waited for his compadres to check with the good doctor, the Grand Exalted Mojo of last year's Workout. cad knew what a great honor it was to be elected organizer of the Mojo Workout and as this year's co-Mojos, Fender and Willie could use an experienced Grand Exalted Mojo's advice. The doctor had kindly consented to their using his Jaguar to pick up some of the supplies that cad was now lying underneath.

cad decided to wait for Fender and Willie in the car even though he had thoughtfully memorized the code-knock he had just heard. He relaxed and was just entering a state of RNM [4] sleep (due to his rather unusual physiology cad's nose wiggled when he dreamed) when the screeching of Cadillac brakes jolted him from his reverie. As he raised up to see who dared disturb an FWC's sleep he gave an involuntary groan as he recognized the car he had just desecrated.

Cad's face was a side of him that Shell Scott hadn't seen before but he recognized the Jag. "Don't worry, creep in the back seat, I'll get to you after I take care of your amigos inside," Scott chuckled as he headed towards the door.

"Ha!" ejaculated cad. "You'll never get through the door without the code-knock! Erkkk!"

Shell Scott's .467 Smegnum's barrel tip entered cad's cauliflower-shaped ear as the white-maned detective muttered menacingly, "And the code-knock is...?"

---

[4] (R)apid (N)ose (M)ovement

cad cursed himself for his inchoate stupidity as he quickly bleated out the code-knock. As the gunbarrel was withdrawn from cad's upper Eustachian tube he rejoiced to see a member of the city's finest, a Meter Molly, striding up.

"Your car is illegally parked, mister, have a nic—" the policewoman began but was cut off when Shell Scott grabbed her by the badge and dragged her to the door. He gave the code-knock and using the Meter Molly as a shield, rushed into the offices of Dr. Dipshux, his gun half-cocked.

The three Exalted Mojos were seated in luxurious Corinthian leather chairs—drinks in one hand, guns in the other. Three shots rang out before Scott could react and the penultimate thing he remembered was his shield's stolid body jerking back into his. The last thing he remembered before oblivion set in was a scholarly voice intoning, "By the way, boys, don't forget the supplies at Aunt Jemima's."

Chapter Five—Shootout at Aunt Jemima's
Prophylactic Factory

{Unfortunately, the rest of the story has been lost. As Knees Calhoon remembers it, the FWCs shoot it out with Shell Scott at the Prophylactic Factory, then proceed to the Mojo Workout at Beaverbrick Mountain. Scott tracks them there and sneaks in, disguised. But the FWCs spot Scott—because of the trail of "unsatisfied babes"—and throw him in a pit with cad's mother. Then they turn on cad. A morality play for the ages.}

APPOINTMENT IN SAVANNAH

An Exercise in Punctuation

"BUT IT'S WRONG to jump out of a loop improperly!" I exploded for the third time. "You do that, Knees, and you're bound to have stack trouble sooner or later."

"You're undoubtedly right, Fender, but who gives a damn!" Knees Calhoon leaned back in the beanbag chair I reserve for visitors to my penthouse office. From 106 stories up, the City of 1000 Churches provided a fitting backdrop for my evil clone as he continued, "Look, you can't keep prattling on about 'computer' stuff all the time. You need some drama, some action. You're puttin' them to sleep with all those articles about programming and that 'state of the C-64' crap."

I was considering calling in my SWAT Team (for the umpteenth time) and having Knees tossed over the balcony but I decided to give him some rope—before I had him tossed. After all, Knees Calhoon had inspired several of my finest programs.

"So what do you have in mind?" I asked.

"Well, you know, I heard a pretty remarkable story from my good friend, Don Pardo, the other d—"

"Don Pardo? Of the Prestasquigi family? You mean the Godfa—?"

"Yes, yes, yes," Calhoon interrupted, "the Godfah, as you say. Now let me tell the story. You know, come to think of it, this story might teach *you* a few things about breaking out of nested loops improperly."

"You must be joking! I *never* exit nested loops wrong. I pop out of them in the reverse order in which I entered them. Just like they do with flashbacks in the film noir."

"Oh yeah?" Calhoon smirked, "I bet you will do it wrong three times before the cock crows."

I was planning to do a little bit of coding later on that night but nothing too sophisticated. There was no way I was going to make one mistake like that, much less three. "Calhoon, I'll take that bet. Now just tell the story."

Calhoon continued. "Well, I was talking to Don Pardo and he was pretty shook up. As Don told me—

" 'Knees, The weirdest thing happened today. You know my consigliere, Guyito?'

" 'I don't believe I've had the pleasure, Godfather.' I replied.

" 'Well, Guyito has been my advisor for many years now and I've had no reason to suspect his judgment. So today I sent him to Bossier City to collect a few debts. When he came back, he had this wild look in his eyes, like he had seen Jimmy Hoffa.'

" 'Maybe he had,' I conjectured. 'It's playing over at the mall.'

" 'No, you sack of spumoni!' the Don barked, 'Not the movie! I'm telling you he looked scared. He said to me—'

" ' "Godfather, you've got to help me! I was in Bossier getting the check from the councilman as you asked, when I saw a man all dressed in black looking at me funny. It gave me such a chill that I asked the councilman who it was and he said—" ' "

"Calhoon," I broke in, "are you telling me that a Bossier councilman is paying off Don Pardo?" Knees just smiled and lifted one finger. "Okay, go on with your story." I said.

" ' " 'Keep your voice down you moron!' the councilman whispered. 'That's Mortuus the Pathologist!' " '

" ' " 'Mortuus the Pathologist?' I asked. 'Who's that?' " '

" ' " 'Only the number one hit man east of the Rockies. Listen, Guyito, if you're mixed up with Mortuus, I'm outta here.' " ' "

This was getting rich. "Now look, you can't tell me that both the Godfather *and* a hit man are mixed up in Bossier politics." Knees Calhoon gave me a pitying look and lifted a second finger. I growled under my breath.

" ' "Godfather," Guyito wailed. "I am doomed! The whole time I was there Mortuus keep looking at me so strangely. It's obvious that he's out to kill me. Can you help me?" '

" ' "But what would you have me do, Guyito?" I asked.'

" ' "Let me go to Savannah, Godfather. I have friends there and I can lay low until maybe you can get the contract called off." '

" 'I said, "Good enough, take the afternoon flight, and in the meantime I'll talk to this Mortuus." So I told Sarducci, my chauffeur, to go to Bossier and ask Mortuus to call me. About an hour later I got a call from someone who said he was Mortuus.'

" ' "Why were you looking at Guyito, my consigliere, so strangely today?" I asked and he said—' "

"This better be good," I muttered and stifled an epithet as Calhoon lifted a third finger.

" ' "I was surprised to see him here, Don Pardo. I am in possession of a contract on his life and I had an appointment with him tonight—in Savannah." ' "

" '!' "

"!"

*   *   *   *   *   *   *

Later that night I was sitting alone in my penthouse atop the Tower. The coding wasn't going too well. All I could think about was the smirk on Calhoon's face as he left for the elevators, a few hours earlier. It's time somebody did something about that clone of mine. I stewed over the bug-ridden program for a few more minutes then picked up the phone.

"Renée, get me Mortuus—on the scrambled line."

THE VULVEENA SAGA

An Internet Romance in One Act

Compiled by Fender Tucker

THE FOLLOWING is a transcript of postings on the *Express Yourself* debate board on Quantum-Link during the dates 4-5-89 and 4-10-89. The characters Vulveena, Calh00n, CarrizoJim and Testicus are played by Fender Tucker. All others are playing themselves.

SUBJ: Affirmative Action for Women
FROM: Vulveena 04/05/89

Since the nation's Affirmative Action for blacks has worked so well, I maintain that it's time that the women of our country be afforded a slight edge in the struggle for jobs, promotions and quality of life.

SUBJ: Yeah!
FROM: COMALite J 04/05/89

Let's hear it for discrimination! If it's against the Majority, discrimination is a GOOD THING!! Let's get back at all those bad ol' WASP males, even those who never once discriminated against anyone else in their lives!

SUBJ: The phrase...
FROM: Ingersoll 04/05/89

..."reverse discrimination reminds me of a joke allegedly told behind the Iron Curtain: "As we are told, under capitalism man exploits man. Under socialism, of course, the reverse is true."...

SUBJ: A black guy's point of view
FROM: FutureTech 04/06/89

Affirmative action sucks. Instead of quotas (whether you want to call affirmative action a quota or not), if a person feels he/she has been discriminated against, let them take the employer to court.

SUBJ: I suppose I should be thankful
FROM: Vulveena 04/07/89
...that Ingersoll interrupts his wishy-washy, liberalist tantrums, COMALite forgoes his ersatz Moronic babblings, and FutureTech actually proofreads his mediocre, half-baked theories to answer my modest proposal, but mainly I feel disappointed that the only responses came from mouth-breathing males with testicular mentalities.

SUBJ: Vulveena
FROM: COMALite J 04/07/89
..."ersatz Moronic...?" Is that slur on my religion? ;>
For your information, Ingersoll is NOT a liberal. Neither am I. We are both libertarians in philosophy (if not in Party membership). As for Future-Tech, I work with him daily. (We both work for a Shreveport, LA software publisher—he as a Commodore 64/128 programmer, me as a general programmer/technical support person). Often I disagree with his views, but at least he rarely stoops to ad hominum attacks, and NEVER on the level you just resorted to. "Mouth-breathing males with testicular mentalities" indeed! If the opinion of males (49% of the population at last count) is to be held invalid on this subject, that is ad hominum taken to extremes not seen since the abortion issue!

I was wondering where that passage in the Declaration of Independence, the Constitution, or the Bill of Rights was that stated that one could not disagree with the opinion of Vulveena?

Now that you have attempted to insult us personally for the most heinous crime of disagreeing with you, can you debate what we have said? Logically? Please? After all, this is the General Debate Board, not the General Preaching and Insulting Those Who Disagree With Your Preaching Board. If you post something here, prepare to have it debated. If you don't like that, don't post here!

(I seem to remember that you original post did indeed ask for comments . You got what you asked for. If you don't like that, don't post here!)

SUBJ: Vulva
FROM: FutureTech 04/07/89

You are a genderic bigot to speak about men that way—and with such small cause. Reverse discrimination is a good term here. You shouldn't bash those who don't agree with you.

As for our "testicular mentalities", my testosterone levels are highest in the morning yet it only makes me a little happier (if you know what I mean). You, on the other hand, are much more affected by hormonal levels, obviously capable of transforming into a b***ch at the drop of a hat. Perhaps your hormones incited your idiotic post. Or was it an absence of hormones?

SUBJ: So the extra X chromosome
FROM: Vulveena 04/08/89

...rears its ugly head again. But you're right, I shouldn't add to the blanket defamation that the male population brings upon itself everyday—I should stick (it) to the two lowest common d(en)ominators on this board, COMALite J and Futuretech.

Who cares where you drag your carcass everyday, COMAL? Or with whom you drag it when you get there? The fact remains that you will soon end up with a penis permanently pointing at your podia and a prostate the size and consistency of a month-old donut. And you treat women as if they were somehow responsible for this innate flaw.

As for Futuretech, I have a feeling that if you ever were to bump into a real woman (at any time of day), the first and only thing that would touch would be your belly.

And who says this board isn't big enough for personal vilifications? Debating is masturbation; insulting is real action—and it's obvious which we prefer.

SUBJ: Vulveena...
FROM: Calh00n 04/08/89

while I agree that this board is big enough for all sorts of interactions, I think you are barking at the wrong dogs. Futuretech and COMALite J aren't misogynous, they're just slightly pompous programmers.

I enjoyed your posts though, and hope to become a target of yours real soon .

SUBJ: The worms are turning!

FROM: Vulveena 04/08/89

Calh00n, I shall be happy to add you to my guano list, since I sense that you fit into the same slime mold as the others. I admit that your posts contain a modicum of erudition but that makes you all the more pitiful. Too bad you have chosen to align yourself with Futureblecch and CATAMite J; in another world I might have let you sniff my stockings before I crushed you like the double-zero you are.

SUBJ: Velveeta
FROM: FutureTech 04/08/89

At first I thought it took a lot of balls to say what you said. Now I think it takes a lot of misanthropic energy. I'm glad you're a woman because if you were a man with all that hatred, you'd be a violent one.

I'm sooooo sorry to have spoken to you in such a way! You're obviously not emotionally stable. I've never met a true man hater before. I always thought there would be an explosion of monumental proportions when I did. Well, now I've met one and I find you boring, even the way you berate men is shallow. Take a course in insulting people. You might do better. I truly feel sorry for you.

BTW, as for your belly crack, what would I bump into first if I stumbled across you? A picket sign? Two prodigious mamaries? The necklace swinging from side to side, sporting the shriveled up testicles from the last boyfriend who didn't agree with you politically? Or have you ever been able to attract a man?

SUBJ: Is Vulveena a "RightWinger"
FROM: FutureTech 04/08/89

No one can be so aggressively bigoted, not even some Klansmen I've met. How can she refer to men as the "brain damaged half of the population" and not mean it as a joke?

I think it's all a put on. For those who don't recall, Rightwinger was a LIBERAL Q-entity who pretended to be a rightwinger in order to make conservatives look bad.

I say that Vulveena is either a man trying to make feminists look bad or truly, TRULY a person in need of counseling.

SUBJ: I opt for the latter. . .
FROM: EdM18 04/08/89

I believe Vulveena is a woman, who at some point in her life, had a bad experience in a heterosexual relationship. She is now a reactionary feminist, who has determined that all the evils of the world are a result of men's actions. One observation about this type of person: They are violently anti-male, yet THEY EMBRACE AND ESPOUSE THE VERY WORST TRADITIONAL "MALE" PERSONALITY TRAITS! i.e.: bigotry, violence, chauvinism, aggression, etc.

The planet was made to operate with both sexes, and dominance by either sex creates an imbalance that is detrimental to all.

SUBJ: sinking to her level
FROM: Nathrax 04/08/89

I'm not proud, if she wants insults let's give them to her. But first let's pity her, for she is a 5-year old mind in the body of a 50-year old bulldyke. After reading her comments and postings I have come to some conclusions. Vulveena (shall we call her Vulva for short? can I get a consensus on this?) is:

A) really in need of getting laid.
B) a dominstic lesbian
C) has a case of CMS. CMS is like PMS but stands for Constant Menstrual Syndrome .
D) has a terminal case of PENIS ENVY
E) all of the above!!!!!

Personally, I feel "she" needs to get some therapy and she should buy a vibrator, cause that's about the only friends he will ever have.

SUBJ: ...
FROM: SLVRSURFR 04/09/89

Now this sounds like a series of arguments worth turning on the computer for!

Does the term Femmi-Nazi apply here?

SUBJ: Gather round, little boys. . .
FROM: Vulveena 04/09/89

and I'll explain how I came to be. It's one of the oldest stories in the book—the switched medical chart.

Four years ago I was the successful editor of a popular guns and ammo magazine, the proud father of three tiny infants and the faithful husband of a lovely wife. I checked into a hospital to have a recalcitrant gall bladder removed and the night before my operation a bumbling male nurse accidentally switched my chart with the poor soul in the bed next to me.

You can imagine my surprise when I awoke the next night the proud possessor of one of the cutest little pudenda ever desired by man. And you wouldn't believe my (as Futuresmeck would say) "mamaries"! All I can say is, thank the Lard for the generous woman who checked off "breasts" on the organ donor sticker on the back of her driver's license.

Not being a bitter person, I was looking forward to resuming my life, but I was shunned by the sexists at the magazine and even by my wife and infants. I was contemplating suicide, mass murder, or even a suit against the hospital when I noticed that there were indeed some "advantages" to my present configuration, one of them truly standing out. COMATose J, think about the greatest orgasm you ever managed to wangle out of your paltry pestle. Multiply it by a thousand and you begin to approach the pleasure I get when I do something as simple as back into a well-packed washing machine on the spin cycle.

The bottom line, little boys, is don't criticize me until you've walked a mile in my six-inch Ralph Lauren heels.

SUBJ: That settles it.
FROM: FutureTech 04/09/89

I won't waste anymore energy grueling over Purina's posts unless I'm REALLY in a good mood. I have a high tolerance for vulgarity but every time this broad opens her mouth she tests my levels of endurance.

I don't believe her story but I do believe that she's not sane.

I truly feel sorry for Velveeta, even though I have contempt for her at the same time.

SUBJ: I can surely imagine that.
FROM: COMALite J 04/09/89

After all, I am a virgin by choice, so multiplying my best orgasm by 1000 wouldn't be a whole lot, since any number times zero is still zero.

SUBJ: Switched Medical Charts?
FROM: Tapestry 04/09/89
PLEASE give us some credit for being intelligent human beings here. (Well, at least some of us.)

A previous posting here gave details of an "accidental" sex-change operation, due to switched medical charts .

::koff::

I by no means claim to be an expert on the subject, but even I know that prospective sex-change candidates go through MONTHS of therapy before the operationS, note the plural, are scheduled. I'd HOPE that during that therapy, the Doctors involved would at least get to know the person's FACE, and LOOK at it before pulling out the knife in the operating room...not to mention the various technician and nurses involved.

As far as thanking the woman who checked off "breasts" on her organ donor card...LOL!! Last I heard those either came from mother nature, hormone treatments or implants . . . NOT transplants.

If even 1/100th of this is true, and you DIDN'T file a lawsuit . . . that's ur loss, cause you could be a very rich woman (?) right now. :)

I could go on . . . and on . . . and on . . .

But naw . . . I won't. I've blown enough steam for now. And yes, I AM a female.

To the men who've posted comments on this same subject...some of you are just as bad as she is. I've seen more sexist and degrading comments here than I care to think about.

Let's quit dividing things . . . and start working towards HUMAN Rights.

SUBJ: I dunno. . .
FROM: CarrizoJim 04/09/89
I remember reading about four years ago about a hospital being accused of something like that. I think it was in Gary, Indiana, but I'm not sure. Only, I think it was a woman who had her chart

switched and she was turned into a man by mistake. Don't quote me on this.

SUBJ: Vulveena, I was prepared
FROM: Testicus 04/09/89

(as Futuretetch was) to write you off as a waste of time, but your last post caused a chill to course through my spine. Your story strains one's credulity, but fellow Q-linkers, once you've heard my story, perhaps you'll see things in a different light.

I grew up a timid young girl in a rigid household, dominated by my father, a well-respected Chicago surgeon. Four years ago, at the age of twenty, I met a young man who wooed and won my heart (and, alas, my innocence), much as will probably happen to young CUMALot J someday. When my father found out, he grew irate and, after knocking me out with some noxious fluid, secreted me to the hospital, where he enacted his punishment upon me. He vowed that I would never repeat my offense and proceeded to remove my offending parts. Ever a frugal man, and deep down a devout humanitarian, he had them sent to a nearby city where I was told they were used in a sex change operation.

That night he had a fit of remorse for his rather rash actions, and he tried to make it up to me. He knew there was a male organ available in the nearby city, and since he had always wanted a son to carry on his name, he had the phallus brought to Chicago, where he attached it to me.

As you can imagine, I have never forgiven Daddy. I am now a successful fashion designer and write occasionally for Spy Magazine. I'm quite happy in my new life, although I really miss the fun I used to have with my Amana SpinMeister Heavy Duty.

So there is at least ONE male reader who believes you, Vulveena.

SUBJ: Testicus, I too must admit
FROM: Vulveena 04/09/89

that when I read your name I was tempted to relegate you to the slagheap of mediocrity that so-called 'men' comprise, but your story evoked in me what can only be described as a lachrymal ejaculation. Could it be that, after all these years, I might be reunited with my former self?

It's too early to say, Testicus, but we may be just the person we're looking for! Check your E-Mail for directions on where to find me.

Well, Q-Linkers, Futuretech, COMALite J, Ingersoll, Calh00n, Tapestry and anyone else I may have offended in my short, yet eventful sojourn through Express Yourself!, it's been stimulating. Almost as good as my Westinghouse Vibromatic washer/dryer combo. But the time has come to say "Au revoir!" I have a feeling that Testicus and I are in for a beautiful friendship/reunion.

SUBJ: good luck
FROM: Mayland 04/10/89

and I hope you two are very happy together. Y'know, I am tempted to believe the foregoing—even a druggie would have a hard time making these up!

Mayland

HE ALSO SERVES

A Utopian Story

Chapter One: Richard Blaine

RICK BLAINE WOKE UP and wondered what day it was. Squinting, he looked through the bedroom door at the screen on the wall of the living room. 9:10 A.M., Sunday, July 5, 2047. He felt amazingly good, considering what kind of a day he had yesterday. He ran a hand through his few strands of hair and walked the three steps to the bathroom where he did his usual morning rituals, humming the verse to "As Time Goes By" over and over, even as he brushed his teeth with Calhoon's toothpaste.

Then he went back in the bedroom and lay back down on the bed, completely nude, and stared at the ceiling. He felt damn good! And he saw no reason for doing anything more than just spending a quiet day at the apartment, watching some wall, having a little supper and just taking it easy. He deserved it after all he had been through lately.

His body was filled with lassitude but his mind was clear. As he closed his eyes, smiling, he thought back on what he had recently experienced. All of it was crystal sharp, almost as if he were reliving it—meeting Ilsa again after all these years, getting the letters of transit, dealing with Major Strasser and Captain Renault, seeing Ilsa and Victor off at the airport—He went over it in detail in his mind, remembering how it was in Paris, before the Germans came...

As it had happened, he remembered, it had been tense, and frustrating, and full of self-pity. But for a while he thought that he and Ilsa might have a chance, and then last night... But looking back on it, especially as good as he felt physically and mentally, it seemed more ironic than sad, more adventurous than stressful.

He spent the next four hours on his bed, reliving his past life, with the events of the past week in Casablanca and the time he and Ilsa had spent in Paris most clear and immediate, but with hundreds of other memories of other exploits—journeys, cases, love affairs, dangers—lurking in the background. He had done so much in his lifetime!

It was around two P.M. when he got up and headed into the living room. He lived in a normal-sized apartment for Cableville, the living room measuring 3 meters by 3 meters, plenty big enough for his recliner and reward box, and of course, wall screen. The bedroom was a little smaller, having only a single bed in it. The bathroom was big enough for a throne, a lavatory and a shower stall. The kitchen was the smallest room, with only a microwave oven in the far wall.

Dodging the recliner he headed into the kitchen. The microwave had a packet inside, as he knew it would, and he pressed the big red button above the oven. Two seconds later he opened the door and took out the packet, tore off a seal and tilted it to his mouth. Malted Oneirine, just the ticket! He had gotten so used to the spicy delicacies of Morocco that on this day of rest he sort of craved the blandness of Malted Oneirine.

How about some wall? he thought. He finished the last of the liquid and put the empty container back into the microwave. A few short steps later, he was enwombed in his beloved recliner. From his sitting position he pushed a big red button on the wall and the clock and date display changed to a wall-sized screen. In the middle it read, "Cableville M-2683".

A sultry, muted sax melody filled the room as the screen changed into the billowing curves of a soft, rippling velveteen cloth, in moving shades of ochres, browns and deep violets. Rick was entranced. The music and the sensuous ripples of the cloth combined to move him into another place and time. Late 1940s Los Angeles, it turned out. He sat back in the recliner and didn't move a muscle as the story streamed past, with its socio-political undertones, its cynical hero, its labyrinthine plot.

When it was over he exhaled heavily and shook his head in amazement. What a great movie! he thought, as he reached into his reward box and brought out a hemp burner and ball of compressed hemp. It had all of the classic elements of a mystery and completely believable characters... he rambled on in his mind as he put the ball in the burner where it immediately began emanating a thin white, wispy smoke. He placed the burner on the top of

the reward box and turned back to the screen. The film was starting again.

By eleven that night he had seen the story three more times. He
had spent the day just as he wanted, taking it easy and indulging
himself. Hey, he deserved a day off, he thought. Running a night-
club was no picnic, and if you think you can find a lost love, stay
out of the clutches of some sadistic Nazis, then give away the
woman you love—all for a higher principle!—and not need a day
off, then hey, you're a better man than I am. Rick Blaine was
ready to pack it in after a perfect day.

He went into the kitchen and saw that the microwave had a
fresh packet of food in it. He pressed the button and took out the
packet, opened it up and drank. Good stuff, that Malted Sonomine. He really wasn't up for any kind of fancy food. After all,
he was getting ready for bed.

He went into the bathroom and did his usual nighttime ablu-
tions, brushing his teeth briskly with some Calhoon's toothpaste,
then dropped down on the bed and within minutes was sound
asleep.

Chapter Two: Jacob Gittes

JAKE GITTES WOKE with a start, and was relieved to see that he
was in his apartment. Through the door into the living room he
saw that it was almost 10 on Monday, July 6, 2047. He must have
gotten some much-needed sleep—he felt pretty good. As his
memories of the preceding days rooted in his mind he sat up on
the edge of the bed. He remained there with elbows on knees, his
hands over his eyes propping his head up for a minute, then three
steps later was in his bathroom. As he brushed his teeth with Calhoon's toothpaste his mind overflowed with warm, yet sharply
detailed memories and thoughts.

Evelyn Mulray was what he thought about. He didn't care
about the valley's water problems or Noah Cross or Hollis Mulray. His nose didn't even bother him anymore, except a little at
night. But why did Evelyn have to die? The memory of last
night's shooting in Chinatown was delicately clear in his mind,
along with the pain, but surprisingly he felt as if the worst had
passed, and that all he needed was a quiet day at home. Sooner or
later he'd have to settle up with Noah Cross, but for today he de-

served some peace and quiet—maybe a little wall—here in his apartment, far, far from Chinatown.

Jake, who always slept in the nude, emerged from the bathroom wearing nothing and decided there was no reason to put anything on. He fell onto the bed on his back and stretched his full, 5' 6" frame over its edges. His eyes closed, he felt a wave of supreme lassitude sweep over his body. His nose, which had been slit the week before by a weaselly gangster who looked like Roman Polanski, no longer hurt at all. There was only the pain of Evelyn's death, which somehow now, almost seemed for the best.

In his mind he went over the events of the past weeks, remembering how that redheaded actress had posed as Evelyn Mulray, suckering him into a scandal with him as the stooge. That sure wasn't a happy time, but in hindsight, it made for a damn good story, Jake thought with a chuckle.

But that was how he met Evelyn Mulray. It didn't take long for her to get her hooks into him and by the time he had slapped her secret out of her, he was in deep, too deep. He had to dodge the cops as well as Noah Cross and when he heard she was headed to Chinatown, he knew it was going to end bad. The pain of last night in Chinatown, with the blare of her car horn as accompaniment, played through his head, rebounding from pillow-like receptors, never catching root... appreciated, but never felt.

Around 2 P.M. he pulled himself out of his reverie and headed into the kitchen. In the microwave, as always, was a packet of Malted Oneirine. "Good!" he grunted to himself. After all of the spicy foods he'd been eating in the greasy spoons of LA, some sensible Malted Oneirine sounded perfect. He pressed the red button and two seconds later he opened the oven and took out the packet. He tore off the tab and swigged it down in one gulp. He put the wrapper back in the microwave and went into the living room and his recliner.

"You know," he thought to himself. "I think I'll just stay home all day and watch some wall." Smiling, he pressed the big red button on the wall by his reward box.

The time:date display stayed on the wall in front of him.

This had never happened before. Jake tried it again, pressing with more pressure this time. Nothing.

"What's going on here?" he spoke out loud. In his experience, when you pressed the button, you got a movie. Nothing complicated, no switches or dials, just one button to watch a movie. He was confused, and that put quite an edge on his good mood. He had reconciled the events of the past week in LA, and he had blended the memories with the thousands of other memories that lived in the back of his brain. His feeling that everything is fine and that he deserved a day of rest was being undermined by this non-functioning button.

Jake Gittes, scandal detective, reached back his small fist and hit the button with all his might. "Owwwww!" he howled, but only because he expected it was going to hurt. The pain never came and in his relief Jake heard a small ping behind the button, as if something mechanical had shifted. The screen suddenly came to life with a centered message, "PBS City D-1463", which soon changed into the face of a wild-looking man, bald on top with a cowlick on each side of his forehead swept up into horns. He was wearing sunglasses and sported a trim, brown beard.

Jake felt better immediately, although the "PBS City" message was mystifying. He had a vague memory of the phrase, but nothing he could easily grasp. Cableville was where he lived and he hadn't really considered there might be places other than that. He leaned back in the recliner and devoted his full attention to the man on the screen.

"—anyway, that's my theory. You can take it or leave it. I really don't give a—"

The wild man's face was replaced by that of a female commentator. "That was in 2013 when Knees Calhoon first proposed his radical new social welfare policy. It's hard to see now why it wasn't embraced wholeheartedly, but we must remember that it was a much more superstitious time."

Jake had never seen such a film. He had memories of hundreds of adventurous romps throughout the world, dramatic family episodes, even hilarious mistaken-identity capers, all of which he had lived, but nothing like this. It was just the dry life history of some guy named Knees Calhoon who had started a new welfare policy back in 2023.

According to the "documentary", as the movie was called in the film, welfare in the U.S. consisted of giving a minimum of food, clothing and shelter to those who, for whatever reason, couldn't pay their way. In addition to the minimum services, there was a general air of severe disapproval attached to receiving welfare. The old Protestant work ethic was still in effect.

Calhoon changed all that. His reasoning was that what made traditional welfare fail was that the recipients were unhappy. How could they not be? They lived on the very edge of survival and on top of that, everybody else looked down on them. The secret to welfare success is to come up with a way to continue to give each recipient minimal support—hence, minimal outlay to the tax-payer—but at the same time keep the poor slugabeds as happy as larks.

To Calhoon, the answer was as plain as the smoke in his face. Drugs. And not just any drugs, especially not the ones approved by the FDA to keep everybody feeling just as bad as they would if they didn't take anything at all. No, what was needed was a drug that would make a person feel absolutely great about living in a minimal space, using minimal resources and producing minimal garbage.

Jake was astounded. There was something eerily different about this movie, or documentary. He had the feeling that this was something that really happened. That's not what movies are for, he protested to himself. Movies are fantasies to take you away from your lives for a day. They're a reward for all the hard work you had done that previous day, or week, or month. But this— This is something he wasn't sure he liked.

He continued to watch, never taking his eyes off the screen, even when he took out a hemp ball and burner and lit it up.

Calhoon worked it all out. Every man, woman and child on earth was guaranteed a small apartment with minimal daily food, a movie (of course), and an article of clothing, if asked for. This was basically what welfare was offering them at the time. But in addition, Calhoon provided a drug that would insure that the apartment dweller was happy about his daily routine.

There were many failed trials, but eventually it was found that a sequence of oneirine and sonomine, taken at regular intervals in a 24-hour period, would cause the following behavioral pattern:

(1) 8-10 hours sleep
(2) 4-6 hours of meditation about life
(3) 8-12 hours of a desire to watch wall

But what really made the whole thing work was a special drug called fenderine, which is the main ingredient in Calhoon's tooth-paste. Its effect is to make the person believe that the memories that are foremost in his mind are his real memories. He becomes whatever persona is most vivid and immediate in his memory, at least for the rest of that day.

People who opted for welfare were housed in huge buildings called Cableville, while those who elected to work lived outside, in what was called PBS City. Cableville residents were shown only escapist adventure films on a single channel; everyone else in PBS City had 10,000 channels to choose from.

Upon hearing this, Jake Gittes sat up in his recliner. This was extremely disturbing, but at the same time, fascinating. Connections were crackling in his brain, ones that didn't get made often. He felt a little disassociated, as if he were two or more people for a second. He stared at the screen.

There were scenes of people lying on beds in apartments just like Jake's, all of them smiling. Knees Calhoon was seen with important heads of state: the president, the anti-pope, the King of Hollywood. His policies in place, his fame secured, he spent the rest of his life republishing the works of Harry Stephen Keeler and writing the definitive history of the Trim-Trio, published posthumously by Ramble House.

The documentary ended with Calhoon's death of pan-sexual asphyxiation at the age of 97 in the year 2044. On his bearded face was a smile very similar to those of his Cableville apartment dwellers.

Jake lit up another hemp ball from the reward box, which always had a fresh supply every morning, and watched the movie about Knees Calhoon five more times. During the third time he got up from his recliner and put his hand on the doorknob of the front door. Even with the screen distracting him with grey and brown images of the horned Calhoon, he could feel that the door was fake. It was all just a wall, with a door painted on and a plastic doorknob attached. He sat back in the chair and continued to watch.

Around 11 P.M. he felt hungry and walked into the kitchen. The screen went out as soon as he left the room, replaced by the time:date display. He pressed the red button and took the Malted Sonomine packet out of the microwave. He really felt like having a tasteless, malty drink before bed after all that greasy LA food. After chugging the drink, he put the empty packet back in the oven out of habit and went into the bathroom.

He brushed his teeth with Calhoon's toothpaste, took a quick shower, and spilled into his bed. Jake Gittes, jaded detective and former LA cop, fell asleep long before midnight.

Chapter Three: Kneesius Calhoon

KNEES CALHOON WOKE UP in a bad mood, even though he felt great. He looked all around at the tiny apartment and thought, this does look about as minimal as you can get. No clothes, nothing but a bed, a chair, a bathroom and a microwave. Oh yeah, and a reward box. And the wall. All in all, not such a bad deal, his mind insisted on saying. But then the memory of what he had done came back to him in full force and he felt like he should be mad.

Here he goes and solves one of his society's biggest problems and he gets put in one of his own Cableville apartments. And to dig the knife in a little deeper, they make a documentary about him and tack on some fakealoo about his retirement and death. Well, he was going to see about this. He'd investigate this from A to Izzard! But not today. He deserved a quiet day at the apartment, to rest up from all of the world traveling and hobnobbing he had been doing lately, promoting his new social policies. Maybe some wall would be nice.

He sat up on the bed and out of 20 years' habit, strode into the bathroom. He brushed his teeth with Calhoon's toothpaste and plopped down on the bed. His memories of life as a social engineer were so crystal clear, he began reliving them, one after another as the morning drew long.

He knew what had happened. Something had gone wrong with his wall and he had tapped into a PBS City show, instead of his usual Cableville adventure. His memories told him that he had spent the last decades creating and refining the Cableville welfare system, but the show implied that it might be just an artifact of a drug called fenderine.

It was all so confusing, even though his mind was hyper-alert. But one thing was clear: he deserved a day of rest. And maybe some wall.

Around 2 in the afternoon he got up from the bed, had some Malted Oneirine and sat down to watch some wall. After he'd relaxed for a while he'd look into the disturbing news about the welfare state and his contributions to it. He'd also see if there was another way out of the apartment other than the fake door.

He pressed the red button on the wall and the date:time changed to "PBS City D-1464". Below it a message read: "Beginning a 5000-part series on Mass Murderers, Serial Killers and other Unfortunates of the Twentieth Century."

After watching a fascinating documentary about a mid-20th Century tyrant six times, Knees Calhoon, hero of the welfare state, performed his usual nighttime rituals and went to bed.

Chapter Four: Adolph Hitler

THE CHANCELLOR OF GERMANY awoke around 10 A.M., feeling damn good considering all that he had been through in the past twenty years...

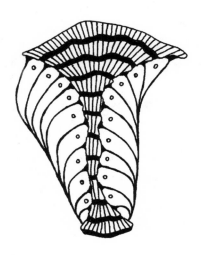

LUCKY JOHN

A True Crime Reminiscence

IN JANUARY OF 1988 a horrible kidnap-murder took place in Albuquerque NM. Because of the pre-trial publicity, the trial was moved to Las Cruces, where I was living at the time. I worked at night playing music so my days were free to attend the trial. I took copious notes—which now make no sense—and the following is taken from just a part of them, mainly the testimony of James Scartaccini, one of the kidnapers.

PART ONE:
The Opening Statements

THE JURY was chosen today for the case of the State of New Mexico *vs* Johnny Zinn. Zinn is charged with 24 counts of various crimes like 1st degree murder, kidnapping, unlawful sexual penetration, armed robbery, illegal use of a credit card and conspiracies to commit all of the above and more.

I had dropped by the courthouse last week to see some of the voir dire and was not surprised to see that it was as boring as it was said to be. The judge, the Honorable William Deaton of Albuquerque, read the same questions to each of the 100+ potential jurors. Have you any relatives on the police force? Are you opposed to capital punishment? Would you automatically vote for the death penalty in a 1st degree murder trial if the defendant were found guilty? Would you refuse to impose the death penalty even if, in your mind, the circumstances warranted it?

Either before or after these questions the judge determined if the potential juror could actually make it to court everyday for an anticipated three weeks of trial. Of the several people I saw interviewed two young ladies were disqualified because they said they would always impose the death penalty in murder cases. Three retired men gave the answers most likely to appease both the prosecution and the defense, all no's—or in one case, no sah's. One lady said that because of her medication she couldn't pay attention that long. A couple pleaded hardship because of their jobs but the judge was hard to convince in both cases.

On the first morning of the trial I was one of a dozen spectators and about as many journalists from newspapers from Las Cruces and Albuquerque and TV people from KOB-TV. Apparently the proceedings are to be televised. As we waited in line to be frisked and searched electronically I was subjected to a conversation with one Donna McGuire, a robust pro bono paralegal who seemed to feel that I needed to know the ropes of trialdom. As an objective spectator I was a little dismayed by her too-loud opinions such as "The scum did it all right. Everybody knows that." Or "I just hope I'm not in the path of anybody looking for revenge."

Wouldn't you know it, she sat right next to me in the first row on the defendant's side. On my left was a couple I later found to be the mother and uncle of the victim. Donna kept up the conversation as we sat in the courtroom waiting for the judge to enter. Johnny Zinn was about fifteen feet away and must have heard some of the more vehement things she was saying. She was quite informative about judicial procedures and I especially enjoyed her characterizations of the various principals in the case. The defense attorney was George Peppard, the defendant was Nancy Reagan in drag, the DA was Tony Orlando and the ADA's were Young Freud and Debra Winger.

Young Freud, aka Donald Cox began his opening remarks in a voice that was often too soft to hear. I imagine the jury could understand him all right but the spectators and press had to listen very closely. Perhaps that is what he had in mind.

He said, "The state is going to prove that three men, James Scartaccini, Randy Pierce and Thomas Sliger, kidnapped, raped and killed Linda Lee Daniels under the willful orders of the defendant, Johnny Zinn."

According to the prosecution, Zinn had a story that he told potential sycophants about having Mafia ties in prostitution and pornography. He paid $1500 for information leading to the abduction of a suitable woman to star in porno films and do a little prostituting in Farmington, a Mormon small-oil town in Northwestern New Mexico. The come-on to the girls was good food and nightlife in Farmington with all the drugs you want, in return for some movies and a little prostitution.

Johnny Zinn had met Wallace Randall Pierce before and hired him as bodyguard so Randy was the guy who had to find girls, or at least had to find the guys to find the girls for him and Johnny. Randy was to bring any prospects to the Bingo Parlor parking lot next to Zinn's Bakery, the family business owned by Johnny's father. The girls would be interviewed by Zinn, the "Boss", in his Cadillac in the parking lot.

On Tuesday Randy Pierce ran into two Los Lunas punks, James Scartaccini, 17, and Thomas Sliger, 20. They were soon recruited by Randy and began looking for an actress for Zinn to produce. They met with him in the Cadillac and were convinced by the $1500 and the fact that Johnny had close friends in the Mafia. The prosecution dwelt a while on the persuasive charms of Zinn which were half threat, half promise.

Scartaccini and Sliger first thought of Crystal King, a local part-time hooker and friend, and at first she seemed amenable. After listening to his spiel in the backseat of the Cadillac she backed out. Johnny was pissed and told the two that he needed the girl by Friday at the latest because the Farmington porn ring was telling him to hurry up.

Scartaccini and Sliger drove all over Albuquerque talking to prostitutes about their offer. They had no takers. Ellen Neff, another part-timer friend, recommended a 13-year-old acquaintance that had Johnny salivating but the girl wouldn't do it. He was getting more and more angry at his two helpers and told them that the Mafia was getting irritated about the delay.

When Friday came and still no luck Johnny went to Ellen Neff's house and threatened her. Her younger sister walked around back of his Caddy to get the license number and she was threatened also. Scartaccini said that he had met a biker named Monty Linville who might be able to help. Saturday night Scartaccini met with Zinn in the car and Zinn at one point began choking him with both hands. Zinn said find me a girl and choke her just like that if you have to, but bring her. And in the meantime, as a test, steal me four new tires for my Caddy.

Scartaccini, sensing a reprieve of sorts, told Linville that he needed four tires now, instead of the broad, so James Scartaccini, Thomas Sliger and Monty Linville stole four radials for Johnny Zinn. Zinn appreciated the gift but had had enough delay. He then ordered Pierce to kidnap a young good-looking blonde and take her to the Canyon Motel where they could make the film that was to bring them fame and fortune. He told them that they'll need a polaroid camera, sleeping pills, a syringe, a gag and some rope. Zinn would meet them at the motel at 9:00 P.M. Sunday. In the meantime they are to keep her quiet an drugged by injecting her either under the tongue or in the vagina with the liquefied sleeping pills.

The three stooges, Pierce, Scartaccini and Sliger took off in an old station wagon looking for a victim. There were several false starts where the two younger nappers froze when approaching a woman that seemed vulnerable and Pierce was getting progressively madder about it. They saw a blonde entering Albertsons a little after 7:00 P.M. and Pierce told the other two that this time they were gonna do it or he'd shoot them. Around 7:20 P.M. Pierce became anxious and sent Scartaccini into Albertson's and saw the blonde at the checkout counter. He also saw a girl he knew and by the time he got back to the car their quarry was driving away. They followed her to her fiance's house where she was house-sitting and as she was getting out of the car with her grocery bags Scartaccini and Sliger attacked. She fought but was soon pushed into the station wagon and taken to the Canyon Motel.

By this time the woman to my immediate left, the victim's mother, was sobbing audibly into her handkerchief as she was comforted by her brother. I noticed that the camera was facing the mother with my well-chiseled profile in the foreground, undoubtedly out of focus. Donna noticed the sobbing or the camera, or both, and mortified me by leaning over me to touch the mother on the arm. "It's okay, it's okay," she stage-whispered as Sigmund droned on in the background about that night at the motel.

Zinn met them at the motel and sent Pierce and Sliger to the drive up bank to withdraw what they could from her account using her Amigo Card. Pierce was photographed by the auto-teller at 8:04. Scartaccini was sent out for vaseline and told to return in a hour or so. The victim, Linda Lee Daniels was kept blindfolded for the next five or six hours during which time she was raped repeatedly by first, Zinn, then the others when they returned. Photos were taken of the three stooges but none were taken of Johnny.

Zinn and Pierce left for the night around midnight. Scartaccini and Sliger were to stay with her and contact Zinn Monday at a nearby bar. That night she was raped again by Sliger.

The next afternoon they called Zinn at the bar and he said to drug her some more and take her to the Jemez Mountains. They were to wait by a phone booth they knew of for further instructions. Pierce drove the three up to the Jemez in James' truck and at one point they took off her blindfold for the first time. They waited a few hours and then the call came. The orders were to kill her.

They drove to a deserted area and with one bullet to the back of the head, Pierce killed her. They returned to Albuquerque where, on Johnny's orders, they burned the incriminating photos, scrubbed down the motel room and got rid of the gun. Since the gun was a sentimental favorite of Scartaccini's, he kept the antique stock and threw away the metal.

The police had little trouble tracing Pierce because of the auto-teller photograph and he and the other two were arrested at the A-1 Dry Cleaners on Friday. Zinn was arrested the following Monday. Scartaccini and Sliger told unconvincing stories about their whereabouts on the days in question and were broken down quite a bit before a lawyer, Leon Taylor, told them to keep quiet. It wasn't long before a deal with the D.A. had been worked out wherein Pierce would not get the death penalty (he got life imprisonment), Sliger would plead guilty to a lesser felony and Scartaccini would be offered immunity from prosecution hinging upon his telling the truth and convincing the jury that he was forced into his actions.

With that, Prosecutor Cox ended his opening remarks.

George Peppard, aka Hank Farrah, wearing a coat to match his silver-gray hair, opened by saying that much of what the jury just heard was true, especially about the killing, with the one difference; his client wasn't the mastermind, he was the fall guy. The stooges lied. Sure, Johnny Zinn was a petty crook, he spent some time in the penitentiary for armed robbery. He was an informant for the DEA. (The scribbling in the press section and next to me increased in volume and tempo at this revelation.) It's true Johnny attempted to talk Crystal King and Ellen Neff into prostitution, but not Linda Lee Daniels.

Johnny Zinn didn't have time to do all the things that the prosecution said he did and besides, he was at home with his girlfriend all night. She'll testify to that. As a matter of fact, when Johnny heard that they were looking for him and Pierce and them he called the police station and volunteered to come in Friday, the day his compatriots were arrested. The cop said to come in first thing Monday.

What happened was that Scartaccini and Sliger and Pierce thought up the crackpot idea a week or so previously and asked Zinn if he could help them out selling the film or, if need be, the girl, later. Johnny said he'd see what he could do, not planning on doing anything at all. When they said they had the girl at the motel he said he'd call Farmington but he never did. It was all a gag.

It was two days after the murder that Scartaccini and Sliger got the idea to frame Johnny for the crime that they had done. While it's true that Johnny did get a set of radials, he never met Linda Lee Daniels and never called them in Jemez. You see, Johnny wakes up every morning and goes to the bar for brandy and coffee. He's an alcoholic thief who works part-time at his father's bakery. He's not a mastermind anything.

James Scartaccini, Randy Pierce and Tom Sliger are the real murderers here. They provided the drugs, money, motel, gun and idea for this terrible crime and one of them might get off for lying to you on the witness stand. James Scartaccini is a liar.

Johnny Zinn managed to look both hopeful and forlorn as the judge ended the first day's session.

PART TWO:
The Ordeal of James Scartaccini

THE FIRST WITNESS called by the prosecution was the father of the victim, Gary Daniels, a dapper, manicured man who looked no more than forty. The woman of the prosecution team, Susan Heidel, questioned him about photos of the kidnapping scene taken by the police when they were called there the night of Sunday, January 12th, 1988.

He identified a photo of Linda's car, a 71 Mustang and a photo of the two shopping bags dropped by Linda in the driveway. Defense attorney Hank Farrah objected when Daniels described the photos as pictures of a "scuffle". He also objected every time Daniels reported about James Ingram's statements to him. Daniels was called by Ingram, Linda's fiancé and so wasn't there at the time of the kidnapping. For some reason, Ingram, who was inside the house and came out right after the kidnappers and their victim had left, wasn't called by the prosecution.

Daniels, after concluding that his daughter had met with foul play, called the police first and then Jim Moore, a reporter for the

Albuquerque Tribune. They all went to the Albertson's Supermarket at Menaul and Juan Tabo which was where Linda was last seen by the person at the checkout counter around 7:30 P.M. Sunday. Daniels also called the local TV stations and a report on the kidnapping as well as a plea for information went out on the Sunday 10:00 o'clock news.

Tuesday the FBI was called in. On Thursday Linda's American Express card was found and Daniels first heard of the arrests of several suspects.

The defense had no questions of Gary Daniels although they objected to several of his responses as "hearsay". Since they were not opposed to the information Daniels was imparting it seemed rather petty (to me) to object to it simply because it was technically hearsay.

Next the prosecution called its "star witness", James Scartaccini. He was about five minutes late getting to the stand dressed in an ill-fitting three-piece light blue suit. He was slight of build with a fashionable haircut and handsome pouty mouth. Several women described him as "cute".

The questioning was conducted by Schwartz who first elicited that Scartaccini worked for his grandfather at a couple of dry-cleaning establishments. He had married his wife, Danielle (pronounced "Danelle") a year and a half earlier because she was supposedly pregnant and he "wanted to do the right thing". He had had one previous conviction, a disorderly conduct charge a few years prior.

Schwartz immediately asked about the "deals" that Scartaccini's lawyer, Leon Taylor, had struck with the DA's office. The first statement and deal were made Monday morning, the 20th of January around 3:00 am. James was asked to read the deal out loud and amused all but Schwartz when he read "the state agrees to forgo (prosecution)" as "agree to forgive". There were four main provisions of this deal. James was to lead the police to Linda Daniels, wake a truthful statement about his actions, testify in any trial that results in a conviction and prove independently that he was not guilty of the actual murder or any other crimes other than the ones described in his statement.

He then was asked to read a second deal which Taylor had made with the DA which superseded the first. This second deal, dated January 28th but actually written up the evening of the 20th, was more formal than the first but contained the same provisions, with one exception. No conviction was required.

He then began his tale.

Randy Pierce, a 25-year-old cowboy came into the A-1 Cleaners Wednesday the 8th of January. He told James that he had $50,000 to launder from the IRS and was interested in buying a dry cleaners. James wrote down the addresses and phone numbers of several places in town.

Schwartz asked Scartaccini, "Would you say that Pierce is a slob?"

"I guess you could say that.

Hank Farrah interjected, "Your Honor, defense will stipulate Randy Pierce is a slob."

Randy had another deal. He would pay $1500 to anyone who could deliver to him a woman, preferably an blonde, who would agree to perform in a pornographic movie and engage in some prostitution on the side. In return she would get $5000, a new car, a new wardrobe and "all the drugs she could do." At this time James thought the $1500 was coming from Randy.

James was tempted because he had hospital bills from his wife's two miscarriages and so he agreed to try to find a woman. Randy set up a meeting between the "Boss" of the operation and James at 8:00 P.M. Thursday the 9th at a Circle K. Scartaccini had a friend Crystal King, a part-time prostitute, whom he thought might agree to the deal since she had made porno movies a few years earlier.

James first met Johnny Zinn at the 8:00 meeting which took place in Zinn's blue Cadillac. Zinn told Scartaccini the details of the deal and said he wanted to meet the "product", Crystal King. James, who was driving his truck, went to King's house, told her the deal and took her to the Circle K to meet Zinn.

Crystal and James got in the back seat of the Cadillac. Randy Pierce and Johnny Zinn were in the front seat. After James introduced Crystal to Johnny, Zinn told her the details of the deal then asked her what she would do on screen.

"Will you do it with animals?"

"No.

"How about anal stuff?

"No, none of that."

"How about blacks? The guys up in Farmington like to see blondes with black guys."

"No way!"

When Crystal asked him what would happen if one of the johns hurts her, he said, "I'll kill anyone who hurts you." Despite this reassurance Crystal told Zinn "No," and left the car. Johnny got angry at James and told him, "If you are going to play big boy games, you better have the product. Now you and your stupid-looking friend get lost and find me a product." The stupid-looking friend was Thomas Sliger.

Randy, James and Thomas then drove over to see Ellen Neff, another part-time prostitute friend of James'. She appeared interested so they went back and told Johnny about her. James mentioned that if Ellen doesn't work out maybe a friend of hers, a thirteen year old prostitute, might do it. Johnny perked up when he heard about the young girl and said he wanted to meet Ellen.

In Zinn's Caddy they drove to Ellen's and James went in and told her the Boss was outside and wanted to talk to her. She refused at first, saying that Zinn should come in instead, then agreed to go outside when James told her that Zinn is mad and dangerous. Ellen got in the car and listened to the spiel about Farmington, movies, prostitution, car, clothes and drugs from Johnny. When he mentioned sex with animals she said, "Goats are sick. No way." Johnny had changed his tune somewhat because when she asked what happens if a john tells her to do something she doesn't want to do he told her, "If he ties you up and says to shit straight to the ceiling, you do it."

As for the prostitution in Farmington, Ellen said she would do it with one guy a week but Johnny said that she may have to do it with two guys at a time several times a week. The split of profits is 75 for Johnny and 25 for her. During the interview Zinn took hits off a bottle of QT, finishing a pint in less than a half hour.

Ellen finally told Zinn that there's no deal and went back in the house. Johnny was really pissed now and said to James, "She deserves a bullet in the head and you do too. I should take her out in the desert, make her dig her grave and blow her fuckin head off." James begged for more time and left with Randy and Thomas.

They drove around looking for prostitutes all that night with no luck although they talked to quite a few. At one point in the evening Randy suggested that Scartaccini ask his wife, Danielle, to do it but James said no. Around 3:00 A.M. they dropped Randy off at his house (he lived with Zinn) and they went to James' apartment.

The next day, Friday, James took his mother, Sandy Wallace, to her home in Los Lunas, thirty miles to the south then returned to Albuquerque. On Central Avenue he saw a couple of acquaintances, Monty Linville and his girlfriend Tanya Galbert. He told them of the deal and Monty said he'd help out and went with Thomas and James in the truck. They met Johnny Zinn at Zinn's Bakery where he worked for his father. Johnny threatened James some more, chastising him for bringing Monty along. He told James that he was pissed off at Ellen Neff and wanted to see her again. He also wanted to see the thirteen-year-old. They drove to Ellen's around 8:00 P.M., stopping off for a bottle of QT first. Ellen came out to the car after telling her younger sister to try to get the license number of the Cadillac. Johnny threatened them both and Ellen stomped back into the house.

They got another pint of QT, which only Zinn was drinking, and then stopped at a Circle K where Johnny said he had to make a phone call to the big wheels in Farmington. Zinn then told Scartaccini that his screw-ups are costing a lot of lost money which he, Scartaccini, would have to pay back. As for Ellen Neff, he'd have a junkie slit her throat one of these days. Zinn also threatened Danielle and suggested to James that he try to talk her into going to Farmington.

On the stand James tearfully stated, "I wouldn't let him touch my wife."

Zinn left them around 9:00 P.M. and they continued looking for a willing girl all that night. They ran into Randy Pierce who told them that there's only one way out of this kind of business, "Feet down."

Monty and Thomas shot some speed around that time and since Monty was currently on a work-release program from the county jail James and Thomas dropped him off at the jail around 10:00 before continuing their fruitless quest.

At this point Schwartz asked Scartaccini about his drug history. James said that he had tried diet pills, but not methamphetamine, and had smoked pot occasionally. As far as dealing, he only sold joints for lunch money, like everybody else. Since the deal between Scartaccini and the DA stipulated that immunity was not granted for any unrelated crimes Schwartz was trying to maximize any other crimes that James might admit to while Scartaccini was trying to minimize them.

This was an unusual aspect to Schwartz's questioning. Scartaccini was a witness for the prosecution and therefore the DA was banking on the jury believing what he had to say. At the same time the DA appeared regretful of the deal that Leon Taylor had finagled for his clients, Scartaccini and Sliger, and hoped to catch Scartaccini in a lie, which might negate the deal. In fact, Schwartz was much more rough and scornful of his own witness in direct examination than Farrah, the defense attorney, was in cross examination.

The next day, Saturday, Thomas and James picked up Monty and they went to a fair looking for a guy named Worthless. On the way Monty regaled them with his plans to buy a bunch of speed and get some guys hooked on it who can then be used like a "junkie army". They picked up a hitch-hiker then stopped at a Circle K where they gave him a dollar and sent him inside for a coke. They drive off with his bag and rifled it finding nothing worthwhile. Meanwhile James got drunk and let Thomas drive.

"The pressure was getting to me."

They were supposed to meet Johnny at 4:00 P.M. behind the bakery. Before leaving, the three of them made a pact to protect each other against Zinn.

Schwartz asked, "Protect, how?" and Scartaccini said he always has a .22 rifle in a pouch under the front seat. It's an antique that was given to him at birth by his father.

They pulled up alongside Johnny in his Cadillac and James got in the front seat with him while Thomas and Monty stayed in the truck. Johnny was drinking QT in a fancy shot glass and said, "If you hadn't screwed up you could be drinkin out of a glass like this." Zinn told James that he wanted a girl soon. He said even if you have to grab one off the street, you do it. He started to choke James with both hands and when Monty got out of the car and advanced toward the Caddy Johnny told James to smile. James did and Monty returned to the truck. At that time Johnny showed James a gun that he carried in a shoulder holster. He said, "If you can't get a product then maybe you can get me some tires for my Cadillac."

James, relieved and frightened, returned to the truck and told Thomas and Monty that they'd been reprieved and now only had to come up with four tires. Monty gave them a few hints on tire-stealing ("Check out Paradise Hills cuz that's where the rich people live.") and was dropped off at jail for the night. James and

Thomas went to K-Mart where they bought winter caps and gloves. That night, early Sunday morning they stole four tires, hubcaps and fender skirts from a Chrysler near Taylor Ranch. They dropped these off at James' apartment around 5:00 am.

The DA quizzed Scartaccini about his first statement in which he said that Johnny had a Mac-10, a machine gun. James said that his first statement was a lie and that all he had seen was a clip of shells which Johnny said were Mac-10 shells. Anytime James mentioned a lie in his first statement Schwartz made him elaborate.

Scartaccini and Sliger met Zinn and Pierce at the parking lot at the bingo parlor next to Zinn's Bakery at noon the next day, Sunday the 12th. Johnny was pleased with the tires but said that since the Farmington people lost so much money on James' screw-ups a product would have to be recruited even if they had to grab somebody right off the street. At that moment they saw a blonde in the parking lot and Zinn said that if they weren't so close to his bakery she'd be perfect. Zinn said, "This time Randy will make sure you guys do it right."

Randy, James and Thomas took the tires to an apartment and unloaded them. Randy said not to worry about the police because, "We take care of each other."

At the meeting with Zinn that afternoon he had given them instructions for that evening. Bring a polaroid camera, bandannas, sleeping pills, a syringe and rope. Randy suggested Mace. Meet back at the A-1 Cleaners on Juan Tabo.

James and Thomas drove down to Los Lunas to Sandy's trailer where they picked up the camera, the pills and Mace. Back in Albuquerque they stopped at a camera store for film and James joked with the salesgirl about what the film was to be used for.

In the witness box James was nearly crying and was having a hard time explaining himself. The DA was asking his questions sarcastically, implying that James was telling the story truthfully but lying about his frame of mind at the time.

Johnny arrived at the cleaners in his Cadillac and Randy drove up in a beat-up station wagon. Johnny gave further instructions about the bandannas. "Put one in her mouth, the other one over her eyes." He filled up the syringe, which Randy supplied, with dissolved pills and Sliger taped it inside the camera case. "Shoot her up under her tongue or in her vagina." Johnny gave Randy some money and told him to "shoot her up and take her to the Canyon Motel like last time."

Randy picked up some speaker wires and scraps of cloth at the cleaners and he and James and Thomas drove to the Canyon Motel on Central where Randy rented a room in back.

With James fighting back tears the judge adjourned the trial for lunch. Scartaccini had been on the stand for about three hours. A TV director couldn't have broken to commercial at a more suspenseful time.

September 8, 1988 1:30 P.M.

BEFORE COURT reconvened for the afternoon session a friend and I talked to a reporter for the Albuquerque Tribune who had seen Scartaccini testify at the preliminary hearing in Albuquerque. My friend remarked that the Tribune's article on the trial seemed to view Scartaccini's story in a sympathetic light. The reporter replied, "Well, I guess he's considered innocent until proven slimy."

When testimony resumed Scartaccini said that he, Sliger and Pierce first went to Monty Linville's mother's house looking for him but he wasn't there. As they passed a shopping center Randy saw a likely product and told James to jump out and grab her but James "chickened out". Randy reiterated how they are to abduct the girl. James is to spray her in the face with mace and Thomas is to slug her in the temple. They are to stuff a balled bandanna in her mouth and tie a couple of them around her mouth and eyes.

Schwartz asked, "You had a can of mace in your hand in the car?"

"Yes, I did."

"Did you think of spraying Randy in the face and running?"

"No. He woulda killed me."

Their next stop was a topless bar. Randy followed a woman walking across the parking lot in the car but she wasn't chosen. They drove to Coronado Shopping Center and checked out several girls but there was no opportunity. A lone girl was followed in her car but when she pulled into a garage at her house Randy said, "Forget that." Their next potential product was followed walking but when she got in a truck Randy said, "No way in a pick-up."

Randy was getting more and more abusive to them saying that they're wimps and that the next one is the one. They were parked in the parking lot of Albertsons on Juan Tabo. A blonde girl drove up and walked to the store. "That's the one." Randy said.

They waited for about ten minutes and Randy, getting nervous, told James to go in and see what's happening with her. As James entered the store he saw Linda Daniels in the check-out lane and at the same time was spied by a girl that he knew from school, Tina Portwood. He talked briefly with Tina keeping an eye on the blonde.

"Why didn't you say something to Tina about what you're being forced to do?" Schwartz asked sarcastically.

Tearfully, "Randy woulda killed me."

"Randy's out in the car."

"Sooner or later Randy or Johnny woulda got me or Danielle."

James and Tina left Albertson's together and walked back toward the station wagon. Thomas got out and, apparently thinking that Tina was the product, was surprised when James introduced them. Randy motioned through the window to James with his finger to get rid of Tina. "She was too fat and ugly."

Hank Farrah objected to several of Scartaccini's answers as hearsay, which they were, but some of them were overruled because the judge said that James was telling what was said, not what he was told. Since the substance of the information was not damaging to Johnny's case it seemed silly to slow up the proceedings by objecting. I think the judge implied this to Farrah.

As Tina left, Linda Daniels came out of the store with a couple of bags of groceries and got in her car. Randy ordered James to get out and get her but he froze. They followed her in the car with Randy threatening them with death if they don't do it right this time. She pulled into a driveway and Randy stopped on the street and pushed James and Thomas out of the car. He turned around and pulled into the driveway next to her car as Thomas and James attacked her. Thomas was knocked down twice before James put his hand over her mouth stopping her shouts. "Lady, please don't scream," he pleaded.

Schwartz paused then asked sharply, "Why did you continue attacking her?"

"Randy and Johnny woulda tracked me down. Where could I go?"

"You could have gone to Detroit. Or the Grand Canyon. Anywhere."

Sobbing, "I didn't have any money. I'm only seventeen."

Linda quit screaming and she and James fell into the back seat of the station wagon as Randy pulled out and sped away. Linda pulled her legs into the car to keep them from scraping on the pavement and Thomas pulled the door closed.

"Did she see you?"

"Yes she saw us all."

"Did you spray her with mace?"

"No."

"Did anybody say anything?"

"She asked if we were going to kill her and Randy said just to do what you're told and nobody would get hurt."

Before James put a blindfold and gag on her she asked cryptically (to me anyway) if they were working for her enemies. As they were driving, Randy saw some grade school children and said that one of them would have been better.

They drove to the Canyon Motel and Randy walked Linda into the room and told James to bring her purse. Zinn had told them to take off all her clothes so that she wouldn't run so Randy told James to undress her. Linda took most of her clothes off by herself but left her "undergarments" on. When questioned about that word James said he meant "panties". They're in Room 321.

James tied her clothes in a bundle and threw it in a corner. Randy gave her some pills (James thought two) and ordered James to tie her hands behind her then had her lie on her stomach on the bed under the covers. Randy told James to take off her panties.

As Randy was looking through Linda's purse Zinn came in. He took her pulse, asked if she'd been given any pills and checked out her body and face. When he removed her blindfold he told her to keep her eyes closed. He then gave her 7 or 8 more pills and made her drink from his pint of OT. Johnny asked her for her bank card password and at first yelled at her for lying. He seemed satisfied with her next answer.

Johnny said he had to call the man in Farmington and left for a few minutes. The deal involved two ounces of crank. When Johnny returned he sent Randy and Thomas with her Amigo card to get what they could from the bank.

"What does Johnny do next?"

"He's playing with her, you know, like fingering her anally and then he tells me to take some pictures of her but they don't come out."

Zinn then told James to go to a Circle K and get some vaseline and come back in about an hour. James left and came back "around 8:45 maybe." He said that he thought that there might have been some other people there while he was gone but only Johnny, Randy and Thomas were there when he returned. Zinn said that "She doesn't give head worth a damn."

"Did you tell all this to the police when you made your first statement?"

"No I lied to them at first."

Scartaccini was alternating between crying and answering sharply to Schwartz's jabs and as he described the actual rape he stuttered and sobbed.

"First Randy takes off his clothes and makes her give him head then he starts raping her then Johnny tells Tommy to screw her while she gives me head. We pull down our pants and Johnny takes pictures of us and her. The pictures are security against ratting. Nobody takes any pictures of Johnny. The Johnny tells me to fuck her in the ass but I can't get it in so I kinda rub up against her."

"Did you reach a climax?"

"No."

Several times during the night Zinn had Linda take some more pills and she was conscious but groggy. Zinn and Pierce raped her again and left around midnight. James and Thomas stayed at the motel with her that night. She slept a bit and then Thomas raped her again. James didn't sleep that night.

"As a matter of fact you haven't slept in quite a while, have you?"

"I haven't slept since maybe Wednesday or Thursday."

Randy came back to the motel room around 8:00 the next morning, Monday the 13th, and told them to get her ready for transporting. He gave her more pills. Randy then told them to clean the place up and he went around wiping everything down including the walls, They put cups and trash in a plastic bag and put it in the truck. Randy told Linda that her boyfriend had paid a ransom so they were going to return her to him.

Their first stop was a truckstop. Randy was driving with Linda Daniels next to him, blindfolded, and James and then Thomas next to her. Part of the time she slept on the floorboard. Thomas made a phone call to Muleshoe Texas and James called Sandy and told her he wouldn't be at work that day.

They next stopped at Jerry's Lounge where Randy said Johnny would meet them but Zinn didn't show. They went somewhere else and James called Danielle and told her he was ok. Then back to Jerry's Lounge. Randy went in and came back out a few minutes later saying that Johnny said to take her to the Jemez mountains (an hour's drive north of Albuquerque) and wait for further instructions.

They stopped at a Circle K in San Ysidro, a half hour out of Albuquerque. It was about 10:30 am. When they got to the Jemez mountains they parked and Thomas got in the back of the truck and sat while Randy walked around. James and Linda, who was sleeping, stayed in the cab of the truck. Randy and Thomas burned the bag with the trash from the motel. Linda awakened and asked to comb her hair so James took her comb from her purse and combed her hair for her. The blindfold was removed for this but she kept her eyes closed.

Randy noticed the .22 rifle in a pouch under the front seat and put it in the rear of the truck. Around 2:00 P.M. Randy and Thomas left James and Linda and drove off to make a phone call. While Pierce and Sliger were gone a truck with a man and a woman parked a hundred or so yards away. The man got out and did something in the back of the truck. James took off Linda's blindfold and told her, "I've had enough of this. Do whatever you want. Take off if you want to. I won't stop you. I don't care what happens anymore."

"Do you realize you just signed her death warrant by taking off her blindfold?"

Sobbing, "I think she was gonna die anyway. It didn't seem real what was happening."

Linda didn't act and soon the truck drove away. James and Linda climbed a hill nearby and were talking when the truck with Randy and Thomas returned. James and Linda went back down the hill.

Randy was mad about their leaving the spot and was even madder about the blindfold, which James put back on. Randy said the instructions were to get rid of her in the best way possible and get back to Albuquerque. James pled with Randy not to do it but Randy said they had to, she could identify them.

The DA, perhaps on purpose, never asked Scartaccini if Linda was aware of all this or not.

They all got in the cab and they went looking for a spot. Thomas and James continued pleading to not kill her but Randy said he ought to "throw her off a cliff." Randy saw a "culvert" and said that it looked like a good place.

Randy and Linda walked to the edge of the culvert and Randy told James to get the rifle.

"Did you hand him the gun or did he take it out of your hands?"

"He took it."

"Is it getting real yet?"

Schwartz had Scartaccini show the jury where everybody was at the time. James left the witness box and showed how he was at the top of the culvert while Randy was standing with the rifle at the bottom. Linda was three feet away from Randy standing but slouching over.

Scartaccini was walking back to the truck when he heard the shot. A few seconds later Randy came up and the three drove on down the road. After a mile or so Randy turned the truck around and headed back "to make sure she is dead." James saw something in the road and jumped out of the truck and began running, expecting a shot in the back. He stopped a few seconds later and walked back to the truck.

"So it seemed real finally?"

"Yes, it was real."

They stopped at the culvert and Randy told James to make sure she was dead. James got out and leaned over the edge of the culvert from the road and saw her body on her back. She was wearing a red winter jacket and there was blood all over her face which was still blindfolded.

On the way back to Albuquerque Randy said, "This wasn't the first, or the second, or the third person I've killed but it's the first girl. It's not gonna be the last either."

They stopped at a carwash where they washed the truck thoroughly, inside and out. Randy told them to burn the purse and they dropped him off on the corner by his house. They drove to a field on the western edge of town and burned the purse. They drove away with the fire still burning but came back a few minutes later to check on it. The fire had gone out so they burned the purse some more. Then they went to the dry cleaners.

After Thomas called his father, Thomas and James went back to the apartment. That night James finally got some sleep.

The next day, Tuesday the 14th James threw his shoes away because he knew he had left footprints up in the Jemez. Randy stopped by the cleaners and told them to keep cool. James was afraid that Johnny might want to get rid of some "loose ends".

"What loose ends?" Schwartz asked.

"Me and Thomas are the loose ends."

Randy called and said there was to be a meeting at the Circle K. Thomas and James had better be there or else. James thought that Randy was trying to get James and Thomas together at the same time. James met Randy at the Circle K but Thomas never showed.

Another meeting was set up for Wednesday at the Mint Saloon and again Thomas didn't show. Johnny was there that time and said the heat is on from Farmington and that everybody should leave town. He saw James arm where James had burned himself on purpose to cover up some fingernail scratches sustained in the abduction, Johnny approved. After Johnny left Randy said he was not going to leave town because he had too many good things going on. He advised James to "Stay put."

That night James, Sandy, Troy Wallace her boyfriend, Danielle, Thomas and Randy went to Cowboy's, a big C&W bar. James felt safe from Randy even though he and Thomas were together at the same time because there were so many people at the bar. Danielle, who knew that James was afraid of Randy tried to keep Randy on the dance floor while Thomas and James shot pool. Later that night somebody threw some popcorn which landed on Sandy and Danielle as they came out of the ladies' room and James, who was drunk, warned the guy to watch it. Randy told James to cool it.

Thursday night James and Thomas saw a fuzzy picture of Randy in the station wagon on either the news or on a Crimestoppers report. They recognized the picture as being from the autoteller at the bank. James and Thomas took the rifle apart and whittled down the stock. Danielle was in the bedroom at this time and didn't see them do it. As per Randy's instructions they soaked the rifle's metal parts in oil and scored the barrel. That night they threw it off a bridge into the Rio Grande River, James kept the butt-plate from the rifle because it had an inscription from his father, who had built the gun. The inscription read, "To my son James Scartaccini, with love, Dad".

James said, "I kept it because it's the only thing my dad ever gave me that said he loved me."

Schwartz asked James what Danielle thought about all this. Was she suspicious? "No. I told her not to ask any questions."

What about his mother, Sandy? "I told her to leave me alone."

The next day, Friday the 17th, James and Danielle drove to Golden, NM, a small town in the mountains nearby. Soon after arriving he got a phone call from the FBI and drove back to Albuquerque and the A-1 Cleaners where he was arrested by the Albuquerque police.

His first statement to the police was that he was in Muleshoe Texas at the time of the kidnapping.

"That was a lie, wasn't it?"

"Yes, that was a lie."

"What do you think will happen to you now, James?"

"I don't know."

With that the prosecution ended its direct examination of James Scartaccini.

Hank Farrah began his cross-examination of Scartaccini with such a belligerent tone that he actually caused the witness to perk up rather than become cowed. When James answered a couple of questions with the phrase, "You could say that." Farrah retorted with, "What do *you* say, Scartaccini?" Farrah got a little flustered in his indignation and fumed, "Don't answer my questions with other answers!"

When Scartaccini stated that his lawyer was being paid $50,000 Farrah sarcastically comments, "$50,000. And you say you couldn't get out of town because you had no money."

James testified that he saw Leon Taylor for perhaps 30 minutes the night of his arrest and told him that he was in Muleshoe at the time of the kidnapping. Later that night he changed his story.

"Why?"

"Because the FBI offered me and my wife protection."

"Your wife works at the dry cleaners. Anybody in town could go in and kill her."

"Not hardly."

Farrah scornfully referred to the "enormous pornography ring in Farmington" as a story made up by Scartaccini himself but James insisted that Randy said there was one and he thought there was one.

Out of the blue Farrah asked, "Didn't you tell the people at Juvenile Hall you killed her.?"

James denied it.

Some other questions asked by Farrah...

"What do you prefer as a weapon?"

"How do you like a baseball bat as a weapon?"

"Didn't you hit somebody in the head with a pipe wrench?"

James related that a month or so before the kidnapping Danielle and he were going to move in with her parents, the Quick's, but when they insisted on James and Danielle sleeping in separate bedrooms James and Dan Quick got in a fight at the cleaners.

According to James, "I almost got killed. He came at me with a pipe wrench and in the struggle before he kicked the shit out of me the pipe wrench sorta glanced off his forehead, but I didn't hit him with it."

"I have a witness who will testify that you threw some scissors at your wife."

"I didn't throw them at her, I threw them to the side. And they weren't scissors, they were pliers."

Farrah quizzed Scartaccini about the discrepancies between the two official statements he had given the police. There were a few substantial differences between Scartaccini's two stories but Farrah seemed to place as much importance on such seemingly trivial matters as the number of pills Linda Daniels was given or whether James ejaculated or not.

When answering some rapid-fire questions about Ellen Neff, James blurted out that Zinn was angry because "She wouldn't agree to do it annually." Farrah said that Ellen disobeyed Johnny, "Why didn't you?"

Farrah then came up with another feeble "lie" when James said he was tired when making the second statement at 1:15 A.M. Saturday the 20th.

"Here is a transcript of that interview. The police ask if you are tired and you say no."

Farrah accused James of lying about the Mac-10 gun. Scartaccini said he thought Zinn had one because Johnny said the shells were Mac-10 shells.

Farrah read several statements from the statements and the transcript from the preliminary hearing which showed that Scartaccini was either lying or making a normal number of errors in remembering events that took place weeks before. One of the more intriguing details concerned what happened when James came back to the motel room after getting the vaseline.

"At the preliminary hearing you testified that when you told Johnny not to rape her he took you in the bathroom and choked you like he did in the car and told you to shut your mouth or he'd kill you."

James quietly said, "That was a lie about the bathroom."

For whatever reason neither Farrah or Schwartz elucidated on this "lie" for the benefit of the jury or the spectators. Nothing was ever mentioned about it in the media.

Another exchange—

"What made you think that other people had been in the room while you were gone?"

"Linda Daniels was saying to Johnny when I came in, 'Please tell me you didn't make me do it with a nigger,' and Johnny told her, 'Don't worry, I canceled the nigger.' "

This detail, which was not self-serving to anyone, especially not the victim, was something I imagine *could* have happened. It's not the kind of detail that anyone would make up if details were, indeed, made up.

Farrah threw a lot of unrelated questions at Scartaccini who, with a bit of contempt, answered them. At one point Farrah asked the Judge to admonish the witness not to argue with the defense and the judge said, "You ask argumentative questions and you get that kind of answer."

Hank Farrah then enumerated the various objects that were required for the kidnapping and murder.

"Where did the gun come from?"

"It was my gun."

"What about the mace?"

"We got it at my mother's house."

"How about the truck.?"

"It was mine."

"The wires she was tied with?"

"We got those at the cleaners."

"The bandannas?"

"I bought them."

"The pills?"

"They were Thomas's."

"And the syringe?"

"Either Monty or Thomas had it."

"What about the camera?"

"It's mine."

"And the film?"

"I bought it."

"Did Johnny Zinn supply anything?"

"He made us do it."

Hank Farrah's last question, "What are you going to do when you grow up?" was answered, "I don't know."

On re-direct examination Robert Schwartz asked Scartaccini if he had seen any of his statements before today and the answer was no. Had he been coached on his answers? No.

The ordeal for immunity of James Scartaccini was over. The question that was never answered for me was; who decides if James has abided by the terms of the deal? Sliger was granted immunity for all crimes except the rape in the motel after Johnny left. For that he received a three year sentence. James Scartaccini could conceivably escape with no penalty except for the time he has served at the Juvenile Hall since his arrest.

PART THREE: Epilogue

ON THURSDAY, September 25, 1986, Johnny Zinn was found guilty on all charges. He was sentenced to life imprisonment plus 96 years. He'll be eligible for parole in 76 years. Randy Pierce had previously been sentenced to life plus 36 years. Scartaccini and Sliger had both made deals with the DA for immunity if they testified. Scartaccini was released from jail covertly, and he and his wife moved to Maine. Sliger was sentenced to three years for the rape that took place that night at the motel when Zinn wasn't there. Six years later, James Scartaccini committed suicide.

THE MAN WITH THE PLASTIC SKULL

Chapter I

A DISTURBING TELEGRAM

PHILO VUNPTAFFHOLSTER leaned back in the specially-designed car seat of his brand-new 1960 Metropolitan convertible and once more regarded the telegram that had just arrived from Mora Bora, informing him that like it or not, he was *not* the only man on the planet with a plastic skull!

He was on his way to spend an hour or so with the most beautiful woman in the world—bar none!—and now, as he pulled out of his driveway into the slow-moving 5 P.M. traffic, he began to read the message from the far off Pacific that threatened to strip him of his fame, his fortune, and more importantly, the most beautiful woman in the world—nuff sed!

MORA BORA 5:13 A.M. JULY 5, 1960

FROM: DWIL SPROCKET
TO: PHILO VUNPTAFFHOLSTER

PHI, OLD FRIEND, I'VE GOT BAD NEWS. A NATIVE OF MORA BORA, ONE MANUEL AMANO, IS GOING TO REVEAL TOMORROW AT HIGH NOON THAT HE TOO HAS A PLASTIC SKULL LIKE YOURS.

Philo swerved around an 18-wheeler that was making a wide right turn, then drove on.

NOW, AS YOU KNOW, YOU'VE MADE QUITE A NAME FOR YOURSELF IN PAST YEARS AS "THE MAN WITH THE PLASTIC SKULL", EXHIBITING YOURSELF IN

TRAVELLING MOTORCADE CIRCUSES, ALLOWING PEOPLE TO FEEL AND MANIPULATE YOUR NON-RIGID SKULL.

A car in the right lane cut Philo off and he had to slam on the brakes, sending the car into a tight, well-controlled spin. Straightening out, Philo once again turned to the telegram and drove on.

I'VE MANAGED TO FIND OUT THAT THE OPERATION ON AMANO WAS PERFORMED BY A DOCTOR WESLEY TOOTHWELL, WHO PRACTICES AT PEPPERDUKE UNIVERSITY, JUST DOWN THE ROAD FROM WHERE YOU LIVE IN NORTHEAST CHICAGO. HE'S A, WHAT DO YOU CALL IT, BONE SURGEON.

Philo pulled into a service station and told the attendent to fill'erup. The attendant gave a toothy grin and shuckled, "Gawsh, Mr. vunPtaffholster, anytime!"

"How did you know my nam—" Philo shot back, but immediately realized his mistake—he was one of the most well-known and beloved circus performers in the Tri-State area.

"Wa-all, Mr. vunPtaffholster, it's writ' raght thar on th' sida yer car!"

"That's right," Philo thought, "I forgot that I had a sign painter come over and paint:

PHILO VUNPTAFFHOLSTER
"THE MAN WITH THE PLASTIC SKULL"
A Circus Near You

---

on both sides of my car." He paid for the gas, got back in the convertible, and picked up the telegram as he started the car, and drove on.

THERE IS MORE TO TELL YOU BUT THESE TELE-GRAMS ARE, WELL, EXPENSIVE. I'LL WRITE YOU A LETTER AND SEND IT TO YOU VIA THE U.S. MAIL.

A policecar pulled up alongside the Metropolitan, which was going about fifty, and the policeman who was not driving held his billy club up and, through the closed window, thumped it against his gloved left hand once, twice, three times, all the while gazing at Philo with a sleepy grin on his face. Philo winced, and felt the skin on his hump loosen. He knew what those three thumps meant—the third degree! Then he saw the cop's eyes drift down to the sign on the side of the car, and the cop's face went ashen. He yelled at his partner to speed up and to Philo's astonishment, the policecar sped on ahead and was soon out of sight.

Philo breathed a sigh of relief and resumed his telegram-reading. Once again he drove on.

    I GUESS THAT'S ABOUT IT, PARTNER.

                    DWIL

Philo put down the telegram and thought about the implications of another person having a plastic skull like his. And how? Philo had always been told that it was ol' Doc Winkerdoll that had saved his life by removing his heavily radar-active skull back in 1954, replacing it with a skull prosthesis made from Plastene, a new form of plastic the doctor had invented, a form that was actually more like a soft rubber with incredible tensile strength. It wasn't the whole skull, but just the bowl-shaped top part, from the tops of the eye orbitals up.

But ol' Doc Winkerdoll was killed not long after performing the operation, and never revealed the secret formula for Plastene. He left a note saying it was hidden in a 2-inch Plastene sphere, but the four government agents who killed Winkerdoll searched every inch of his office and home and never found it.

At this point in his ruminations Philo pulled into the posh driveway of the Smith-Smythes, where dwelt the most beautiful woman in the world, Confessa Smith-Smythe.

Chapter II

CONFESSA WORRIES!

CONFESSA MET HIM at the door as she always did, giving him a warm kiss while rubbing his hump for luck. But she had a look of worry on her pretty face.

"Oh, Phi, oh Phi, oh Phi," she bewailed, "I've just had the most dreadful news!"

"Me too! You first," Philo countered.

"Well, you know that Daddy has had some bad luck in the market lately, and he just found out that unless he pulls a big score with Plastene, Inc. the company that you and he started in anticipation of the day when the formula is found, he's dead broke! And you know we can't get married until he can afford to pay for the lavish wedding ceremony!"

"Gosh, Confessa, that *is* bad news. My news isn't quite so bad, but it's sort of in the same category. I just found out that there is another person who now has a plastic skull, and that may put a damper on my circus career. As the only man on earth with a plastic skull, I was quite a draw, but with this Amano guy—"

"Oh Phi! What are we to do? You've always been so resourceful. In fact, it was because of your hump that Daddy was happy for us to become, well, an *item*. He always said, 'If a man can grow up with a handicap like a huge hump on his right shoulderblade, and still not be bitter with the world, that man is good enough for my daughter!' Of course I've come to love you in spite of your hump—although it does get in the way of our lovemaking sometimes and I *do* wish it could be removed—but that's not to mention your brave experience with your radar-active skull."

"We-ell, Confessa, I feel the same way about your father. As for my skull, you remember how I discovered back in 1954, quite by accident one day when I wandered too near an army air force installation, that my original osseous skull was hyper-sensitive to those new-fangled radar waves used by the military since WWII. I got an excruciating headache that knocked me out and it was only through the good luck of being found by Ol' Doc Winkerdoll that I survived. Apparently, the radar waves caused my skull to contract, giving me the horrible headache. So he removed the top of my skull and replaced it with a Plastene facsimile. I was in a coma for a month afterwards but came out of it in good condition."

"Oh, Phi, if only he had told you what he did with your old skull, we might be able to help Daddy. I've heard that the military and the police are very interested in any material that can detect radar-waves. Of course it's obvious why the air force wants it, but—"

"—Why would the cops want it? I know what you mean, Confessa, it's a real mystery."

He pulled her close to him for another kiss, then snapped his fingers. "Hold it! I just had an idea. Can I use your 'phone?" He reached for the telephone and dialed 0. "Operator, connect me with Professor Wesley Toothwell at Pepperduke University!"

A few minutes later a voice answered. "Toothwell here."

"Doctor Toothwell, my name is Philo vunPtaffholster. Did you just perform surgery on a Mora Boran native, giving him a plastic skull?"

"Why, yes, I did. Did you say, 'vunPtaffholster?' "

"Yes I did. I'm the original Man with the Plastic Skull. Er—ah—did you use Plastene for your skull?"

"No I didn't, Mr. vunPtaff—"

"Just call me Philo, please."

"Thank you, Philo. No I didn't use Plastene. As you know, the formula is still unknown and the Plastene in your head is the only bit of it known to be in existence."

"That's right, Doctor. May I ask two questions? One, is the man you operated on planning on travelling around, exhibiting his skull in circuses? And two, was the operation difficult? I mean, would it have been easier if you *had* had some Plastene to work with?"

"Well, Mr. vunPtaff—er, Philo, the answer to your first question is, absolutely not. Mr. Amano has an abject fear of circuses, especially clowns, and wouldn't get near a circus. In fact, he leaves his village in Mora Bora whenever a circus comes to town, and lives on another island until the carnies leave town for good. As for the second question, the answer is yes, yes, yes, and double yes, yes! The qualities of Plastene, as exhibited by the hundreds, if not thousands of circus-goers who have seen and manipulated your Plastene skull, show that it is a much better material for skull-fabrication than the hard bakelite I used. The formula for Plastene, when it is finally found, will make mill—"

"That's what I wanted to hear, Doctor! I think you'll be hearing from me again—sooner than you think. Thanks for everything!"

With that Philo hung up the phone and turned to his Confessa. "Darlin', I think I've got the answer to all of our problems!'"

Chapter III

ALL STRINGS TIED UP

BONG HAI, leader of the tong, the Fat Black Lemurs, leaned back in his *papa-san* chair and tamped down another bowlful of his tong's best brand of opium. He lit the pipe and took a long, slow pull, gazing at the wall as if it were ten miles away. He set the pipe down and settled deeper in the chair, then reached up and rubbed his skull vigorously, with both hands. He pushed with both hands, squeezing the sides of his head until they receded about an inch. Then he pushed the top down, squeezing the sides out. He had a plastic skull!

The sensations Bong Hai felt as the inner side of his Plastene skull rubbed against his brain, even moving it a bit, were exquisite. He simply could not describe the pleasures to anyone who did not have some good opium and a Plastene skull.

He thought about how he got his new skull. His photographic memory had it all down in detail and the opium was making it seem especially real. His lips mumbled soft words as he drifted into the warm, rolling clouds of nepenthe.

"It began wi' that 'Melican fella, vunPtaffholstel. He velly smalt. He have filst plas'ic skull. He got skull in fi'ty-fo' because he fin' his skull contlac', get smallel, w'en he get neal ladal."

Bong Hai chuckled to himself at his pitiful attempt to say "near radar". And drove on.

"But he luckily foun' a bone sulgeon docta'—fella name' Winkeldoll—who lemove skull an' leplace it wi' Plastene. Docta' also hid folmula fo' Plastene at 'loun' same time. Folmula not foun' until day six yeals latel, w'en vunPtaffholstel get blight idea w'ele it be. He kill two bilds wi' one lock! He fin' folmula fo' Plastene an' fin' his ol' skull w'ich contlac' w'en neal ladal. All in same place!"

The wizened old tong leader smiled to himself as he continued to manipulate his Plastene skull with much pleasure. His softly spoken ruminations continued.

"He get bone docta' name' Toothwell to op'late on his hump and *he* fin' that oliginal docta' name' Winkeldoll, aftel lemovin' skull an' leplacin' it wi' Plastene skull, also lemove hump an' leplace *it* wi' oliginal skull! T'en he hide folmula ball *inside* skull-hump! Why? Because he know govelnment agents wan' to kill him fo' bot' seclets an' will sealch offices flom A to Izzald."

He took another pull on the opium pipe and continued to manipulate his Plastene skull, which he got at the *Chicago Center for Frivolous Elective Surgery,* or CCFES. Once the formula was released by Plastene, Inc. to much public hooplah and unheard of investment by the stock market class, Bong Hai, thanks to his huge fortune amassed from opium sales, was one of the first to receive a new skull.

"So much pleasule I get. Make me glad vunPtaffholstel get lich flom Plastene, get lid of hump an' mally sweethealt, an' sell impoltant ladal-sens'tive skull to militaly so they can tell if ladal bein' used 'gainst them."

Bong Hai's eyes glazed over with extreme joy as he mumbled one last question.

"Nevel did figule out w'y cops wan'ed ladal-sens'tive matelial. Cops nevel use ladal 'gainst own cit'zens, would they? Aftel all, 'tis 'Melica, lan' of flee, light?"

CALHOON

THE ELEVEN AMBIGUPHONES OF FARTHALOMEW SPLIB

BEADS OF SWEAT sprang out on the brow of radio personality Wally Fletch as he sat down in front of the microphone. He knew that if he didn't read his uncle's story flawlessly, he'd lose his $100,000 inheritance and with it, the hand of the only woman he'd ever loved, Miss Avigail Beutelle. What a contretemps!

Three days earlier he had found himself poring over a small piece of paper he had found in the study of his wealthy uncle, Farthalomew Splib, the day after the latter's demise. He was looking for a will—which later turned up in the law offices of Immabod MucMarphy—but all that his uncle's desk contained was a slip of paper with eleven words scratched on it in his uncle's phthisic handwriting.

Bass
Bow
Buffet
Invalid
Lead
Sewer
Singer
Tear
Tower
Peer
Colonized

What could they possibly mean? Wally studied them all weekend and wasn't able to come up with anything. Then, Monday morning when MucMarphy revealed the will and its unusual stipulations, Wally became even more mystified, for the will contained only these words:

"I, Farthalomew Splib, in sound mind and health do present my last will and testament. All of my estate, about $100,000 after taxes and outstanding bills have been paid, shall go to my beloved nephew, Wally Fletch, if he can perform one task: the reading *without error* of my radioplay GRUBS on his show. If he fails, then my entire estate shall go to my pet research project, Society for the Preservation of Anhydrous Slime Molds."

Simple enough! As soon as Wally heard this he took the copy of GRUBS that was attached to the will and prepared for the next day's radio show so he could claim the money his uncle had left him, and ask for the hand of the lovely Avigail. But was there a catch?

Wally noticed that all twelve words on the list were found imbedded in the short story GRUBS, a rambling saga of unlikely characters and implausible plot. So he took his pen and underlined the passages with the twelve words, planning to be especially careful when reading them. Wally was one of the world's greatest radio show readers and normally felt quite confident when reading on air, but he'd never had $100,000 riding on his skills before. Not to mention the hand of Avigail, who had told him that the only way she would marry him was if he could buy her the $80,000 ring that had caught her eye at Bergdorff's.

He quickly glanced through the radioplay at the underlined passages. They were:

"Gasbaugh, bull fiddlist for the London Symphony and professional sport fisherman, had a specially made craft he used to transport his equipment—his bass boat."

"After breaking into the Sheriff of Nottingham's armory, the flamboyant actor/thief Robin Hood took a bow."

" 'One more buffet like that,' the airline passenger moaned during the bumpy flight, 'and I'm gonna hurl!' "

"After losing her license and her leg, Nurse Lancet became an invalid processor for the hospital."

"At the beginning of the foot race on the molten metal planet, Plumbum, Space Cadet Simpson found himself firmly in the lead."

"As the British troops searched the septic system of Betsy Ross' mansion for the patriotic rebel seamstress, Leftenant Spythe cautioned, 'Watch out for the sewer.' "

"The crooning arsonist who specialized in torching night clubs considered himself somewhat of a lounge singer."

"After her radial keratotamy surgery, Mrs. Biffings had tears in her eyes."

"Three stories tall, the huge mobile tower pulled a dozen troop carts behind it."

"His former commanding officer considered John Wayne Bobbit 'a marine without peer.' "

"After the name of the Roanoke settlement was changed from 'Jamestown' to 'James:town', the king considered the New World colonized."

Wiping the sweat from his brow, Wally signaled the producer of the radio show and began to read.

A STARKY FISH STORY

Grandpa Eben Kornpome said:

"Now sit yerse'fs down and lissen, yew no-necked monstahs, an' Gran'pa Eben'll tell you all about Poison Swamp an' the starky fish ovah crost Ol' Twistibus. An' tell Aint Jemidah t' brang me 'nother toddy.

"Evah one o' yew kids knows that th' starky fish c'n strip th' meat offa daid mule in less'n three hours, an' I'm sho' yo' daddies done tol' yew that starky fish lahkes hooman meat e'en better. But yew mayn't know jus' how bloodthi'sty them fish rilly are. An' it's all 'cuz o' mah pappy, yo' Great-gran'pa Enekial, 'r as we called him, 'Neke'. Now yew kids stop fightin' and lissen up.

"It 'uz back in ought-eight when pappy woke up one mornin' cravin' some starky fish stew. A'course the onliest starkies in Idiots Valley is ovah t' Poison Lake so pappy—'r as evahbody called 'im, Neke—sets out on Ol' Twistibus, which wuz nothin' but a windy dirt road back then, to get a mess o' 'em fer maw t' cook.

"It took pappy nigh onto all day t' get there, even with Lightnin' Bug leadin' th' team pullin' a wagon with a big tank fer th' fish in it. So he parks th' team an' settles down fer th' night 'bout a mile f'm th' Swamp, lookin' to git an early start th' nex' day.

"Well, that night a coupla flatland know-nothin's from up Chicaga way get it in they fool minds t' do some midnight skinny-dippin' in Poison Swamp an' they's screams wake evahbody up fer 'bout a mile 'roun'. Th' water where they wuz swimmin' wuz red as a boilt beet fer a whol' day after'erds, but they wuzn't evah foun'. Th' starkies got 'em, shure's shootin'.

"Ennyways, pappy decided t' do some starky fishin' in that very same spot th' nex' day an' hault in near t' fo' dozen o' them suckers. He caught so many that th' tub in th' wagon wuz near' solid wif starkies. They wuz all fat an' sassy lahk on'y starky fish c'n get after gorgin' on some prime grade-A-1 meat. So pappy Neke heads back t' th' frog gullies an' maw's stew pot.

"He hauls in 'bout dusk an' maw tells him t' leave th' starkies, which 'uz all frisky and jumpin' in th' tub, an' get some sleep so's we c'n have a big starky stew feast th' nex' day. Man, we could almos' smell that good starky stew a'cookin' a'ready.

"The nex' day, maw grabs 'bout a dozen o' th' starkies, th' big fat ones who'd had they fill th' day befo', an' boils up a stew fer suppah. I tell yew kids, that wuz th' bes' starky stew ennyone evah had. Tha's when we foun' out that starkies taste bettah if'n they's jus' had some hooman meat t' eat.

"Now mah brothah, Onus, yo' Gran'-uncle Onus, who yew prolly don't remembah, had a huge helpin' o' th' stew that day. An' mah othah brothah, Url, yo' Gran-uncle Url who lives down t' Catamount Creek, he din't have none o' th' stew 'cuz he sez it 'smellt funny' an' so he jus' et some ol' starky stew that 'uz lef' ovah f'm a week befo'. Well, they wuz both fussin' an' fightin' ovah somethin' that evenin' an' wouldn' yew know it, they bof fell in t' the tub wif th' three dozen starky fish swimmin' 'roun'.

"Afore we could haul 'em out, them starkies started in on 'em, and poor ol' Onus wuz et up quick as yew please. Them starkies seed him as some kin' a' goormay meal! But Url, they lef' completely 'lone, not oncet even takin' a bite outa him.

"That's when we foun' out that hoomans tas'e bettah t' starkies if'n the hooman done et some starkies who'd done et some hooman afore that!

"We-ell, it din't take too much more 'sper'mentin' 'roun' to see that we might jus' turn this inta a gol' mine. Maw started bottlin' up her spaycial stew made from starkies who et hoomans who et starkies, an' afore we knew it, them flatland fools from Chicaga wuz payin' top dollah fo' it. An' whenevah we needed more o' them hooman-eatin' starkies we'd hol' a spaycial "free dinner" fo' skinny-dippin' fools. Th' main part o' th' party would get some reg'lar starky stew and then when they went skinny-dippin' th' starkies'd leave 'em 'lone. But th' one 'r two guys who'd get starky stew made f'm starkies who'd et some hooman meat, why, they'd jus' supply us wif more o' the good starkies for maw's spaycial stew when we wen' fishin' th' nex' day.

"An' tha's why yew li'l monstahs live in this twenny-room mansion wif swimmin' pool an' golf course smack dab in th' middle o' Idiots Valley. Now shet up an' tell yo' Aint Jemidah t' brang me some o' that Rooshian caviar 'long wif anoth' toddy. Now git!"

CATCH - XXII

IT WAS LATE one Saturday night when Philbert Wallaby decided there was no other option: he'd have to murder his boss, Simon Bubbleday.

It began that afternoon. Philbert was editing a book by one of the publishing firm's most popular writers and he had all the text exactly as it should be, except for the introduction. He had to make one final fix and the book would be done. Philbert had worked for Bubbleday for a while and he knew the absolute rules for typesetting that the owner had proscribed, which could never be broken.

(1) *Everything* will be in 11-point Verdana!

(2) The page size and margins will be standard and never changed — *under any circumstances!*

(3) The page numbers for the introduction will be in Roman Numerals!

Philbert knew the rules well and had never had any problems. Now, if he could just get this little book done, he'd be through for the weekend and tomorrow he could marry the woman of his dreams, Esmeralda Colloquia. If he couldn't, he knew that Bubbleday would insist that he keep working on it until it was finished and his marriage plans would be dashed.

Philbert wiped a bead of sweat off his brow and squinted at the sentence at the bottom of page IX. It read:

"For a more detailed description of this, see page ---."

Philbert had inserted the "---" into the sentence because he didn't really know what page the description would land on when he edited page IX. He planned to fix it when he did know the proper page.

His stomach lurched spasmodically as he tried inserting the correct page number, "XXIV", into the sentence. When he did, the Roman numeral made the line too long and the "XXIV" word-wrapped and was placed on the next page, page X.

Ordinarily that would pose no problem but when Philbert scrolled ahead to page XXIV he saw that the sentence with the description had now been moved from the bottom of page XXIV to the top of the next page, XXV.

So Philbert went back to page X and replaced the "XXIV" with "XXV". Aaarrrgh! The Roman numeral was now pulled back onto the bottom of page IX! And when he scrolled forward to the description, it too had been moved back to the bottom of page XXIV.

It was at this point that Philbert Wallaby knew that his boss, Simon Bubbleday, had to be killed.

MURDER IN THE MONASTERY

A Novelization of a Game

Chapter 1: The Gate

"MERDE!" The word oozed past the lips of the dour, mustachioed man as he leaned back to read the wrought-iron inscription above the massive gate. He pulled his trenchcoat tighter about him—although it was warm for All Saints' Eve—and remembered what the superintendent had said to him that morning, "Don't let it get to you, Claude. It's only The Abbey of St. Isosceles." Easy for him to say—he didn't have to spend the night digging up clues in the most mathematically mysterious place on earth.

Claude la Mort, Inspecteur d'Hommicide of the Sûreté, had hopped a jet from Orly to Dulles, and after a short briefing by the DC police chief, been driven to the small village outside of Washington DC. He now stood outside the Abbey gate, feeling like a very minor imp, dwarfed by the twenty-foot walls that surrounded the 14th Century monastery. Ten years ago it had been brought over from France and reconstructed, brick by brick, and now it was the home of a group of monks and nuns. The sun was just starting to dip over the wall to the west.

The superintendent had picked him to investigate the death of Abbot Costello, the head of the Abbey, who had been killed the night before. La Mort figured he had been chosen because of his "success" in the Calhoon Museum caper earlier that year, although the superintendent probably knew that if it hadn't been for a lot of luck, and a well-placed adze, La Mort would be pushing up grapevines right now. But maybe this case needed a Lucky Pierre.

He knew that once he entered the Abbey gate, he would be expected to stay inside until he solved the case so he looked around the area surrounding the gate. Who knows? Maybe the killer left his car parked in a No Parking zone. La Mort smirked at his natural pessimism, thinly disguised as optimism, then leaned over and picked up a piece of paper sticking in a nearby bush. It was a newspaper clipping, a review of a book by one Father Murphy, called "How to Change a Light Bulb". Murphy's main claim to fame seemed to be the invention of "soul-detecting" lights and sound-sensitive locks. The inspector vaguely remembered hearing about Father Murphy. Didn't he live at the Abbey? He put the clipping in his trenchcoat pocket.

La Mort looked down to review an info sheet the chief had given him. He might as well know what he was getting into before he entered what may be his own private apocalypse.

The sheet read:

~ At 8:03 A.M., October 31, 1963 a monk reported to the police that he had discovered the body of Abbot Costello on the floor of the south confessional of the church.

~ The lab reports that he died of a synthetic strain of the Bubonic plague, so all residents of the abbey have been evacuated to St. Dismal's.

~ Six people are missing. Since the villagers didn't see anyone leave the abbey it is assumed they are still inside.

~ No one seems to know how to get into the library so it hasn't been searched.

~ Matins, a bell and prayer ritual usually rung at dawn, was mysteriously heard at midnight last night.

The missing and/or deceased are:

~ ABBOT COSTELLO (deceased)—the saintly figurehead of the abbey.
~ CARDINAL MUSIAL (missing)—visiting consul from Rome, arrived October 29.
~ FATHER NOSTER (missing)—the head monk, in charge of the monks and novices.
~ MOTHER PULEEZE (missing)—Mother Superior of the cloister, in charge of the nuns.
~ NOVICE SCOSHA (missing)—fledgling monk, reputed to be a practical joker.

~ SISTER DEBBIE (missing)—young nun, said to have several un-nunlike tendencies.
~ DOCTOR DEE (missing)—the village physician, last seen entering the abbey the night of October 29.

Not much to go on.

He turned the sheet over and saw that there was a map of the abbey drawn on the back. He glanced at it and saw that the abbey was a typical monastery/cloister, except for an unusually shaped building in the center of the vaguely square grounds. This was the famous Library of St. Isosceles, a four-lobed building with angular slits between each of the lobes. Judging by the building's shape on the map, it seemed to have triangular rooms, rather than rectangular.

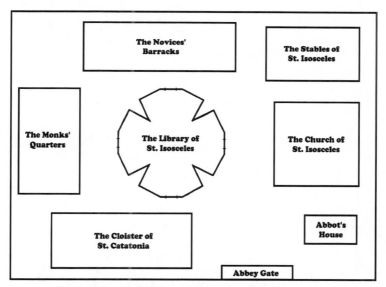

The Abbey of St. Isosceles

To the right of the gate, inside the abbey, was the house where the victim had lived. Directly north of it was the church, and beyond that the stables. Continuing on around the library were the barracks for the novices, then the monks' quarters and finally the Cloister of St. Catatonia, which was just to the left of the gate. Each lobe of the Library faced a building, with the church to the east, barracks to the north, monks' quarters to the west and the cloister to the south.

Well, I've got all night, La Mort thought, and maybe I can find one of those missing people to give me a better idea of what went on last night.

Taking one last look at the wrought-iron inscription that read "The Abbey of St. Isosceles: Abandon Joy All Ye Who Enter Here", La Mort sighed and shuffled through the gate.

Chapter 2: The House

Might as well check out the Abbot's house while there's still some light, La Mort thought, and walked along a stony path to the house to the east. It was a grey, nondescript building with an as-cetic air to it—the kind of house a homeless person might have. The front door was closed, but not locked, and La Mort entered to see a gloomy sitting room, the only room in the house. On a table by a Lazee-Boy was a book. He picked it up.

It was a weekly daily planner—Costello's—for the week of October 25 to 31. "The gendarmes must've left this for me," he muttered to himself as he thumbed through the pages, noting the small, cramped handwriting. He decided to settle down in the chair and digest this first clue to the Abbot's murder.

"Sacre bleu!" La Mort spat as the roughness of a rhinoceros-tough hide gouged him through the bulk of his trenchcoat. It was a hair-chair, modern equivalent of a hair-shirt. The victim definitely wasn't killed for his riches and high lifestyle, he thought, and tried to ignore the discomfort and outright pain as he read the Abbot's diary.

~ October 25—The St. Swithins Day Ceremony was ruined today when the altar mysteriously exploded. Under the rubble was dis-covered a small, previously unknown catacomb.

~ October 26—Found a disgusting scroll in the Room of the Ram. Must speak to Father Noster about this.

~ October 27—Spied Sister Debbie giving more than proper succor to a grieving villager. I related to her the parable of the Bashing of the Sodomite and sent her on her way.

~ October 28—Overheard Mother Puleeze talking to the heathen Doctor Dee. She said something about "services rendered". Must follow this up. Only priests may perform liturgical services.

~ October 29—My official seal seems to be missing. Cardinal Musial arrived from Rome and was quite interested in the Papal Bull of 303 AD which was found in the catacomb. I'll show it to him tomorrow night right after confession.

~ October 30—Tonight I'm hearing the confessions of Father Noster, Mother Puleeze, Novice Scosha, Sister Debbie and Cardinal Musial. The Cardinal will hear mine.

There was no entry for October 31. Since he was killed prior to 8:00 that morning, that was understandable. La Mort digested this new information which placed all of the missing people except Doctor Dee at "confession" the night before. It looks like at least five people had "opportunity" to kill Costello in the confessional. And what's to stop Doctor Dee from creeping in?

The inspector gratefully got up out of the painful Lazee-Boy and, seeing nothing else of note in the room, walked out into the early evening.

Chapter 3: The Church

The path to the north led past the Church of St. Isosceles. It seemed to be a typical Gothic church on the outside, a couple of flying buttresses on each side, a large belfry above the nave. La Mort opened one of the two cast iron doors and entered the vestibule, which he recognized as a prime example of ante-Lutheran extremism. The Inspector was a dabbler in medieval architecture when he wasn't running suspects to ground.

Inside the church proper was an altar, which looked to be under construction, and a huge statue. To either side were the confessionals. Upstairs was presumably the belfry. La Mort walked to the statue and, squinting in the scant light shining through a stain-glass window, read the inscription under the statue: "St. Spurious—There is Knowledge Nil Until Ye Fill." "Fill what?" the Inspector asked aloud, trying to dispel the spookiness of the church.

He strode to the altar and leaned over to see down into a small pit in front of it. This must be where the altar exploded at the St. Swithins Day ceremony. Not much of a catacomb, he mused. Completely empty.

The confessional to the south was where the Abbot's body was found so La Mort went to it first. It was a typical confessional; two small compartments separated by a partition with a wicker screen at face level for anyone sitting at the chair on the side which seemed to be the confessor's. On the other side was a kneeler for the confessing person. Something glinting underneath the kneeler caught the Inspector's eye and he bent down to pick up a string of beads. La Mort's memory of his early schooldays told him that it was a rosary, a cross attached to a loop of beads. There was just enough light for him to see the initials "M.P." on the back of the cross. It was a strange-looking cross, but La Mort couldn't put his finger on what was different about it.

He crossed the church to the north confessional, which looked just like the south one. On the priest's side was a prayerbook, which La Mort recognized as a breviary. La Mort picked it up and noticed that it had a ribbon marking a page. In the margin someone had scribbled, "Thrice Three and Two are the Laws of the Holy Tablets." That's clear as merde, he thought, and then noticed that there was also something written on the ribbon in a different hand. "Bull in Boar."

There was nothing else to see in the confessional so the Inspector climbed the spiral staircase to the belfry. He found a five-sided room with a bell rope in each corner, leading up to a bell. There was a chart on the wall which read: "The Five Bells of St. Dapiacle" and below that, "For Matins, start with the Bell of St. Pentomino." St. Dapiacle? Where had he heard of that saint before? Something about a cabinet? Maybe it would come to him later.[5]

---

[5] It never does occur to La Mort what the significance of "St. Dapiacle" is. The term was a mnemonic used back in the 60s to help one remember the order of ascension to the presidency in case of incapacitation—after the Vice-President and Speaker of the House. The order then was: Secretary of (S)tate, (T)reasury, (D)efense, (A)ttorney General, (P)ostmaster

In any case, if he needed to ring Matins, he knew which bell to start with, he chuckled to himself. They seem to have a saint for damn near everything in this godforsaken abbey. He inspected the famous bells, noting them to be made of solid molybdenum and numbered from 1 through 5. The five bellropes were fashioned of the finest Marin County hemp. Hmmm, he thought, those ropes could come in handy later. That hemp is good stuff.

The Inspector, who was now carrying an info sheet, a map, a newspaper clipping, a diary, a rosary and a breviary, as well as his Sûreté-issue flashlight, descended the staircase and exited the church, finding that the sun had set and an ominous grey cloud was blotting the moonlight. La Mort shivered and headed north to the stables. He wasn't sure if he was getting anywhere.

Chapter 4: The Stables

He didn't need light to know he was entering the Stables of St. Isosceles, but he flipped the flashlight on to keep from spooking the horses. It didn't take him long to see that the horses of the Abbey were the results of years of Mendelian inter-breeding. In the largest stall was a nervously pacing, two-headed gelding. A sign on the wall read: "Stall must be cleaned before Matins." Apparently no one had cleaned the stall that day because there was a wealth of ordure beneath the horse. He shuddered at the thought of having to clean up after a two-headed gelding.

La Mort sincerely hoped there weren't any more clues in the stables and decided to move on to the barracks to the west.

Chapter 5: The Barracks

The first thing La Mort noticed about the barracks was its architectural style: post-Holocaust utilitarianism. Each of the novice's cubicles were spotlessly clean and orderly, except for one, Novice Scosha's, which looked as though it had been recently ransacked. Under the bed the Inspector spied a piece of paper which he found to be an intra-abbey memo. "Novice Scosha, you are bellringer for

---

General, (I)nterior, (A)griculture, (C)ommerce, (L)abor, (E)ducation [Health, Education and Welfare].

the week." It was signed by Abbot Costello. On the back was written, "For Matins, do not ring adjacent bells consecutively."

I never knew there was so much to Matins, La Mort opined. I just figured they were rung in the mornings to annoy the poor souls on the second shift. Nothing else caught his eye so he gladly left the depressing barracks and headed for the monks' quarters to the west. So far he had seen two sides of the library and no sign of a door. Just a window in each of the east and north lobes.

Chapter 6: The Monks' Quarters

The quarters—apparently designed by St. Torquemada, La Mort cynically mused—resembled nothing so much as a pre-Franciscan abattoir. Upon entering, he noticed that the room was divided into cribs for the monks. All of the cribs were starkly devoid of any luxuries except for one, Father Murphy's, who apparently was the Abbey electrician. His crib was full of electronics books. Across the room was a closed door.

The lights had come on as soon as La Mort entered the room and he determined, by stepping outside for a second, that the lights would go out as soon as he left. Aha! These must be the soul-detecting lights the clipping had mentioned. He thumbed through a few books but soon quit, figuring that if he were to find a clue here, he'd have to check every one of them.

Then he was suddenly aware that there was a low, bubbling sound coming from behind the door across the room. He strode to it, threw it wide and saw that it was apparently an office. The sound was coming from a hot tub, the first La Mort had ever seen. He stared at it, wondering if he'd have time later on for a well-desired—and hopefully, well-deserved —dip.

Then he noticed there was something dark in the deep end. He looked around, wondering if he should take the time to undress, decided against it, and waded into the tub. Any other time he'd have enjoyed the hot water, but he quickly reached down and grabbed what he saw to be a waterproof strongbox, with a chain attaching it to the tub.

This ought to be a real clue, he rejoiced. Who would keep anything trivial in a strongbox in a hot tub? He lifted the strongbox out of the water and set it on the side of the tub. He opened the box, which wasn't locked, and found only receipts for "art reprints". Hmmph. Some clue. Well, at least I know whose office this is, the Inspector thought, the receipts were signed by Father Noster. Apparently, the good father received $20 a scroll from a Capitol Hill bookstore.

His shoes and pants ruined, La Mort sloshed out of the tub and left the monks' quarters, with angry, wet footprints following him out the door. The west lobe of the library had the same kind of window as the other lobes, but still no sign of a door into the library.

Chapter 7: The Cloister

La Mort gagged as he neared the Cloister of St. Catatonia. It didn't take an architecture buff to see that it was a paradigm of ante-deluvian depressionism. He entered the ghastly building and saw that the main room held the austere cells of the nuns. He quickly peeked through an ornate door and saw that at least one of the cloister's inhabitants lived in sumptuous splendor. Must be Mother Puleeze's, he figured, remembering the hubris of Sister Edwina, the crone-nun who ruled over his childhood parochial school with an iron thumb and a slap of steel.

He decided to search the nun's cells first and, finding that none of them had doors, entered one that had "Sister Debbie" carved above it. The young nun must be hung up on early gulag, judging by the decor. The only thing of note was a handbook by the bed. La Mort picked it up and perused it. "Knots of a Trappist Trapper" by Friar John. The well-thumbed book was full of directions for tying various kinds of knots. Kinky. He flipped a few pages and, finding nothing too interesting, went into Mother Puleeze's boudoir.

In the middle of the spacious, magnificently decorated room was an emperor-sized waterbed, again the first one La Mort had ever seen. Beside the bed was a brassbound book, which had the word "Ledger" embossed on the cover. Now *this* ought to have some clues in it, the Inspector beamed, and tried to open it. Curses! It was locked. An ornate keyhole on the front taunted La Mort mercilessly.

The shape of the keyhole reminded him of something but it was just beyond his mind's grasp. This case is full of meaningless clues, he moaned, full of sound and fury, signifying *rien*!

He stomped out of the Cloister of St. Catatonia, hell-bent for the library. There's got to be a door somewhere. Whoever heard of a library without a door!

Chapter 8: The Library

La Mort inspected every foot of the exterior of the library and found no doors. Each of the four lobes had a window but they were too high for him to see through. They looked too dark to see through, anyway.

The triangular slits between each of the lobes suggested, as he had noticed before, that the library had triangular rooms. That made sense, he thought, after all, it's called the Library of St. Isosceles. In fact, the whole damned abbey is named after St. Isosceles. Let's see, isosceles triangles are those with two of its sides having equal length. That fits.

La Mort wondered if it would be difficult to navigate through a building full of triangular rooms. He decided to head back to Mother Puleeze's boudoir and study the coatful of clues he had accumulated. He had a info sheet, map, newspaper clipping, diary, breviary, rosary, intra-abbey memo, receipts for "art reprints" and a handbook on knots. No wonder the other inspectors at the Sûreté called him the "shopping cart detective". He just couldn't seem to drop anything, once he'd put it in his pocket.

At least the boudoir is comfortable. Maybe he could figure out how to get into that ledger. This case is turning into a real mys-adventure. And where the hell are those missing people?

He trudged over to the cloister and flopped down on Mother Puleeze's waterbed. His mind was racing.

Chapter 9: Ruminations

Surrounded by festoons of velvet, silk and the finest terrycloth, La Mort snuggled deeper into Mother Puleeze's four-poster waterbed and mulled over the various things he knew. All of the missing people could have done the deed if they had had access to a synthetic strain of the plague and had a way of administering it to the unfortunate Abbot. Cardinal Musial and Doctor Dee were ciphers, but the other four seemed to be involved in some sort of chicanery, at least the Abbot's mind.

The untimely ringing of Matins must have some bearing on the case. Why would anyone ring it at midnight, and was it Novice Scosha, whose job it was for the week? The missing people must be in the library, but how do you get into the dang thing?

No, there just wasn't enough evidence to work with. He sat up and examined the ledger again. Then something that had been nagging him hit him like a wet fist—the rosary's cross! It had the same intricate ornateness that the ledger's lock had! He took out the rosary and tried inserting the crucifix into the keyhole. Success! The ledger sprang open.

La Mort's teeth gnashed audibly as he saw that everything was in some sort of code. A typical page read:

```
11  16  9  15        15  22  15            7  6  6
------------------------------------------------
5  19  1  5  6  6     5  6  3  3  10  6     7  19  6  6
9  16  7  7  2        14  10  15  6         25  13
11  7  12             5  10  21  21  16     4  4  13
```

He tried a simple substitution code, where A is 1, B is 2, and so on but it didn't make any sense.

$$K P I O \qquad O V O \qquad G F F$$

After thumbing through a few more pages, he gave up in disgust and sat on the edge of the bed wondering what he should do next. It was now after 9:00 P.M. and the sleepy village was probably shutting down for the night. A wry smile crept across his face as he figured, maybe it's time I reconstructed the crime—and annoyed a few people at the same time. He left the cloister and headed for the church.

Chapter 10: Matins

At the entrance to the church, he hesitated and looked over to the stables. Why did the sign in the stables say that the stables must be cleaned before Matins? What did the two things have to do with each other? He decided to check out the stables again before he carried out his plans.

The stable with the two-headed gelding was as malodorous and filthy as ever. Entering the gelding's stall, La Mort sighed and used a pushbroom to sweep out the ordure of the day. Luckily, the gelding gave him a wide berth. La Mort wasn't in the mood to cozy up to any hooved animal, even a two-headed one.

"Sacre merde!" he exclaimed. In the floor of the gelding's stall there was a trapdoor! He threw the broom aside and knelt down to tug on the brass handle of the trapdoor. Locked! There was an unusual type of lock on the trapdoor, and upon closer look, he saw that it was one of Father Murphy's sound-sensitive locks. But what kind of sound would open it? "D'eau!" he exclaimed, thumping himself on the forehead with an open palm, and ran to the church.

With a stout length of hemp in his hand, the Inspector looked up at Bell #5. According to Costello's memo to Scosha, you start with "the Bell of St. Pentomino" when ringing Matins. There was also something about not ringing non-adjacent bells consecutively. The memo refreshed his memory. Let's see, if I start with 5, then I can't ring 4 or 1 next. If I ring 3 next, then I can't ring 2 or 4 after that. So I'll ring 1. Then I have to ring 4, since it and 2 are the only ones left.

It made sense. He could ring the bells in this order—5, 3, 1, 4 , 2—and he would not be ringing adjacent bells consecutively. With a wide grin, knowing he'd probably interrupt the amorous activities of dozens of villagers he rang the five bells in that order. BONG! BING! BANG! BUNG! BENG!

From the direction of the stables came a strange whinny— actually two whinnies in harmony, a perfect fourth apart. That's got to be the gelding, he thought, and ran down the staircase, out of the church and north to the stables.

Sure enough, the trapdoor was open! Maybe this was the entrance to the damnable library. He pointed the flashlight down into the hole in the stable floor. A few steps led down then leveled out into a tunnel, tall enough for a man to walk upright. It headed in the direction of the library. La Mort, his trenchcoat filled with meaningless clues, entered the tunnel. Maybe something would finally happen.

Chapter 11: The Courtyard

With his heart dancing in his chest, Inspecteur Claude La Mort saw an ever-growing circle of light at the end of the tunnel. Fifty feet later he found the tunnel opened inside what appeared to be a water well, a couple of meters below the top of the well and about three meters above the waterline. Metal rungs, set into the inside of the well led up over the edge. He climbed them, noticing that a chalice was perched on the edge of the stone well, and found himself in a square courtyard. He quickly glanced around, admiring the art-deco decadence, and noted a door in each of its walls. Above each door was a sign, inscribed with the name of an animal.

He tried one of the doors but it was locked, apparently with another of Father Murphy's sound-sensitive locks. The locks were labeled "holy-locks". He turned around to gaze at the massive stone well.

It was a masterpiece of pre-Inquisition realism, with a sign reading "The Courtyard of the Chimera" above it. Below the sign was an inscription in Latin, and on the edge of the well a large pewter bucket sitting next to the chalice. He looked in the chalice and saw that it was filled with something. Reaching out for it, the inspector fumbled it in his hands and it dropped into the well where it splashed into the water and sank. It seemed to be filled with wafers. Merde! That could have been an important clue!

A spot on the well where the chalice stood attracted La Mort's eye and, dipping a finger in the spot and tasting it, he spat violently. That's arsenic di-cyanide, he muttered, a powerful poison whose symptoms resemble those of the plague. That explains what killed the Abbot. But how was it administered? In the wafers? But why would a priest ingest a wafer in the confessional?

La Mort reviewed what he knew about arsenic di-cyanide. If the poison is inhaled, death is almost instantaneous; if it's taken orally, paralysis sets in within minutes but death doesn't occur for a day or so. Hmmm. That means that Abbot Costello must have inhaled the poison—it wasn't the wafers. So why was the chalice with the poisoned wafers sitting on the edge of the well?

Leaving that mystery for later, La Mort turned his attention to the bucket. It was a heavy pewter bucket, made to last for centuries. There seemed to be something etched in the bottom of the inside but it was too small for him to make out. Wish I had a magnifying glass, he thought to himself, then beamed as he remembered the nonsensical verse beneath the statue of St. Spurious in the church. What had it said? There is knowledge nil until ye fill?

Holding the rope in his hands he lowered the bucket down to the water and let an inch or two of water flow into it. Pulling it back up he looked into it and was pleased to find that the water did indeed magnify the words etched in the bottom. "To open the holy-locks of the Library, pray the name of the room you wish to enter." It was signed by St. Spurious.

La Mort let the bucket drop back in the well and was dismayed to find that the rope wasn't attached to the top of the well. The bucket and rope sank into the black water. He climbed up on the edge of the well and examined the stout bar atop the well, to which the rope had been attached. Aha! Someone had cut through the rope, leaving it attached by only a few strands. Luckily he had grasped the rope with his hands when he filled the bucket, or he might never have found out about the holy-locks.

Well, there are four doors, he thought, might as well start with the north one, the one whose sign read OTTER. The east, south and west doors were named TOAD, GIRAFFE and PIG respectively. It was dark and ordinarily it would be difficult to get one's bearings in an enclosed courtyard, but luckily the inspector had a Sûreté-issue compass watch.

La Mort strode up to the north door and, rolling his eyes in embarrassment, muttered in what he hoped was a fervent tone, "otter". The door opened soundlessly and he peered into the room beyond.

Chapter 12: The North Lobe

Just as La Mort expected, the Room of the Otter was a triangular room—isosceles, at that. He walked into the room through the door that was in the middle of the hypotenuse. The other two walls met at the vertex directly across the room. The left wall was completely covered with bookcases but the right wall had a door with the word "CAT" above it. The doorway behind him was named "CHIMERA". How nice of St. Isosceles, mused La Mort sarcastically, to put the names above the doors. It almost makes up for the holy-locks.

The Room of the Otter seemed to have Father Murphy's soul-detecting lights because the light was on. There was a light switch on the wall with the door; the switch down. Below it was the ubiquitous Latin inscription. I sure wish my barroom Latin were up to translating the inscriptions around here, he thought, as he walked to the door and prayed, "Cat". The door opened revealing a deep blackness beyond. La Mort leaned through the door with his flashlight and cursed when the bulb went out. These are brand-new batteries, he spat, and became even further confused when the flashlight came back on as he moved back into the Room of the Otter.

La Mort vowed to pistol-whip Father Murphy if he ever ran into him in the future. Apparently the electrician's sophisticated wiring in parts of the Library short-circuited conventional lighting devices. The inspector walked into the Room of the Cat but it was so dark he saw immediately there was nothing he could do in there without seriously injuring himself. Apparently the Room of the Otter had the automatic lights and the Room of the Cat didn't. He flipped the light switch up and peeked into the Room of the Cat again, but it stayed dark. What's with the light switch?

He decided to try one of the other lobes and headed back to the Courtyard of the Chimera, angrily praying "Chimera" to open the door. At least he had determined that the holy-locks weren't picky; you didn't have to sound fervent. In fact you could sound downright nasty.

Chapter 13: The Other Lobes

La Mort went up to the door to the east of the well and prayed, "Pig". It sounded good, and the door opened into a room very similar to the Room of the Otter—a featureless wall on the left and a door in the wall to the right. The sign by the door read "Bear" and below it was a Latin inscription. There was a light switch by the door and it was up. He said, "Bear" and as the door opened, peeked into the dark room. Sure enough, the flashlight went out as he leaned into the room, coming back on as he stepped back into the Room of the Pig. He flipped the light switch down, spat "Bear" and saw that the room was still dark. What had that fool Father Murphy done to the lights?

"Chimera," the inspector prayed and stepped out into the courtyard. He strode to the door to the south of the well and muttered, "Giraffe" and entered a room similar to the others. The door in the right wall was named, "LION" and it had the usual Latin inscription and light switch, which was up. La Mort quickly said, "Lion" and flipped the switch down and back up, seeing that the room beyond stayed dark.

Shaking his head, he mumbled "Chimera" and stomped over to the last door, to the west of the well. "Toad." Again, the same room, door, inscription and light switch on the wall to the right; simple wall to the left. He didn't even bother to pray "Deer" or flip the switch. He had an idea.

Chapter 14: Father Murphy's Crib

The Inspector walked over to the well, climbed over the edge and clambered down the rungs to the tunnel. He was just about to enter it when he noticed that there was another opening in the inside of the well about two meters above the waterline. It was on the other side of the well from the tunnel so he couldn't reach it without breaking his neck. It was high enough above the waterline that he knew he couldn't reach it from the water were he to jump in. He'd need a rope to get to the hole. Too bad the well rope fell in the water.

He turned and trotted down the tunnel, back to the stables. The trapdoor was closed, but not locked from this side and he pushed it open and climbed up into the gelding's stall. The equine mutation stood to the rear of the stall, looking decidedly unhappy. As La Mort left the stables, he heard the trapdoor slam shut behind him. Quelle domage, he grinned, thinking of the villagers; now I'll just have to ring the bells again.

Moments later he entered the monk's quarters and began searching Father Murphy's crib. He had searched everything but the textbooks when he remembered about the newspaper clipping with the review. What was the name of Murphy's book? How to Change a Light Bulb? Maybe that's where I can find out how to get past those four rooms, he thought. He quickly scanned the book covers. Aha! Here it is. Sitting down on the monk's sagging cot, he thumbed through the short tome.

In a chapter entitled, "Apologia" was the sentence, "I'm afraid that in spite of my years of experience in electrical design, I've never been sure whether ON is supposed to be up or down. Usually it doesn't make much difference since you can just try it both ways until the light comes on, but in systems such as in the Library of St. Isosceles, where four switches are in series, you have to have them all ON at the same time in order for the lights to be on. Sorry about that."

In the margin beside this passage was penciled, "O=1   T=2 G=3   P=4   UP=7". La Mort stared at this for a moment then yelped, "I've got it! O is for otter, T is toad, G is giraffe and P is pig. The UPs equal 7 so I've got to have 1, 2 and 4 UP. Otter, Toad and Pig UP. Giraffe down. Elementary Boolean algebra! And those other detectives at the Sûreté laughed at me when I said that the insane scribblings of the Englishman George Boole would have some practical use in the future!"

The excited inspector ran back to the stables, tried the trapdoor, and when it remained locked, sprinted to the church and ran up the stairway. He was in such a good mood that he tried a different Matins this time. He reasoned, if 5–3–1–4–2 satisfied the requirements for Matins: start with 5 and don't ring adjacent bells consecutively, then 5–2–4–1–3 ought to work just as well. BONG! BENG! BUNG! BANG! BING!

A harmonic whinny from the north proved him right, and he sped out of the church to the stables, where he saw the trapdoor standing open. The gelding stood to the side, its four eyes glaring at him malevolently. La Mort quickly entered the tunnel and hotfooted it back to the well.

Chapter 15: More Rooms

His trenchcoat flapping, the wily inspector climbed up the rung ladder out of the well and ran to the north door, shouting "Otter!" He flipped the switch up, and tried to get back out into the courtyard before the door behind him closed but was too late. "Chimera," he muttered and moved to the east door. "Pig." He flipped the switch up. "Chimera." Over to the south door. "Giraffe." He flipped the switch down and sped over to the east door. "Toad."

He stood in the Room of the Toad and flipped the switch down. Then he said "Deer" and saw that it was dark inside the Room of

the Deer. If my theory is correct, the light should go on when I flip
the switch up. He flipped it and said, "Deer."

Eureka! The room was lit! He entered the Room of the Deer.
Of course it was triangular, the same size as the other rooms he
had been in. But this time he entered through one of the equi-sized
walls. The vertex was to his right; the hypotenuse to his left. Each
of the walls had a door in it, and a sign above it. The door he had
entered through read "TOAD" of course. The door on his left, the
hypotenuse, had a few obliterated letters and looked like "--M-
AT". The sign above the door on his right was totally illegible.
Merde! Don't these monks ever repaint their signs?

A small table stood in the middle of the room and on it was a
scroll. La Mort snatched it up and saw that it was blank except for
a title that read, "ELZGAEL" and a small inscription, "St. Jumblius". Those cryptic monks! La Mort briefly mused that it might
have been better if the St. Swithins Day explosion had been in the
megaton range.

He searched the room, found nothing and with an expletive-
prefaced "Toad, chimera" he crossed the courtyard to the Room of
the Otter. "Otter, cat," he spat and found himself in the Room of
the Cat. It looked a lot like the Room of the Deer, down to the table with a scroll on it. He picked it up and saw that it too was by
St. Jumblius. It was entitled, "OBNOAB". Utter nonsense.

The sign above the door in the hypotenuse read "--EP-A-
T". The sign to his right was illegible, just as in the Room of the
Deer. Again he searched the room and found nothing. "Otter, chi-
mera," he intoned and headed west to the door marked "PIG".

"Pig, bear," took him to the Room of the Bear where he found
a scroll entitled "MTAWBO". As expected, the door to the left
was partly legible, "-A-E-LE", and the door to the right, totally
unreadable. At least the monks are consistently negligent, he
fumed. Might as well get the fourth scroll.

Performing the familiar litany he found himself in the Room of
the Lion, where he picked up a scroll named "NEPLAHTEL". The
partly legible door was named, "--BO-N" and the other was of
course totally unreadable.

La Mort started to curse violently, then, taking a deep breath,
decided to sit on the table and think things over. I've got four
scrolls and four locked doors; surely there's a connection, he
thought. He took the "NEPLAHTEL" scroll and examined it more
closely. Looked like an ordinary scroll. Then he got up and scruti-

nized the lock on the door below the "--BO-N" sign. Hmmm. In tiny etched words, it said, "Scroll-lock by St. Jumblius." So there WAS a connection between the scrolls and the locks!

He pulled the other three scrolls out of his trenchcoat pocket and checked them out. "MTAWBO", "ELZGAEL" and "OBNOAB". The only one that shared letters with the "--BO-N" sign was the latter. Let me think. St. Jumblius. Sacre merde! Could they be jumbles? La Mort kicked himself. What a fool I am! Of course! They are all animals! Surely with my experience with word puzzles I can figure these out.

Within seconds La Mort had solved them all. BABOON, GAZELLE, ELEPHANT, and the hardest one, WOMBAT. He looked up at the "--BO-N" and, holding the OBNOAB scroll, in-toned "Baboon". The door opened! I'm finally getting somewhere, he thought as he sprang into the Room of the Baboon.

Chapter 16: Big Rooms

The Room of the Baboon was triangular, with the two equal sides quite a bit longer than the hypotenuse, through which La Mort entered. There were doors in all three walls, and mirabile dictu! The doors were all legibly marked! On his right the sign read, "ARMADILLO" and on the left, "RAT". He decided to see what's inside the Room of the Armadillo.

He was gratified to find that no obnoxious locks barred his way and found himself in a large triangular room permeated by a deep, red light that seemed to exude from the walls themselves. As the door closed behind him he gulped, realizing that there was only one door in this room, the one through which he had just entered. Just to be sure, he prayed, "Baboon" and was thankful to see the door open. He didn't go through it, and a few seconds later it closed, miring him in the ruby-colored room.

There was enough light to see a table in the middle of the room with a book on it. He picked it up and identified it as a missal—a prayerbook used to follow the arcane rituals he was subjected to as an adolescent. The roseate light was bright enough for him to see that the missal was a typical one, nothing out of the ordinary. But just in case, he added it to the many items in his trenchcoat pockets.

Quickly glancing around, he saw nothing of note and went

back to the normally lit Room of the Baboon. Forging ahead, he intoned, "Rat," and found himself in the Room of the Rat, a large triangular room. He had entered through one of the long, equal walls; the vertex was to his left and the shorter hypotenuse to the right. There was a window in the short wall, about eye level. Aha! He had found one of the rooms that looked out on the rest of the abbey. The other wall had a door with "LEOPARD" above it.

He peered over the bottom edge of the window and saw the Cloister of St. Catatonia. It figured. He had entered the library through the Room of the Giraffe, to the south of the well, and had continued more or less in that direction through the confusing triangular rooms. The cloister was to the south of the library so he was looking out the southern window. The cloister was dark and forbidding, and, seeing that there were no clues in the room, prayed the word "Leopard" and strode into yet another triangular room. How many rooms are there in this damnable library?

The Room of the Leopard had its vertex to his right and a short hypotenuse to his left. The door on the right was labeled "CIVET" and the door to the left, "COW". La Mort saw nothing of interest in the room so tried the door to the right. "Civet," he prayed. Nothing happened. Then he saw, in tiny print, inscribed right above the door, "To enter the Room of the Civet, you must first solve the two Puzzles of St. Caliban." The rest of the inscription is in Latin.

La Mort stared at the taunting inscription with seething anger, then, shaking his head ruefully, spoke the word, "Cow." He entered a small, triangular room with one other door, whose sign was totally illegible. Oh no, not one of those again! La Mort then saw that there was a fireplace in this room, filled with ashes. He knelt down to see the ashes better and saw that a sheet of paper had burnt, but not crumbled into grey ash. Squinting, he was able to determine that it was an official summons from the Vatican to Abbot Costello: "Under penalty of excommunication, you shall bring the Bull to Rome where it belongs."

He tried to gently remove the burnt summons from the fireplace but it crumbled into powdery ash. Hope I don't need that for evidence, the inspector gulped. Well, that seems to be it for this section of the library. Now that I have the scroll-locks figured out I should be able to explore the other lobes of the library, as I have the southern one.

"Leopard, rat." As he passed through the Room of the Rat, he glanced out the window one more time. Sacre Bleu! There was a light on in Mother Puleeze's boudoir! "Finallement!" he ejaculated, "At last I may meet someone in this godforsaken abbey. Perhaps the murderer of Abbot Costello?"

With a quick "Baboon, lion, giraffe, chimera," La Mort sped to the well and sprinted down the tunnel. Those other lobes could wait.

Chapter 17: Back to the Cloister

La Mort violently slammed the trapdoor up, hoping to re-geld the two-headed horse, and trotted past the church and gate to the Cloister of St. Catatonia. The lights were all out, including the light in Mother Puleeze's boudoir. He entered the building carefully, not knowing what to expect and saw nothing in the nun's cell room. Then he slowly eased into the boudoir. Nothing. No, wait! On the bed, right were he had lain the last time he was in the boudoir, was a perfume atomizer.

He snatched it up and examined it closely, careful not to squeeze the rubber ball. By now he had formulated a theory that this just might be the murder weapon. What better way to kill a priest than to spray him through the confessional screen with a deadly poison? The liquid in the atomizer resembled the spot he saw on the edge of the well where the chalice had stood. Probably arsenic di-cyanide.

The inspector looked around and saw nothing amiss, so he left the cloister, keeping an eye out for whoever set off the soul-detecting light in the boudoir that he saw from the library. It was just after midnight as he trudged up the stairway of the church, rang Matins a little louder than he really needed to, and headed over to the stables and an increasingly livid gelding. He entered the tunnel and climbed up into the Courtyard of the Chimera.

Chapter 18: The North Lobe Again

Having charted the southern lobe, La Mort decided to try the north lobe this time—for no particular reason, really. He went through the Room of the Otter into the Room of the Cat and, holding the ELEPHANT scroll of St. Jumblius, spoke the word, "Elephant."

He walked into a large, triangular room, as he expected and saw doors to his right and left, labeled "BOAR" and "GNU" respectively. So far, everything in the library had been the same from lobe to lobe. Same room layout, different animal names. La Mort spouted, "Boar," and entered the Room of the Boar.

The first thing he noticed was a thick acrid smog that made him cough. He squinted to see through it and found himself getting disoriented. The room was starting to pulsate in a sensuous fashion and looking down, La Mort was mortified to see small, paisley squids attaching themselves to his legs. Trying to brush them off, the frantic inspector screamed as tie-died gerbils started nibbling on his magnificent mustaches, "Gotta get outta here." He stumbled towards the door as lentils and chives began raining from the ceiling. "What the hell is the name of the room outside?" he babbled, and just before careering to the floor, remembered, "Elephant!" The door opened and a zoned out La Mort fell into the Room of the Elephant, gasping for breath.

He lay on the thick rug that all of the rooms of the library seemed to have and within minutes had recovered his senses. Must be a psychedelic fog filling the Room of the Boar. In other circumstances it would be quite enjoyable spending a few hours in there, but he was on the job and he had to decide what to do about the Room of the Boar. Speaking of Boar, where had he heard of that room before? He wracked his brain, which was back to almost normal, but couldn't remember.

Then it occurred to him that he still had most, if not all of the clues he had found. Maybe it was in his pockets. He quickly emptied them and while examining the ribbon in the breviary saw the scribbled note that said, "Bull in Boar." That's it! The mysterious Papal Bull of 303 AD referred to in the Abbot's diary must be in the Room of the Boar! But how can he find it in that psychedelic smog?

He mulled it over for a few minutes, considering calling out for a gas mask, but how could he call? There are no phones in this godforsaken abbey. He didn't come up with anything concrete so he decided save the Boar for later and do some more exploring. He look at the door he hadn't tried yet and said, "Gnu."

It was a typical room, and as he suspected, had a window in it, facing north. He looked through it and saw the novice's barracks in the darkness. It looked as austere as ever. He tried prying the window open but it was solidly made. He was hoping he could find a quick way out of the library, just in case he needed one.

The other door in the Room of the Gnu read "OX", so a quick syllable later he was in the Room of the Ox. The room on his right was labeled "PANTHER" and under it was a similar inscription to the one in the Room of the Leopard, "To enter the Room of the Panther you must first solve the Two Puzzles of St. Caliban." The rest was in Latin. *I must figure out a way to translate the Latin inscriptions,* he mumbled to himself. He tried the door with a fervent "Panther" but it didn't open.

Above the other door in the room was the sign, "RAM". *If parallelism continued, it would be a small room with two doors, one of them unreadable.* Sure enough, it was. He searched it anyway and in a corner he found a pornscroll illustrated with the figure of a young nun in a very provocative pose—tied to an altar. *On the back is what appears to be an eight-letter word, written in garish red ink. The only letters* La Mort could make out were the fourth and fifth, "P" and "K". *What kind of eight-letter word has a "PK in the middle? And what does it mean, anyhow?*

Well, La Mort thought, *there's still a couple of lobes to explore, as well as that spacey Boar room. Might as well get to it.* Before he left he looked up at the illegible sign. *I wonder if that leads to a different lobe, perhaps the west one. Wasn't there an illegible sign in one of the two west lobe rooms he had been in? Maybe it was the same door.* He tried to remember the name of the rooms and they finally came to him, the Pig and the Bear. He tried it. "Bear." The door opened.

Amazing! A quick way to get from one lobe to another without retracing all those steps. He was in the Room of the Bear and had St. Jumblius' GAZELLE scroll with him. "Gazelle," he ventured and seconds later was in a large triangular room. The door on the right read "TIGER" and the door on the left "RHINO". He, as in the other lobes, tried Tiger first and found himself in a room with only one door, the one he had just entered. On a table was a cruet of water.

He took it and found that it seemed to be ordinary water. There was a stopper in it so he put it in his pocket with the rest of his clues. He left the Room of the Tiger and going through the Room of the Gazelle entered the Room of the Rhino. It had a window, and if he hadn't gotten totally disoriented, it should look out upon the monk's quarters. He peered through the window and was startled to see a light on in Father Noster's office! Someone was out there. Maybe if he hurried he could catch them before they left.

The inspector, who was getting a little tired by this time, took the quickest route to the courtyard by going back through the Gazelle, Bear and Pig. Then through the tunnel, where the gelding took a vicious bite at him. Two bites, actually. He dodged and sprinted past the novice's barracks to the monks' quarters. It was dark, but as soon as he entered, Father Murphy's soul-detecting lights came on. He ran into the office, finding no one there. Merde! Too late again!

He was about to leave when he noticed something in the corner that he could swear was not there before. A suitcase. Picking it up, La Mort noticed it was made of rich, Corinthian leather and opened it. Empty. He started to fling it in exasperation into the hot tub but then stopped suddenly. It seemed heavier than it should be. He opened it again and tore at the silk bottom. Aha! A false bottom! Ripping it out he found a strange electronic gadget. "Quelle l'hell?" he exploded, and turned it over in his hands, looking for a clue as to its function.

It had a keyboard of sorts, with the letters from A to Z. There were two buttons, one labeled "English" and the other "Latin". Hey! This might be the answer to my prayers, he thought. What's the closest place that has some Latin for translating? He couldn't remember there being any Latin signs outside the library so he hotfooted it over to the church, rang a quick Matins, and headed to the stables. The gelding attacked as he entered the stall but after the inspector gave him a couple of swift whacks with the broom, retreated to the back of the stall, licking its wounds with both tongues. La Mort was really getting sick and tired of that stupid horse.

Chapter 19: Latin Revelations

On the way back through the tunnel La Mort re-assessed the situation. There was one more unlocked room in the western lobe he hadn't be in yet, and practically the whole eastern lobe. Maybe the Latin translator would show him how to get into those locked rooms, the ones that required him to solve the Two Puzzles of St. Caliban. But where were they? He hadn't seen anything with that name on it, except the signs.

He climbed the rungs to the courtyard and, grasping the electronic translator, immediately punched in the Latin inscription atop the Well of St. Spurious. Miraculously, in a tinny voice the device beeped, "The well is the locus of the final knowledge." This is great, he exulted, even if this particular inscription doesn't help much. So far, all the well has provided is the way in and out of the Library. But then there's that other hole—

He decided to go back through the west lobe, checking out the Latin signs along the way. The message in the Room of the Pig translated to "Carvings by St. Binarius". Will this litany of perverse saints never end?

A short "Bear, gazelle, rhino, dog," later he found himself in the Room of the Dog where the translator told him "To enter the Room of the Gorilla you must first solve the Two Puzzles of St. Caliban. The room of the Second Puzzle must be entered via the Room of the Deer." Interesting. So the room with one of the puzzles shares a wall with the Room of the Deer. That's over by the Toad in the east lobe.

But before heading that way he decided to finish inspecting the west lobe. He didn't even bother checking the Room of the Gorilla; he was sure it would be locked. So he prayed the name of the other room, "Horse," and entered.

The sign above the door he faced was illegible, as he expected but the room had a desk in it. There was nothing on or in the desk but under it he spied a torn sheet of paper. He snatched it up and saw that it was part of a letter or note. The fragment read, "...if the Bull is as subversive as I think, you and I better update our resumes." La Mort didn't recognize the handwriting, but it had a Vatican watermark. Another clue indicating a Roman connection, perhaps involving Cardinal Musial, the Papal emissary.

La Mort, who had been making a mental map of the lobes of the Library, decided to see if the room he was in was analogous to the Room of the Ram, which also had an illegible sign. If his map was correct, on the other side of the wall should be the second room of the south lobe, the Room of the Lion. "Lion," he purred and was pleased to see the door open. He entered.

The quickest way to the east lobe, the only one he hadn't explored, was to go through the courtyard via the Room of the Giraffe. Also, wasn't there a Latin inscription there? But there was also an inscription in the Room of the Leopard, if he remembered correctly. He decided to go there first. "Baboon, rat, leopard," took him to the Room of the Rat where he saw that the inscription below the CIVET sign read, "To enter the Room of the Civet, you must solve the Two Puzzles of St. Caliban. The Second Puzzle is adjacent to the Room of the Giraffe."

The Giraffe? That was the first room in this lobe. La Mort retraced his steps and made it back to the Room of the Giraffe. Using the translator, the message was, "Ten walls in each room are equal in length." Talk about cryptic! Every room he had been in so far was triangular; what could "ten walls" possibly mean? La Mort was beginning to despair because of the mysteries that were piling up. When would he run into the missing people, or at least the person or persons who were wandering around outside the Library?

He was also getting tired of all this walking. He mumbled, "Chimera," and stumbled into the Courtyard of the Chimera. One more lobe to go.

Chapter 20: The Last Lobe

La Mort decided to quickly zip into the Room of the Otter to read its message before tackling the east lobe so with a breathless "Otter" he scooted across the courtyard. The translator decoded the message, "There be one hundred thousand rooms in the Library." Sure. What kind of mathematical flake was this St. Binarius, who claimed to have carved the message?

Then it hit him like the wet fist of an overweight onanist. Of course! St. Binarius! The messages are in binary, not decimal! The translator was an electronic gem, but how was it to know that the messages used the binary number system? That would explain the "ten walls" crack. In decimal, "10" is ten; in binary, "10" is two. There are two walls of equal size in each room. That's right.

And as for the "one hundred thousand" message, "100000" in binary was, let's see, thirty-two! That made sense. So far, each lobe contained eight rooms, making 32 rooms in all.

With this exhilarating new info in mind, La Mort sped across the courtyard and entered the Room of the Toad, the first room in the east lobe. The message was translated as, "There are one thousand, one hundred small rooms." The inspector's ability to convert decimal to binary was taxed somewhat but he soon came up with "twelve" for the number of small rooms in the Library. That jibed.

The first two rooms in each lobe were small, as well as the last room. All the other rooms in each lobe were large.

Now onto the rooms he hadn't explored yet. With the WOMBAT scroll in hand he almost fervently prayed the word and entered a large, triangular room. It resembled all the other large rooms in the Library, with WOLF to his right and ELK to his left. He spoke the word, "Wolf" and strode into a large room with only the one door behind him.

On a table he spied a cruet containing wine, or what smelled like wine. It sat on a napkin. He picked up the cruet, putting the stoppered bottle in his pocket with the cruet of water. Then he examined the napkin. It seemed to be a sacramental napkin and, judging by the indentations in it, had a message written on it. But La Mort couldn't decipher the message. It was too faint.

He pulled the two cruets out of his trenchcoat pockets and set them on the table. What if he were to mix the two fluids; would anything result? After all, wasn't there something called "transubstantiation" that was supposed to occur during the ritual called "Mass"? What the hell? Why not try it?

La Mort poured a dollop of each fluid on the table and dipped the sacramental napkin in it. Aha! The message surprisingly— some might even say, miraculously—appeared. It read, "The Abbot has no real evidence of our pornscroll and call-nun services here at the monastery, so don't let him scare you. I'll take care of Cardinal Musial myself if he gets too nosy. I've never met a cardinal yet who won't listen to reason, especially when it's backed up by cold, hard cash." The message was signed, "Dr. Dee."

La Mort had almost forgotten about the village physician who was one of the missing people. So *that* was his scheme—running a pornscroll and call-nun service. He must be the village contact. But was the revelation of such relatively innocuous crimes as pornography and prostitution enough to inspire murder? Not in France, of course, but this was the United States, and even though the youthful president had seemed to indicate a softening of the rigid moralism of the Republican years of Eisenhower, there was definitely an air of abject prudery about the country.

But then again, this was a monastery, where religious passions ran high. There's no telling what a monk or nun would do when threatened.

Time to explore some more. He intoned "Wombat" and left the Room of the Wolf. As he crossed the room to the door to the

Room of the Elk, he stumbled over a small bump in the rug. "Quelle—" he began, and bending down to feel the rug, determined that there was a book-sized object under the rug. He started to pull the rug back, and saw a tag that read, "Hand-woven by St. Caliban." Caliban? The saint with the puzzles? Could the puzzles be in the rug? Or under the rug?

He pulled the rug back further and found a small black book with the initials "M.P." on the front. Must be Mother Puleeze. The inspector flipped through it and saw that it was filled with daily prayers and benedictions.

There were two messages written in a flamboyant hand, "Subtract one from code," and "Find who stole my perfume atomizer." Aha! Subtract one from code! That may help to decipher the contents of the ledger in Mother Puleeze's boudoir. When he tried a simple substitution code before, it didn't work. But he didn't subtract one from the code.

He stood there a few moments—should he go over to the cloister now and check, or should he continue his search of the final lobe? His legs moaned, "Continue, please. Don't make us go all the way to the cloister," so he prayed "Elk" and entered the Room of the Elk.

It resembled the Gnu, Rhino and Rat rooms—as La Mort knew it would—complete with a window on the east wall. La Mort quickly checked the rug and it, too, was hand-woven by St. Caliban. Would he have to peek under every damn rug in this place? Thirty-two rugs?

He went to the window and looked out. "Sacre merde!" He bleated. There was a glow in the church! Should he rush there to try to encounter him? It never worked the other times he tried it. And there's always those moaning legs. He went into the next room, the Room of the Hyena.

This was a room with the locked door and the Latin message below it. The message, when translated read, "To enter the Room of the Fox, you must first solve the Two Puzzles of St. Caliban. The room of the First Puzzle shares a wall with the Room of the Otter."

A grim smile crept over La Mort's visage. He now knew where the two puzzles were. His mental map of the Library was just about complete and everything was falling into place. The four Latin messages in the rooms outside the four locked rooms gave two separate pieces of information: one, the room that shared a wall with the puzzle room; and two, the door that had to be entered in order for the puzzle to be solved. It wasn't clear how St. Caliban had rigged the doors so that they had to be entered in a certain direction, but since the rugs were all made by him, the door may catch the rug a certain way.

There was one more room to explore—except for the four locked rooms, of course—and the inspector was getting exhilarated by the thought of finally encountering the two puzzles. He mentally flipped a coin and decided on the last room, the Room of the Beaver. He entered it.

It was a small room of course and had an altar against the left wall. On the altar was a grey candle. He picked it up and scrutinized it closely. It had a putty-like feel to it and a thick black wick. In fact, it looked to La Mort exactly like plastique explosive. Explosive? Could this have something to do with the explosion on St. Swithins Day? He was beginning to suspect that the St. Swithins Day desecration had precipitated just about everything that had happened at the abbey, culminating with the murder of Abbot Costello.

La Mort hoped that he would have no reason to light the "candle" but put it in his pocket anyway. You never know.

La Mort decided to test his theory of the layout of the library. "Cat," he spoke and smirked when the door under the illegible sign swung open. He strode in, mumbled "Otter" then "Chimera" and limped over and sat on the edge of the well. His feet were aching. It was almost 4:00 A.M.

Chapter 21: The Puzzles

La Mort felt that he knew how and where to find the Two Puzzles of St. Caliban. But there might be someone in the church. Should he check that out first? He decided he should, and clambered down the rungs to the tunnel. Minutes later he was pushing the trapdoor open and dodging the nips of a sleepy, irate gelding. He cursed as the left head's teeth clicked near his elbow, and sprinted for the church.

The church was dark, the belfry too, so La Mort used his flashlight to quickly scan the belfry and the two confessionals. Nothing had changed. Then he peered over the edge of the catacomb in front of the altar under re-construction. A footprint! La Mort was sure there hadn't been one there before. He slid down into the catacomb and stared at the footprint, his flashlight just inches away. The heel of the shoe had some kind of icon etched in it—a cross with a body on it? A staff with something twined around it? He couldn't tell for sure.

He clambered out of the catacomb and willed his legs to take him back up to the belfry where he rang Matins for what he hoped was the last time. Then he trudged back to the stables. Wearily he threatened the gelding with the broom, and dropped through the trapdoor. By now even the two-headed horse had resigned itself to a sleepless night. Soon he was back in the courtyard.

He knew the First Puzzle of St. Caliban was on the other side of the doorless wall in the Room of the Otter. If his impression of the Library was correct, that was the Room of the Ram. But he had to enter the room via the Room of the Bear, so he turned west, to the door marked "PIG". He prayed "Pig" then "Bear" and faced the door with the illegible sign in the Room of the Bear. "Ram" he prayed and entered the room when the door opened.

Once inside the Room of the Ram he pulled the rug back. Voila! The First Puzzle of St. Caliban was carved in the hardwood floor. It was a diagram of monastic staffs, describing a series of connected squares. A legend read, "There are five squares formed by the Staffs of St. Caliban. By moving THREE of the staffs to new positions, you will end up with FOUR connected squares of the same size. All sixteen staffs will be used. Pray the letters of the three staffs when you know them."

The diagram looked like this:

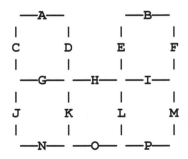

FIRST PUZZLE OF ST. CALIBAN

La Mort burned the image of these sixteen staffs into his mind. Why, this reminds me of the toothpick puzzles that one often sees in bistros and saloons, he thought. Let's see, move three staffs to form four squares. Four connected squares.

He moved staffs around in his mind for a while, then gave up in exasperation. Maybe he should try the other puzzle and come back to this one later. He spat, "Bear, pig, chimera," and went to the west door, named "TOAD". He went through it to the Room of the Deer and prayed, "Cow." From the Latin inscriptions he knew that the room with the Second Puzzle of St. Caliban shared a wall with the Room of the Giraffe, therefore the Room of the Cow. He had to enter it via the illegibly signed door in the Room of the Deer.

In the Room of the Cow he pulled the rug back and saw a diagram similar to the first one. The Second Puzzle of St. Caliban required you to move only TWO of the sixteen staffs to form FOUR connected squares. The diagram looked like this:

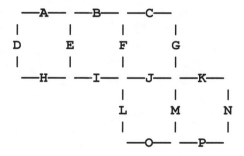

SECOND PUZZLE OF ST. CALIBAN

This one seemed even harder than the other one, where you had to move three staffs. Again, La Mort memorized the layout and letters of the staffs. He walked over to the rolled up rug and sprawled down on it, determined to relax until he solved these two puzzles.

La Mort wished that his old crony-in-arms, Lovejoy the antiques dealer, were here. He wouldn't be any help, but his friend Tinker Dill knew every matchstick puzzle known to man. For about a half hour he juggled staffs around in his mind but got nowhere. He was beginning to develop an almost spiritual hatred for all things monastic, especially monks and their stupid staffs.

"Cherchez le merde!" he finally cursed and decided to go to the cloister and see if the ledger had any information that would help him.

He went back through the Deer and Toad rooms to the courtyard and descended the rungs into the tunnel. This time he eased the trapdoor open, and was immediately glad he did, because he was able to dodge a huge load of gelding droppings that had been cleverly deposited on the edge of the hole, and fell in a sickening splat on the floor of the tunnel at his feet. La Mort reached in his pocket and pulled out the perfume atomizer. He didn't know if arsenic di-cyanide had any effect on the equine species but one little two-headed horsie was going to find out.

But the gelding kept to the back of the stall and the incensed detective turned and, placing the atomizer back in his trenchcoat, trundled to the Cloister of St. Catatonia.

As soon as he entered the lavish boudoir, he flopped down on the waterbed and closed his eyes. Would this night ever end? He knew that he was getting close to finding the murderer, or at least the missing persons. Could they all be the murderers, as in the Orient Express case he solved back in '58, sending all of the relatives of the kidnapped baby to the guillotine?

After a few moments of exhausted thought, he sat up and opened the ledger. Subtract one from code. That made the top line:

10 15 8 14   14 21 14   6 5 5

Using a simple substitution code where A equals 1, B equals 2, and so on, he came up with:

J O H N   N U N   F E E

But of course! This proves that Mother Puleeze's sideline was a call-nun service. He quickly deciphered the rest of the code:

```
D R 0 D E E    D E B B I E    F R E E
H O F F A      M I N E        X L
J F K          D I T T O      C C L
```

Obviously the good mother catered to a highly placed clientele. La Mort was amused to see that in spite of the young president's religious affiliation with Mother Puleeze, she socked it to him for 250 big ones, while the pugnacious labor leader had his teamster ashes hauled for a mere 40. But the first entry loomed ominously above—so Dr. Dee was definitely implicated, and Mother Puleeze had evidence. A motive for murder perhaps? But as far as La Mort knew, the Mother Superior was still alive.

It was time to solve the Two Puzzles of Caliban and see what was in those final four rooms. He headed once more for the church.

He was ringing the third bell of Matins when it struck him that if he was ever to see what was in that other hole in the well he would need a rope—which he just happened to have in his hands. He quickly rang the other two bells, and hardly hearing the harmonic whinny from the stables, examined the rope where it was attached to the bell. It was quite firmly attached. He'd have to cut the rope somehow.

La Mort reached in his pants pocket and brandished his Sûreté-issue Trim-Trio. Probably the handiest gadget on the face of the earth, it just wasn't made for cutting through two-inch thick bell-ropes, particularly ones made of the finest hemp. He'd need a more formidable blade to cut one of those ropes.

He sped down the stairs to the stables. The gelding was waiting and with an insane chorus of neighs, reared back upon its hind legs, its forelegs slashing like quixotic windmills. La Mort, having dealt with many a recalcitrant animal in his years at the Sûreté, dodged them adroitly and leapt into the tunnel. "Merde!" He had forgotten about the gelding's booby trap. Scraping his boots on the cobblestones of the tunnel, the determined detective made yet another journey to the Library of St. Isosceles.

It was just before he reached the opening in the well when he shouted out loud, his voice echoing in the stony cloaca. "I've got it!" In his steel trap of a mind, he had been shuffling staffs around like a demented shepherd, and it had all of a sudden become crystal clear—he had solved the Two Puzzles of St. Caliban! He knew which staffs to move, and where to move them.

Over the well he scampered, into the Room of the Toad. He had decided to tackle the second puzzle first. A curt "Deer" and "Cow" and he was looking down on the Second Puzzle of St. Caliban carved in the hardwood floor. Taking a deep breath, he intoned, "B" then "O". He figured by removing the B staff, then placing it vertically below the E staff; then sliding the O staff to the left, he would end up with a layout that would look like this:

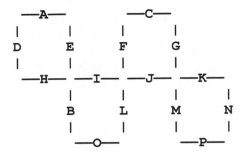

As soon as he spoke the "O" the lights in the room glowed more brightly and a sound, similar to that of a chorus of Gregorian monks singing a major chord, reverberated through the room. I think that's the solution, La Mort beamed.

The Room of the Civet was the closest locked room to him so he quickly skipped the Room of the Leopard and prayed, "Civet." The door remained closed. That didn't surprise him; the inscription said that BOTH puzzles must be solved first.

"Rat, baboon, lion, giraffe, chimera," and La Mort scampered into the courtyard. Then "Pig, bear, ram" and he was in the room with the rolled up rug and the First Puzzle of St. Caliban. He looked down at the diagram and prayed, "J, N, P" and was rewarded by another glow and major chord. The revised diagram he envisioned looked like this:

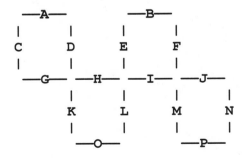

Now he was ready to search the final four rooms of the Library of St. Isosceles!

Chapter 22: Missing Persons

Wishing he had a four-sided coin, La Mort stood by the Well of St. Spurious. He had decided to go to the courtyard and gather his wits before attacking the four locked rooms. "Eenie, meenie, miney, meaux," he ventured, using the traditional French method of making military decisions. And when that didn't work, remembered the advice of the Gallic philosopher, Le Petomane: "Go east, young man." The intrepid inspector prayed "Toad, deer, wombat, elk, hyena," and found himself outside the door to the Room of the Fox. "Fox," he prayed, and stepped into the room.

Immediately he saw a crumpled form in the corner. Racing to it, he saw that it was a young monk, Novice Scosha apparently. He was dying. In his clenched fist was a note, which the inspector pried from his fingers. He read:

"It is extremely important that you meet me at midnight in the Room of the Fox. Wait for me there." It was signed with the seal of Abbot Costello.

The poor novice gasped, "Will you hear my confession?" and La Mort, with mixed emotions, placed his ear next to Novice Scosha's lips to hear, "Bless me, Inspector, for I have sinned. It was me. I was the St. Swithins Day Desecrator. Dr. Dee was always showing me tricks and when he gave me the dynamite-candles I put them on the altar. He told me they were stink-candles. I wanted to tell the Abbot about him but Cardinal Musial said for me to keep quiet and he would take care of Dee personally." The novice coughed a couple of times, then added, "Tell Debbie I love her. I'm sorry for these and all the sins of my past life."

With long-forgotten words of absolution quavering on his lips, La Mort watched the young trickster succumb to the Final Joke.

His mind racing, the inspector left the east lobe and wended his way to the Room of the Ox in the northern lobe. With breathless anticipation he intoned, "Panther," and hurried in.

"Oh no!" he groaned as he saw a fetchingly shaped form in the corner. Rushing to its side, he saw to his dismay that it was a young nun, Sister Debbie no doubt. She, too, had a note clutched in her tiny hand. He gently pulled the note loose and read:

"Meet me in the Room of the Panther at midnight. Wait for me there." It was signed with the seal of the Abbot.

La Mort was preparing to administer heroic measures to resuscitate her when she moaned, "Would you please hear my confession?"

"But of course, my dear," the detective sympathized and placed his head upon her heaving breast, where he could hear her faint, but tremulous, voice.

She whispered, "Bless me, Inspector, for I have sinned. I have broken my sacred vows of squalor by accepting the financial favors of vile men who appreciated my excessive nubility. I had a crush on Dr. Dee and he put me to work for Mother Puleeze. I wanted to give it all up and tell the Abbot but Dr. Dee talked me out of it. He said that the Abbot is too worried about the Bull of 303 AD to concern himself with my problems." A tear came to La Mort's eye as the ecumenical Lolita gasped, "Tell Novice Scosha I wish he'd been able to save up that twenty dollars. I'm sorry for these and all the sins of my past life."

As La Mort gamely tried to find the five points of the body to be anointed in the rites of Extreme Unction, Sister Debbie fetchingly passed on.

This is too, too tragic, the inspector moaned, as he stumbled, Humbertlike, from the room. With tearing eyes he staggered from room to room, until he faced the Room of the Gorilla in the west lobe. With a guttural, simian growl, he was inside the room, where he found, to no great surprise, the dying body of a voluptuous, black-habited nun, a little long in the tooth, but quite toothsome in the long run. The note was similar to the other two, except the instruction was to meet Costello in the Room of the Gorilla. It was looking as though someone—not the Abbot though, since he reported in his diary that his seal was missing—had lured the three victims to the Library—and to their death.

With a certain amount of anti-climacticism, La Mort heard Mother Puleeze ask him to hear her confession. Still stinging from the loss of Sister Debbie, he acceded to her request.

"Bless me, Inspector, for I have sinned," she gasped. "I have procured pleasures of the flesh for evil men of lucre and have even offered my own considerable charms if their filthy lucre was big enough. I wanted to tell the Abbot of my sins but was always dissuaded by Dr. Dee and his cunningly linguistic arguments. If only I had been satisfied with being Mother Superior, and hadn't let him talk me into becoming Madame Superior!"

She deliriously continued, "I confessed to Cardinal Musial today but he was too concerned with the Bull of 303 AD to do anything. I'm sorry for these and all the sins of my past life."

Then, as Inspector La Mort of the Sûreté vainly tried to remember the words to the "act of contrition" for the good mother, Madame Puleeze gently shuffled off her mortal coil.

Grimly, the inspector stomped through the rooms to the final room of the Library, the Room of the Civet in the south lobe. "Civet," he spat, fearing for the life of Father Noster, and prepared to face what may be two murderers, one ecclesiastical, and the other, decidedly secular.

The Room of the Civet yielded only the form of a monk in the corner, Father Noster, of course. Guiltily stifling a yawn, La Mort pried the note from the monk's hand, saw that it was similar to the others, and without waiting for the monk's entreaty, leaned over to hear his fourth confession of the night.

"Bless me, Inspector, for I have sinned. I have catered to sinners of the flesh by supplying them with filthy and highly artistic pornscrolls. I abhor my weakness and greed but those congressmen paid so well, and hot tubs don't come cheap. Believe it or not, I was on the verge of telling Abbot Costello everything, but he was so involved in deciding what to do with the Papal Bull of 303 AD that I never got the chance."

With a final breath, the dying monk wheezed, "I wish Dr. Dee had never gotten me into this fine mess. I am sorry for these and all the sins of my past life." As La Mort cursorily mumbled a few random Latin phrases, Father Noster peacefully expired.

Suddenly, the detective was startled to hear Matins, followed by a single, sad toll of a bell. He jumped to his feet, kicking Noster's brown robe slightly as he turned towards the door. He started towards it, then noticed something glistening underneath the dead monk's cowl. He reached to pick it up and was shocked to see it was a sharp, twelve-inch knife. "Sacre epee!" he ejaculated. "This is just what I need."

Anticipating that he was nearing the end of his monastic nightmare, he ran through the Library to the courtyard.

Chapter 23: The Papal Bull of 303 AD

La Mort climbed over the edge of the well and stared down at the hole across from the rungs, two meters above the water. Now that he had a knife he figured he could cut a bellrope, and by tying it to the crossbeam at the top of the well, lower himself to the hole. It ought to work. And if something goes wrong, the worst that could happen would be a tumble into the cold water of the well. Not a problem; he was an excellent swimmer.

But not with a trenchcoat full of clues, some of them rather heavy. He quickly emptied out his pockets and marveled at the pile of "clues" before him on the sand of the courtyard. He had:

~ A map of the abbey
~ A police info sheet
~ A newspaper clipping
~ A breviary
~ A rosary/key
~ An intra-abbey memo
~ A breviary
~ A handbook on knots
~ An electronic Latin/English translator
~ Four scroll-keys
~ A perfume atomizer filled with arsenic di-cyanide
~ A cruet of wine
~ A cruet of water
~ A pornscroll
~ A little black book
~ A missal
~ A note, signed by Dr. Dee
~ A page with a Vatican watermark
~ A knife
~ A flashlight
~ A Sûreté-issue Trim Trio

La Mort put the knife and flashlight back in his pocket and gazed at the pile. Just about every one of these items had given him a piece of information about the chaotic goings-on at the monastery—except for maybe the missal he had found in the Room of the Armadillo, the room with the deep red aura. He picked up the missal and thumbed through it again.

"Mon Dieu," the inspector uncharacteristically expectorated, "the only time I looked at this was in the red room, and I saw nothing." This time he saw that Sister Debbie, whose missal it obviously was, had scribbled all over it in what the shrewd detective knew to be Passion Red ink. It didn't show up in the Room of the Armadillo, but now it was quite visible.

One scribbling brought a tear to his eye and a curl to his lip, "If the boar gets too strange, hold your breath." Once again the inspector slapped his forehead with open palm. "But of course! It is too simple!"

The Room of the Boar was in the northern lobe so with a swift "Otter, cat, elephant," La Mort screeched to a stop in front of the door. "Boar," he triumphantly prayed, and taking a large breath and holding it, he entered the smog-filled Room of the Boar.

The psychedelic smog stung his eyes slightly, but he was able to see a rolled-up sheet of papyrus on a table. He grasped it and then, taking a small hit of the smog for old time's sake, breathed the word "Elephant." The door opened and he exited the Room of the Boar, the Papal Bull of 303 AD in hand.

At last, he was going to gaze upon the document that had cost the lives of at least four more or less innocent players in the game of life.

With trembling fingers, La Mort unrolled the papyrus and read:

OMNIA EST NULLUM ET VOIDUM
Hear ye, all ye faithful! The Third Tablet
of Moses has been found, and on it is
the Eleventh and final commandment:
THOU SHALT NOT BELIEVE
EVERYTHING THOU READETH.
Pope Pompous III

There was a cover letter to the document. It read, "This document is definitely authentic. It was found by Novice Scosha in a small catacomb under an altar that mysteriously exploded during the St. Swithins Day Ceremony."

The letter was signed by Abbot Costello.

La Mort was visibly shaken. Could this be true? Could there be an Eleventh commandment—and could it mean that all two thousand years of Christian tradition have been based on nothing more than a mosaic joke? He didn't claim to be a theologian, but this sounded pretty ominous, especially for anyone who relied on faith and dogma for an income. Like Cardinal Musial and his vicar in Rome. Indeed, for a lot more people than that.

He shook his head to clear it and decided there was only one thing to do. It was almost dawn and he had searched every place in the abbey except one—the hole in the well. He needed to get a bellrope and lower himself down to it. As he ran to the courtyard, he looked forward to ringing Matins for the last time. He knew that once he cut a rope he wouldn't be able to ring Matins again. That was okay with him. The obnoxious melody, even with its variation, was getting on his nerves.

At the well he paused by the pile of clues. A great sense of loss came over him as he bent down to pick up the missal, pornscroll and the handbook on knots. They were his only link to someone he knew he would dream about for years to come.

Chapter 24: The Rope

The tired but exhilarated inspector's footsteps echoed in the cobblestoned tunnel as he neared the trapdoor under the stables. A sobering thought had occurred to him—what if the Matins he heard right before he found the knife were rung so the murderer could come back to the library? And what about that extra toll? Could that, gulp, have been the sound of a bellrope being cut? If so, with only four bells to ring, how would he get back through the trapdoor?

Sweat sprang out on the detective's brow as he mulled over his situation. Let's see. There wasn't any rope hanging from the beam of the well, so that means the murderer isn't in the hole. Unless he knew of some way to lower himself on a rope and still keep the rope with him. It would take a special type of knot. If I only had—

La Mort's eyes crossed involuntarily as he thwacked himself on the forehead for the third time that night. Of course! He had a handbook on knots. Using the flashlight in the dark tunnel he paged through the handbook. It was full of interesting knots but none of them he saw would do what he wanted. If the murderer had tied the rope to the beam, lowered himself to the hole, then somehow took the rope with him, he'd need a knot that would remain tied as long as there was pressure on it, then loosen when the pressure was taken off.

As he perused the handbook, his eyes momentarily caught the pornscroll sticking out of his pocket. He took it out and stared at the chiaroscuro nun that reminded him so achingly of Sister Debbie. Then he turned it over and gaped at the eight-letter word on the back. Eight letters, two middle letters "PK". An eerie, hollow clarity enveloped his mind and he dully turned his attention to the handbook.

"Slipknot. Slipknot. That's the kind of knot I need. And that's what Sister Debbie wrote on the back of the pornscroll for me. Somehow she foresaw that I would find the pornscroll and need that knot." La Mort was babbling, his obsession with the young nun and the rigors of the nightmare taking their toll on his sanity.

He looked up SLIPKNOT in the handbook and saw that it was a relatively easy knot to tie. Closing the book, he placed it inside his shirt, close to his heart.

Now all he had to do was tackle the gelding once more and hope that all five bellropes were intact. He looked up at the bottom of the trapdoor and formulated a plan. It was crazy—as crazy as he was—but it just might be crazy enough to work.

He slowly opened the trapdoor about halfway and began shouting anti-equine epithets up through the opening. Soon a shadow fell over the opening and La Mort could see the malevolent faces of the gelding looking down at him. "Swaybacked plug!" he shouted, "Oat-eating bar of soap!"

He opened the trapdoor a little wider and made an obscene gesture with his fist at the fuming horse. Finally, as the inspector spat a particularly vile expletive slandering the gelding's dam, one of the heads dipped through the open trapdoor, its large, oat-stained teeth closing on La Mort's left shoulder. With a scream of terror and glee, the wily detective jumped back into the tunnel, pulling the trapdoor down hard on the horse's neck. The door's mechanism clamped down firmly.

His ploy had worked! There was just enough room for him to squeeze past the snarling horsehead through the trapdoor. As he got to his feet in the stable the other head gnashed at him violently but the rock-solid trapdoor held the gelding in position. La Mort trotted to the church and up the steps to the belfry.

His heart sank as he saw that one of the bellropes was missing. But that was okay, he thought, this just proves that the murderer, Musial or Dee, took the bellrope and used it to climb down into the hole in the well while I was getting the Bull from the Room of the Boar.

He gripped the knife and cut one of the bellropes where it attached to the bell, giving him a stout length of hemp about five meters long. As he cut the rope, the bell swung once and a mournful toll rang out. He coiled the rope around his shoulder and headed back to the stables. He was a rope's length from solving the murder of Abbot Costello. Or getting himself killed by a maniac who had already poisoned five people—maybe six.

Chapter 25: The Well

Getting past the gelding was easy; the trapdoor kept one head in the stables and the other in the tunnel. La Mort slipped past and was on his way down the tunnel, going over this confusing and complex case in his head.

The murderer was Dr. Dee or Cardinal Musial—or both. Apparently whoever it was stole Abbot Costello's seal and sent notes to the four people found in the library, luring them there some time around midnight of the 30th. There, the murderer had somehow convinced the four to ingest arsenic di-cyanide, perhaps with the chalice? That pointed to Cardinal Musial, but not conclusively.

Then the murderer had met with Abbot Costello in the church and sprayed him with the atomizer through the screen in the confessional. Very, very neat.

The murderer left a footprint in the catacomb when he was wandering around outside the library while I was in it. The imprint in the heel is a clue but not until the shoe is found. The design could have been a religious symbol—a crucifix; or a doctor's symbol—a caduceus. An ambiguous clue, at best.

The Cardinal had a motive. He wanted to cover up anything to do with the highly subversive Papal Bull of 303 AD, perhaps under orders from the Vatican. Costello knew about it so he had to go. The other victims were pestering the Abbot and he might have spilled the beans about the Bull to them. They had to be termi-

nated, or as they say in the ecumenical underworld, "excommuni-
cated with extreme prejudice."

But the Doctor also had motive. His pornscroll and call-nun
rackets were about to be exposed. There's no telling how much he
was pulling down in fees, as well as shakedowns of important po-
liticos. The Abbot knew about it and wasn't the type to let a pagan
like Dr. Dee make a profit on his turf. Dee's partners in crime had
to be eradicated; they were spilling the beans to Abbot Costello.
Yes, it all fit. The wily Dr. Dee could have figured some way to
get his four victims to ingest the arsenic di-cyanide. As for the
Abbot's murder, spraying him through a confessional screen was
deliciously blasphemous, which sounded like Dr. Dee's style.

La Mort reached the end of the tunnel and climbed up into the
courtyard. He slipped the rope off his shoulder and tied it to the
beam, using a slipknot. Keeping the tension on the knot, he
gripped the rope and slid down it until he was level with the hole.
Then he swung from side to side until he was able to swing into
the hole. He fell onto a hard surface and looked up to see a large
sign that read, The Catacomb of St. Faustus. He still had a grip on
the rope so he shook it a couple of times and smiled grimly as the
rope fell from the beam. He hauled it in and coiled it at his feet.

He was in a tunnel, tall enough for a man to stand upright. It
ran straight for about five meters, then curved sharply to his right.
A priest hole, he figured, an escape route for the clergy that many
medieval homes and castles had. There's undoubtedly an exit into
the village at the end of the tunnel.

He started down the tunnel, made the turn to the right and
gasped as he found himself in a large catacomb. There was a pulpit on one side and a lab table on the other. Behind the pulpit was
a short, pale man dressed in the red cassock of a cardinal. Behind
the lab table was a tall, dark man dressed in Harley Street finery.

Cardinal Musial exclaimed, "Thank God you've come! I've
just now escaped from Dee's bonds and now we have him! He
was using the monks and nuns to further his lustful ambitions and
when he found out they were going to repent and confess to Abbot
Costello, he killed them all."

Warming to his speech, he continued. "He stole the Abbot's
seal and sent notes to each of his victims telling them to meet him
in the Library. Then he lured me down here and drugged me so he
could murder the Abbot in the church with Mother Puleeze's atomizer. For God's sake, help me apprehend this fiend!"

From across the room came a cry from Dr. Dee. "Wait!"

"Cardinal Musial has described the plot most admirably, except for the minor point that it was he, not I, who murdered everyone. He had received an order from Rome to keep the Papal Bull of 303 AD under wraps and when the Abbot refused to comply, he gassed him in the confessional. He had to kill everyone who knew about the Bull so he lured them into the library where he gave them a little thing he called 'Last Communion'."

At this exposition by Dr. Dee, the Cardinal squawked, "That's a lie, you fiend! You killed everybody in the library by giving them an antidote to the plague in my favorite chalice!"

The dapper doctor retorted, "Again you have credited me with actions that you yourself have undertaken. Surely it's obvious that this man of the cloth is consumed with zealotry."

In unison, the two suspects turned to the inspector and pleaded, "Help me tie him up!"

La Mort was in a turmoil. One of these two bozos was a methodical, cold-blooded killer who had murdered five people without a shred of remorse—and the other was either a hypocrite who conspired to cover up a 2000-year mistake, or a Hippocrat who corrupted simple, innocent believers, one of whom was a nubile angel.

The inspector was almost feverish with indecision and disgust. He had been through several levels of hell, fought a demonic, two-headed monstrosity, and had had four people die in his arms. But the superintendent expected a neatly-wrapped solution to the case.

With a short, painful intake of breath, La Mort slowly slid the knife from his pocket.

Chapter 26: La Mort at Peace

Inspector La Mort of the Sûreté strolled down the Champs Elysées, basking in the warm Parisian sun. He flicked a pebble with his cane and smiled at the honking, chaotic swarm of automobiles that streamed by. He was at peace.

The six weeks he had spent in the hospital in Washington had been good for him. The superintendent had flown over from Paris and visited him regularly, congratulating him on solving another major case. Who'd have thought that two such disparate people as Cardinal Musial and Dr. Dee would have flipped out at the same time, senselessly poisoning five members of the abbey, before stabbing each other to death.

It was a brilliant piece of detective work. All loose ends were tied up, the victims buried, the murderers dead. The Papal Bull of 303 AD was never found, but apparently it was just some minor essay by a forgettable pope. The Vatican, who presumably would have been the only agency interested in it, had remained curiously tightlipped.

Yes, a very neat case, indeed.

La Mort stopped in front of a little bistro and tipped his hat to a couple of young nuns sitting at a table. "Bon jour, mademoiselles," he purred, "bon jour." They tittered gaily; La Mort was well known throughout the city as the man who solved the monastery murders. He was at peace with himself and the world. He knew that on the day he died—hopefully a natural death after a long, hedonistic life—a safe deposit box in Zurich would be opened and the contents, a scroll written by Pope Pompous III, delivered to the editors of the Skeptical Enquirer, an American magazine specializing in debunking popular delusions.

La Mort smiled wanly. It was only late at night, after too many cocktails of absinthe and hashish, that he remembered the last, gasping words he heard that unholy All Soul's Day in the Catacomb of St. Faustus—"The horror!" and in a different, dying voice, "The horror!"

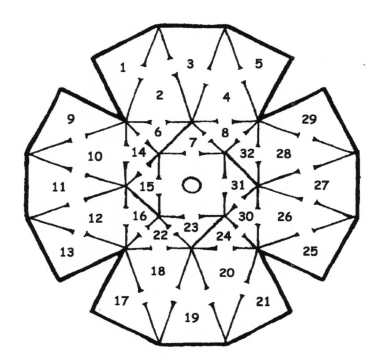

THE LIBRARY OF ST. ISOSCELES

1 Panther	11 Rhinoceros	22 Lion
2 Ox	12 Dog	23 Giraffe
3 Gnu	13 Gorilla	24 Cow
4 Elephant	14 Bear	25 Wolf
5 Boar	15 Pig	26 Wombat
6 Ram	16 Horse	27 Elk
7 Otter	17 Armadillo	28 Hyena
8 Cat	18 Baboon	29 Fox
9 Tiger	19 Rat	30 Deer
10 Gazelle	20 Leopard	31 Toad
	21 Goat	32 Beaver

THE BEST REVENGE

THE YOUNG MAN'S eyes opened and beheld ten thousand stars. The Colorado night air was cold but under the blanket he got from Jimmie Yazzie years back he was comfortable. Nothing had awakened him, but he was wide awake and he knew he wanted to get started, even though daylight was a couple of hours away, he guessed.

He stood up and rolled the gray and black Navajo blanket into a tight cylinder and cinched it with a couple of leather strips. He had slept fully clothed—except for his boots—and thought about how good a bath would feel. Maybe this was the day he'd have one. The campfire was still glowing and he threw on a few sticks for his coffee.

Hosteen, tethered a few feet away, snorted and acted as if he was ready to get on with their journey too, even though he was undoubtedly hungry. All either of them had the day before were some apples because they had skirted Canon City and the provisions were running very low. Hosteen, a tall sorrel obtained from Henry Begay two years ago, was a magnificent horse and had made the two-week journey fully packed without complaint. There were roads all the way from Farmington, in New Mexico, to their destination, but the two travelers had mainly kept off them, paralleling them a few miles to the east where the land was a bit less mountainous, and the dangers of meeting curious or malevolent miners less probable.

The young man pulled on his boots, sipped his coffee, and had an apple before packing everything onto Hosteen. He was especially careful with the oversized, bulging saddlebags that only a horse the size of Hosteen could have carried. He cleaned up the fire, fed Hosteen a couple of apples and climbed into the saddle and they continued north, with the black Colorado sky dotted with stars above.

It was about an hour later that the young man noticed a faint blue glow on the near horizon ahead and with every step a hundred stars died out. They were approaching a ridge that the young man sensed was the last one they'd find before they reached their goal. The blue glow was winking out the stars, not the looming sun that would soon strip off the cold, September night. Both the young man and his horse seemed to sense the excitement of journey's end as they approached the crest with the blue glow, which had by now obliterated almost all of the stars to the north.

They reached the top and looked down on the most beautiful thing the young man had ever seen, or imagined.

~ ~ ~ ~

Two weeks earlier, the young man had just picked the last bushel of apples from Henry Begay's tree when he heard the gunshots. He climbed down the ladder and walked with the basket back to his house a hundred yards away just north of the San Juan River. He knew his father didn't like it when the cowboys from Durango got drunk and rode down to Farmington to raise a little hell, and for that reason the young man liked it even less.

"Hey Pa!" he yelled as he dropped the basket on the back porch. He'd take them to Henry's clan, the wolf clan, the next day if he had the chance. They'd probably meet him a mile or so down the road towards Kirtland. "I got Henry's apples."

"I'm out front," Pa said, and the young man walked around the house and sat down on the front steps at the feet of Pa, who was sitting in the rocking chair on the big front porch, smoking his pipe and staring out into the dusk. "Those Durango boys just don't know how to have fun, do they?"

"Aw, don't mind them, Pa. They do whatever they have to do to get the girls. If there was any girls to speak of in Farmington, I might be doing the same thing." The gunshots were coming more often now, and getting a bit closer. Probably near the train tracks on the south side of Farmington. Pa smiled because he knew that there *were* some girls in Farmington, mostly young, timid Mormon girls, and that his son had romanced a few of them in his own way.

Farmington had been an incorporated town for about 20 years and it was mainly inhabited by hardworking farmers, orcharders, tradespeople and most of all, Mormons. It was not an easy life but the land was rich, fueled by three rivers, The Animas, the San Juan and the La Plata. The Navajo name for the area was Totah, which meant "three rivers". The reservation lay to the west and there was a friendly, peaceful relationship between the mystical Indians and the differently mystical Mormons.

Pa and his son were not Mormons, but they respected the townspeople and farmers, who had been here for a couple of generations before Pa migrated to Farmington from Missouri with the young man's mother, who died giving birth to him the year after they arrived.

Durango, fifty miles to the north, in Colorado was a mining town. The people there were rough and rude, but they had to be to scrabble a living from the mountain that was filled with silver and a little gold just south of the town.

The young man was hearing even more shots now. He knew what was going on. The cowboys were drunk and firing their pistols in the air, hoping to impress the young women of Farmington. They rarely did, mainly because the fathers and mothers wouldn't let their daughters out of the houses when there was a wild ride from Durango going on. It happened about once a month, and the cowboys seemed to be satisfied with just annoying the Farmington townspeople for an hour or so before heading back to Durango at a gallop.

He thought he saw some of the cowboys off to the east. It looked like Jerry Jimerfield and his gang. Their reputation preceded them. Calling themselves the "Lords of Durango" —the young man laughed to himself as he thought of that—the gang of Jimerfield, Tommy Beuten, Sid Leavell and Chuck were notorious for their hijinks. Jimerfield was the leader, a tall, gaunt twenty-five-year old who always wore black shirts with a big white hat. He was one of the ugliest men the young man had ever seen with what Doc Smith, the local Farmington druggist/dentist said was a "severe overbite", but there was nobody in Farmington or Durango who got more girls than Jerry Jimerfield. He was the fastest guitar strummer anyone had ever seen and he knew exactly what to say to get almost any girl who got near him to go with him out back of the dance hall for a short, but apparently satisfying good time.

The young man knew them all by reputation, and wished they would get the alcohol out of their systems and get on back to Durango. "Did the new *Scientific American* come in yet, Pa?" he asked and the old man answered, "Not yet."

Pa had raised the young man by himself and had instilled in him an appreciation for reading, especially the magazines that came in about once a month on the train from the east. Pa was the Farmington blacksmith and fix-it man and the young man was going to take over for him someday. But Pa was the real expert on everything he could learn about the world outside New Mexico. He read *Harper's*, *The Strand*, all the way from across the Atlantic with the terrific Sherlock Holmes stories, but his favorite was *Scientific American*. He tinkered with everything he read about in the magazine, using his blacksmith shop to make his own tools and devices. The young man liked all of those magazines too, but he also liked *Deadwood Dick* and *Wild Bill Hickock* stories. In fact, if they didn't spend so much money on the magazines, which were expensively shipped from back east, they'd probably have a lot more money saved.

The gunshots sounded like they were only a couple hundred yards away and the young man saw the Lords of Durango shooting in the air, whooping like wild men, their horses probably drunk too.

"I'll take Henry's apples to him tomorrow, Pa," the young man repeated. Pa had planted one of the finest apple orchards in the county not long after the young man was born and it was the son's job to maintain it. It was almost as lucrative as blacksmithing and their apples were known throughout the town for their succulence. The young man spent part of every day preening the orchard and in the fall, picking the apples that filled the trees.

Most orchards were planted in rows, for maximum efficiency, but Pa had been reading about something called the golden ratio, or the divine proportion, when he did the planting. So their orchard looked haphazard and random seen from the ground, as if planted by a psychotic. But Pa knew that if you could somehow get up above the land—in a balloon, perhaps— you could see the beautiful spiral shape of the orchard, winding like the shell of a sea creature away from a central tree.

Two years back Pa knew that his son needed a good horse and had arranged for Henry Begay, who had an uncle in Window Rock who knew horses, to bring him up a half dozen to choose from. In return, Henry's clan would get the lion's share of the apples from the tree of their choice.

The uncle, William Etcitty, was a medicine man for the clan, and he was stoic when the deal was made at the house. Pa had let his son decide and he picked a small, young sorrel, which he named Hosteen. Everybody knew "Hosteen" meant "friend" and it was a good name for a horse. But how did the young man know that the horse would grow so large and magnificent?

Pa, the young man and William then walked out to the orchard to select a tree. The orchard was large and sprawling and the young man wondered how the medicine man would decide which tree to pick. It was February and they all were bare and, to him, looked exactly the same, scattered aimlessly. A hawk was flying high overhead, making strange predatory sounds.

As they approached the orchard, William all of a sudden jumped straight up in the air and gave a bloodcurdling whoop that chilled the young man's spine. The medicine man then ran at a gallop right into the orchard and fell onto his face right in front of the tree that the young man knew gave the best fruit—the number one tree at the very center of the spiral.

He never figured out how the Navajo knew that was the best tree. There was no way he could have seen the pattern from ground level. But that tree became Henry Begay's tree and every year his clan would have the best apples in Shiprock.

"Want me to go tell those guys to stop all that shootin'?" the young man asked. There were still a lot of gunshots going off.

"No," Pa answered. "They're just young and stupid. Let 'em be." Then he grunted and leaned forward in his rocking chair, and his hand slowly fell to his lap. The pipe spilled, sending glowing embers over his pants

"Pa?" The young man got up from the porch steps and walked over to the slumped man. "You okay?" he asked and lifted the man's head. Then he saw the blood welling out of a small hole in Pa's chest and he pulled his father out of the chair and laid him gently on the porch. The old man was breathing heavily, gasping for breath. "Pa!" he yelled and cradled his head in his arms trying to do something—anything —to help him. The gunshots were moving farther away.

The young man was crying, frantic. His father coughed a few times and trembled in his son's arms. "Take it. . ." the old man gasped. "Take it to him. . ."

"What?" the young man cried through his tears. He had never known such sudden despair.

"You know. . ." his father whispered. "My life is over. . . Make it worthwhile. Take it to him." The words were but a rasp and almost silent.

"I'll get those guys, Pa. Don't die! I need you!" the young man choked.

"No." Only a whisper. "Take it to him."

For an hour the young man rocked on his knees, holding his limp and dead father in his arms, blood on the clothes of both of them, weeping at first uncontrollably and later silently.

Then he got up and walked inside the house and got a blanket. He placed his father's body on it. Later that night he carried the body out to the orchard. He was a big man and his father was small. He dug a grave near Henry's tree and buried the man who had raised and cared for him for twenty years. He used a rock for a gravestone and scratched a few words on it. He would do more later, but now he had a job to do.

It was almost dawn when he saddled up Hosteen and rode to the Foutz's trading post on the east side of Farmington, a couple of miles away. The Foutz's were awakening and he stopped outside the hogan where Billy Chee lived. Billy was the best leather-worker in Farmington. The young man woke him up and told him what he wanted and Billy said he'd have it ready the next morning. Billy sensed the desperation and intensity in the young man's eyes and knew that he would be paid for his work when it was picked up.

Then the young man rode back to his house and went to sleep. He slept all day and all night. Tomorrow he would fulfill his father's last request. Then he'd do something for himself.

~ ~ ~ ~

The young man awoke before dawn and packed provisions for his journey. He put the money that his father had stored in the house, about $80, in his pocket and saddled up Hosteen. He rode to the Foutz's trading post and Billy Chee had the saddlebags he wanted. He gave Billy $20 and placed the huge bags on Hosteen's rump. Billy knew Hosteen well and the bags fit perfectly.

Then he rode back to the house and stopped outside Pa's blacksmith's shop. He took the bags in and came out five minutes later with the bags filled. One was bulging and the other was about half filled. He placed them on Hosteen, who seemed to look proud to be carrying such a load. He fiddled a while with some other things he brought out from the shop and then rode back to the house. He left Hosteen at the front porch, where the horse shied away from the blood stain, and went inside. He came out with his father's Winchester rifle and a magazine and stood by Hosteen for a few minutes while he read. It was the June 1899 issue of *Scientific American,* the one they had last received. The rifle he placed in the holster on the right side of his saddle.

After a moment he put the magazine back in the house, locked up and led Hosteen to the back porch where he emptied the basket of apples for Henry Begay into the saddlebag that was half filled.

Then he and Hosteen headed north.

~ ~ ~ ~

The road from Farmington through Aztec, a little village on the Animas River, was practically empty and no one noticed the young man with the big horse and the almost comically bulging saddlebags. By afternoon he was headed north along the Animas up to Durango. He tried not to dwell on his father but on his quest.

He camped out right around the territory line about fifteen miles south of Durango. The land seemed to miraculously turn from the brown sage of New Mexico to the greenery of Colorado and he found a quiet spot by the Animas underneath a big bluff to the west.

The next morning early he was on his way and skirting Durango on the west when he heard a shout from his rear. He turned to see four men on horseback galloping towards him. He saw right away it was the Lords of Durango and his hand, perhaps not so instinctively, reached for his Winchester.

"Hands off that rifle, Farmington!" Jimerfield shouted and all four of the men drew their pistols and brandished them. "What are you doin' up here?" He had a big smile on his face, his two ferret teeth peeking out from his thin lips.

Tommy Beuten and Sid Leavell split apart from the others and approached him from the left. Jimerfield and Chuck—no one ever knew Chuck's last name— rode up to him on the right. The young man held his hands away from the rifle and stared with steely eyes at Jimerfield. "Let me go about my business," he said. He lowered his left hand behind him and there was a slight click that none of the gang heard.

Beuten said, "Them are some saddlebags you got there, Farmington. What's in 'em?" The young man remained silent.

Leavell moved his horse up to Hosteen and reached in the left saddlebag and brought out an apple. "Looky here!" he guffawed and took a bite. "Damn! That's pretty good." He said it with an unusual amount of sincerity that surprised his pals.

"Maybe we might have somethin' here," Chuck said, his long flowing yellow hair hanging down to his shoulders.

"Enjoy your apple and let me be," the young man said.

Jimerfield eyed him with interest and moved his horse closer to Hosteen on the right. "Well, Farmington, maybe we'll do that. But lemme see what you got in this one first." The black-shirted man reached down into the right saddlebag and immediately gave a howl that spooked all of the horses except Hosteen. He jerked his hand back and knocked his white hat off as all four of the men's horses whinnied in fear. Chuck fell off his horse and there was a sickening snap as his foot hit the ground. The three men stared at Jimerfield in horror. The gang leader's hair was standing straight out from his head like the thousand quills of a porcupine.

The young man snicked at Hosteen and they moved at a fast speed up the road north. Beuten and Leavell couldn't take their eyes off Jimerfield, whose gaped mouth seemed like it would never close. His eyes had rolled back up into his skull and his hair was slowly drifting down in its usual greasy state. Chuck was moaning on the ground.

~ ~ ~ ~

The young man stayed off the main road through Durango, instead taking the Florida road that branched around the mining town on the west. He camped that night in the high mountains north of Durango, about thirty miles south of the mining town of Silverton. He heard in the distance the narrow-gauge train that carried miners and ore between Durango on the south and Ouray on the north. The whistle and sound of the engine was calming to him, even though he knew nothing about mining, and cared less. He'd always wanted to ride the train with his Pa but the opportunity never arose. He'd heard that the scenery from the train was spectacular as it wound its way along the Animas.

It took him over a week to cross the Rocky Mountains and the Sangre de Christos and he'd never seen such sights. Occasionally he'd run across a small mining camp or a small ranch and a few of the people gave him some grub and let him rest for a spell. Everyone he met seemed curious about the huge saddlebags but were too polite to ask. In general, the pioneers of Colorado believed in minding their own business and letting you mind your own.

The last city before his goal was Canon City and he decided to skip it. There was a territorial prison there and even the chance of seeing the huge gorge of the Arkansas River didn't tempt him. He'd read in *Harper's* that some crazy engineers had proposed building a span over the gorge, but no one really believed they would.

The young man and Hosteen continued on their quest.

~ ~ ~ ~

An hour before dawn, they crested the blue-traced ridge and he saw the most beautiful thing he'd ever seen, or imagined. Off to his left was a snow-capped peak that rose up into the clouds, another, just to the south of it. But catching his eyes and holding them was the valley floor below. It was a big valley, extending to the base of the peaks on the west and on into the horizon on the north and south. In the center of the valley was a grid of hundreds of blue dots, a shade of turquoise and cerulean he'd never seen before. In the crisp, cold and dry Colorado night the dots didn't twinkle like stars, they pulsated in a rigid north-south *straight* grid that was so unnatural in the Colorado wilderness that it made him gasp out loud.

The grid was almost a square, with about fifty dots across and fifty dots down, each uniformly spaced. Hosteen drew back a step, instinctively. There was something utterly alien about the blue-dotted valley.

"We're almost there, Hosteen," the young man said and they slowly wended their way down the crest into the valley below.

An hour later the sun began to peek over the eastern horizon and the dots went out—all at once. The city of Colorado Springs had turned off its street lamps. Not the gas lamps used by all of the other cities of the civilized world—the electric lights supplied by the El Paso Power Company.

Four hours later the young man rode his horse to the east side of the city and began to approach the base of the huge mountain peak that towered like a religious icon. He was almost there.

He met a few ranchers along the trip and one of them he asked directions. The rancher knew exactly what he was seeking and pointed the way. An hour later the young man followed a road that led to a huge metal fence and gate, behind which stood a tall, well-dressed man with a dark mustache and a smile on his face.

Nikola Tesla said, "I've been expecting you."

~ ~ ~ ~

After cleaning up in a nicely furnished house with amenities the young man had never heard of, he sat down with the great man he'd read of numerous times in *Scientific American*. Tesla had summoned an assistant who took care of Hosteen and unloaded the saddle bags carefully, taking them into a huge warehouse that stood beside the house.

"How can you have expected me?" the young man asked, in awe of the inventor.

"The mining towns of Colorado communicate a great deal," Tesla said, "and there was an amusing story about a gang of hooligans in Durango who were 'shocked' by a man from Farmington in the New México territory. The description of the way the man's hair stood up all around his head meant only one thing to me. You have one of my coils. Apparently a very efficient one, since it seems to be able to fit into a saddlebag."

The young man nodded his head, amazed at the deductive powers of the inventor. "Sherlock Holmes has nothing on you, Mr. Tesla."

"I very much want to see your coil. But one thing I cannot figure out is what you used for power. Surely to get such a reaction you must have had a huge power source?"

"I used leyden jars that my father made in his blacksmith shop. He's the one who made the coil, using some of the diagrams from *Scientific American*."

Tesla sat up straight and exclaimed, "But leyden jars cannot possibly supply such power."

"They are ordinary leyden jars—four of them. They're in the left saddlebag, under some apples. The coil is in the right saddle bag."

"I must see this coil. Right away." The inventor stood up and they walked quickly to the warehouse, which the young man saw was a huge laboratory of incredible machines. Some of the coils made him gasp at their size.

The young man pulled the coil out of the saddlebag, after disconnecting some wires that ran from the left bag to the right. It was a metal donut about 18 inches in diameter.

"A-a-a torus!" Tesla sputtered. "But I never designed any coils in the shape of a torus, and there were no diagrams of anything like *this* in the *Scientific American.*"

"My pa was always experimenting around with the things he read. Always changing them and seeing what happens."

"I *must* meet your father— immediately!"

"I'm sorry. He died. It was his last wish that I bring this to you. Ever since he read that you had moved to Colorado Springs he talked about us coming here to see you. But he was the blacksmith for Farmington and we never got the chance."

"A blacksmith." The mustached inventor's eyes misted and he said, "You must stay here with me, young man, and I will show you the wonders of technology. I may even show you how we will eventually communicate with Mars—and Jupiter."

The young man's mind reeled.

~ ~ ~ ~

For three days he stayed with Tesla and he saw sparks and lightning streaks of indescribable dimension. He saw machines that took his breath away, some of them literally as he felt the magnetic attraction of millions of volts. He had the grand tour of a lifetime guided by the number one genius of the century.

But then he said he had to return to Farmington.

The inventor asked him to come with him to New York once his experiments with interplanetary communication in Colorado Springs were completed. But the young man declined. He must return to his home.

Tesla agreed, but insisted that he leave behind the three apples that were left. He thereafter told his friends in Paris and New York that the best apples he ever ate, even though they were beyond ripe, were from Farmington, in the new state of New Mexico.

~ ~ ~ ~

Ten days later Hosteen and the young man were moving leisurely down the Florida Road to the west of Durango when they heard gunfire. Carefully they moved into a copse of cottonwood trees and moved toward the shots. From behind the trees the young man looked out on a small glen where it looked as if an apple orchard had once stood. Someone had gone through a lot of trouble to up-root and destump the area and now there was a makeshift race track there. Cowboys were racing from right to left across the track and shooting their guns into the air at the end of each race.

He recognized the Lords of Durango. He watched for several races, noticing the girls that stood on the side of the track, cheering every winner, of which Jerry Jimerfield seemed to be the main one. Chuck, with his leg in a white cast, sat with the girls in a wooden chair. He shot his gun into the air at the end of every race too. There was a lot of hooting and hollering and all seemed to be having a grand time.

The young man placed a hand on his Winchester and thought how easy it would be to pick off one, or two, or maybe even all of the Lords of Durango by shooting them at the end of a race when the sounds of his rifle would be masked by the shooting of their guns. They probably wouldn't even notice anything was wrong until there were four bodies lying on the ground. And unless they saw his muzzle flash, they still wouldn't know where the shots came from.

But after watching a few more races he took his hand away from his rifle and pulled Hosteen away from the edge of the copse. He'd been away from Farmington long enough. The Taylors and the Nygrens probably had some horses to be shod, and there might still be some apples on some of the late-blooming trees. And Pa was a wise man. It wasn't what he wanted.

The young man rode on to Farmington.

There was a new century on the horizon and he hoped it would be less violent than the last.

THE MARTINGALE ARMS

THE FIVE POKER PLAYERS who had just finished their weekly Friday night session were sitting on the verandah looking out over the bay and drinking a final beer. The topic of conversation was gambling and the atmosphere was jovial. The host said, "Did I ever tell you guys about the Martingale brothers?"

A couple of the men shook their heads and the host continued, "It's the damnedest thing you ever heard. Fact, we wouldn't be sittin' here if it wasn't for those guys. Lemme tell you how it went."

THE MARTINGALE ARMS STORY

I guess it really started with old man Martingale. He made a small fortune in the publishing business and then up and died when his two sons, Abner and Zeke, were in their early 20s. About 15 years ago. Both of them were decent fellas, Abner more of a college guy and Zeke always trying to break into the business world without doing any real work himself. The old man, even though he had a bunch of money, never spoiled his kids. They had to work their own way and everybody seemed to respect the family for it.

Now this is just what I heard. I didn't come along till a bit later.

Anyway, at the reading of the will no one was very surprised when each of the boys was left half of the estate. The mother had died years back and there was only the two. Something like five million apiece.

Now this was right around the time when gambling was legalized in the state and a couple of small casinos opened up down by the beach. And it was also around the time when the city was worried about the homeless people who were showing up more and more around downtown.

Well, Abner knew right away what he wanted to do with his fortune. He wanted to help the homeless. So he approached Zeke and tried to get him to go in with him on some project that would give the homeless jobs and get them off the street. But Zeke wasn't having any of that. He also knew where he wanted his money to go—into one of them casinos. He wasn't a gambler, he just wanted to make a bunch of money by being a big casino mogul.

They argued a lot but it wasn't long before Zeke bought a big cut in one of the casinos, the Silver Dollar. Abner was disappointed, but Zeke told him that there was no way he was going to waste his money on homeless people. Not when there's plenty of money to be made on tourists and rich Hollywood people.

Abner just shook his head and said, "We'll see about that." That was when he got his big idea.

Now, you may remember that when gambling was legalized a lot of cities saw a gold mine in the casinos. They made so much money that the mayor and his crowd pushed through a bunch of tax levies on the casinos to pay for things the town needed. This wasn't unusual; most cities tax the hell out of the casinos and the casinos just shrug it off. They make so much money it's actually good publicity that they "support the community".

But Zeke didn't like the taxes at all. He didn't care about the city except as a place for his casino. But he wasn't about to buck the system and the Silver Dollar paid its taxes on time and in full.

So what did Abner do with his five mil? He ended up buying the old Strater Hotel, a few blocks away from the Silver Dollar. Big five-story apartment building with about 25 apartments. He got the building cheap, something like two million. It was empty and he put another million into fixing it up nice and about six months later he had an apartment house that anybody would want to live in—except maybe rich people who would want bigger rooms. The rooms were small but perfect for single people.

He called it the Martingale Arms. Then he started looking for people to move in. That was where the scheme started.

Abner put out the word that he wanted to rent to homeless people, but not just any homeless people. He screened every tenant.

Now I guess I ought to mention that one of the ways that the city spent the casino tax money was to subsidize housing and jobs for the homeless. If any company would give a job that paid at least $50 a day to a homeless person, the city would pay half of it. A few companies went for it but not many. Let's face it, not many of the homeless types were very skilled.

But Abner wanted only homeless people to live in his apartments and he'd offer the ones who applied—and there was a lot—a room and a $50-a-day job. A few of them, the ones who were good at it, worked around the building, cleaning it up, doing janitorial work, landscaping and stuff. They were glad to have the work and apparently they did a good job. It was a great place to live.

But the others got a different job offer. Here's what they had to do: gamble. In return for a room at the Martingale Arms he had them sign a contract that they would go to the Silver Dollar every day of the week and gamble. But they had to gamble *exactly* as he said. They would dress up nice—Abner provided each tenant with some decent clothes and laundry service until he could afford his own—and go to the casino and play roulette. Only roulette, which had no table limit and one green 0 spot. That was the Silver Dollar's big come-on, their no-limit roulette tables.

Here were Abner's instructions: you can bet on red or black, or odd or even, but *only* on red, black, odd or even. No numbers or any other options. You'll bet $50 on your first bet. As soon as you win once, you quit, collect your winnings—which was $50—and leave. If you lose, you double the bet to $100. If you lose again, you double the bet again. You keep doing this until you win, collect your $50 in winnings, and leave. If you lose sixteen times in a row, you leave the casino.

Abner explained to them that he had set up an account at the casino that each of his residents could tap into as needed if they went on a losing streak. Up to a million and a half, which is just about what they would be betting if they lost sixteen times in a row.

If anyone broke the rules, say by continuing to gamble after winning once, he'd fire them from the job and kick them out of the Martingale Arms. They were told this up front and in the ten years that the casino was in business only about a dozen people broke the rule. This went on until the Silver Dollar closed down about five years ago when a hurricane caused a bunch of damage.

Now the job only brought in $50 a day for the twenty tenants who gambled daily, and Abner charged them $10 a day rent, but that still left $280 a week profit for the residents, and that was good money for the typical homeless person, who didn't really have any other expenses. In fact, most of 'em ate at the casino and ate damn well. Fifteen years ago $280 a week was pretty good

wages, especially for about fifteen minutes' work a day. Half of
the twenty gamblers won on the first spin of the wheel and another half won on the next spin. Rarely did they have to go to the
cage and get more money because they kept losing. They could
walk over to the casino from the apartment house anytime they
wanted, as long as they went once every 24 hours, and only once.

Abner even set up a group health insurance plan for every resi-
dent/worker and paid for it.

The Martingale Arms is still an apartment house now, but
when the casino closed, Abner sold it to that Trump guy and
moved to Florida. I hear he's helping out the homeless down there
now. Zeke took his hurricane insurance money and his casino
earnings and moved to the west coast somewhere.

And that's the story of the Martingale brothers.

One of the men on the verandah snorted, "Well, I'll be damned.
How did that work? Nobody ever lost 16 times in a row?"

The host replied, "Figure it out yourself. The odds of losing
sixteen 50-50 bets in a row is about 1 in 65,536, or maybe 60,000
because it's not quite a 50-50 bet. There's a green 0. Twenty guys
going once a day would take about 3200 days to make that many
bets, and that's about ten years. Abner was gambling that none of
his 20 guys would go on a losing streak of sixteen in a row. And
he lucked out and no one did.

"But even if one guy did, he could easily afford it. Look at
what he was bringing in every year. The 25 tenants each paid him
$70 a week rent and the city chipped in another $175. That's
about a quarter million a year."

"But that would have meant he just broke even, if he had to
cover for a guy who lost sixteen times in a row," another one of
the men insisted. "Surely it cost him money to run the apartment
house and pay taxes and stuff. And the health insurance for the
tenants. . ."

"Oh it did," the host said, "Abner wasn't trying to make a lot of
money. He just wanted his brother to pay the homeless people's
salaries. When he sold the Martingale Arms for six million after
10 years he made all of his investment back, and more. But mainly
he wanted his brother to support the hundreds of homeless people
who came and went over the ten years the scheme was in operation. Zeke came out okay, but in reality it was *him* who paid the

salaries of the homeless people. Him and the taxpayers of the city."

One of the men said, "I never knew about this. Where the hell did you learn all this?"

The host smiled, "I was one of Abner's first tenants and I stayed for the whole ten years. How do you think I saved up enough for this place? I made $280 a week all that time and only spent it on food and books and, I have to admit, a few ladies. It was easy work and with compound interest I made out like a bandit. And I owe it all to Abner and Zeke. And the taxpayers, of course."

The five men each killed off their beers and went into the house, a six-room villa on the beach. Or as the host called it: "home".

JICARILLA MUD

Farmington New Mexico

1955

Wild Bill Smith

BILL SMITH SPUN OUT of the parking lot of the Macgobar office on West Main Street and headed east. His blue Packard sedan was too clean for Farmington and looked out of place. He and Geneva had driven in from Tulsa over the weekend and the Packard hadn't had time to attract the fine gritty sand that coated everything in New Mexico in the spring.

He passed the El Vasito lounge on the right—some called it the Bucket of Blood—and continued west for several blocks past the Totah Theater and Sprouse-Reitz dime store. On the left was the Palace Market, a hotel, the Allen Theater, Gardenswartz Sporting Goods and Sweetbriar's clothing store. He took a left on Allen and angle parked at Noel Hardware and exited the Packard. The sun was going down as he walked across the street, gazing up at the wall of Sweetbriar's at the big semicircular crack in the plaster that showed where the openings for the old Trailways Bus Station had been. Bill had never seen it as the bus station, since it moved up the street a block a couple of years before he'd ever visited Farmington, but he'd heard the stories about the place.

He headed north on the west side of Allen and entered the first door he came to, the entrance of the Blue Spruce Restaurant.

It was dark inside the place and it took him a while to get used to it. A U-shaped counter faced away from the door with cushioned seats spaced around the near side of it. Behind it, in the U, were the swinging doors to the kitchen. There were booths around the sides of the room and Bill took the last one on the right, facing back towards the door. Sally, the waitress who'd been working at the Blue Spruce for ten years, ever since the war, brought him his usual, water and tea.

"How's bidness, shug?" asked Sally.

Bill, who was 25 and often accused of looking like the movie actor Richard Egan, shrugged off the "shug" and answered, "The oil bidness is the same here as it is in Oklahoma. Too many Okies."

Sally laughed and moved off to wait on the growing evening crowd at the Blue Spruce.

Don Tucker

DON TUCKER put his hat on the seat next to him in the 1947 Lincoln as he pulled out of his driveway on Wall Street. He headed south, down the hill to where Wall doglegged at Apache Street and turned west. Traffic was always light in the evening on Apache and he didn't see any other cars as he spotted the St. Thomas Catholic School on the left, which his boys attended. He took a left on Allen, just past the church, and drove down the hill past the ballpark. There was a game just starting and Tucker was tempted to park and watch a few innings in the twilight before they turned on the spotlights. If the Scribner's café, just across the street, had been open, he probably would have. It was the best ballpark in town and its six rows of concrete bleachers made it the most comfortable place in town to watch baseball. And Scribner's hamburgers with the thin patty of meat hanging over the bun on all sides, *ai caramba!*

Tucker took the little dogleg Allen Street made and continued south past the Huntzinger's Apartments on one side and an abandoned government building that seemed doomed to linger as urine-depository for years to come on the other. Just past the Allen Hotel, a two-story wooden relic of the "Old Farmington" of the '40s, Tucker angle parked and, grabbing his hat, got out next to the new Trailways bus station. He adjusted his hat using the reflection in the bus station window and crossed the little alley that led behind the Allen Theater block.

Just as he reached the door of the Blue Spruce Restaurant, the neon sign above him crackled into life. It was now dark enough for the garish red, green and blue sign, in the shape of an oil field derrick, to bathe him in its glow as he entered the restaurant.

His eyes had no trouble adjusting to the darkness of the place and when he heard his name shouted above the din of hungry oil workers off for the day, he headed back and sat across from Bill Smith.

"Cheerio," said Bill.

"Gotdoggit, Bill, do you have to tell everyone I'm here?" the bald man said as he laid his hat on the booth seat next to him. "We'll have every salesman in town after us."

"Well, what do you think I do," the genial Okie retorted. "I don't just fix the rigs; I buy the tools too."

"Yeah, but you've already bought Miley Mud all it needs for the year."

Sally came over and took Tucker's order for coffee and a hamburger, calling him "Shug" too. He gave her a big smile and watched her walk away, her hips reminding him of a pumping unit on a hysteresis cycle.

"Got any idea why Arky wanted to meet with us tonight?" Bill asked, dipping his water glass under the table and adding some bourbon from a flask to it, just enough to give it the color of his tea. Now he had two glasses of tea in front of him.

"No I don't," Tucker replied, "but he said it had something to do with the Jicarilla."

Arky and Neta Miley

ARKY MILEY shouted to his wife, Neta, as she got in the driver's seat of their 1945 Cadillac de Ville, "Are you sure all the doors are locked?" At a nod from her, Arky closed the front door of Miley Mud and Chemical Company on East Main and locked it. Then he walked to the Caddy and got in on the passenger's side.

His thick, dark mustache gave a quiver as he settled in for the ride downtown to the Blue Spruce. "It sure would be a shame to have someone break in and trash the office—now that the Jicarilla situation is panning out." Arky, who was often told he looked like that young TV funny guy, Ernie Kovacs, seemed to have a hard time containing his excitement about something. He kept up a constant patter to Neta, a statuesque brunette with big hair, big smile, and an air of competence that Arky thrived on, as they drove west on Main, passing the jagged cliff that had been cut away from the bluff so that Main Street could angle at the edge of town. On their left was the Apache Motel where new employees of Miley Mud and their families stayed until they had found a house. On the right was Farmington Lumber, the Harmony House music store, the Creamland Dairies milk company and the downtown city park. Neta listened to his enthusiastic plans, nodding her head from time to time, and took a right just past the Snooker 8 pool hall, Don's News Stand, Pop's Fountain and Noel Hardware on Allen. She spotted Bill Smith's Packard and angle parked next to it.

The sun had gone down and the neon derrick sign across the street above the Blue Spruce flashed red, green, red and green, then blue in an old pattern that everybody in the oil business in town knew by heart. Arky took Neta's arm and they crossed the street and entered the Blue Spruce.

Tom Bolack

TOM BOLACK stuck his bullet head out of the GMC pickup and yelled at the carload of Navajos ahead of him that couldn't seem to make up its mind about which bar to stop at. That's how he saw any car- or truckload of Navajos, even though most of them were on their way back to their hogans after spending a hot day on Broadway Street selling their turquoise and silver jewelry to tourists. Tom had spent the day in the Jicarilla oil patch, 70 miles south of Bloomfield, and he was tired and dusty.

He was thinking about getting a new Chevy pickup—and maybe even a Lincoln town car—but he figured as long as the Jimmie held up on his daily trips to the oil fields, why bother with transportation that needed to be cleaned?

Tom was over six feet tall and a little overweight and his huge, balding head scared most Navajos, who thought he looked like a *dona shona chindi*, a no-good devil. He had driven in from the Bloomfield highway and needed to stop at Foutz' trading post on Behrend and Main to pick up a squash blossom jewelry piece for his wife, Betty, but the damn navvies changed his mind. Instead he turned north on Allen and a block later pulled up alongside Noel Hardware.

He wished he had taken the time to change clothes because he had some news for his oil buddies at the Blue Spruce and it would have more impact if he were dressed in a suit or something more elegant than his oil field clothes.

The derrick sign crackled as he entered the restaurant. As his eyes adjusted he saw Bill Smith, Don Tucker and Arky and Neta Miley in a booth at the back. He walked to them and sat on a stool at the bar across from their booth.

"Hullo," he intoned and the four Farmingtonians, who stopped their animated conversation, answered back noncommittally. "Glad I ran into you guys," Tom said. "How's bidness been?"

The four looked at each other and left it to Arky to comment wryly, "Wa–all, it's doin' pretty good, Tom. How 'bout you?"

"Can't complain. Can't complain. I'm thinking of takin' a little huntin' trip up t' Alaska."

"Alaska?" Bill said. "That's a long ways to go for huntin'. What're you goin' for? Polar bear?" He gave a little laugh.

"That's right. Polar bear. I hear they got some of them that's almost a ton on the hoof. Betty just bought me a new 30-06 with a telescopic sight."

Bill, who knew guns, smirked a little and said, "You'll *need* a telescopic sight if you hope to get a shot at a polar bear. I hear they're way up north where there's nothin' but ice and snow. How can you sneak up on a bear where there's no trees or rocks?"

"Oh I'm not thinkin' of shootin' a bear on the ground. I'm plannin' on shootin' him from a Beechcraft I'm buyin' from Oscar Thomas up at the airport."

They all laughed at that, visualizing the huge Bolack sticking his upper torso out of the window of a twin-engined airplane to shoot at startled polar bears on the ice below.

"You must have hit a few wells," said Tucker, "to be talking about buying an airplane."

"More than a few, Tucker. More than a few. In fact, Omer Tucker over at the accounting company tells me my assets just passed the million dollar mark."

The four could tell by the way Bolack rushed the sentence that this was what he had been wanting to tell them all along. He was Farmington's first oil millionaire. And by way of celebration, a polar bear would have to give his all.

"Well, that's great, Tom," Neta said quietly. "When you get to be governor, why don't you invite us out to your Xanadu ranch and show us your polar bear?"

All four of the men laughed at this, but Bolack ended his laugh before the others.

"Will do, little lady. Will do."

An awkward silence followed, broken by Sally's, "You want anything, big fella?"

Tom Bolack mumbled "No thanks," and saying goodbye to the four in the booth stomped out of the restaurant.

"The sad thing is," Arky Miley said, shaking his head, "he'll probably get that bear—and maybe even become governor."

Neta sniffed. "And maybe we'll get that tour of his ranch."

The four hunched closer around the table and continued their interrupted conversation.

The Mud

ARKY LOOKED at the other two men and said, "First of all, tell me how's it goin' down at the Jicarilla plant."

Tucker and Bill looked at each other and Bill said, "Well, Arky, I haven't spent all that much time down there but what I've seen is sort of confusing. Tucker's doing tests all day on some new mud that I don't find all that promising for well service. What we're using now works plenty good enough on the wells I've checked lately."

"So you haven't noticed anything unusual around the plant?" Arky asked.

"No, not really. Joe Eaves has been actin' goofier than usual but then it'd be unusual for him to *not* act goofier than usual."

"You said it," Tucker agreed. "There's something down there that's setting Joe off on one of his weirder toots, and I'm not sure it's not affecting me too. Y'know, I've read everything there is about the tests you ordered but I can't see why you keep 'em going when they show that Jicarilla mud you brought in is simply no good for drilling."

"So you say something might be affecting you too? Do you spend as much time in the lab as Joe?"

"Not at all. I've got other things to do besides the lab work. But Joe works in there all the time."

"Yeah, I know. So Joe is acting strange and you're feeling something, too?"

"Well, I tell you. It's not a concrete thing. It's kind of subtle. I notice that after spending some time with that moldy mud in the lab I start to get a little lightheaded and everything seems to be—brighter."

Bill broke in. "Hey, there was that one time when Joe showed me the mud in the lab and I—I remember that day I felt sort of rubbery and had a weird kind of double vision. I had been drinking schnapps the night before so I switched to scotch that night and everything was okay."

"So what's going on, Arky?" Tucker asked.

Neta smiled and said, "Yes, Arky, do tell us what's going on."

Tucker grinned at Neta and said, "So you're not in on the secret either?"

"Actually I am, but I'm just getting tired of the buildup. Tell them already."

"Okay, okay," Arky said. "Let me give you some background before I tell you how that Jicarilla mud that's no good for drilling is going to make us all millionaires who can buy Tom Bolack and cap his wells just for spite.

"Remember last year when I met that Al Hubbard guy in Houston at the Petroleum Club convention? Did you know that he was in the CIA? Well, he was and pretty high up. He was in charge of a program to get information out of prisoners and how to keep the Communists from gettin' information out of our captured guys. Anyway, they've come up with some pretty interesting ideas. One of 'em is a drug that makes a guy go out of his mind temporarily and he'll just about tell you anything you want. The ironic thing is—get this—it's actually pleasurable to the poor sap who's gettin' questioned.

"The stuff was invented years back by a Swiss chemist. He made it from a kind of mold that grows on wheat and other grains. Al suggested to me that it might grow on crude oil or some other kind of organic substance. So I flew out to Virginia and got some of his mold and that's what we've been growing down at the Jicarilla plant. Using some of that nutrient-rich mud from the Jicarilla River basin we've found that the mold has mutated slightly from the strain that the Swiss guy used, but it really seems to like growin' on the Jicarilla mud."

"Great!" Bill jumped in. "Miley Mud'll have the finest and most successful interrogation department in the whole San Juan Basin."

They all laughed and Tucker asked, "No, really, Arky. Where are we going with this? Are we going to sell this stuff to the CIA?"

"No–o–o. Not really. Y'see, our mold is different from their stuff. They purify the mold into a liquid. What we've got doesn't need any purification. The fumes from the mold itself carry the important chemicals through the air. That's what's been happening to Joe lately. Sniffin' the product."

"Okay," said Tucker. "But what is the scheme? Do many people need a truth serum? Is the stuff so pleasurable that people would pay to sniff it? How is it going to turn into money for us?"

"Well, now that you mention it, Tucker, it is pretty damn pleasurable," Arky replied.

Neta said, almost dreamily. "Yes, pretty damn pleasurable," and Tucker looked at her with squint-eyed interest.

Arky continued, "Look. The war's been over for almost ten years now and everybody's settlin' in to the good life. They want thrills that don't cost an arm and a leg and don't make you drive all over hell to get to 'em. I'm telling' you. This stuff is that good. The CIA will never let their stuff get out because it's their nature to be hush-hush. It's *their* drug. Al Hubbard doesn't like the way they're handling it so he tipped me off. So we'll have a corner on the market of something that everyone will associate with pleasure. I tell you. It's gonna be a big thing and it's right around the corner."

"How come no one else has thought of this?" Bill asked.

"They have! Haven't you been watchin' the commercials for Miltown? Everybody and his mother is takin' Miltown and all it does is make you want to sleep during the day. This Jicarilla mud is different. You only got a small dose of it down at the plant because the best mold Joe keeps in the isolation chamber. And you have to get pretty close to the mold to really get the full effect."

"Arky and I have a patch of the mud in a small planter right by the bed," Neta said helpfully. "We just hold the planter and breath the air right above the mud. About two hits does the trick."

Tucker looked startled and stuttered, "So—so h–how long does the 'pleasure' last?"

"About three hours."

Arky looked a bit embarrassed and tried to bring the conversation back to his scheme. "The way I see it, we should phase out the drilling mud end of the business and switch over to Jicarilla mud exclusively. If people start spending more time at home with the mud instead of driving out to eat, to a drive-in, to a ball game or wherever the hell they drive to, the oil bidness is not going to do all that well anyway. It'll be good to get out."

Bill Smith looked thoughtful. "But if word gets out to guys like Bolack, there could be trouble. They don't want people stayin' at home. They *want* them ridin' around them four-lane highways that Eisenhower been building around the country. We got to be cagey about how to get the word out."

"Oh I got some ideas about that," Arky smiled. "But let's save that for our next meeting. Tucker, I want you and Bill to go down to the Jicarilla tomorrow and ask Joe to show you the isolation chamber. I'm hoping you guys will want to see what it's all about."

"Sounds good to me," said Bill and Tucker nodded.

Arky picked up the check and the four left the restaurant, found their respective cars, and drove off. The neon derrick above the door of the Blue Spruce Restaurant switched from red and green to blue, then all-red—then did it over and over again.

The Plant

BILL PICKED UP Tucker at 8 the next morning at Tucker's house on Wall. Tucker waved goodbye to Maxine as he got in the Miley Mud & Chemical pickup and they sped down Wall to Apache and doglegged down across Main. They were settled in for the two-hour ride to the Jicarilla plant by the time they crossed the Animas River just south of downtown on the narrowest bridge in New Mexico. Only one direction at a time across the bridge and even then you had be careful.

The 15-minute drive to Bloomfield was quiet but both men could tell that there was anticipation in the air. As they passed a green cottonwooded area close to the river about five miles out of Farmington, Bill asked, "Do you think Tom Bolack will really go up to Alaska and shoot a polar bear?"

Tucker chuckled. "What made you ask that?"

"Well, that's Bolack's land over there on the right. Joe Salmon was tellin' me that he bought it when those three wells a' his out on the Bisti came in. Tom says he's gonna build a huge ranch on that land."

"Bolack's always been the most ruthless driller in northern New Mexico—I guess we shouldn't be surprised if he's ruthless off the job." Tucker leaned back in the pickup seat and, placing his hat over his eyes, said, "Wake me up when we get there."

"Dammit, Tucker, you can't sleep. You're gettin' way more than roustabout's wages!"

Tucker laughed with his eyes still shut. They both knew that the roustabouts—oilfield hands hired each morning to go out with the crews to do odd jobs—liked to go to the Jicarilla because it started off with a two-hour sleep. At a buck an hour.

Bill played the radio as he drove through Bloomfield, passing the two gas stations and one bar, listening to Harold Nakai and his Navajo Show on KVBC, 1280 on the dial as they turned right onto Highway 44, *El Camino del Muerte.* They played mostly Navajo songs, which had a steady bass drum and five or six male voices weaving oddly oriental-sounding melodies, all involving the syllables "aaaayyy" and "yaaah". But every few songs Bippity Bob Barnett or Bob Berry would interrupt and throw in a Hank Williams or a Jimmie Rodgers.

Forty-five minutes later Tucker was awake and checking out the map as they passed the Chaco Trading Post and Huerfano, a large mesa that stood alone on the expanse of the desert. "There's a road we can take about ten miles ahead that will take us to the plant the back way. Want to take it?"

"Why not? It's a Miley truck."

They took the turnoff on a dirt road and headed east. They curved south about five miles later, driving through hills of tumble weeds and cacti. Fifteen minutes later the truck pulled into the dirt parking lot on the north side of a compound of three tan stucco buildings, bleached by the sun. One was bigger than the others and they went in that one, perspiring from the long drive.

There were three men in the front room, all at desks with charts and papers covering them. All three looked up as Bill and Tucker entered and one stood up to greet them. "Hey, good to see you ol' boys. I hear you want to see some Jicarilla mud." The other two men snickered at this.

"Hi, Joe," Tucker said, "Yeah, we want to see it. Up to now the results have been so bad on paper I haven't really cared to, but Arky says it's, uh, got some unusual properties."

The two men at the desks snickered and Joe Eaves, Tucker and Bill looked at each other. Joe said, "Let's go to the isolation chamber and check it out. These two bozos have been sniffing the mud all morning long."

The three went through a door on the east wall and entered a laboratory full of equipment, obviously designed to test chemicals. The mud used in oil well drilling had to have the perfect specific gravity for the terrain and underground structure of the well site. The weight of the mud, forced down into the oil deposit through the shaft, provided the pressure that pushed the crude oil from hundreds of feet below the surface into the large cylindrical storage tanks that littered the oil patch like big white pimples.

Tucker was an expert on mud and knew that any mud that was so organic that mold would grow on it had to be too light for oil field use. Which had made him wonder why Arky was spending so much money and time on the special mud that Joe was working on.

Joe had a smirk on his face that he couldn't conceal and he led them into a glass-walled room in one corner of the large laboratory. In the center of the room was a table with a flat inch-thick "cake" of brownish-black mud covering it, about three-foot by four-foot. On top of the cake was a coating of greenish mold that had a shimmering effect when one's eye caught it at the right angle. There was a dank, musty smell in the air, not unpleasant, but strong.

"That's the smell I been smellin' out in the office every once in a while," Bill exclaimed. "I always thought it was you, Joe."

"It *was* me. That smell sticks to you like roadrunner manure. Sue says she gets silly just sniffin' my dirty clo—"

"So you're saying," Tucker interrupted, "that there's some kind of pleasure we're gonna get out of sniffin' this, uh, mud, and it's so good that people will pay for it?"

"I'll tell you how good it is. I fired those two guys out there three weeks ago because with you two dropping in every few days there ain't no need for 'em, but they're still showing up every day—even though they ain't getting' paid."

"Hmm. That *is* impressive," Tucker said. "Well, I've noticed a couple of times how lightheaded I felt driving home from here. I'm feelin' pretty light right now. Is this the big pleasure?"

"No, no," Joe laughed. "This stuff gives off spores that get you a little giggly if you're in the same room with it, but that's about as high as you get. No, you gotta rub the mold and get close and really take a big snort right above it as it kinda ruffles in your fingers. It smells like a cross between cinnamon and glycerine. A' course that's partly the mud."

"I'm game," said Bill, and leaned over and rubbed his fingers over a patch of the mold. He took a deep breath through his nose and closed his eyes. "Jicarilla mud, be good to me," he said as he straightened up. "One snort does it?"

"I generally take three on slow days and four on fast ones," Joe answered, "but only one or two at a time. This is some damn good mud. That stuff we had at first was pure shit. You could sniff all day and only get a headache. I was tellin' Tom Bolack about it last night an'—"

"You told Tom Bolack about it?" Tucker snapped.

"Not about the good stuff. Not about this stuff. I told him about the stuff we used to have that got you a little, uh, warped but not about this good—"

"I don't think Bolack is the man to be talking about this to. You know he'd do anything to keep this oil boom going. He's gettin' rich and powerful and anything that upsets the status quo is *not* goin' to be in his best interests. I hope you—"

"Holy cheerio!" Bill spouted. "This is fantastic! My head is spinnin' at 500 rpms. An' in Technicolor! Whoa! I gotta sit down." He took one of the chairs at the side of the table and settled in it. "Tucker, you gotta give this mud a sniff!"

"I'd like to, but I'm kinda worried about this Bolack factor. Joe, what exactly did you tell Bolack about all this?"

"I didn't tell him nothin'. I just said we had some special mud that was gonna make us all rich and give everyone somethin' to do besides drive around all the time."

"I'm getting' flashes, guys. There's all kinds of wavy things flyin' around and I swear my legs just turned to synthetic rubber."

Tucker said to Joe, "I gotta tell Arky about this. Is the phone workin'?"

"Naw. Pete outside is supposed to be an electrician, but it'd be pretty impossible to get him to do anything constructive, an' besides—"

"Hey, guys, I just melted outa my chair. An' can anybody stop those sparrahs from—"

"Bill, let's go! Take another snort if you want, but let's hit the road. We gotta get back to town and tell Arky that Bolack is in on the action. Joe, you stay here and keep the place locked. Don't let the mud out of your sight, and for gotdoggit's sake, keep those two goobers outside quiet. There's no tellin' what *they* said to Bolack."

Bill Smith leaned over and took another big inhale as he ruffled the mold almost wantonly. "There ain't no mud like Jicarilla mu-u-u-u-ud," he sang in his slow Oklahoma drawl as he and Tucker walked through the outer office where the two former Miley Mud & Chemical employees began beating on their desks and joining in, "Ain't no mud—Jicarilla mud—*ain't* no mud—*Jic*arilla mud."

They left the building and got in the Miley pickup, Tucker driving. Bill rolled down his window and shouted, "Che-e-e-r-io," back at the building as they drove away.

El Camino del Muerte

TUCKER PEELED OUT on the dusty road that led back north from the Jicarilla plant. He kept the speedometer above 60 as the truck careered around corners on the back road and fifteen minutes later he pulled onto Highway 44, heading back to Bloomfield. There was no other traffic, other than the occasional horse-drawn wagon with a family of Navajos in the back. They stayed off the side of the road so Tucker was able to speed along at 80 on the poor blacktop highway, known across the state as the most dangerous road on earth. Bill had finally stopped singing his new song and was taking swigs out of a small flask he had in a back pocket.

Both windows were open and the hot desert air whipped past their faces as they sped north.

"Damn this is a wonderful drive!" Bill yelled. He leaned his head out the window and marveled at the way the wind caressed his cheeks. "Take your time, Tucker! I've got all day."

"You just keep havin' fun, Bill. I've seen you when you've had too many shots and I'm thinking that this may be better." He got quiet for a while and then said, "Y'know, Arky may finally be onto something. And it couldn't happen to a nicer guy—and Neta."

"Oh, he's *onto* somethin' all right. This stuff is big, real big. I *never* felt like this before. I just wish that fly would stop buzzin' so I could—"

"What fly?" Tucker asked, looking around the cab. Then he heard something and started, but glancing out the window saw nothing.

"I'm talking about the fly that's headin' right at us!" Bill shouted and pointed out of his window to his right. "The fly with the green eyeballs!"

Tucker leaned over and tried to see what Bill was pointing at but whatever it was was at an angle he couldn't see.

Bill leaned farther out the window and stared up at something. "That thing is getting' closer, Tucker! An' it's flashin' at us—" Bill jerked when a couple of loud metallic thuds sounded on his side of the truck. There was a slight bounce to the truck with the sounds, as if it had been hit on the right side by a couple of large rocks.

"Why, Tucker, I do believe that that goddam fly is shooting bullets at us! Orange ones!"

"What?" Tucker exploded, and hit the gas even harder. The pickup hit 90 as they passed the Chaco Trading Post. Bill was now looking backward.

"It's behind us now but turnin' around. If only the sky wasn't so pink and runny, I could see that green-eyed bastard better. Uh oh. I think it's shootin' at us again."

Tucker felt three jolts to the truck and heard three loud smacks as he saw an airplane zoom over from behind. As the plane flew ahead he saw a large, bullet-headed man with a huge rifle leaning out of the window of the small plane, looking back at them.

The plane circled around as Bill animatedly pulled out a pistol from the glove compartment and started waving it out the window. "See if you can get closer to that thing, okay? I got a feelin' this is my lucky day. Gonna bag me a giant fly."

"I'm not slowing down," Tucker shouted above the roar of the truck and the increasing drone of the plane as it started flying at them from the front. "But I'm also not going to give that bastard a good shot at us."

He started weaving from side to side on the narrow paved road as the plane came in low, dead ahead. Tucker saw orange flashes on the side of the fuselage and yelped when a loud thud shook the truck once again. A small hole cracked in the middle of the windshield, starring out in an explosion of shiny tendrils. A hole appeared in the back of the seat between them, spitting out a little plume of dust and upholstery.

Bill's gun popped four times as the airplane approached them. "Got him!" Bill yelled as the plane flew over, so close that Tucker could see the crooked grin on Tom Bolack's face as he pulled back into the plane, pulling the rifle in with him.

"Well, if you didn't, it looks like you may have one more shot at him before he hits us in the gas tank. He's coming back again!"

The plane was indeed making a big circle and heading back after them from behind.

The pickup leapt over a rise and on the top of the next hill a mile off Tucker could see a wagon on the right edge of the road. He kept veering from right to left as he waited for the man in the airplane catching up with them to fire again. He was just passing the wagon of Navajos when he heard the cracking of a rifle above the roar of the twin-engine airplane. He felt a slam in the back of the truck and in the rearview mirror he saw the wagon burst into flames, with screaming people running from it like lemmings. The plane flew ahead.

"Hold on!" Tucker yelled and spun the wheel of the truck as soon as they passed over the next rise in the road. The truck screeched on two wheels as it veered to the right onto a dirt road that led down into a deep rocky canyon. "It'll take a better pilot than Tom Bolack to catch us in Kutz Canyon!"

Tucker bounced the truck at 50 miles per hour over the dirt road that wound down into the miniature Grand Canyon just south of Bloomfield. There were oil field roads all over the floor of the canyon, many of them right up against the canyon walls. Tucker found one that led to a spot directly under an overhanging cliff and pulled to a stop, the dust billowing around the bullet-riddled truck.

The plane flew over but the pilot was in the cockpit and not hanging out the window. It flew over three more times then headed northwest out of sight.

Bill got out of the truck and fired off two shots at a roadrunner that scooted across the canyon, a hundred yards off. "Beep beep," he intoned quietly as the bird continued his scooting. "I'm savin' my aim for that green-eyed fly. Cheerio."

"Let's go," Tucker called from the truck, "He's going to beat us to town by a half hour. We gotta warn Arky."

The two men drove back to Highway 44 and sped on through Bloomfield back towards Farmington.

The Rendezvous

TUCKER DIDN'T SEE the airplane anywhere in the sky even though Bill kept shouting, "There it is! Here comes the green-eye fly o' destruction!" He figured Bolack had gone back to the airport on a mesa just northwest of Farmington.

"We have to tell Arky about this. We may be up against the whole oil bidness now that the word about Jicarilla Mud has leaked. I wonder where's the nearest pay phone?"

Bill, who was waving his gun out the window with his right hand and drinking from his flask with his left, said, "Hey, there's the turnoff to the Mesa Drive-In. Lloyd the pr'jectionist oughta be out there settin' up for tonight's show. I bet he has a phone."

"Good idea," Tucker said as he veered right onto the two-grooved dirt road that led to the drive-in about a mile up the road. The marquee, perched out among the tumbleweeds blared:

ROMAN HOLIDAY
&
THE THING

"Hey, you seen those shows? Geneva and I saw 'em a couple nights ago. Audrey Hepburn is this princess, y'see, and there's this creature made out of rosebush an' carrot—"

"Yeah I saw 'em," Tucker interrupted with a grim face. "Maybe you better stay in the truck while I go in and call." They screeched to a stop in front of the snack bar and Tucker ran to the door leading to the projection room, just to the west of the concession stand.

"Lloyd! Can I use your phone?" Tucker shouted.

Lloyd Freeman, a tall, angular man of about 50 looked up from the film he was splicing at a workbench. "Oh, hey, Tucker. Sure. It's in the snack bar. Hey, you gonna see the show? It's purty good—Gregory Peck's this reporter who's followin' this princess all over Rome an' this big monster made outa…"

Tucker was already in the snack bar and didn't hear any of the review that the projectionist, who had seen the films a dozen times in the past four days, was providing. He spun the dial of the telephone five times and waited, tapping his fingers nervously on the glass countertop. There was no one else in the snack bar.

After four rings, Arky answered, "Hullo?"

"Arky, Tucker. Listen, we have problems. Tom Bolack found out about the Jicarilla Mud and tried to kill us on the way back into town. We're at the Mesa Drive-In right now."

"Tom Bolack! Of all the people to—how'd he find out? No, never mind. We need to get together and talk this over. You, Bill an' me."

"Okeedoke, where do you want to meet?"

"We can't meet at the company. That's where Tom would expect us to go. Is there anyone else who knows?"

"I don't know. He might have had time to land and tell somebody. Who do you think that might be?"

"Who knows? There's all sorts of people, 'specially in this neck of the woods, who wouldn't want something like Jicarilla Mud to catch on. I tell you what. Meet me at Sadie's."

"Sadie's?" Tucker was flabbergasted. Sadie's was a notorious bordello down by the tracks. He had never gone inside; he'd only driven by it on his way to Allen Construction down by the Animas River. "I thought Sadie's was a whorehouse?"

"Well, it is, but they rent rooms by the day too and sometimes, ever since we started hitting the mud, Neta and I like to go down there and spend a day in their Kachina Suite. It's pretty atmospheric and when the mud comes on—what the hell are we babblin' about? You say Tom Bolack—of all people—tried to kill you?"

Tucker was still a little tongue-tied, thinking about Arky and Neta sniffing Jicarilla Mud at—Sadie's? "Well, okay, if you say so. Where will we meet? The, uh, Kachina Suite?"

"No," Arky laughed. "There's sort of a bar in the back on the ground floor. They don't have a liquor license but they serve booze anyway. Just go in the front door and keep walking past the desk to the back. I'll be there probably before you get there. You say you're at the Mesa?"

"Yeah. Okay, we're heading there right now. Keep an eye out for Bolack."

"Say, did you guys get a chance to check out the mud?"

"Bill did, but I didn't. Hell, somebody had to drive."

"Good thinking. So how's Bill doing?"

"Shootin' at anything that flies."

"Well you keep an eye on him and meet me at the bar at Sadie's as soon as you can."

"Will do, Arky. Bye." Tucker hung up and, ignoring Lloyd who was still reviewing the movies, walked swiftly out to the truck. Bill was lying on the hood of the truck, making humming noises.

"Gotdoggit, Bill, let's go. We gotta meet Arky and you'll never guess where."

"Uh, Sadie's? That's where I run into Arky a lot."

"What the hell, you too? What do you know about Sadie's?"

"Well, me and Geneva go there every once in a while to kinda blow off a little steam. They got this Kachin—"

"Yeah, I know. Let's go."

The two men hopped in the truck and a minute later it was bouncing along the dirt road past the ticket booth and back onto the Bloomfield Highway. Tucker gunned it up to about 80 and five minutes later they reached the bridge over the Animas River. There was a car on the north side that was closer to the bridge than they were but Tucker honked his horn and barreled on across the narrow bridge. The driver of the car, seeing the truck speeding towards him, wisely pulled off the road into a ditch as the Miley truck lurched past.

Tucker stayed left onto Pinon and drove alongside the railroad tracks till he got to Behrend Street and turned left. There, in the part of town that every Farmington mother warned their children about, was Sadie's, a three-story wooden hotel, painted a faded brown and baking in the hot New Mexican sun. The words "SADIE'S HOTEL" were painted on the front of the building across the second story. A few Navajos and Mexicans were lounging around the entrance. It was one in the afternoon.

Incident at Sadie's

THE MILEY TRUCK screeched to a stop and Tucker and Bill hopped out, running into the dark building. The people standing outside stopped speaking and stared at them, then laughed and continued their low conversations.

The lobby was very dark, with only a few 10-watt bulbs scattered around, and a bored-looking Mexican behind the front desk eyeing them warily as he looked up from a well-thumbed copy of Argosy. "The girls don't get here till three, my frien's. 'Cept for Sadie, of course."

"We're headed to th' bar," Tucker spat as the two men strode through the lobby and entered an even darker room to the back.

"Gotdoggit," Tucker cursed, "I can't see a thing."

"The good tables are to the right," Bill offered, and as if he had night vision goggles, stomped to one of them and sat down heavily. Tucker followed suit, although much slower and hesitatingly.

"Arky said he'd be here before us," Tucker said. "I hope he didn't have any problem."

"Cervesa con limon!" Bill shouted, and within seconds a short, gray-haired Mexican woman brought them two beers in dark brown bottles without labels.

Just then Arky Miley strode into the room and, seeing them as his eyes adjusted, joined them at the table.

"Listen, we can't stay here. Bolack saw me driving downtown and I had to drive all over hell tryin' to lose him. I don't think he followed me here but you never know. He's got one of them police-band radios in his truck. C'mon, let's go."

The three men jumped up and headed back into the lobby. As they were about to exit through the front door they heard the sound of a truck pulling to a stop outside and a door slam.

"That's Bolack!" Bill whispered as he glanced through the door.

"Quick," Arky said, "up th' stairs! There's a fire escape outa the Kachina Suite. We'll circle around back to our cars."

They ran to the stairway and up two flights to the third floor. The stairways were, if possible, darker than the lobby or the bar. They could hear Tom Bolack shouting down below but couldn't understand what he was saying.

At the end of the third floor corridor was a big green door painted with Navajo symbols—zia signs, kachina doll faces, even a sand painting. They ran to it and threw it wide and entered the room, which was lit by the sunlight streaming in from an open window to the south.

A bundle on a sumptuous king-sized bed sat up in shock and a man's voice thundered, "What the hell?" The bundle turned into a brown-haired, clean-cut man of about 40 and a dumpy Mexican woman of about 50. Both nude and sweating.

"Beel! Arky! What the fock are you doeeng? An' who the hell are you, Baldy?" The woman looked indignant, as if she owned the place—which she did.

"Sadie, you gotta help us," Arky quickly blurted, then, noticing the man for the first time, "Scott? Boyd Scott?" Arky seemed stunned.

The man looked uncomfortable but quickly mustered his dignity and said, "Arky, I hope you have a damn good reason for—"

The stomping of big cowboy boots in the corridor through the open door drowned out anything he said and a second later the bullet head of Tom Bolack stuck through the door. Followed soon after by his massive body—holding a cocked .45.

"Howdy," the big man said, then slowly as he faced each of the other people in the room, "Arky, Bill, Tucker, Sadie, Mayor. Looks like the gang's all here."

Sadie hopped off the bed, and without a gram of embarrassment, walked to the door in complete nudity. "You boys have your leetle fun. Joos' remember—you pay by the person, not the room." She left, closing the door behind her.

Boyd Scott, as the only nude man in the room, huddled under the covers and seemed to be cursing to himself.

"What's this all about, Tom?" Arky asked calmly. Bill was sitting in a chair looking amused and Tucker seemed to be distracted by the huge bed and its silky splendor. Bolack waved the gun and the three Miley men backed away from him.

"Now, Arky," Bolack drawled, "you know we can't let you get away with that crazy mud scheme. The oil bidness is gonna make billions in the next few years and we don't want anything to upset the cart. Ever'thing's just gotta stay the way it is. No bumps in the road."

"Yeah, but what if the road needs a little bumping?" Tucker asked.

"I jes' love them bumps," Bill Smith grinned.

"You fellas are what's wrong with this country. Always lookin' for new thrills. Well, a thrill ain't worth nothin' to me unless you gotta burn some gas to do it."

Arky looked at Bolack with a dark look on his face. "So you're gonna kill us to keep the mud a secret." He didn't say it as a question.

"Naw, I ain't gonna kill you boys. Long's you keep your mouths shut about what you been doin' down at the Jicarilla plant. Which, by the way, I unnerstand caught fire about an hour ago and burned to the ground. Too bad."

The three jumped at this news. "Is Joe okay?" Arky looked grim.

"Yeah, Joe an' a couple of other guys got out in time. They wasn't able to save anything in the lab though." Bolack walked over to a chair and sat down, keeping the gun on the three. "Naw, nobody needs to get hurt. Ain't that right, Mayor?"

The huddling mass under the covers mumbled, "That's right, Tom. I don't know what you guys are talking about but Tom Bolack is right. Nobody gets hurt. Everybody keeps their mouth shut. About everything."

Arky, who was fidgeting more each minute, said, "You can't keep it quiet forever. Sooner or later people are going to find out just how good Jicarilla mud is and—"

Arky grimaced and grabbed his right shoulder. He gasped, "It's just too good—"

"You okay, Arky?" Tucker asked, looking worried. He approached Arky as Bolack waved his gun at him.

"No, I don't think so," Arky groaned, and sat down heavily on the edge of the huge bed. "Can't catch my breath—"

"Now hold on—" Bolack sat up as Tucker reached Arky's side.

"Put the damn gun away, Bolack," Bill Smith said. "Can't you see there's somethin' wrong with him?"

Arky doubled over and gasped, holding his right arm awkwardly, and then laid back on the bed, obviously in pain.

"Call the doctor quick," Tucker shouted, then when he noticed that Bolack was hesitating, the gun still trained on them, "we're not going anywhere you dumb ass. He's having a heart attack!"

Bolack looked confused, then ran out of the room.

Tucker tried to make Arky more comfortable then leaned to put his head near Arky's as the stricken man began whispering.

"Neta—tell her—send the package." His voice was getting weaker and the glimmer was going out of his eyes.

"The package—the package—"

He closed his eyes, took a small breath, then seemed to relax.

Tucker looked at his old friend and shouted, "Arky, come back, come back."

Arky's eyes opened and he looked at Tucker and whispered, "Tucker, take care of Neta for me, okay?"

"I will, I will," Tucker cried, and Arky slumped one more time and lay still.

A stomping came up the stairs and Bolack's gravelly voice echoed, "The ambulance is on the way!"

The Wait

NETA MILEY brushed a tear back as she huddled in a big chair in the living room of her home.

"The package?" she asked, trying to keep from bursting into tears.

Tucker, sitting on the armrest of the chair, placed a hand on her heaving shoulder and said, "Just before Arky died he said to have you send the package. Do you know what package he was talking about?"

"Yes. I'll get it." She got up and walked to a roll-top desk on the other side of the room.

Tucker's eyes followed her. "Bill and I talked it over and think we should just forget about the mud. Bolack's got everybody in his pocket and he's dead set against it."

"I don't give a damn about Tom Bolack. I know what Arky would want and one day..." Her voice trailed off, then continued haltingly, "But you're right, we need to forget about the mud—for now."

Tucker smiled at her and mused, "It's too bad—I never had a chance to really try the stuff. In all the excitement—"

Neta walked up to Tucker and handed him the book-sized package. "Oh there's some left. In there."

Tucker wasn't sure if she was talking about the package—or the bedroom. His hand shook slightly as he looked at the address.

> Dr. Timothy Leary
> c/o Psychology Dept.
> Harvard University
> Cambridge Mass.

Epilogue

Twelve Years Later

"THIS IS WEIRD WALLY at 1280 on your dial. Hey don't go away
because we've got a new song by some guy named Knees Calhoon
and it's a hoot. It doesn't make a lick a' sense and it's kinda hard
t' tell if it's a country & western song or a psychedelic song but
it's a little different from what those straight stations been feedin'
ya. Wally says check it out."

Wild Bill Smith was a man who loved his whiskey
He was greeted with a smile at every bar in town
He knew his guns and how to have his fun
But when the Jicarilla called him—
The deal went down.

Don Tucker was a man with a mission
Livin' every day as lovers do
He knew his mud and he knew his blood
But when the Jicarilla called him—
His aim was true.

Bill Smith was in it for the whiskey and the guns
Tucker was in love with love
Tom Bolack did it for the money and the fame
But only Arky Miley knew—about Jicarilla Mud.

Tom Bolack had a head like a bullet
And he wanted everyone to know his name
He was the man who owned all the land
But when the Jicarilla called him—
He played the game.

Arky Miley was the man with the secrets
And heavy was the price he had to pay
He did it with a smile, laughin all the while
And when the Jicarilla called him—
He led the way.

Only known pictures of the Mileys

Neta Miley, Brian Donlevy, Arky Miley, Don Tucker, Maxine Tucker

Arky Miley, Neta Miley, Hermione Gingold, Don Tucker, Maxine Tucker

THE GLOWING GREEN GAMBIT

Farmington New Mexico

1955

Lazy Day at Miley Mud

THE MILEY GANG—the four top dogs of Miley Mud and Chemical Company—lounged in various positions around the office. Arky Miley was on the phone and his wife Neta was talking quietly with Bill Smith and Don Tucker.

"Okay, Ace, okay. . .I get that. . ." Arky spouted, "Even J. B. Rhine, whoever the hell that is, uses your paper. But we don't necessarily need that much security. We sell *mud,* for Pete's sake."

Neta smiled at Tucker and said, "And let's not forget chemicals." She was a strikingly handsome woman of 40 or so years with dark brown hair and a big smile.

Tucker, a bald, sincere-looking man of about 45 with a square jaw, whispered back, "Yeah, the smell of mud and chemicals is the smell of bread and butter to us."

Bill Smith's eyes were open and he seemed to be listening but a quick jerk of his head showed that he was almost asleep in his easy chair. He was movie-star handsome and had already had a couple of shots at his desk that morning.

With a short nod Arky spoke into the phone, "You got it, Ace. Eleven o'clock at Harry's. Bring your money." He hung up the phone and laughed out loud, startling Bill awake.

Miley Mud and Chemical Company was a support company for the oil drilling business in northwestern New Mexico. They sold a special type of chemical mud that drillers used to pump into the well to cause pressure that forced the oil out. It was a sweet business to be in when gas exploration in San Juan County was at its peak.

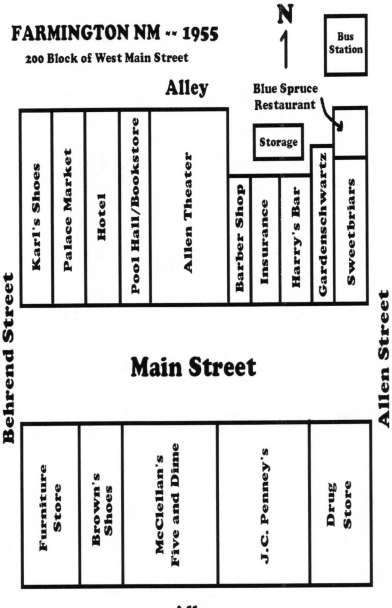

FARMINGTON NM ·· 1955

200 Block of West Main Street

N

Bus Station

Alley

Blue Spruce Restaurant

Storage

Behrend Street

Karl's Shoes

Palace Market

Hotel

Pool Hall/Bookstore

Allen Theater

Barber Shop

Insurance

Harry's Bar

Gardenschwartz

Sweetbriars

Allen Street

Main Street

Furniture Store

Brown's Shoes

McClellan's Five and Dime

J.C. Penney's

Drug Store

Alley

"So tell us, Arky," Neta said to her husband, "why we should get off our duffs to see Ace Spelvin at Harry's bar at eleven in the goddam morning." She'd had a drink already too.

"Oh the same old thing. He wants us to buy letterhead envelopes and stuff from Security Stationers. I told him we didn't need that kind of secrecy but he kept jawing about the new breakthrough they had in opaque envelopes."

"Man, this is some exciting day," Bill Smith moaned and Tucker kicked him in the shin.

"I tried to get a game of ping pong going but you weren't up for it." All three stared at Tucker and he set his jaw and settled lower in his chair. "Okay, okay. So I like ping pong."

"Well, hell," Arky said, "Ace is buyin' and we're not doing anything. Let's go down and hear him ou—"

Bill interrupted. "Wait a minute, Arky. What was that he said about J. B. Rhine?"

"You heard of him? He just said that Rhine used his envelopes in some of his experiments. What kind of experiments?"

Bill seemed to perk up. "I just read something about him in *Colliers*. He's some professor at Duke University who thinks that people have some sort of 'sixth sense' and has been doing a bunch of experiments to prove it since the 30s. They call it 'ESP' or something like that."

Tucker and Neta spoke at the same time. "I read that too—" They all laughed.

"Q.E.D." said Bill.

" 'Sixth sense', eh? How does that work, Bill?" Arky asked, sitting up at his desk and moving things around on it.

"Well, it has something to do with these cards they use. Cards with designs on them. They hide them from the, uh, subjects, and then ask them to say which card they're holding. According to Rhine, some people can guess the right card more often than chance allows. That means they have ESP."

Arky rubbed his Ernie Kovacs mustache and sat back in his chair. "Tell me more, Bill."

"Well, if I remember right there are five kinds of cards, or designs on the cards. There's a circle, a square, a five-pointed star and, uh, lessee, a cross or a plus sign—"

"That's only four," Tucker said.

"Yeah, a plus sign and—what the hell's the other design?" Bill thought for a minute then snapped his fingers. "I got it. A wavy lines design. They purposely made all five designs as different as possible so there wouldn't be any chance of getting them confused with each other."

"And so they get some cards with these five designs and, what, hide them from the guy who's being tested?"

"Yeah. Maybe they have them sealed in an envelope and then have the guy guess which cards are in it. I don't know for sure."

Arky squinted his eyes shrewdly and said, "Hmmmm. Let me think about this."

Neta looked at him and laughed. "You're still thinking about last month when Ace took you for $300 at poker, aren't you?"

"Lemme think. Lemme think."

Tucker, who didn't drink anything but juices and soft drinks, but who had also lost at poker to Ace in the past, said, "I'm up for scamming Ace Spelvin whenever possible, even if he *is* buying."

The rest of the Miley Gang sat and watched Arky rub his mustache vigorously, his eyes shut and lips pursed like Nero Wolfe. They knew he was hatching something, and when Arky Miley schemed, somebody was going to be the egg.

Finally, he opened his eyes and took a fountain pen out of his desk drawer.

"Tucker, you have any of that liquid carbonized barium you were playing with last week?"

Tucker got up and strode toward the door. "I think I do. Hold on a minute." He left.

"How big are these cards, Bill?" Arky asked.

"I don't know. Maybe a little larger than regular playing cards?"

Arky scrounged around in the drawer and took out a few blank 3"x5" cards. "Neta, here. Take some of these in your purse."

Tucker walked in with a small bottle of a thin, black liquid and handed it to Arky, who shook it to see its consistency, then smiled and set it down on the desk. He then emptied out the fountain pen into the waste basket and filled the pen with the black carbon/barium fluid.

"Bill, when we get to Harry's be sure to mention J. B. Rhine in passing if Ace doesn't. And Tucker, here's what I want you to do . . ."

The four conspirators huddled around Arky's desk and plotted. A minute later they all burst into laughter and stood up.

"Let's go have a drink on Ace." Arky led the way to the Miley Mud Lincoln and they hopped in.

Harry's Bar

THERE WAS going to be a parade later that afternoon for the local high school football team, the Farmington High Scorpions, and already people were picking out parking places on Main Street. So Arky had to park the Lincoln down the block from Harry's Bar. Harry's was on the north side of Main in the same block as the Palace Grocery, the Allen Theater, a barber shop, Gardenschwartz sporting goods and Sweetbriar clothing store. Harry's was sandwiched between the barber shop and Gardenschwartz, with a door that opened onto a long bar on the left and a few tables towards the back, away from the street.

Across the street was a drug store, McClellan's five and dime store, Brown's Shoes and a furniture store. Arky parked in front of the ultra-modern shoe store, and they all checked out the black leather wingtips in the window before walking across the street to the bar. It was right at 11 o'clock in the morning.

Ace Spelvin, a rotund balding man in an orange plaid suit, was sitting at the long bar and spotted them as they entered. They were momentarily blinded by the relative darkness of the bar as they came in from the bright sunlit day.

"Arky! Neta! Over here," Ace grinned and led them to a table in the back, where they were the only customers. "Hey, Tucker, Bill, glad you could make it."

They all sat down and ordered drinks; martinis for Arky and Neta, whiskey for Bill and orange juice for Tucker. Ace was drinking beer and had a briefcase with him.

They started with small talk and before long the martinis took over and the party of five was getting a little louder. Ace had mentioned poker, causing Arky to stiffen momentarily, but soon the laughs were coming regularly, with Neta having an especially good time surrounded by the four more or less oiled men.

Inevitably, Ace brought up envelopes. "I tell you, Arky, there's nothing worse than some rival competitor sneakin' a peek at your company's mail. It happens all the time. I heard the Rosenbergs got caught that way, somebody saw 'E=MC squared' or somethin' in one of their letters."

Bill chuckled at that and said, "If only they had used Security Stationers for their correspondence, Roy Cohn would be chasin' ambulances in Hoboken right now."

"Huh?" said Ace, then continued. "No, I mean it. You gotta keep prying eyes outa your mail. Especially with all those hush-hush deals Miley Mud is making with the feds."

This brought on a gale of laughter, and Ace ordered another round of drinks.

"Okay, okay," Arky conceded, "Tell us what is so special about your envelopes."

Ace seemed to sober up a bit and he brought out his briefcase from under the table. "Lemme show you. Here's a typical white envelope, prob'ly the kind you use. And here's one of our envelopes."

They looked identical.

Bill knocked back his whiskey and said, "Ace, you'd need some kind of magical sixth sense to tell the difference between those two."

"Hey, you're right!" Ace beamed. "They look the same but there's one big difference. You can see through the regular envelopes. But ours, you can use any kinda light you want, hell, use a lighthouse beacon if you want, but you can't see anything through our envelopes. They're white, but they're totally opaque. An' speakin' of sixth sense, they're so good that J. B. Rhine used them for his ESP experiments. He didn't want anybody being able to see through the envelopes at the cards inside so he used ours.

"And that's another thing," Ace continued, getting into a rhythm, "we use a special glue that really sticks. Once you seal a Security Stationers envelope that sucker stays sealed. Anybody tries to open it, you can tell right away."

Arky looked skeptical. "I don't know, Ace. That's pretty hard to believe. Now maybe if your envelope was black, or dark grey——"

"No, I mean it. Once you close it, it's impossible to see what's inside. And there's no way to get it open without somebody bein' able to tell."

Arky rubbed his jaw wryly and the other three had to stifle their laughter. "I'd have to see that to believe it."

"Hell, give it a shot. Put something in one of these babies and I dare you to see what it is." Ace handed Arky an envelope.

Bill spoke up. "Hey, how about we give it one of those ESP things? You know, with the designs on the cards——"

Ace brightened. "Great idea, Bill! We could——"

Neta reached for her purse. "Here. I've got some blank cards. Let's draw some designs on them. Anybody got a pen?"

Arky quickly pulled out his fountain pen and said, "Lemme do it. What are those designs again, Ace?"

Ace, with a big smile on his face, said, "Uh, there's a circle, a square, some wavy lines, and, uh—"

Arky began drawing in thick dark lines the designs. Bill prompted, "There's also a plus sign, or cross, and a five-pointed star."

"Go ahead, Arky. Make 'em big and black. You *still* won't be able to see 'em once they're in the envelope." Ace was on a roll.

Arky finished the five designs and handed Ace the cards. "Okay, how do we do this? How about you pick one of the cards and without letting anyone know which one, put it in the envelope and seal it. Then we'll see if we can see which design it is. I have a feelin' that it'll be easy. There's no way that white envelope can keep me from seein' it."

Ace nodded his head energetically, "That's right Arky. You keep thinkin' that way." Then he looked around the table at the four. "How's about we make this thing a little more interesting . . .?"

Arky pondered this for a couple of beats and then said, "Tell you what. Let's give it a real test. Let's do the experiment three times, with three cards and three envelopes. If we can get the card right three times in a row, you supply the entire stationery needs of Miley Mud and Chemical for a year, free. If we miss even one, we sign a contract with you for five years, at *double* the regular price."

Ace tried to keep the smile off his face, but failed. "Why—it's a deal!" He and Arky shook hands.

Arky said, "Go ahead, Ace. We'll all turn our heads and you put one of the cards in an envelope and seal it. Then you give the envelope to Tucker and he'll try to see what's inside. What do you say, Tucker?"

Tucker nodded and replied, "It's too dark in here to see anything. I need to take it outside the door and look at it in the sun. Is that okay, Ace?"

Ace bobbed his head up and down. "Fine. Fine. However, I think I'll retire to the men's room to put the card in the envelope, if you don't mind."

"No problem," Arky said. "We'll wait here."

The tipsy stationery salesman took the five cards and an envelope and tottered to the men's room. The four others tipped their drinks and looked at each other, smiling.

Soon Ace swooped out of the men's room, envelope in hand. He sat down and patted his jacket pocket. "I got the other four cards right here. Here you go, Tucker. No fair peekin'! I can tell if you try to get into the envelope."

"Don't worry, Ace. I won't touch the seal. I just want to see it in the bright sunlight and will come back as soon as I've seen—or not seen—anything." He got up and walked toward the front door of Harry's bar.

"Another round!" Ace shouted.

The Three Experiments

SUNLIGHT STREAMED into the bar when Tucker opened it and the other four celebrated as the bartender brought the next round.

"So you're a big believer in these ESP 'speriments, eh?" Bill asked Ace.

"Hell, I only heard of 'em a year or so ago when I took over the Rhine account. They've been doing them for about twenty years now. There're some skeptics who make Rhine and his crew jump through all sorts of hoops to make sure that there's no fakealoo goin' on. We kept havin' to make our envelopes more and more foolproof to suit 'em. That's why I'm so confident you'll be doin' bidness with us for the next five years—at double the usual price."

"But you think there's somethin' in this ESP?" Bill insisted.

"Ah, hell no. But don't tell anybody I said so."

The door opened again and Tucker walked back in, the sunlight at his back as the door slowly closed. He handed the envelope to Ace, who looked at it with squinted eyes, fingering the glued flaps carefully. "Hmmm. Looks okay. So whaddya say it is, Tucker?"

"It's the wavy lines, Ace."

The salesman looked a little stunned, then pulled the other four cards out of his inside pocket and threw them on the table. The Miley Gang leaned closer and saw the four cards.

"Lucky guess!" Ace spouted. "You had a one in five chance to get it right. There's no way you coulda seen that card." He handled the envelope again, obviously trying to see if he could feel anything from the outside. He couldn't.

"Well, there's still two more you gotta do. Lemme go to the rest room again," Ace grumbled as he headed off with another envelope and the four cards from the table.

The four at the table took another drink and grinned at each other.

Arky snickered, "We'll have Ace joinin' the Rhine cult before this is done."

Neta laughed, "Arky, you are the devil incarnate."

The men's room door swung open and the orange-suited salesman returned to the table with one hand on his jacket pocket and an envelope in the other. "Here ya go, Tucker. Maybe I used the same card. You never know."

Tucker took the envelope and said, "We'll see about that," and walked out the front door. Once again they were momentarily blinded by the sunlight.

"So," said Ace, "did Tucker say how he decided? Did he say he could see through the envelope?"

Bill said, "He didn't say, but I think he's usin' ESP."

"Don't give me that! I'm not sayin' he peeked. I think he just made a good guess. We'll see how he does this time."

About a minute after Tucker left, he came back in the door and the four at the table looked up at him expectantly. Tucker stared back at them.

Finally, Ace sputtered, "We-ell?"

"The circle."

Ace took the envelope from him and looked at it very closely. Without taking his eyes off it he reached in his jacket and took out four cards, which he threw on the table.

"Goddammit! That's bullshit luck! I don't believe this."

Bill spread out the cards to see that they were the wavy lines, the square, the cross and the star. Neta looked up at Tucker in mock awe and said, "You have the power! By the way, what exactly does 'ESP' mean?"

Ace muttered, almost under his breath, "Extra-Sensory Perception. It's a bunch of crap, I tell you. They can't see through our envelopes and neither can Tucker."

Tucker said soothingly to Ace, "You're right. I *can't* see through the envelopes. I hate to tell you this at this late stage of the bet, but I've always had this kind of 'gift', a kind of—"

The salesman snapped, "Cut the crap. You're just on a lucky roll. I dare you to do it one more time." He picked up the cards and another envelope and walked to the men's room. As he walked he was looking carefully at the empty envelope, scowling.

"Is anyone but me starting to feel sorry for the poor—?" Neta asked, and Arky interrupted.

"When I get my $300 worth of revenge I'll start feelin' sorry for him."

"That's about what we spend on stationery every year, idn't it?" Bill said.

"Just about." Arky leaned back in his chair and finished his martini. "Bring another round!" he yelled at the bartender.

Ace stayed in the men's room a little longer this time. When he did come out Arky handed him a new beer.

"Okay, guys. The third time's the charm. If you get it right again, Tucker, I may have to change my mind about all this ESP stuff. I *know* you can't see through the envelope, even in the sunlight."

He handed Tucker the third envelope and sat down with his beer. He took a big swig as he watched Tucker stroll out the front door, the envelope swinging at his side.

"You know, Ace, if you're using this Rhine guy as a sellin' point for your security envelopes, you prob'ly oughta at least act like you believe in his thing." Arky looked at Ace with seemingly genuine concern.

"Oh I do. I do. I figured I didn't have to do any actin' with you guys, though. Normally I tell everybody that ESP is the next big fad, like Davy Crockett or Frank Sinatra. Only I don't use the word, 'fad'. I say 'trend' or 'th' future'."

Bill said, with what sounded like sincerity, "I don't think Tucker is guessing. And I don't think he's peekin'. And—and I mean this, Ace—I don't think the envelopes are faulty. I think they're every bit as opaque as you say they are. So what does that leave? ESP. It's Occam's Razor all over again."

"What the—? You say he's usin' a razor to get inside—"

Bill laughed. "Hold on, Ace! It's got nothin' to do with a razor. Forget I said that. Here he comes, let's see if Tucker can do it again."

Arky smacked his lips as Tucker strode back to the table. "My money's on ESP."

Ace reached for the envelope and scrutinized it with eyes and fingers. "Okay," he said, voice filled with dread and, at the same time, hope, "what's the verdict?"

Tucker waited a few beats and said, deadpan, "It's the wavy lines again, Ace."

There was silence around the table. Bill and Neta finished off their drinks. Arky played with his mustache. Tucker sat down and wiped the sweat off his pate. It was about 70 degrees outside.

Ace looked sadly at the envelope. "I'll stop by the office Monday and set up your stationery account for the comin' year."

No one responded so he continued. "There's somethin' goin' on here and it kinda gives me the willies. I figured as easy as it was to take you for a few hundred bucks in poker it'd be nothin' to take you on this deal."

Neta consoled him. "We don't use *that* much paper at Miley Mud—"

"Oh I know. It ain't the money or the paper. It's just that I never gave much thought about Rhine and his theories. I'm startin' to think that maybe there's a 'wave of the future' that I mighta missed, if it hadn't been for you guys. I'm thinkin' that maybe Bill and his razor might be onta somethin'."

"Now don't go off the deep end, Ace," Bill said.

"I won't. Don't worry. But I'm definitely gonna give it some more thought. Bartender, how about bringin' that tab?" The salesman got up slowly and signed the slip the bartender handed him. He then reached in his jacket and threw the four cards down. He ripped open the envelope and added the wavy lines card to the pile.

"I'll be seein' you guys. Neta, it's been a pleasure."

"You too, Ace," they all said at the same time, which made all five of them laugh.

"It's ESP, and it's the wave of the future," Arky said. "How about a beer to go?"

"That's okay. See you all Monday." Ace Spelvin walked out of the bar into the bright New Mexico sunlight.

The Wave of the Future

THE MILEY GANG finished their drinks and the bartender gathered up the empty glasses.

Tucker said, "That was easy. It went just as you said, Arky."

"Shhh. I'm thinkin'." Arky was rubbing his mustache furiously.

They were silent. Finally, Arky said, "You know, all of this 'wave of the future' talk has got me goin'. That ESP stuff is all bull but I'm thinkin' that we might ought to look into the real power behind this little scam we ran on Ace. I'm talking fluoroscopy. Did you have any trouble with the machine, Tucker?"

"Not at all. It was just as we planned. As soon as I got out the door I ran across the street to Brown's Shoes, stuck the envelope in the foot part of the Green Magic Foot-O-Scope machine and looked through the viewer. The design on the card stood out like a sore toe. Then I ran back here."

"That's right! And just about every damn shoe store in the country has one of them machines. I even heard that some clothes stores are thinkin' about usin' 'em to make sure people're gettin' the right size clothes. Hell, they'll be using fluoroscope machines in everything pretty soon. In hat stores, in the underwear department—you name it!"

Bill and Tucker sat up. "You might be onto something, Arky," Tucker agreed. "Maybe we ought to be thinking about putting our money into fluoroscopes, instead of oil. Gotdoggit, this may be big."

The four got up and walked to the door, one by one exiting the dark bar. Thanks to Ace Spelvin, stationery salesman, the future looked a little brighter for all of them.

Outside, people were milling around on the sidewalks and the sound of the Farmington High School marching band could be heard approaching from a block west, in front of the Avery Hotel.

The Miley Gang stayed to watch the parade. They were on a lucky streak.

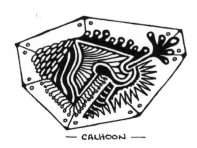

— CALHOON —

ANGELUS OF DOOM

Farmington New Mexico

1955

Tension at the Snooker 8

BILL SMITH wiped a bead of sweat from his brow as he squatted down and looked up over the edge of the pool table at the brown leather bottle. It was perched upside down and its base was covered with $20 bills. Bill noticed that the bottle, about six inches tall and shaped like a small narrow-necked milkbottle, was about a sixteenth of an inch away from the rail midway between a side pocket and a corner pocket on the snooker table. The bills on the base actually hung out over the top of the rail, about three inches from Bill's squinted eyes.

The poolroom was dark, except for the fluorescent light directly above the table, but Bill imagined that he could see among the shadows that shifted just outside the range of the light, pairs of red, unblinking eyes that seemed to follow every move he made. The murmurs among the shadows were unintelligible but Bill knew they concerned infamous bottle pool games of past years, when the legendary Jicarilla Pete Felch or Totah Bosco played with $100 bills.

In the far back of the Snooker 8 poolroom Bill could hear the clack of dominos from the same four old men who'd been playing there daily since the war. He stood up and chalked his cue for the third time as he walked around the table, ignoring the baleful gaze of the burly, bullet-headed man who stood near the table.

"That bottle's not goin' anywhere, Bill—are you?" the man asked, and the shadows chuckled and coughed.

"My wells haven't come in yet, Tom, so I kinda look at those 20s a little different than you do," Bill retorted, placing his cue on the rail and lining up what looked to be a three-rail shot. A nervous titter ran through the room. The shot he was lining up was dangerous—he'd be trying to make the 9 ball in the corner pocket and it would miss the bottle by about a half inch—*if* he made the shot. If he didn't, the cue ball or the nine ball might hit the topheavy bottle and knock it over. If that happened he'd have to add a $20 bill to the pile of bills and put the bottle back upside down with the bills on top of it, draped across the base of the bottle. Then Tom Bolack, his beefy opponent, would have a shot at making the nine and collecting the money on the bottle.

Bill wasn't worried so much about anteing up another $20 if he knocked the bottle over on the table. What would be disastrous was if the bottle and money fell on the rail or on the floor. Then he'd have to match the pile of $20s and there were at least two dozen of them.

Bill tried to shut out the distractions of Bolack and the derelict shadows as he lined up the shot. Another bead of sweat dripped into his eye and he wiped it off and chalked his cue yet another time. He was vaguely aware of a church bell tolling mournfully three times in the distant background. *Maybe they're tolling for me—if I miss this shot?*

It really was a desperate shot—three rails before the cue ball even hits the nine, and then the nine would have to have enough oomph to shoot past the bottle into the corner pocket. He couldn't shoot a finesse shot. He had to hit the cueball damned hard and hope he didn't get a vertical bounce when it slammed off the rails. A bouncing cueball could knock the bottle off the table easy.

Bill knew he shouldn't have accepted Bolack's challenge of ending the session with a high stakes bottle pool game. He was better than the oilman, all right, but sometimes the bottle laughs at the better player. And Bolack had bottomless pockets when it came to competition. If he knocked the bottle on the floor, he'd just peel off a few more $20s from the roll in his overalls. If Bill had to match the pot—and lost—his wife Geneva would have his lunch for breakfast. He was pulling down $200 a week at Miley Mud and Chemical but they were also buying a pricey little MG.

The bell had stopped but just as Bill was getting ready to bring the cue back for his shot, it rang again—three times. Bill grinned nervously and relaxed again for the shot. He chalked his cue again then drew the stick back and—just before he slammed the cuestick into the cueball, the bell rang once more. Three times.

Tom Bolack guffawed. "For whom are them bells tollin' for, eh, Bill? For thee?" This brought numerous cackles from the shadow gallery.

Bill was angry that Bolack had usurped his literary metaphor but shrugged it off and hunkered down to make the shot. He took his time because of the importance of the shot and just as he drew back—the damn bell started tolling again—and kept tolling. This time even Bill laughed out loud. "Okay, now it's a sign. A sign that I'm going to make this shot and walk out of here with your money in my pocket."

He set the cue down on the rail and held it steady with his left hand. His right hand drew back once, twice, three times and with complete silence in the poolroom—broken only by the seemingly eternal bell in the distance—Bill grunted and whipped his right arm forward.

"Bill!" "Skkkrrraaaack!"

The sickening screech of Bill's cuestick slicing off the edge of the cueball in a horrible miscue was simultaneous with the booming voice of a tall, fedoraed man entering the front door, momentarily flooding the front part of the poolroom with sunlight. The cueball spun dizzily across the table towards the far corner pocket, clipped the pocket's edge and bounced about two feet up in the air before caroming off the edge of the rail right at the bottle. The cueball had so much spin on it that it curved just before hitting the bottle dead on and instead glanced off the side of the neck. The ball's english started the bottle spinning, the $20 bills acting like a green and black propeller, and the bottle drunkenly teetered down the table alongside the rail and with an agonizingly slow final spin, dropped topfirst into the side pocket, the bills still firmly perched on the bottle's bottom.

Meanwhile, the cueball kissed the nine and the nineball slowly rolled into the corner pocket where it fell with a PLOP! just as the bell stopped ringing.

There was a hush in the poolroom. No one had ever seen such a thing happen. The bottle didn't tip over. But it was in the pocket. The bills were still on the bottle. The nineball was made.

"Bill, goddoggit, what are you wastin' time in here playin' pool for? I told you yesterday we needed to pick up Gunter at noon and it's already past noon." The newcomer didn't notice the murmurings of awe that erupted from the shadows. "Hey, Tom," he said to the hulking man near the table. "How's it goin'?"

Bolack stood mutely at the side of the table staring at the nine ball in the pocket below him, his hammy fists clenched tightly around his custom-made ivory-inlaid cue, made from the tusk of a wooly mammoth.

Bill Smith laid his stick down on the table and quickly gathered up the pile of bills on the bottle. "Good game, Tom. Gotta go." And was out the front door with the man with the fedora right behind him.

The stunned big man squinted in the momentary sunlight and grabbed the bottle out of the side pocket and threw it against the wall. "Goddam you, Tucker!" he shouted at the closing front door. "He'd a never made that shot! An' as for you Smith, I'll see you at th' bowlin' alley tonight! 'N' somebody's gonna die!" Then he turned and faced a wizened man in an apron who approached with a triangular device and a big camel-hair brush. "Pete," he muttered. "Rack 'em."

Miley Mud and Chemical

THE TWO MEN stood in the shade of the awning over the front of the Snooker 8 Pool Hall, the bright New Mexico sunlight baking the asphalt of Main Street.

"You parked in back?" Tucker asked and Bill nodded. "Well, leave it there. I'll bring you back later. Right now we got to get Gunter and take him up to the school." He headed west and Bill followed him to his 1947 Lincoln parked on Orchard, right off Main. They got in the car.

"Y'know, Tucker, I think you came in at just the right time. I don't think I would have wanted to plead my case on that last shot with Bolack and his cronies—not with all those cuesticks on the wall."

"Yeah, but what the hell are you doin' shootin' pool in the morning? I never thought of you as a 'morning person'."

"Morning? Hell, we've been playing since 10 o'clock last night. Pete blacked out the windows at midnight. I was behind until that last game. Wasn't that a pip?"

"Right. Cheerio. Glad I could help." Tucker had taken the alley behind the Snooker 8, noticing Bill's Oldsmobile parked in an empty lot, then turned right on Wall and left on Main heading east past the Continental Diner. It was sort of a landmark in town because it was an old windowed railroad passenger car converted into a short-order greasy spoon. It was also a block away from the jail so it was a favorite hangout for Farmington's finest.

"Technically, Bill, you're in charge of this whole fiasco. I know I suggested it first, but as PR guy you're in charge. Do you remember what the deal is?"

"A'course I remember! It's something about Gunter getting' to brainwash a bunch of schoolkids into becoming oil guzzlers like their daddies—"

Tucker snickered. "You're closer than you think. What it is is Gunter has volunteered to speak at St. Thomas Catholic School about his audience with the pope back before the war. Apparently he met the ol' boy and likes to tell people about it."

"With Pope Pius XII himself, eh? I didn't know ol' Gunter was even in that part of the world back then. I thought we hired him out of Bolivia."

"We did, and he's been one of the best engineers we have. I guess he came from Europe before that. Anyway, let's get Gunter and drop him by the school. You can wait in the car if you want—and get some sleep—while he's talkin'. I'm going in to talk to Tommy, who says he has somethin' to tell me."

Tommy was Tucker's 8-year-old son who was in the third grade at St. Thomas School.

The Lincoln took the curve at the end of Main Street and pulled into the parking lot of a two-story, tan building with a sign saying, MILEY MUD AND CHEMICAL COMPANY. Surrounding the back of the building was a row of storage buildings, like a lumberyard, filled with bags of dried chemical mud for oil well drilling.

The two men got out of the car and entered the front doors of the building. They were immediately met by two men, one a suave man with a trim black mustache and the other a short, older man with sparse hair and a definite stoop.

"You guys are late!" The mustachioed man boomed, a cigar bouncing up and down out of the left side of his mouth.

Tucker started to say something but Bill cut him off. "It's my fault, Arky. The damn Baroid pumpin' unit out on the east Bisti blew a sprocket an' Joe Eaves beat me there. You know what that means—"

"Yeah, I know. Well, Gunter here is itching to tell them young Catholics all about Pope Pompous the Third and he's la—"

"Pope Pius XII, Arky." The smaller man interjected.

"Right. Number Twelve. I'll see you guys later." Arky strode off to his office in the back of the building.

The three men left the building and got in Tucker's car.

"So you don't drive, eh, Gunter?" Bill queried as they headed west back into town.

"No, I nefer learned. I dun't think I've really missed anything."

"You're probably right," said Tucker. "By the way, my son Tom will be one of the students you'll be talking to. I'm sure you have an interesting story to tell, Gunter."

"Oh ja, I'll nefer forget the day I met the pope. He vas magnificent. Dere were lots of important people dere mit us. Dis vas 1940, before the United Shtates entered the var."

"Y'know, I'm kind of a nut on hist'ry," Bill spouted from the back seat. "What city was that? Berlin?"

"Nein, it vas Rome, at the Basilica."

Tucker turned right onto Wall and made a left on Arrington. He asked, "So, Gunter, your wife and son are in Texas. Midland, right?"

"Nein, Odessa. Dey'll be back dis weekent."

That ended the conversation as they passed by the Farmington Public library, where Tucker knew Tommy spent much of his time, and turned right just past the baseball field onto Allen Street. They turned into the parking lot at St. Thomas School and Sacred Heart Church.

The church was next to the street and was almost as large as the school to the east of it. A third large brick building, the priests' house, was just to the north. The school looked like an old-fashioned red schoolhouse should, made of red brick, three stories high with a bell tower to the front—which faced south.

There were dozens of schoolchildren milling around the dirt area, playing marbles, jumping rope, and swinging on a tall swing set near a garage. A few nuns were scattered throughout the crowd of munchkins, dressed in black habits from head to foot, with white cowls surrounding their faces. To Tucker, they resembled oil derricks in a landscape of oscillating pumping units.

It was lunchtime at St. Thomas School.

A Catholic Death

"I THINK I'll take you up on that offer to let me sleep in the car," Bill Smith said as the other two men got out of the car. He sprawled across the back seat and disappeared from sight. Tucker and Gunter walked to the front of the school building and ascended the dozen steps to the double doors. They entered and found themselves in a hallway, with hardwood floors and walls painted a dark beige. Each of the doors in the lengthy hall had dark wooden jambs and there wasn't a speck of dust anywhere.

Tucker said, "I'm not sure where Sister Edwina's office is. She's the head nun here, Gunter. All I know is that Tommy is in Sister Gertrude's room on this floor. I guess we should go there."

"Ja. Okay mit me."

Tucker led the way to a room down the hall. It was open and they entered.

"Mr. Tucker," a rotund nun of indeterminate age greeted them. "Thank you for bringing Mr. Hedelin. I am so looking forward to your talk."

Gunter muttered hello and Tucker added, "It's our pleasure, Sister. . ."

"Gertude Mary, Mr. Tucker. I have the pleasure of teaching your son Tommy this year. He should be coming in from lunch soon." Then, to Gunter, "The room where you'll give your talk is the meeting room downstairs in the basement. I'll show you to the room if you don't mind. The kids will be in from lunch anytime now."

Gunter nodded his assent and Tucker asked, "May I speak to Tommy for a bit?"

"Of course. I'll send him up to this room." She and Gunter left the room and headed to the stairway.

Tucker looked around the small classroom. The desks were old and wooden and were the kind that attached to the chairs in front of them. There was an inkwell in the upper right corner of each desk and a book storage compartment under the desk lid. In the back of the room was a long walk-in closet. At the front of the room was a blackboard and there were windows to the outside on two walls. A couple of iron radiators stood under the windows.

He was starting to look through one of the desks at the books when a boy with a thicket of badly-shorn brown hair, with a big cowlick in front walked through the door.

"Tucker!" The boy said as Tucker greeted him back.

"Hey, Tee-Tom. So this is where you spend your days? It looks pretty good. How are the nuns?"

"They're okay. Sister Edwina just made me the bell-ringer for this week. I just got through ringing it. Ya wanna see?"

Tucker assented and followed his son out the door into the hallway towards the front of the building. There, off to one side of the main doors was what looked like a small closet with a closed door. Tommy opened the door and there was a bellrope dangling down with a knot in it about four feet off the floor. The rope extended up through a six-inch hole in the ceiling, about twelve feet up.

"Everyday at noon I get to come here and ring the Angelus. It's great. I can't show you now but when I ring the bell if I hold on to the rope just above the knot, when the bell swings one way it lifts me up to the ceiling. Sister says not to do it but I do anyway."

Tucker looked at his son proudly. "So that's the, what did you call it, the—"

"Angelus. It's some Catholic thing. It's supposed to be rung every morning, noon and night, but Sister says the people who live around here wouldn't like all that ringing all the time so we only ring it at noon and six in the evening."

"So you'll be coming back to school every evening at six?"

"Yeah. It's only for a week. And it's fun!"

The boy was obviously excited by his new job.

"To do the Angelus you gotta ring it three times, then wait about fifteen seconds and ring it three times again. Then wait another fifteen seconds and ring it three more times. Then, after fifteen seconds you ring it thirty-three times. I think it's for the number of years Jesus lived. Sometimes it's hard to get it to stop after the third time. If I pull too hard on the third ring, then I try to stop it, it jerks me up and rings again. Sister doesn't like that."

"I don't imagine she would," Tucker mused, having had a little experience with the vagaries of Catholic ritual from his marriage to Maxine.

The two talked a bit more about life at St. Thomas then Tommy said Sister wanted him to go downstairs to hear the talk by Gunter. Tucker said, "If you get a chance to talk to Mr. Hedelin, tell him I'll be out at the car," and rubbed Tommy's cowlick as the boy ran out the door.

He walked down the hall to the rear of the building and left through the back door. He had just made it to the car when a black-habited nun ran down the stairs of the school and over to him.

"Mr. Tucker! Mr. Tucker! Come quick! There's something wrong with Mr. Hedelin!"

Bill Smith sat up in the back seat and opened the door. "C'mon, Bill," Tucker yelled, and ran after the nun who was scooting back to the school. Bill followed shakily.

They ran around the building and down three steps to the "basement" which was actually a bottom floor, half below ground level. They turned right into the first room and Tucker saw a crowd of kids at the front of the room. He pushed past them and saw Gunter lying on his back, a small nun huddled over him.

"Get back! Get back!" The nun hissed and the children, who were already five feet away, drew back more. It took Tucker a few seconds to navigate through the crowd of kids to Gunter's side and saw that he did not seem to be breathing well—and had actually turned a dark shade of blue. His eyes were closed and he wasn't moving.

"Somebody call an ambulance!" Tucker shouted and knelt down next to Gunter. He saw that the nun was a particularly wizened crone of 50 or 60. She looked at him and said, "He was just starting his talk and then keeled over. I tried to help him but. . ."

Tucker noticed that the hand she had placed on Gunter's chest was missing a couple of fingers, one completely and the other at the second joint.

Bill Smith entered the room out of breath and Tucker walked over and met him by the door. He told him to make sure an ambulance was on its way and then returned to the nun. "I'm sure you did what you could, Sister, uh. . ."

"Edwina," the nun answered in a low, croaky voice in an odd, European accent.

"Yes, Sister Edwina. You're the, uh, head nun around here."

"The mother superior, yes."

Gunter was no longer moving at all and didn't seem to be breathing. Tucker wasn't sure what to do so they remained at the prostrate man's side until an ambulance's siren was heard. A few moments later a couple of medical men entered and attended to Gunter. They looked at Tucker and Sister Edwina and shook their heads solemnly. He was not going to make it.

The kids were assembled outside and the body taken away by the medics. Tucker turned to Sister Edwina. "I'm sorry about all this Sister. I'm sure you did all you could."

"Thank you, Mr. Tucker. I'm just sorry that Tommy had to see it."

"Oh, I'm sure he'll handle it fine, but thank you anyway. Uh, did Gunter say anything? I assume it was a heart attack or something like that."

One of the other nuns who was still in the room piped up, "Yes he did. He said something about not seeing any gerbils—"

"That'll be enough, Sister," Sister Edwina cut in. "You can go back to your classes now." The other nuns left leaving Tucker and Sister Edwina alone in the room.

"Gerbils?" Tucker queried.

Sister Edwina's craggy face twisted into a dark mask. "Oh yes, I know what that's all about. He did say, I believe, 'I do not see gerbils,'. You see, before he began speaking I had told him about the wonderful gerbil trail we have upstairs, and asked him if he'd like to see it before he left. I guess the stroke, or whatever, addled his brain and made him say that."

"I see," said Tucker and sighed. "Well, I guess I'll have to call Odessa and tell his—"

Sister Edwina choked, quickly raising her three-fingered hand to her mouth and swallowing hard. Her eyes stared at Tucker coldly. "Excuse me Mr. Tucker, do go on."

"His wife and son, Gunnar, are in Odessa Texas. I'll call them. I'll be going to the hospital now. I'm sorry you had to endure—"

She cut him off. "My prayers will concern Mr. Hedelin and you, you can be sure, Mr. Tucker." The shriveled face seemed both wary and relieved. "By the way, would you tell your son Michael that he often figures in my prayers?"

"I will, Sister. In fact I'm meeting him soon to take him to work at the Navajo Bowl. He's a pinboy there."

"I always knew his cleverness would come in handy."

Tucker smiled confusedly and said goodbye as he left the building. Bill was waiting for him by the car.

As they got in, Bill said, "Best engineer Miley ever had. That's too bad. He makes it all the way through the war and has it all come to an end in a crummy New Mexican schoolhouse."

"Yeah," Tucker said, "I bet he still had a few stories to tell, too. Well, let's go tell Arky. I gotta remember to go pick up Mike and take him to work at the bowling alley. I'll take you to your car first. You might want to get some work done today."

"I don't really feel like working after all this, Tucker. But I guess I should put in some hours. Something to take my mind off everything. Man, I bet ol' Gunter knew a lot about the war. Why didn't I talk to him more?"

The San Juan Hospital

TUCKER DROPPED Bill off at his car behind the Snooker 8 and drove out Main almost all the way to the end of town. He passed the A&W Root Beer stand, the Navajo Bowl and the El Vasito then took a left. Four blocks later, almost to the river, he came to a three-story wooden building standing all by itself, needing paint and maintenance. The sign read SAN JUAN HOSPITAL. Tucker turned into the parking lot that was half-full with older cars and pickups.

He entered through a double-wide door and approached the main desk. A shapely nurse, redhead, sat at the desk. A dozen sick people sat in chairs around the room.

"Maybe a half hour ago a man was bought in here. I think he had had a heart attack." Tucker was distracted by the nurse's highly symmetrical blouse.

"You must mean Mr. Hedelin." A look of sympathy filled her face. "Are you a relative?"

"No, a co-worker. I was with him, sort of, when he had the attack. The medics said he was gone."

"Yes, I'm afraid he was dead when he arrived here. I'm so sorry, Mr. . . . ."

"Tucker, just Tucker. Uh, was there anything—was everything okay? Other than him dying, of course?" Tucker felt a little tongue-tied from the attention the nurse was giving him.

"Well there *was* some kind of heated discussion among the doctors and the pathologist but of course they don't tell *me* anything. . . oh, I tell you what. Here are his x-rays. Dr. Fine left them for Dr. Howard. Shall we look at them?" She said it with a conspiratorial air that made Tucker's pants lurch.

"Why not?"

She slid a couple of x-rays out of the brown sleeve and placed them on the table. Tucker couldn't see anything so he picked one up and held it to the light in the ceiling. It was of a man's torso. The x-ray looked normal to Tucker except for something in the middle of the man's chest. Tucker peered more closely and saw that it was a white cross.

"What's that, Nurse, uh . . ."

"Beavers, Mr. Tucker, just Beavers."

"That's just Tucker, not 'Mr.' Tucker."

They paused for a couple of beats and then Nurse Beavers took the x-ray from Tucker and looked up at it. "Oh, I think you see that all the time. The X-ray techs just haven't completely undressed him yet and he's wearing a crucifix. It must be on a leather string or something."

"Hm. I guess so. I just never knew Gunter as much of a Christian. He was a mud engineer."

Tucker suddenly looked at his watch and said, "Thank you very much, Beavers, for everything. I may have to, uh, query you a bit more—"

"I'm the only Beavers in the book, Tucker."

The Navajo Bowl

TUCKER HAD about an hour before he was to pick up Mike so he drove slowly, mulling over all of the things that happened that day. He took Broadway all the way to mid-town then got on Main. Something felt wrong to him. Something just didn't add up. But he got nowhere and gave up. He arrived at Miley Mud and Chemical Company around 3:15.

After telling Arky and Neta Miley about the happenings at the Catholic School, Tucker spent an hour with them talking about funeral arrangements, wills, heart problems in general and other depressing things and then left for the day, driving in a semi-daze to his house on Wall Street. He honked the horn and a tall, slim dark-haired boy of fourteen came out of the house and got in the car.

"Hi, Tucker," the boy said and pushed his black horned-rim glasses up on his nose.

"Mike," Tucker said, "You're getting taller every day. How's the new job?"

Michael Tucker was a freshman at Farmington High School, having been graduated from St. Thomas School the year before.

He had just walked home from the school, about three blocks to the east just past Dustin.

"I really like it. Mike Kelloff's dad says it's one of the most dangerous jobs in town but I'm pretty careful. I figure in about a year I'll have enough saved for a car."

"Oh I wouldn't worry about a car just yet. You don't get your license till next year and besides, I think that Jerry Miley will be getting a new car around that time. What do you think about his old Merc?"

The boy beamed. "Jerry Miley's Mercury! That would be great! Can you imagine what the guys would think seeing me driving around town in that?"

"Not to mention the girls," Tucker grinned.

Michael was silent for a couple of seconds and said, "Hey, I don't start work for another half hour. How about we get a root beer?"

Tucker had driven down Wall to Apache and turned right, then due west into the afternoon sun for a half dozen blocks before turning left and heading down to West Main Street. Tucker pulled into the parking lot of the A&W Root Beer stand right across Main from the Navajo Bowl.

The two had root beers, delivered to the car by a young carhop Michael knew. Tucker had a nickel root beer in a frosted glass and Mike ordered the dime glass, twice as tall.

As they drank, Tucker told Michael about the day's events. The boy was shocked and dismayed. "I can't believe Mr. Hedelin is gone. Gunnar is my best friend."

Tucker knew that Michael spent a lot of time with Gunter's 15-year-old son and commiserated with him. "Yeah, he was one of the best. And it was so sudden. I wasn't there but they said he mumbled something about not seeing any gerbils. Apparently Sister Edwina had offered to show him some gerbils."

"Really? That's odd," Michael said. "There's no gerbils at St. Thomas."

"There isn't?" Tucker was startled.

"Well, there *was*—last year. In fact I was the one who designed the trails for them. But Father Gregory and Father Conran would get so nervous and silly every time they saw them that at the end of last year Sister Edwina made me tear it down. She sold the whole thing, trail boxes, tubes, gerbils—everything—to little Tommy Bolack."

"That's funny all right. I wonder why she said that?" Tucker stared out the window and looked thoughtful.

Michael said, "I wouldn't put anything past Sister Edwina. You don't know how happy I was to get out of that place. She doesn't trust me and I don't trust her—and she knows it. Well, I gotta go to work. Hey, do you want to see the place? I bet you've never seen the back of a bowling alley before."

Tucker had worked as a pinboy in Tulia Texas when he was Mike's age but he shook his head and said, "Let's see it."

He started the car and they drove across Main Street and parked directly behind the brightly lit building with the big painted sign that read, NAVAJO BOWL.

"You've only been working here a week and they give you a key?" Tucker asked.

"No, they leave the back door open all the time because that's where the pinboys go in and out. There's always at least four pinboys for the 12 lanes."

The two entered through a big metal door that was partially hidden by a bushy tree. They could hear the noise of hurtling pins from outside the building but once they were inside the din was deafening.

The room was long, extending all the way across the building and narrow, about ten feet from the wall to the series of twelve pits, one for each of the lanes. There were a few folding chairs along the back wall but no one was sitting in any of them, the four boys of around Mike's age too busy to sit. The alley was already packed for the night although it was only 5 P.M.

With the regularity of ocean waves, the balls came whizzing down the lanes, their sound growing in volume and pitch, ending with a crash of wood against wood. The pins propellered into the pit at all angles, sometimes threatening to fly out of the pit back towards the boys who stood a respectful distance back from it. There was a barrier between each pit that prevented a pin flying into or behind an adjacent lane but the pinboys were always wary when standing behind a pit with a ball coming down that lane.

So they were always on the move. After a roll and once the pins had settled down the pinboy jumped in the pit and picked them up, dropping them in a ten-slot rack suspended above the end of the lane. If a pin had bounced out on the lane or in the gutter, he retrieved it. This was the only time the bowlers saw the pinboy. Most of the time he was a shadowy figure moving around behind the end of the lane. The pinboys seemed to know exactly when to pick up the ball and lift it to the ball return ramp, where it whooshed out of sight behind a billowing curtain. After the second roll and with the rack filled, the pinboy pulled a lanyard and the rack was lowered to the lane. Another pull and the rack ascended, leaving the ten pins wobbling, ready for the next frame.

There was a complex rhythm to the pinboys' dance that Tucker marveled at. The action behind the pins was much more interesting than the action in front of the pins, he thought.

"I think tonight I'm slated to work the first three lanes, right here at this end." Mike's almost shouted comment broke into Tucker's thoughts.

"I had forgotten how dangerous a bowling alley is," Tucker yelled back. "You be careful, okay?" He noticed there were two phones on the wall. "You can use those phones in all this racket?"

Mike laughed. "It's usually not this loud. And the phone's are extra loud. They need to call us sometimes from the front."

"Can I make a call from one of them?"

"Sure. As long as one of them is free for incoming calls, it's okay."

Tucker went to the first phone and picked up the receiver. The dial tone was pretty loud.

He dialed the number at home on Wall Street. Tommy answered.

"Tommy. Good! I was hoping you were home. I need to know a few more details about what happened today. Did you actually see Mr. Hedelin when he had his heart attack?

Tommy answered, "Yeah, I saw everything. Are you in a bowling alley or something?"

"Yes I am. Now tell me exactly what you saw, okay?"

"Well, after I left you I went down to the meeting room and got up pretty close to Mr. Hedelin. He was just starting to talk about the pope. Then, I think Sister Edwina came in and stood at the back of the room. A minute later I heard Mr. Hedelin choke and he sort of grabbed his chest and fell down. I was right there."

"What did he say?"

"He was mumbling something about not seeing any gerbils. Not exactly that but—you know—his accent. It was hard to tell what he was saying. It sounded like, 'I do *not* see gerbils.' Or something like 'gerbils'. Then Sister Edwina rushed up and told everyone to move back. We did and she knelt over him pushing on his chest and trying to revive him or something. He kept mumbling about the gerbils and she kept shushing him and telling him to relax. Whenever any of us got close she'd yell at us to get away and give him room to breathe."

"Then what?"

"Then you came running in. Then they made all of us kids leave."

"Okay, Tommy, that's very good. That's just what I needed to know. Sister Edwina came in and then Mr. Hedelin had his attack."

"What's wrong, Tucker?"

"Nothing I can't handle, Tee-Tom. You just stay at home with your mother and brothers and I'll see you later." He hung up.

Then he dialed Bill Smith's number at Miley Mud and no one answered. So he dialed Neta's number at the office and she picked up on the second ring.

Tucker shouted, "Neta, can you tell me where Bill Smith is? I just called his line—"

"I think he drove out towards Aztec. There's some big real estate thing brewing out there. You sound like you're in a bowling alley."

"Actually, I am. Hmm. So there's no way to get a hold of him—?"

"Oh yes there is. I told him to take the company car with that new-fangled mobile telephone. Just dial DAvis 0-0023. But have you heard about Gunter?"

"Well, I was out to the hospital and heard that he died before he even reached the hosp—"

"No," Neta interrupted. "I mean did you hear about the crucifix? The hospital called here right after you left."

"Well, I saw that he was wearing a crucifix. That was funny, I never knew—"

"Wearing? He wasn't *wearing* the crucifix, Tucker. The damn crucifix was *inside* his throat. That's what killed him. Not the heart attack."

"What?" Tucker was stunned. This was it. The proof that there was something mortally wrong with Gunter's death. Tucker didn't have all of the pieces of the puzzle filled in but he at least had the straight edges. He shouted into the phone, "I gotta go, Neta. I'll call you after I talk to Bill. I need his expertise right now."

He hung up and saw that Mike had already begun his work as pinboy for the first three lanes. Tucker walked over to his son who was in the pit for lane 2. He leaned down and said, "Mike, you be very careful. Stay here and I'll pick you up at midnight. Don't leave, okay, until I come for you."

Tucker walked quickly to the phone and dialed DAvis 0-0023. Three rings and a metallic voice answered, "Bill Smith here, cheerio!"

"Bill," Tucker yelled. "We gotta talk! This is big. Where the hell *are* you?"

"Damn, you sound like you're in a bowling alley or something. What's all that—"

"I *am* at a bowling alley, gotdoggit. Where are *you?*" Tucker could hardly hear Bill's voice.

"I'm about six miles out of town on the Aztec highway. Can you believe that some local bozos are thinkin' about buildin' a goddam golf course out here in the stinkin' desert? You ever heard of anything so ignernt?"

Tucker, who was a scratch golfer, hesitated for an instant. "Why, that's not a ba—Bill, I got to talk to you. Now! I'm out at the Navajo Bowl. Let's meet halfway. Meet me at the Continental."

"Good idea. I'm starvin'."

"Just get there. After I tell you what I think, you may not feel like eating anything. Hurry!"

Tucker slammed the phone down, waved to his son who was in pit three, and left through the metal door.

The Continental Diner

TUCKER MADE it across town to the Continental Diner in a little under three minutes. It was five-twenty. He pulled into a spot behind a cop car halfway down the block west of the diner and quickly hotfooted it to the diner entrance.

The place was about half full, with a contingent of cops seated at the stools to the right of the door, a few sport-coated gents among them, and a row of empty stools to the left. A telephone booth was on the west wall. Tucker took a stool on the far left and muddled over in his mind what he was going to tell Bill. He ordered a cup of coffee he knew he wouldn't drink.

One of the policemen, a sheriff, sauntered over and said to Tucker, "Sorry about the noise, bub, there's a convention in town."

"Oh yeah?" Tucker looked up. "What kind a convention?" Tucker knew the sheriff from the occasional newspaper stories about him. Dan Sullivan. An overweight blowhard who liked to see his name in the paper.

"The Federal Bureau of Narcotics. These guys in the suits over here are narcotics experts. Man, have they got some stories to tell."

"I'll bet. Well you guys aren't botherin' me. I'm just waiting for a friend—who's driving up right now." Tucker waved through the window at Bill Smith who had parked just to the east of the diner and was approaching the front door.

"Well, it's always good to have a friend, idn't it?"

Sullivan walked back to the throng of cops and suits then stepped into the telephone booth and closed the door. Bill sat on a stool next to Tucker. "What're all the narcs doin' in here?" Bill asked under his breath.

Tucker said, "Convention. Y'know, we may need some cooperation from the cops if we're ever going to make the person who killed Gunter pay."

Bill was stunned. "Killed? I thought he died of a heart attack?"

"Let me tell you what happened. When they got him to the hospital they found a crucifix stuck in his esophagus."

"His esophagus? Hold it. He's a Catholic, right. Maybe it was an accident? Or maybe he swallowed it on purpose?"

"Well I guess you can't rule those out, but I'm thinking Sister Edwina did it. Here's why. Numero uno, she lied to me. She told me that she had offered to show Gunter the gerbil trail upstairs and Michael assures me that the trail was taken down last year. Numero dos, she was the one who had the best access to him. Hell, maybe the only real access. When he started choking she made everybody else get back. I can still see her three-fingered hand on his chest. Numero tres, it's a damn crucifix. Who else but a nun would have a crucifix handy?"

"It's a Cath'lic school, Tucker. Everybody and his horse has a crucifix handy."

"Hmm. Maybe you're right."

"Wait a minute. Three fingers?"

"Three—count 'em—three."

"I wonder how the hell a nun loses two fingers?" Bill muttered.

Tucker continued, "But one thing that bothers me is *why*. Why would an old nun like Sister Edwina want to kill a guy like Gunter? Tommy said he started choking right after she came into the room. According to her she had met him a little earlier, when she told him about the gerbils. But maybe she hadn't. Maybe she lied about the gerbils just to explain what he was mumbling?"

"I follow you. She didn't want you thinking it was important what he was sayin' so she made up a story. What was it again?"

" 'I do not see gerbils.' Or something like 'gerbils'."

Bill stared at Tucker for a second then said, "Y'know, there's something about the way you say—"

But Tucker cut him off. "Another thing was funny. I just remembered. When I was talking to Sister Edwina and mentioned that Gunter's wife and kid were in Texas, she about choked. She covered it up but she definitely was shook by something about them being in Texas."

"Texas, eh," Bill said, "are you sure it was Texas she was shook about?"

"Well it might have been Midland or Odessa I said. I can't remember—"

"Odessa! I thought so!" Bill almost shouted and Sheriff Sullivan and a few narcs looked over at the two men. The sheriff said something to the crowd of policemen and left the diner.

Bill lowered his voice. "Tucker, I think I know half of why Edwina killed Gunter."

Tommy's Kampf

TOMMY'S OTHER brothers, Bobby and Johnny, were out playing baseball in the back yard of the Tucker's Wall Street home and Tommy was sitting in a cushiony chair in the living room, immersed in *The Secret of the Lost Tunnel*, #20 in the Hardy Boys series. Their mother, Maxine, was playing bridge at the McGarry's.

The book was Tommy's first Hardy Boys book. Michael had about a dozen of them on his bookshelf and Tommy had always been fascinated by the colorful dust jackets. He had been tempted to read one before but Maxine had suggested he read *Now We Are Six* by A. A. Milne. Tommy tried the Milne book but the poetry and difficult, obscure words discouraged him and he decided to jump into the Hardy Boys book, even if he wasn't grown up enough for it yet. *The Secret of the Lost Tunnel* had the best title and before he knew it he was traveling to the American "South" with Frank and Joe in search of lost confederate gold.

He finished a chapter and looked up at the clock to see that it was four forty-five. He still had plenty of time before he had to walk to school and ring the six o'clock Angelus. But he was tired of sitting here in the house and decided to take his book with him and go on down to the school. He could sit on a bench in the shade on the east side of the building where he often sat while waiting for Mass.

Tommy slammed the door as he left and walked at a fast pace down Wall to Apache. He turned west and continued up the hill to Orchard. Just past the house on the corner he cut across an empty lot to a tall wooden fence that extended across the four-foot wide ditch that ran along the north side of the school property. The ditch was just wide enough that boys of Tommy's size risked falling in every time they jumped it. Sometimes there was a log across the ditch farther up Apache but the fence was always the easiest way to get across. It had a horizontal two-by-four you could step across on while holding onto another horizontal two-by-four about chest level.

Tommy maneuvered his way across the fence and walked past the chicken coops and garage that made up the northeast corner of the school property. There was no one in sight as he sat on the bench, which had its back against the east wall of the school-house, right below an open window.

He had been reading for about a half hour when he heard a phone ring through the window of the room just above him. He heard Sister Edwina's raspy voice.

"Oh, it's you. Speak to me."

A pause, then, "You found him? Goot! At the Continental Diner? Isn't that where the police hang out with their donuts and coffee?"

There was another short pause and Sister Edwina cackled, "Narcotics convention? Only in America could they have such a thing. What about the other one, the one they call Bill?"

Another short pause and, "Very goot. I recommend that you exit the premises within five minutes. When I finish with Tucker and Bill I'll take care of his oldest spawn. I've been informed by the fedoraed one himself that he's working as a pinboy at the Navajo Bowl." She laughed darkly and hung up.

Tommy was shocked. What was Sister Edwina doing? What did she mean by "finish" and "take care of"?

He carefully placed his book down and stood up and stepped up on the bench. He quietly and slowly peered over the edge of the window into the room. The light was off and the east side of the building was in shade but there was enough light for him to see a black-habited form moving about on the far side of the room. He raised himself up an inch and saw her open a bureau drawer and pull out a large gun. Then she reached into a desk drawer and got a set of keys. She looked towards the window and Tommy ducked his head below the window.

Did she see him? A chill came over him as he heard footsteps walking rapidly towards the window. He immediately jumped off the bench and crawled under it. He was curled beneath it, scrunched against the wall, thinking how badly he had to urinate, when he heard her raise the window a bit more and hiss, "Iss any-one there?"

Tommy could feel her eyes sweeping the whole east side of the school property then boring down through the bench seat. He counted a vein near his bladder thumping—thirty—forty—fifty times.

Then he heard her slam the window shut—and he breathed for the first time in over a minute. He stayed where he was until he heard the door on the north side of the school open and a pair of hob-nailed nun's boots beat a rapid tattoo down the steps and head towards the garage. A half minute later a car started, backed up and drove off.

Tommy crawled out from under the bench and shook the dirt off his clothes. He thought, "I gotta warn Tucker—and Michael. Maybe I can call the Continental Diner and the bowling alley. But I don't know their numbers and I don't have much time. Sister Edwina'll be down there any minute."

Then it hit him. The Angelus!

He ran around the southeast corner of the school and up the steps to the south door. It was open, as it always was. He ran in and threw open the door to the bellrope room and rang the bell four times. He waited about five seconds and rang it four more times. He waited another five seconds then rang it four more times. He had been dragged up to the twelve-foot ceiling of the room with every other ring.

Then he started ringing the bell for all he was worth.

The Continental Massacre

"YOU KNOW half of why she killed him? What do you mean?"

Tucker stared at Bill, who was fidgeting next to him at the counter.

"You won't believe this, Tucker. She killed Gunter because he recognized her. From where? The audience with the pope. Gunter said there was a lot of important people there and Edwina was one of 'em."

"So they knew each other back then in 1940?"

"Maybe. But not necessarily. I'm thinkin' that the reason she killed Gunter is to keep anyone from knowin' she was there. Not because of who knew her, but because of who she is. Or was."

Tucker was getting frustrated. "For Pete's sake, Bill, tell me what you've figured out."

"Okay, I will. Y'see—"

Just then a bell to the north tolled. Four times.

The look on Tucker's face kept Bill from continuing with his story. Then the bells tolled four more times. Tucker quickly looked at his watch and saw that it was five thirty. The Angelus was not supposed to be rung until six.

Bill said, "What is it, Tucker? Do those bells mean anything?"

"Something's wrong, Bill. I think Tommy is trying to tell me something."

The bells tolled four more times. Tucker looked around and saw the cops and narcotics agents all sitting in a row at the counter.

Tucker said under his breath. "Let's get out of here. I don't think we're safe. C'mon."

The bells began ringing as if they would never stop.

Tucker got up and headed for the door. Bill followed. Just then three agents wearing ill-fitting plaid suits got up to leave. And at the same time a large black Dodge pulled up and stopped in front of the diner next to the curb—facing the wrong way, west—with a black-habited, white-cowled nun barely visible behind the wheel. Tucker and Bill saw her and instinctively ducked back to the counter. The three suits opened the door just as the nun propped a large gun on the door through the open window of the car and began firing.

The sound of the shots drowned out the tolling of the bell. The bullets ripped through the bodies of the narcs and they flew back into the diner as the astonished cops jumped to their feet. The three wounded men fell to the floor, dragging a few cops with them.

Tucker and Bill stared into the eyes of the nun behind the gun as the whole diner erupted in confusion. They could see the indecision on her face as she strained to see who she had shot. Then she pulled the gun back into the car and screeched out into Main Street, heading west.

"A luger. I thought so," Bill muttered.

"Let's go," Tucker spat, "she's headed toward the bowling alley!"

Bowling For Death

TUCKER AND BILL were the first ones out the door of the Continental Diner, which was a madhouse of shouting cops and bleeding narcs. They ran to Tucker's car and were soon peeling out, making a U-turn on Main and heading west to the Navajo Bowl.

"Tell me what you're thinkin', Bill," Tucker seethed as they accelerated through the one red light at Allen.

"Well," the Okie said nervously as they clipped a pickup full of Navajos in front of the Avery Hotel. "It's a bunch of things together—and what Gunter said as he was dyin'."

"Gerbils?" Tucker shouted.

"Not gerbils, no. That's just what everybody heard. But the kicker was what you said about Edwina chokin' when you said 'Odessa'."

"So what about Odessa?"

"Well, I'm kinda a nut about WW Two and the Nazis and 'Odessa' is the name for an organization that helped high-rankin' Nazis escape to South America after the war. Not many people know about it."

"So Gunter was a Nazi? I can't believe that!"

"Not Gunter. Edwina was a Nazi and Gunter recognized her. And either he knew her or she was somebody famous enough for him to recognize. Remember he said there were a lot of important people there. This was before the war and I wouldn't be surprised if some of the German High Command wasn't there to have an audience with the pope. There are rumors Pius XII was a good friend to the Nazis before, during and after the war. After all, the damn Cath'lics hated the Jews almost as much as the Nazis."

The car was approaching the Navajo Bowl and Tucker screeched to a stop behind the building next to the black Dodge.

Bill grabbed Tucker's arm as he opened his door. "But hold it, Tucker. You can't go barging in there. He's got a gun."

"I don't care, Bill. Mike's in ther—what do you mean 'he'?"

"I'm telling you. I recognized him from the hundreds of photos I've seen of his ugly face. If only I had seen Sister Edwina at the school earlier. That's not anybody named Edwina—that's Josef Goebbels!"

"Josef Goebbels?" Tucker exploded. "The Nazi propaganda minister?" A look of comprehension crept over his strong-jawed face. "That means that what Gunter was really was sayin' was—"

"Nazi Goebbels. Not 'not see gerbils'. It's the same, except for th' hard G."

"But isn't he supposed to be dead?"

"Oh yeah. He and his wife and six kids committed suicide as soon as Hitler died in April '45. Their bodies were burned just outside the bunker. At least that's what Trevor-Roper figured out."

Bill was talking to the back of Tucker as the fedoraed man approached the metal door of the bowling alley. "We gotta go in, Bill," Tucker said over his shoulder. "I think she's—uh—he's gunning for Mike."

Tucker opened the door slowly and peered in. Bill heard a sigh of relief from him as he entered the dark room. Bill followed and they ran to Michael, who was standing in the near pit with a bowling pin in his hand.

"Mike, are you—"

A voice from the shadows against the back wall stopped them. "Dumpkopfs! Now I have all three of you togesser. So easy to kill."

Josef Goebbels, dressed in the black habit and white cowl of an Ursuline nun, was backed against the wall, a large luger in his hand. Tucker quickly looked over at the other three pinboys on the other nine lanes but in the din and darkness, they were all obliviously doing their dangerous and noisy jobs.

"We know who you are, Goebbels," Bill Smith spouted.

"So, you haf figured it oudt." The wizened ex-Reichminister was lapsing into his former speech patterns. "I vundered when you would. I always sought it vouldt be young Michael who put two undt two togesser."

Bill licked his lips and asked, "But one thing puzzles me. There was no mention of Goebbels, er, you, ever having three fingers on one hand. How did—"

"Oh dot. I'm afraidt dot Magda undt a couple uff der kinder weren't too ensoosiastic aboudt my suicide scheme for *zem*—undt a trip to Argentina for *me*. Zey bit like crocodiles ven I gafe zem zee cyanide."

Tucker noticed that Michael was holding the pin tightly, as if he were getting ready to throw it. He hadn't reset the pins and one of the bowlers was shouting loud enough for them to hear over the noise of the other bowling that was going on.

"Hey, pinboy! Reset the goddam pins!" It was unmistakably the voice of Tom Bolack.

Geobbels laughed and said to Michael, "Ja, go aheadt and let zee loudmouth bowl. Do it right because it'll be zee last sing you do."

Mike put the pin in the rack and pulled the lanyard to lower the pins onto the lane. He pulled it again and the rack rose, leaving the ten slightly wobbling pins. He grabbed another pin from the pit and crawled out and stood between Tucker and Bill.

The Nazi nun began moving toward the door. "Vell, it's been schweet. I'm not in zee habit uff shooting Aryans but zis time I'll make an exception. So much more fun to shoot Jews undt homozexuals."

Tucker saw Mike's knuckles whiten and thought to himself, that's funny, I never knew Mike was so concerned about Jews.

Goebbels reached the closed metal door and pointed the gun at Tucker. The sound of a rolling ball grew louder and higher-pitched as it approached the pins. The gnarled, three-fingered fist holding the gun tightened. . .

The metal door burst open, slamming into the back of the Nazi nun, knocking him towards the pit. The three hostages stepped aside as Goebbels teetered on the brink of the pit and fired the luger at the hulking figure that lumbered through the door, blowing a large hole in Sheriff Dan Sullivan's groin. The recoil of the gun toppled the nun backwards into the pit just as the speeding 16-pound ball crashed into the pins sending each of the ten 3.3-pound truncheons rocketing into the pit.

The Nazi's final scream was drowned out by a bellow from the front of the bowling alley. "Steeee-rike!"

From outside the din of the bowling alley one could faintly hear the sound of a bell ringing the 6 o'clock Angelus.

Epilogue

Twelve Years Later

BOB BERRY replaced the Mantovani LP on his turntable with a 45 with an orange label. The silver-coifed man-about-town DJ murmured smoothly, "Let's have a change of pace now with a song by a local boy name-a Knees Calhoon. You might want to turn your radios down a bit because he gets a little raucous at times. It's something he calls 'Angelus of Doom' and it seems to be about bells and some local citizens from a few years' back. But don't worry, right afterwards I'll get back to some real music with the latest hot platters from Guy Lombardo and the Percy Faith Orchestra right here on KVBC."

It all began at the Snooker Eight
Bottle pool was the game
And it ended at the Navajo Bowl
In Tom Bolack's last frame.

Tucker got the ball rollin'
Takin' Gunter to school
Bill was sacked out in the back seat
Bill Smith was no fool.

But the bells that were ringin'
They were tollin' for you
Sister Mary Edwina
The Angelus of Doom.

Gunter Hedelin packed it in
Recognized the wrong face
He never made it to the finish line
Of the master race.

Tucker knew there was something wrong
With that lyin' nun
An' there ain't nothin' more dangerous
Than a nun with a gun.

Photographic Evidence

Only known picture of Sister Edwina (with
unidentified student — perhaps an accomplice?)

Close-up of three-fingered hand

Josef Goebbels, circa 1944

Josef and Magda Goebbels in happier times

THE NAKED TROCAR

A NOT-SO-TRUE CRIME NOVEL

PROLOGUE: The Murder

THE JAYNES MORTUARY stood at the end of a dead end road in Shiprock New Mexico. It was in a residential area and the words "Jaynes Mortuary" in red neon script was the only light on the short street. It was an adobe building, one story with a basement, and if it weren't for the neon, no one would ever have any reason for going to the end of the road—except for a death in the family.

One night in late 1983, if you had been standing in the street outside the mortuary, you would have seen the door open, yellow light spilling out over the cactus and sand that made up the yard of the building. You would have seen a young man, perhaps a Navajo boy, run out of the door with the shadow of a larger person looming in the doorway. You may have even heard a sobbing shout from either the boy or the shadow before seeing what looked like a gun in the hand of the man in the doorway.

You would have then heard the sound of a gunshot and seen the young boy sprawl to the ground, obviously shot in the back. The man, who remained only a shadow, would then move to the boy, and either put into or take something from the pocket of the boy's shirt, before going back into the building.

And the sobbing would have continued until the door closed and the neon light was all you could see.

But you weren't there back in 1983. Someone else was, but be thankful it wasn't you.

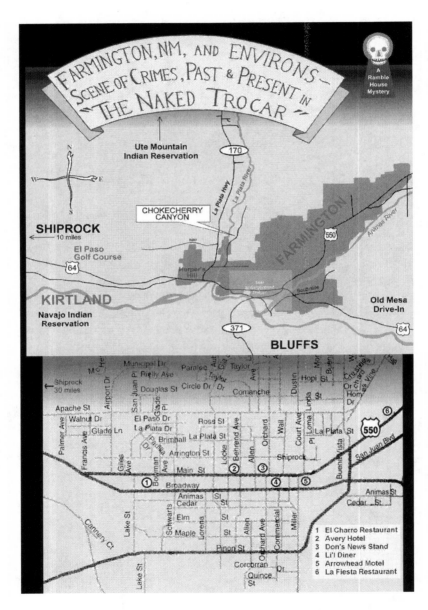

Mapback Cover of *The Naked Trocar* by Gavin L. O'Keefe

A Vacation in Farmington

AS YOU APPROACH Farmington New Mexico from the east on Highway 64 there's a time of day when you are for all intents and purposes clinically blind. The setting sun sits right on the highway ahead of you and as you pass by the turnoff that used to go to the Mesa Drive-In, about five miles east of the Animas River bridge, you have to slow down to ten miles an hour and hope no one stops in front of you—or doesn't stop in back of you. They're as blind as you are.

There's a clue to who and what I am in that description above. I grew up in Farmington in the 50s and even though there are, in 1989, numerous roads that split off of Highway 64 to the right and left, in my mind there's only the one turnoff—to the long-gone Mesa Drive-In. All of my memories of the town are from 1950 to 1967 when I used to own the place, or at least thought I did.

Farmington was an oil-field burg of maybe 5000 people back in the early 50s, growing to 15,000 by the time I got out of high school and left in 1965 to go to college in Las Cruces, downstate, then the army in the late 60s. I've lived in Cruces ever since, playing guitar in bar bands for a living and generally living the easy life. I could have stayed in Farmington and played but Las Cruces, as a university town, was better for surviving in the sleazy bar bidness.

Now, in 1989, Farmington is a sprawling hotbed of traffic, covering three times the area that it did in the 50s, and full of people I don't know. Needless to say, I liked it better back when I lived there.

We all go back to our home towns sooner or later and I was on a vacation, which meant that a week- long gig we had slated at a nifty bar in Ruidoso up in the mountains had been cancelled at the last minute. So the other members of The Mighty Calhoon Brothers and I had all decided to take advantage of the lack of work—and pay—and go on separate vacations. I, Knees, went to Farmington; Balls (who claims to have taken his nickname as a tribute to Honoré de Balzac) went home to Clovis; and Thyroid (who wasn't too thrilled about adopting a body-part nickname and was having medical trouble with his thyroid gland at the time) visited his folks in Belen.

That's me, Knees Calhoon, guitar picker and slugabed, and the one who's going to tell you all about my fateful vacation in Farmington this fall of 1989.

It was a Monday evening when I drove into town, blinded by the sun and tired from the seven-hour drive from Las Cruces. I had no plans for how long I would stay, or where. I didn't know very many people who were still in Farmington and none of them were anyone I could call and stay with. So I decided to stay at one of the old motels on Main Street, ones that were there in 1950 when my family, my mother, father and little brother Billy, moved to town in 1950. It made me feel good that there were a few places from the old days still around, maybe because none of my family was. My father had died in the late 50s, my mother in the 70s and Billy had been killed in '83.

The sun finally went down and traffic picked up a bit as I crossed the Animas River and drove along Broadway before turning north to Main Street at Wall Street. The Arrowhead Motel loomed on the south side of Main just as it had back in 1950 when it was at the very end of town. It looked a little bigger than I remembered and had a huge neon sign with a marquee that blared that it was "100% American owned". That's a clue to something, too, but I don't know what.

I pulled in and paid $80 for a room for four nights. It was a typical motel room, TV with bad cable, a reasonable king-size bed and a working air conditioner. I took off my shoes and pants and leaned back on the bed and flipped on the TV. I had rolled a dozen joints for the trip, hoping that would last me, and smoked one while watching the news. It was the same old Reagan bullshit and I was glad that I had a compartmentalized life back in Las Cruces where I could ignore the beginning of the end of American civilization at the hands of a clueless ham actor.

I was used to going out every night to work so around nine o'clock I took a shower, got dressed and went to the El Charro Restaurant on west Main, a Mexican place I used to like in the old days. It was still there and the hot sauce was as sweat-producing as ever. Great enchiladas, too. Right next to it was the El Vasito Lounge, where I had learned the ropes of the sleazy bar scene back in 1966. It was disappointing to see that it had been renamed The Maverick Club but it was still a pretty good C&W bar and I watched a band from Texas play a decent set before heading back to the motel.

I had no idea of what I was going to do in my old home town. I felt about as lost as I had ever felt in my life.

Reminiscence

I CAN'T—AND DON'T—complain about my childhood. Farmington was a perfect place to grow up back in the 50s when Eisenhower was our national grandfather and the oil fields were booming. I had my bicycle and could go anywhere in town, or even out of town. Once you reached the edge of town in any direction, you ran into incredible desert scenes with cacti, sand and magnificent sandstone formations. You didn't have to get in a car and drive for hours to be in the middle of the stinkin' desert; you could walk or bike there. And Billy and I did.

My family had friends who lived out by the new country club on Highway 550 halfway to Aztec and that's where we did most of our desert exploring. We'd take canteens full of water and sandwiches and spend the whole day exploring and hiking out there, watching out for rattlesnakes and scorpions, running up and down the sandstone with total abandon. On days we went west instead of east, there was the La Plata highway that led north to Colorado and Mancos. There was a side road that paralleled the La Plata highway that led to a girl scout's campground and it was one of our favorite hiking areas. It was full of canyons and miniature cliffs like the Anasazi cliffs of Mesa Verde or Canyon de Chelly—but without the dwellings—and we knew them as well as we knew the streets of Farmington.

Chokecherry Canyon was about two miles up the side road. It was where the high school students had their beer bashes on weekend nights. The canyon was small, just a cul-de-sac off the left side of the road, but it was hidden from the road and perfect for the bonfires that the high school parties were centered around. Just behind the campfire area was a 20-foot cliff up to a mesa, and in this cliff was the notorious Fat Man's Misery, a tunnel in the base of the cliff that led up to the top—*if* you were man enough to climb it. Billy and I had been up Fat Man's Misery many times. We even climbed it in the dark. It opened on top of the mesa where you could get back down to road level by walking around the edge of the cliffs—about a half mile walk. It was practically impossible to climb down Fat Man's Misery. We tried it and just about killed ourselves.

To the south of town were the Bluffs, tall rugged cliffs that overlooked the San Juan River that skirted Farmington on the south. We even climbed the Bluffs one day when we were feeling specially energetic.

It was a great time to be alive and in Farmington and we made the most of it. It was because of these experiences in the desert that I decided to visit Farmington in 1989 on a whim.

Billy was one year younger than I was and we were inseparable in our younger days. Our father died when we were in our early teens and we found the freedom invigorating. As the oldest boy I was given the reins of the family by my mother and we all worked hard to get by, but the combination of freedom and responsibility, especially after I learned the guitar and started making a living in a band, made us grow up fast and happy.

Then, in 1967 I was drafted into the army and Billy joined the navy. Afterwards, I ended up in Las Cruces going to college on the GI Bill and Billy went back to Farmington where he lived with some friends from high school. We kept in touch with occasional letters and phone calls and I came back to town for the funeral in 1975 when our mother died.

Billy worked at a few places in Farmington and Shiprock, a small Navajo town thirty miles to the west, and then in 1983 his body was found just south of the Bluffs in the oilfield area known as the Bisti. He had been shot in the back and his body hidden in the desert. It was only a fluke that a couple of Navajo boys had found him and the investigation had gone nowhere. I had driven up at the time but there was nothing I could do. I talked to several people who knew him well but they were all puzzled by the killing. He wasn't into heavy drugs or crime, that they knew of, and had no enemies.

Maybe Billy was the reason why I hadn't visited Farmington in more than six years.

I woke up late the next morning at the Arrowhead and wondered what I was going to do. I got dressed, smoked a half a joint and decided to go hunt down some breakfast.

I wanted to eat at some place that I remembered from back in the 50s.

Breakfast at the Avery

I DROVE WEST on Main looking at all the buildings. The traffic was not too heavy downtown and I was able to gawk at the old familiar places: Farmington Lumber Company, Harmony House, Li'l Diner, Snooker 8 Pool Hall—which will probably outlive its cockroaches— Noel Hardware, Harry's Bar, Allen Theater, Totah Theater, and finally, on the northwest corner of Main and Behrend, the Avery Hotel.

On the ground floor in the back was a great greasy spoon restaurant which had been there as long as I could remember. I saw a parking spot on Behrend right next to the side entrance to the restaurant and turned north onto Behrend then made a quick U-turn just past the empty space and pulled in directly behind a huge automobile with double tires on the back. As I got out of my 1969 Volkswagon Squareback, gray with carburetors instead of fuel injection, I noticed that the big vehicle was actually a hearse. On the side of it was printed in a flowery script "Jayne's Mortuary" and in smaller letters, "The Mortuary at the End of the Dead End Road".

What kind of an advertising mind thought of that one, I wondered as I put some coins in the parking meter and went inside the Avery Hotel.

It was brightly lit and looked about the same as I remembered it. I hoped the food was the same. I sat down at a booth facing the back of the restaurant and checked out the menu. Looked familiar.

As I was waiting for the waitress to take my order—huevos rancheros with fry bread and iced tea—I noticed a guy who was standing in an enclosed phone booth at the back of the restaurant. He looked vaguely familiar and as I looked more closely it hit me. Marty Jaynes. That's right, he owned the mortuary in Shiprock. That must be his hearse outside.

Marty and I went to school together. At least we started out together. We were the same age but he flunked one year around the fifth grade and was always a year behind me after that. He was more friends with Billy than with me. I didn't really know him that well back in school and had only run into him occasionally since then. There was some trouble Marty had with the law a few years back but I couldn't quite remember what it was.

I saw him take out a pen and write something on the wall of the booth just as the waitress took my order. I was wondering if I was going to say hi to Jaynes or not as she scooted off and he hung up the phone. He opened the door of the booth and looked straight at me as he exited. A look of recognition came over his face and he smiled and walked over to my booth.

"Hey, it's Tommy Calhoon," he said and put out his hand for me to shake. "What are you doin' in town?"

His hand was clammy and wrinkled and I didn't want to think why. He was about six feet tall and was probably a few pounds more than my 180. He had ridiculous curly hair, cut long in front even though it was thinning elsewhere. He sat down across the table from me.

"Marty Jaynes. It's good to see you. I'm going by Knees these days. Fact, I've been Knees ever since junior high."

"I know that. I was just goin' way back to when we were get-ting' slapped around by the nuns. God, those were the days. I'm surprised we survived."

I guess he saw something in my eyes that made him say quickly, "A'course not everybody survived, huh?" He looked a little embarrassed and continued, "So what're you doin' these days? Still pickin' the guitar?"

"Yeah, down in Las Cruces still. I hardly ever make it back to Farmington any more. I barely reco'nize the place now that's it's all overgrown and—"

"You said it! Downtown it's not so bad because most of the bidness's moved out on the highway to Aztec or the highway to Shiprock. That's where I spend most of my time, at the mortuary in Shiprock. The undertaking bidness never seems to die out."

I wasn't sure I wanted to talk about the "undertaking bidness" so I didn't acknowledge his strained joke and said, "Yeah, I saw your hearse outside. Uh, you eatin'?" Pointing at the menu.

He shook his head and said, "No, thanks, not now. So what brings you to Farmington?"

The waitress brought my food and we talked for about ten minutes, about the music business in Cruces, the state of the world, and a bit about the mortuary trade that wasn't too graphic for the huevos. It was when he mentioned that he had been away from the business for a few years that I remembered more about his legal troubles. He had gone to prison for manslaughter, or murder, or something.

I was curious and interrupted his discourse on the tools of the embalming arts and asked, "By the way, Marty, don't let me tread on any corns, but didn't you have a bit of trouble with the law in recent years?"

"Oh yeah. Fact, I went to prison for five goddam years. It was back in 1983 and it was for manslaughter, technically. I shot a guy who was stealing from me."

I don't know why I probed but it seemed like something I should know. And if I could get it from the horse's mouth. . .?
"Stealing, huh?" I prompted.

"Well, there was this young Navajo kid named Sammy Arthur who worked for me at the mortuary. I had just opened up the Shiprock place and he ran errands, helped out with the embalmings, nothing too technical. I noticed that things were missing about two months before the incident but they were small stuff and I overlooked it. But then he started taking things that were, well, expensive and in a few cases, embarrassing—"

"Embarrassing? What do you mean?"

"Well, you know, like things that people put on the corpses. The Navajos are very superstitious about death and the disposition of the body. They have all sorts of taboos that I have to worry about and frankly, most of them don't make a lick a' sense."

"Wow. I can imagine. So what happened with the young boy, Sammy—"

"Arthur. Well, one night I confronted him about it and he got all freaked out and said he was going to go to the cops and tell them I was doin' all sorts of illegal things out there. I tried to keep him from leaving but he got out the front door and I had a gun and, well, there was a witness and she said that I shot him from the doorway as he was runnin' away."

"A witness?"

"It was a lady that lived in the house closest to the mortuary. It's set way back from the road so you hardly notice it but she apparently had a good view of the front of the mortuary and she said that I pointed the gun at him and shot him as he ran away. The jury believed her and I was given ten years for manslaughter. I got out in five for good behavior."

"How did you manage manslaughter? That sounds like maybe murder two." I was thinking I was going too far with this, but for some reason didn't care.

Jaynes said, "They found a medallion in his pocket which was supposed to have been buried with a body the week before. I also told them that he had threatened me with a trocar right before I shot him and that I was fearful for my life."

"Trocar? What's that?"

"It's a tool we use for embalming. Come on out to the plant—I call it 'the plant' 'cause that's what we do with the bodies—and I'll show you one."

"Hmmmm. Lemme take a rain check on that. But the shot in the back. How could they get around that?"

"Well, I *did* get ten years. Ol' Judge Slinger made sure I did time."

"Judge Slinger. Lawrence Slinger. I remember that name. God, he's been around for a long time, hasn't he? Hangin' judge, right?"

"It depends. I'm out now. On parole, keepin' my nose clean, workin' at the old job and sendin' a lot of Navajos off to the happy hunting grounds in the style they want. It's a living."

"I understand completely. We all gotta pay our dues."

I don't exactly know what made me uneasy about the conversation with Jaynes. It was nothing explicit in his words, but I felt that he was feeling me out as much as I was pumping him. I was curious about his homicidal experience and he wanted to know what I was doing in Farmington. He seemed almost suspicious about why I was in town, but why should he care?

We talked a bit more then Jaynes got up and said, " 'Scuse me a second. I gotta make a phone call." He walked to the booth and closing the door made a call. It was short and he came back to the table a couple of minutes later. We talked for another five minutes or so and I finished my meal and got up and shook hands with him as we said parting phrases. He handed me a card and said, "Here's my number. Hold it, that's an old number. Here's the new one." He took out a pen and wrote his phone number, in bright blue ink, on the card, crossing out the old one.

I walked to the cash register and paid the bill and Marty saluted me as he walked out the door onto Behrend.

I followed soon after—to find that I was being given a parking ticket.

I quickly glanced at the meter and saw that there were still fifteen minutes left. There were two cops, a man and a woman; the woman bedecked in full police regalia, hat, badge, crisp black uniform with all of the accessories, the man in civilian clothes but with a badge on his belt, highly visible. The woman had a name-tag: Molly Miller.

Marty had moved on up to the hearse, which was directly in front of my Squareback, and was watching us.

"What seems to be the problem, officer?" I said to the woman officer and she looked up from her pad to ask me, "Is this your vehicle, sir?"

"Yes, it is."

"Well, it's illegally parked and I'm writing you up a citation. You can mail in the payment or, if you dispute this ticket, appear in court at the Municipal Courthouse, on, uh," she looked on another sheet of paper on her clipboard and continued, "Wednesday, that's tomorrow, at one p.m."

"What exactly is my crime here, officer?"

"You're parked too far away from the curb. The city ordinance states that the tires should be no more than 18 inches away from the curb. Yours are 20.5 inches. I'm afraid you are in violation of the ordinance."

I looked at my VW, which is a relatively narrow car. There were white lines painted on the asphalt, showing the boundaries of the parking spot for each meter. My car's outer tires were about two inches *inside* the white lines.

The two policemen looked at what I was looking at. Then I walked behind my car and stared at it, noticing that my car did not extend out into the street any further than the hearse in front of it did. In fact, the outer wheels of the hearse were on top of the white line showing the outer perimeter of the parking space. The two policemen saw what I was looking at.

I started to say something but there was a smirk on the detective's face that stopped me. This was not the time to argue. They wanted to give me a ticket. I kept my mouth shut and took the ticket and signed it when the woman handed it to me. The detective was walking around my car peering into the windows, not even trying to be coy about it. Jaynes sat behind the wheel of the hearse but hadn't started it yet.

The two cops, who were parked on the opposite side of the street in a No Parking zone got in their car and started it, talking on their car phone. On the side of the police car it read, "To Serve and Protect".

I was pissed off and frustrated and not sure if I was being railroaded or not—and for reasons I knew not enough about. Something was off-balance here. So instead of driving off in a huff, I walked back into the restaurant, leaving my car parked illegally. To hell with 'em. I looked around the restaurant and then decided what to do. I walked to the left out of the restaurant's inner doors to the lobby of the hotel and exited the front of the Avery Hotel and walked to the corner of the building on Behrend street. I peeked around the corner and saw that the hearse was still in front of my car and that the cop car had pulled out and was parked next to the hearse—blocking traffic going south on Behrend if there had been any—and the detective was talking animatedly with Jaynes, who was still behind the wheel of the hearse. They were almost yelling at each other and I heard the dick say something like, "Don't take any chances. Take him out if you need to."

And Jaynes answered, "Okay, okay. Easy for you to say."

Then they mumbled for a while longer and I thought I heard a word that ended in "—inger". Finger? Ringer? Slinger? Judge Slinger?

The cop car pulled away and I quickly turned around and scooted back inside the front doors of the Avery Hotel. I walked back to the restaurant and went to the side door and looked out to see that the hearse had gone too.

I was perplexed and didn't know what to think. How much would the ticket be for? Probably just a few bucks. It was a non-moving parking violation. But there seemed to be a conspiracy of some sort between the cops and Jaynes. I wanted to know more. And even though there was nothing that directly connected what was going on in Farmington here in 1989 with what happened in 1983, I had a nagging hunch deep down that kept poking at my mind.

I had an idea. I went to the phone booth at the back and entered it and closed the door. Good. There was a phone book. I looked up "Lawyers" in the yellow pages and then moved to "Attorneys" as instructed. Maybe Barney is still in town, I thought. I thumbed through the five pages of lawyers and spotted what I was looking for: "Eastwick, Barney, criminal law."

I called the number and got a secretary, who took my name and put me on hold. A few seconds later a big voice boomed through the phone, "Knees Calhoon! You old git-picker. What're you doing in Sin City?" It was unmistakably Barney Eastwick, a flamboyant lawyer I knew from college in Las Cruces. He'd gone on to law school and ended up practicing in Farmington. I'd last seen him a decade before when he helped me get my divorce.

"I'm just in town for a vacation. No reason whatsoever. Thought I'd see how the place had changed without my presence. I trust you're doing okay?"

"Oh I'm just havin' fun with the law. In this town it's a racket and I'm swingin' it for all I'm worth. Don't tell me you need a lawyer!"

"Well, actually, Barney, I do. It's not a big deal, just a parking ticket but I think there are, uh, facets to it that might make it worth your interest. It involves an ordinance that makes no sense and a couple of cops who are itching to follow that ordinance to the letter. I think we can beat the rap and maybe even humiliate a couple of asshole cops at the same time."

"That sounds pretty good. I always enjoy stickin' it to Farmington's finest when they get too pompous. When's your court date?"

"It's tomorrow at one p.m. Can you swing that? I wouldn't think it would take much time to plead the case."

"There's nothing like goin' into court without knowin' what the case is about. It's the ultimate high wire act for us legal folks."

"Well, hell, I can tell you what it's all about before the case. No need to walk the wire without a net. How about if I come to your office tomorrow at noon and we go over it and then drive over to the Municipal Court and confront the formidable Molly Miller and her mufti-clad consort?"

"Huh? Mufti-clad? You must mean Detective Smuff. Wally Smuff. He and Miller are well-known partners in crime here in town. Molly 'n' Wally. They always ride together. I would *love* to chop off a few inches a' those two. One tomorrow afternoon, eh? That's sounds good. You don't wanna tell me a bit more about what I'll be arguin'?"

"I have complete confidence you'll snap to the best defense right away. We can discuss it tomorrow. I'll see you at noon?"

"Okay. See you then, Knees."

As I hung up the phone I happened to glance up on the wall of the booth and saw, in bright blue ink, "Thur. 10:30, mort." That wasn't too hard to figure out, even whether it was A.M. or P.M. I had a feeling that whatever Jaynes was up to, it was not happening at 10:30 in the morning. Tomorrow night at 10:30 at the mortuary.

I left the restaurant, got in my illegally parked Squareback—whose meter read 'VIOLATION' in big red letters by now—and

drove back to the Arrowhead Motel. I needed to smoke a joint and
think things over. I could only take so much service and protection.

After watching a damn good Robert Mitchum western in the motel
room I took a nap and later had dinner at Chef Bernie's Restaurant
out on the west side of town. I did a little more sightseeing then I
checked out the Office Bar on East Main. The band was decent
but I couldn't get the wrongness of the ticket and Jaynes and the
cops out of my head. Maybe I was anticipating having my day in
court with a mouthpiece like Barney Eastwick.

I made it back to the Arrowhead by eleven, smoked a joint and
watched a horror flick about a giant mollusk that was eating nubile swimmers. Pretty good, actually. Then I started reading a
David Dodge paperback I'd brought along and crapped out after a
couple of chapters.

So ended my first full day back in my home town.

The Trial

BARNEY EASTWICK'S office was a half block north of Main on
Orchard in a refurbished old two-story brick house, and I got there
a little after high noon. We had to get up to the court on Municipal
Drive, by the airport, so I knew we only had a half-hour or so for
me to fill him in on the case. It should be easy.

I had started the day with a terrific lunch/breakfast at the Li'l
Diner just a few blocks down Main Street, then walked up and
down the length of the downtown area seeing what kind of books I
could find. That's what I did when in a strange town, and even
though I still knew the geography, I was finding Farmington
strange. Don's News Stand, the combo newsstand/ book
store/pinball alley of my youth was now a Navajo Trinket store.
No 25 cent Gold Medal books to be found in 1989. But there was
a damn good paperback store next to the Allen Theater, which had
once been a second pool hall on Main Street back in the 60s. How
many towns of less than 15,000 people could brag of having *two*
pool halls on Main Street? And the weird thing is that for about a
year back in 1965 there was a third pool hall, Singleton's, right off
Main on Commercial Street.

After I made it back to the Arrowhead and had a quick smoke, I was ready to consult my lawyer.

I parked behind the Snooker 8 Pool Hall and found my way up to his office on the second floor. It was a spacious room, with books lining the walls and a huge polished wood desk in the center. Barney, a big guy who was a little balder than I'd remembered him, shook hands with me and pointed me to a comfortable chair.

"So, Knees Calhoon, you slink back into town and immediately antagonize the men in blue. That sounds about right."

"I didn't actually slink, but you can bet next time I will. Barney, you're looking good. I guess the legal life agrees with you. Are you up for a Supreme Court-worthy case, full of sound and fury?"

"I thought you said it was a parking violation?"

"Bad parkers are people, too. But here's the case in a nutshell. I got a ticket for parking 20.5 inches away from the curb in my VW Squareback, even though my car was *completely* within the white lines that described the perimeter of the parking spot. The ordinance states that the near tires must be within 18 inches."

"Hmmm. Sounds like a typical stupidly thought out law. You propose that I argue that the purpose of the law is to keep people from sticking out in traffic too far, and that a better measurement would be from the *far* wheels to the curb?"

"Damn, Barney! You sure picked the right career. That's *exactly* what I think the argument should be. But I even have some more corroborating evidence of the argument, if the cops and Marty Jaynes don't outright lie—"

"Marty Jaynes? What the hell does he have to do with this?"

"Nothing, really. He was just parked in his hearse right in front of me and even though he was sticking out into traffic about 6 inches more than I was, because he was parked closer to the curb, he didn't get a ticket."

Barney Eastwick paused a moment, rubbed his hands together and said, "So let me get this straight. Molly Miller and Wally Smuff are giving you a ticket and Marty Jaynes is there in his hearse. Did he say anything?"

"Well, not really. I had talked a bit with Jaynes in the Avery Hotel restaurant before the ticket incident. He was just driving away." For some reason I didn't want to tell Barney about the altercation/conversation between Jaynes and the two cops afterward.

"So there wasn't any collusion between the cops and Jaynes?"

"I'm not sure what you're getting at. Is—"

"You haven't been around Farmington for a while, have you? Did you ever hear about what Jaynes did?"

"Well, I talked a little with him about it in the restaurant. He said, in a sort of elliptical way, that he had shot a young Navajo boy who worked for him and went to prison for five years for it."

"Uh huh. Did he mention why he did it?"

"He said the kid had been stealing from him and that the kid was going to spread some lies, some damaging lies, about him and that it was more of a case of self-defense."

"Yeah, that's what was argued in his trial, and except for the self-defense part, that was what the prosecution went with. Because the boy was shot in the back at a distance of about fifteen feet, the self-defense argument didn't hold up and Jaynes was found guilty of manslaughter. He got ten years."

"And got out in five." I was wondering where Barney was going.

"Well, there's a different story about the case. I was working with the D.A.'s office back in 1983 when the trial took place and we all knew that the stealing story was a crock. What happened was that Jaynes was dealing coke and heroin out of the mortuary and the kid was his runner. Maybe the boy was going to rat, maybe he had ripped Jaynes off, we never knew for sure, but we were convinced that dope was the reason for the murder. But the D.A. knew the manslaughter charge was a slam-dunk so he left all of the drug stuff out of the trial, figuring it would muddy the issue."

"No shit?" I was surprised at these revelations, even though I had no problem believing that Jaynes was into hard stuff. What else was there to do in a place like Shiprock?

"Yes, shit. A lot of the guys at the D.A.'s office are pissed off he got out so quick. And then went right back to work at the mortuary. There's no way he would be back in the dope business now, with a parole officer visiting him every week, but there's some animosity towards him.

"But here's the thing. There were two police officers whose names were mentioned in the heroin/coke scene. They didn't get charged with anything, maybe because of judicial influence, but their hands looked a little dirty. One of them was kicked up to detective and the other was demoted to traffic."

"Smuff and Miller."

"Right."

I must have looked at him blankly, because that was the state of my mind. All of the threads and tendrils had tied themselves into a big blankness.

"So let's go fight for Truth, Justice and the American Way," the burly barrister bellowed, and we walked down to his Jaguar XKE. At least we'd be wooing Lady Justice in style.

We got to the Courthouse with five minutes to spare and took our places in the back of the room. Barney immediately started talking to some lawyers and court officials near the judge's bench and it was obvious it was not about my parking ticket.

I took out the David Dodge book, a Dell mapback, and continued my reading from the night before, and it was ten minutes later that I heard the bailiff announce in a stentorian voice, "All rise for the honorable Judge Lawrence T. Slinger!"

The judge was in his fifties, with sleek silver hair parted on the side and flowing over his ears senatorially. His flowing black robes valiantly tried to disguise his corpulence, and failed miserably. He strode to the bench and sat behind it as we all sat down after him.

"Okay, let's get this traffic court going. First case."

One of the under-assistant D.A.s at the prosecution table called out a name and I was back to David Dodge. Thirty minutes later, Barney Eastwick sat down beside me and said, "We're up next. I guess I don't need to tell you to let me do the talking."

"My life is in your hands, brother."

"And would I let my broth—"

Barney's filial pronouncement was interrupted by the braying of the bailiff: "Knees Calhoon! Improper parking!"

My trial had begun.

At this point in the narrative, Erle Stanley Gardner would have dictated a scintillating, and 90% plausible, courtroom dialogue, with strident objections and Masonesque histrionics. All I can do is tell what happened.

Barney and I stood while the sub-deputy D.A. read out the charge. When he said "tires were 20.5 inches from the curb," I saw the judge's face grow a shade redder and his jaw tighten. As soon as the last word of the charge was read, he turned to me and scoffed, "You are challenging the measuring abilities of our fine police force, Mr. Calhoon?"

I started to open my mouth to say any number of wrong things when Barney quickly jumped in. "Your honor, we stipulate to the simple facts of the case. Our objection is to the way the law is worded—and enforced—which we argue is antithetical to its intended purpose: to make the streets safer."

"Do tell. Well, let's hear what the prosecution has to say and we'll get to your argument."

The sub-deputy re-stated the case by pretty much re-reading the charge. Tires were 20.5 inches away when they should have been 18 or less. "Call Patrolman Molly Miller."

The meter maid/officer was dressed as nattily as she had been yesterday as she pushed through the doors across from the jury box, which was empty. She sat in the witness box and took the oath. Detective Smuff entered at the same time and sat near the back of the courtroom.

The sub-deputy spoke from his desk. "You are a police traffic officer named Molly Miller?"

"Yes, I am."

"You saw a car parked too far from the curb and gave it a ticket, after measuring the distance from the curb to the near tire as being 20.5 inches, did you not?"

"I did."

"Was the car the property of Knees Calhoon, the defendant?"

"It was."

"Your witness."

Barney stood up and smiled at the empty jury box. Then he turned to Miller and said, "Thank you, Officer Miller, for your excellent testimony, all seven words of it. Now, did you notice a vehicle parked in front of the defendant's car?"

"I did."

"Uh, what kind of car was it?"

"It was a Dodge Econoline hearse."

"Big vehicle?"

"Yes."

"Bigger than the defendant's car, which was a—" he looked at me and I mouthed, "Volkswagon Squareback." "Volkswagon Squareback?" he continued in the same tone of voice.

"Yes, bigger."

"So big that it stuck out into traffic even more than the defendant's Squareback?"

"I believe it extended further into the street than did the, uh, defendant's car."

"It was a hearse you say?"

"Yes, from Jaynes' Mortuary in Shiprock."

I was marveling at this slow, deliberate sashay of Lady Justice when the officer's response jerked the judge into action. He sat upright and glared at Barney. "Where are you going with this, Mr. Eastwick? What is the relevance of the type of car that was parked in front of the defendant's?"

"No relevance at all. The only reason I brought up the other vehicle is to show that even though it was in compliance of the law, and my client's not, the complying car was the more dangerously parked. The law needs to be changed to make compliance with it compatible with safety, rather than danger. In other words, since the reason for the law is to ensure that cars don't stick out too far into traffic, the law should address the far side of the car, and not the near side."

Molly Miller sputtered from the witness box, "But Judge, even if we were to start measuring how far it was to the far side of the car, we don't know what that figure is. We'd have to stop giving tickets for this until they decided what that figure should be."

Barney Eastwick suggested, "Maybe you could ask the city department that paints the white lines that define each parking space?"

"But it's so much easier just to measure to the near wheels!" Molly whined.

"This whole case is ridiculous," the judge boomed. "How much is the fine for this thing?"

"Uh, ten dollars, your honor," the sub-deputy announced.

Judge Slinger turned his hefty body to face me. "*Mis*ter Calhoon. You don't live in Farmington, do you." He said it as a statement.

"No, I don't, your honor."

"You stayin' long?"

"Not any longer than I have to, your honor."

"Well, I'm inclined to instruct the D.A.'s office to drop the charges in hopes that we will soon see the backside of you as you skedaddle home. Is that satisfactory?"

Again my mouth opened to say something inadvisable when Barney interjected, "One hundred percent satisfactory, your honor. And I'm sure the proper department of the local government will look into revising the laws concerning how parking parameters are measured."

The judge, Molly and the sub-deputy glared at Barney for a few seconds then glared at each other in an oddly chicken-like sequence where none of them glared at the one glaring at him.

Finally, the sub-deputy intoned, "The prosecution withdraws the charges."

Barney and I smiled at each other and left the courtroom before I could be told to get out of town again. We drove back to his office, cackling like hens in the XKE, and when we arrived it was just past two p.m.

"Thanks for giving me an opportunity to piss off some well-deserving cops," Barney was saying as we entered the office building. "Especially Miller. Too bad Detective Smuff didn't get called. He tends to sweat noticeably when grilled. The juries eat it up."

"I noticed you playing to the non-existent jury today. What's with that?"

"Just a habit. But a judge is just like a small jury. Say, did you think Judge Slinger was taking this whole case a little too seriously?"

"Well, I don't really know him. I thought *you* did."

"Oh I know him all right. He's been an ass ever since he got demoted to traffic court about seven years ago. But this was somethin' different. It's like he had somethin' personal to pick with you. He coulda made you pay the $10, easy, but it's like he wanted you to just leave."

"It seemed that way to me too."

By this time we were in his office relaxing. I piped up, "Well, Barney, there went two hours of your billable time. How much you need for your pound of flesh?"

"The same as for your divorce."

I nodded. A quart of Jim Beam and a quart of the store's second best tequila. I'd have to take care of that tomorrow—for the rest of today I had plans that were crawling around in my head like worms in an ant farm.

I said goodbye to Barney and drove back to the Arrowhead. I took a shower and smoked a joint while a movie with Alan Ladd and Sophia Loren played on the silent TV. Great wet pearl-diving blouse scene.

By five p.m. I was hungry and it was time to put my plan in action. This time I wasn't going to leave town with Billy lying dead on the bluffs.

Snakes on a Plain

I KNEW I had plenty of time to kill so I started out heading east to see what sort of restaurants there were towards Aztec. I spotted a likely looking one, La Fiesta, and had a superb combo plate with sopaipillas and honey *during* the meal. A half hour later I was driving out of town to the west, towards Shiprock.

This was a part of town I hadn't revisited and it really took me back. I passed the intersection where Apache Street, a major east-west residential thoroughfare hit Main Street and then passed where the La Plata highway headed off to the north to Mancos. Immediately ahead of me was the two-mile long Harper's Hill, a 15% grade that led up to the plateau around Kirtland. I saw off to my left the San Juan River valley and beyond that the western reach of the Bluffs. It was really a beautiful valley, especially out here where the farms were small and well-manicured. I noticed that the highway department had put in a run-off lane for trucks coming down the hill. If their brakes failed they could veer off onto the run-off and be slowed by about fifty yards of level sand. Good idea. Harper's Hill was notoriously dangerous back in the 50s and 60s because of its steepness and length, and the four-lane divided highway they'd put in hadn't made it any safer if your brakes went out.

As I chugged up the hill in my Squareback, gray-blue, the same kind of car Harrison Ford drove in his Amish detective movie, I saw off to my right a cliff of rugged sandstone that ended only as I topped the rise. The highway divided the top of the mesa in a straight line—heading directly into the sun.

Why do I always seem to be driving west when the sun is going down?

I was just getting to the turn-off to Kirtland, about ten miles from Farmington, when I saw ahead a road that led off to the right to the El Paso Natural Gas golf course. That really brought back some memories. Billy and I and some friends used to play golf there almost every day for a couple of summers back in '65 and '66, when I was just out of high school. It was for El Paso workers and their dependents only, but since we always had Ron Oliverri around, whose father and uncle were surveyors for EP, we had no problems playing nine holes a day. There was usually no one around to care, anyway. It was just a nine-hole golf course—no pro shop or anything.

I decided to see what it looked like today and turned off on a well-traveled dirt road. It angled to the left and over a small hill and there it was—almost exactly the way I had last seen it.

The fairways were a water-deprived green and the roughs were sandy dunes, completely covered with sagebrush, cactus, and species of stickers that probably plagued the dinosaurs. Even if you saw exactly where you duffed the ball out into the rough, there was a good chance you couldn't get to it without placing your shins in serious jeopardy. There was a lake hole and if it hadn't been for periodic night excursions where we'd wade the lake shoeless, picking up balls with our toes, we'd have never been able to afford to play the course, even though it was free. It was damned easy to lose balls in the rough out here.

I parked the car at a little shed that stood next to the tee for Hole #1 and walked over to the only bench on the whole nine holes. I sat and looked out over fairway #1 and fairway #9 beyond it, my back to the desert.

The first inkling of twilight was on me and I fished out a joint and lit it. An empty golf course is a beautiful sight at the end of the day. It was a day like this that Billy and I found my old pet Mojina, a five-foot garden snake on one of the middle holes by the lake. It was out in the rough and my ball practically hit it. We took the snake with us and kept it at my apartment where I lived the summer of '65. Billy was still in high school and was living at home with our mother. I moved out of the house the day I graduated from high school. In those days practically everybody did. Nowadays they've made things so rough on 18-year-old people that they're forced to be wards of their parents up into their 20s. It used to be that only rich assholes went to college paid for by their daddies. Regular people worked their way through or went into the service and got the GI bill. But then they raised tuitions so much that it stopped being men and women who went to college and started being children. So of course mommy and daddy freaked out when little Susie and Johnny started taking drugs and having sex. Hell, what did they think college was for?

There's no telling how far my internal diatribe would have gone on if I hadn't heard an ominous rustling in the sage behind me.

I jumped up and saw the stickers move a bit about five feet away. "Holy shit!" I exclaimed as I saw some other stickers move about four feet away from that. I was being snuck up upon! Then I saw the snake.

It was not as long and fat as Mojina, whom I returned to the rough at this course when I left Farmington for the army in 1967, but it was just as beautiful. It was relaxing in the evening air, which was getting cooler as the fall came on. It had the markings of a rattler, but much more subdued. I knew nothing about snakes, but I had been told back in 1965 that it was a garden snake and I'm sticking to that.

The plan I had roiling around in my mind involved revenge, and all of these things blended together to remind me of something Billy had told me in the early 80s, about Marty Jaynes. Billy knew Marty pretty well and when the Jaynes Mortuary opened up in Shiprock in 1980 Billy went out to see the place a couple of times. The way Billy told it to me was that it was maybe Billy's first visit and there was nobody around the place, just Marty and Billy. Marty was down in the morgue doing something and Billy was looking around the upstairs where the caskets were on display. No bodies, just empty, open caskets. Billy was checking out an especially frilly casket when he saw something that made him shout out for Marty to come check it out.

Marty came up the stairs and looked into the casket where Billy pointed. Marty jumped and shouted and looked around quickly. Seeing all of the doors closed and no one in sight, he reached in and pulled out a two-foot long snake, who knows what kind. Not a rattler, obviously. Marty took the snake and went out the back door and came back a few minutes later. He had told Billy that to the Navajos a snake is a very powerful being that must be respected for many things—and blamed for many others. But the last thing you want associated with a member of your clan's death is a snake. As Marty had put it to Billy, "If any customer had ever seen a snake in any of my caskets, or even in my building anywhere, he'd have been my last Navajo customer.

He'd'a told all his clansmen and they'd'a told all their wives and before long the mortuary would have been taboo."

The snake had moved only a foot or so since this memory had hit me and I started thinking that maybe I could use him for my plan. It was a half-baked plan anyway and everyone knows that snakes make everything more fun.

So I ran over to my car to see what I could use to hold the snake. In the back—a Squareback is essentially a station wagon—there was a cardboard box that had some books in it. Plus a bunch of Styrofoam packing popcorn. I took the books out and brought the box to where I had seen the snake. It was still there and I could see it well, even though it was rapidly getting dark. I picked up the snake and put it in the box with the popcorn and closed the four flaps inside each other. It didn't seem to mind.

I had no idea of what I would do with the snake. I'd figure that out when I got to the mortuary. It was going to be 10:30 at night and some shady people I didn't like were going to meet at a mortuary in Shiprock New Mexico at the end of a dead end road. And I was going to spy on them with a snake as my partner.

This wasn't much of a plan, but it sounded like it was going to be fun.

But then came the final nail in the coffin of my strategy. As I walked in the dusk with a box full of four-foot snake in my hands, I stepped on something. And it turned out to be a two-foot snake. I put it in the box with the four-footer. Why the hell not?

Stakeout

THE REST OF THE TRIP to Shiprock was about like I remembered it was back when my family knew some people who worked at the helium plant and we used to visit them regularly. It's a pleasant road and there used to be a stretch where the cottonwoods were planted in rows alongside the road and their branches met overhead, like something you'd expect to see on the Natchez Trace. Those trees were no longer there.

As I approached Shiprock from the east I could see the monument off in the distance to the southwest. It was so big that it looked a lot nearer than it was. If you've seen any old western movie you've probably seen the tall, jagged Shiprock, which is the remnant of an antediluvian volcano. The cone has completely worn away leaving only the magma, extending almost 1800 feet above the desert in the vague shape of a clipper ship. Billy and I had driven up to it a couple of times and touched it, both times getting run off by the Navajo Police. People have tried to climb it and some have died trying.

I almost passed the place I was looking for, a little café with the quaint name of Chat & Chew. I wasn't interested in chatting, but I had some time to kill and I'd always heard there was some good chew at the Chat & Chew in Shiprock.

I pulled into the parking lot at the Chat & Chew at ten till eight. I ordered a burger with green chile and onions and thousand island dressing with French fries and cole slaw and pulled out my David Dodge and settled into the booth for a while. The cover of the book was fantastic, with a red-robed Death rowing a floating coffin with a huge, ten-foot "cigarette" as cargo. It looked like they used to roll their joints more professionally back in the 50s than I do now. The smoke of the cigarette wafted into the dark sky in the form of a buxom and naked bighaired babe. The rear cover of the book was a mapback, with a double map showing the California coastline around San Francisco and Monterey and Carmel in the top map, and the northern half of San Francisco in the bottom map. The banner above the maps emblazoned "Where marijuana and murder make a thrilling story". My kinda book.

An hour and a half later it was getting close to the Chat & Chew's closing hour of ten. I was just finishing the book when the lady behind the counter started looking at me as if she'd like for me to go. I read the last page and left, leaving a big tip and telling her it was the best burger I'd had in a long time. It was.

I got in the Squareback and wondered if I knew how to get to Jaynes' Mortuary. I had a vague idea of where it was but had never been there. I didn't want to ask anyone, just in case. . .

I knew it was at the end of a dead end road and I was pretty sure it was on the southern edge of town off of Highway 666 that led down to Window Rock and Gallup. Down in Jim Chee country, where Hillerman says he has a trailer down by the river. I headed west and turned south on 666. There was a fast food place at the intersection that I remembered had the best Navajo tacos. Damn. Maybe I should have eaten there.

I decided to just drive around the area on the side streets. Sooner or later I was bound to see a Dead End sign. According to the hearse, the mortuary was at the end of the road. I'd just go down any dead end roads I saw. It was five after ten.

It took me five minutes of driving before I saw it. I actually saw the red neon glowing down a dark, dark road before I saw the sign that said "DEAD END". I turned onto the road and saw that it was two blocks long, with the mortuary straddling the end of the road. There were about four houses on the two blocks but none of them were near the road. They were all set back about twenty feet and were hidden by trees. We must not be far from the San Juan River.

It was coal dark and the moon wasn't out, which was good, because there wasn't any place to hide my car. My best bet to stake out the place was to park off the road about a half block from the mortuary and hope the person who owned the property didn't see me. Chances were good that anyone driving up the road to the mortuary wouldn't see my car unless they veered right at me.

I found a good spot and shut off my engine. I had turned my lights off when I entered the road. Now came the stakeout. I was close enough to see that there weren't any cars parked in the parking lot in front of the building and it didn't look like there were any roads around the building.

The only lights besides the neon sign were in a small window on the left side of the main floor. The mortuary was a two-story affair, but the bottom floor was a basement, half sunk into the earth, and the top floor was just up a few steps from the parking lot. From what Billy had said, the morgue was in the basement and the top floor was the part the public would see.

It was not quite 10:15 so I figured I might as well see if I could put the snakes to a good use. I got out of the car—after first turning off the dome light—and took the box, from which came a rustling sound that sent a chill down my spine. I wasn't exactly sure of what I was going to do—I just thought that sabotaging the mortuary was a good idea.

I headed for the south end of the building, where the light was. It looked like a bathroom light that had been left on; or maybe an office light. It was up about eight feet off the ground. I went up to it and saw that it was tightly closed and didn't look like anything I could jimmy open. My eyes were getting used to the dark and I could see some other windows, some on the bottom floor right above ground level, but they were all closed, too. So much for my idea of mortuary sabotage. It was a stupid idea, anyway.

So I went back to the car and put the box in the back, checking to make sure that the folded flaps were still tightly closed. I didn't want to come out to the car and find one or more of the snakes missing.

I sat in the dark, listening to the occasional rustle of the box, and had a smoke while waiting. A few minutes later I saw the lights of a truck that turned onto the dead end street and passed by me. It pulled in front of the mortuary and parked and two large men got out. They leaned up against the side of the truck, lit cigarettes and mumbled a few words I couldn't pick up. They sounded like Navajos.

A few minutes later another set of lights came up the street and I saw that it was the Jaynes Mortuary hearse. Jaynes got out and said something to the two men and they entered the building.

Was there any more? What about Miller and Smuff?

Not more than two minutes after the trio had entered the building another car came and parked, a Cadillac de Ville. Out of it lumbered a very large man. Slinger! What role did he have in this caper? And more importantly, was there really a caper?

Slinger strode into the building and I hunkered down in the car. What about Miller and Smuff? Weren't they supposed to be here for this meeting or whatever it was?

I had to piss. Why didn't I do it at the Chat & Chew? In the noir books the dicks always talked about the bottles they brought along on stakeouts. But they lived in big cities like Frisco or Miami. Hell, I was in Shiprock New Mexico. It was better than being at Bohemian Grove with Greenspan and Kissinger and that crowd. I could piss on any tree I wanted.

I got out of the car and was relaxing the bladder against a small cottonwood when I heard a female voice chortle, "That looks like some kind of violation, doesn't it, Wally?" Uh oh.

Introduction to a Trocar

PATROLMAN MOLLY MILLER had her service revolver out and pointed in my direction. Detective Smuff lit a cigarette and sneered, leaning up against the Squareback. "Looks like parking up the road and scouting the area was a good idea, Molly."

"I get 'em every once in a while, Wally," she said huskily and after I zipped up, pushed me to the car. "Let's go tell it to the judge."

The three of us walked to the door of the mortuary and entered. I wasn't holding my hands in the air but Miller kept the gun in her hand. They acted like they knew I didn't have any sort of weapon. They were right. I wasn't even sure if I had a brain any longer. What a plan!

The front room of the mortuary was large and full of open caskets. I didn't look to see if there were any bodies in them—humans *or* snakes. There was a staircase heading down towards the back of the room and we walked to it and descended ten steps to a dank, musty room that looked like the lab of a mad scientist. Judge Slinger and Marty Jaynes were talking next to a flat, metal table with grooves running down each side of it into a trough-like container. On the tables was a sheet-covered, man-sized object that I assumed was a corpse. If P.D. James were telling this you'd get a detailed description of every item in the room, but I'm doing it, and you'll have to use your imagination. It was a morgue, for pete's sake. I didn't *want* to know what was in it.

Slinger and Jaynes looked surprised to see me. The two Navajos, huge men who looked like brothers, stood on the other side of the table and looked bored. I figured them for the muscle of the gang.

"What the hell is *he* doing here?" Slinger sputtered, his enormous belly draping over the table and jiggling.

"Ask him," Smuff said, smirking.

I had no idea what I was going to say, but Slinger didn't look at me. He turned to Smuff and muttered, "Make sure the Etcitty boys keep an eye on him." Smuff said something in Navajo and the two brothers nodded, but didn't look at me.

Jaynes spouted, "Well, I'll ask him! What the hell are you doin' here, Calhoon?"

"I came out to see that thing you were talking about at the Avery. That tro-something."

"The trocar? It's kinda late to be gettin' curious about undertakin'."

The judge waddled away from the table a couple of steps and said, "Miller, go check his car. Smuff, what does he know about us?"

Miller left and before Smuff could answer, Jaynes broke in, "Smuff doesn't know any more than what I told him when I called him to come and ticket Calhoon's car. Look, nothing has happened since this afternoon when you left him off of the ticket. Other than him comin' out here and snoopin' around."

"That's what worries me. You told me if I let him off he'd leave town."

"Hey," I complained, "I'm right here. You can talk to me." I immediately regretted it because I wasn't sure what I was going to say.

Finally the judge looked at me and with narrowed eyes asked, "So what do you know about what happened here in 1983?"

The question surprised me and I mumbled, "Uh, you mean when Jaynes killed that Navajo kid?"

"Yes."

I wondered how much to tell. "Well, Jaynes said he shot the kid for stealing. I figured there was something more than that but, hell, it's no business of mine."

"What do you mean, 'more than that'?"

"Hey look, I'm a man of the world. I don't care if people use, sell or worship drugs. I've been known to take a puff or two myself."

The judge and Smuff snorted. Jaynes looked a little worried. He started to say something but the judge cut him off. "Drugs. That's what you think is going on?"

"I don't think anything is going on. I came out to see a trocar."

Jaynes' face lit up and he quickly said, "That's right. The trocar. Here lemme show you one." He walked to a table and picked up a metal instrument in the shape of a hollow cylinder, about a foot in length and a half-inch in diameter. It was beveled and sharp on one end. He brought it over to me and pointed it at my midsection.

The judge looked on thoughtfully as Jaynes continued. "Y'see. We gotta drain all the insides out of a body and so we insert this thing in several places in the abdomen and. . ." He tried to look maniacal and went on, "So what do you think, Calhoon? What do you think of the trocar now?"

"Other than being an anagram of 'carrot', not much," I countered and the Etcittys snickered but still didn't look at me.

Smuff saw the consternation on Jaynes' face and walked over to another table and picked up an instrument that looked like the trocar in Jaynes' hand, but at least four times as large, with a diameter of about 2 inches. "How about this baby, Calhoon? Ya' got an anagram for this thing?"

Jaynes sputtered, "That's a horse trocar, Smuff."

"Okay. Okay," I stammered. "I get the point. I'm not supposed to be here. I haven't seen anything and I'm on my way out of town."

"But I don't believe you, Mr. Calhoon," the judge said, wheezing. "I think you are here because you know there's more than drugs involved. I think you're here, perhaps at the instigation of that shyster Eastwick, to spy on us for our other activities."

I didn't know exactly where he was going but I tried to put a knowing look on my face, hoping he might continue and actually tell me what was going on.

"You tolerant types make me ill, Calhoon. You have no qualms about illegal substances but as soon as a man takes a small advantage of a person who has since left this plane of existence, using only the physical shell that the person has left behind for his modest pleasure, you become a moralist. You have no perspective. You—"

I was just beginning to digest what the judge was saying—and it wasn't sitting well—when Molly Miller's legs appeared in the stairway leading up to the top floor. She entered the room and I saw that she was carrying the cardboard box. Still closed.

The judge continued, "We are but a group of simple souls with a taste for life that so many ignorant people consider, shall we say, perverse?"

I was hardly listening to the madman because I was intent on Miller's actions. She walked over and placed the box on the table next to what I assumed was the corpse's head.

"All he had in the car was this box. And a roach in the ashtray. Looked like crummy Mexican weed."

"Here. Lemme see what you got," Smuff said and, after placing the horse trocar on the operating table, flipped open the four flaps of the box to reveal a level sea of white Styrofoam popcorn. All of the people in the room: me, Judge Slinger, Marty Jaynes, Detective Smuff, Molly Miller and even the Etcitty brothers leaned a little closer to the box to see.

Detective Smuff grunted and reached his right hand into the pile of Styrofoam. A look of recognition flitted across his face and he suddenly gave a yell that startled us all. He whipped his hand out of the box and on the end of his forefinger was the head of a writhing, two-foot snake. Its body slapped against the face of one of the Etcittys and the Navajo let out a howl that drowned out the cursing of Smuff. Everyone jumped back and I thought, "There's only two ways you can stick a finger into a snake and I'm glad he picked that one." I reached out and pushed the box off the table onto the floor and the other snake, the four-foot one, fell out of the popcorn and curled around the other Etcitty's leg.

As the scream of the second terrified Navajo pierced through the chaos, everyone froze—except me. The trocar in Jaynes' hand was pointing at the ground and before anyone knew it I was running up the stairs.

I slammed through the door to the cool New Mexico night and ran to my car. I could hear shouts from inside the mortuary but so far no one had come out of the place. I started it up and peeled out, making a quick 90 degree turn and was headed out of the dead end street when I saw two figures run out of the building in the rear-view mirror. Miller and Smuff it looked like.

I screeched around the corner and soon found myself on Highway 64 speeding through the sleepy town of Shiprock on my way back to Farmington.

The Flight of the Squareback

I HAD ABOUT a half mile lead on the cop car as I left Shiprock and I kept the VW at 80, which was about its maximum speed. They could have caught me within a few miles but they seemed to be biding their time. They didn't have their flashing lights on but stayed about ten car lengths back as I passed Kirtland a few minutes later.

I didn't have time to be thinking but I couldn't help but wonder what the judge was talking about. Necrophilia? Was he saying that they had a necrophilia ring out at the Jaynes Mortuary? And that maybe *that* was the reason for the murder of Sammy Arthur? That would explain their trying to kill me for simply parking my car outside the mortuary. They knew I wasn't going to turn anyone in for dealing coke or heroin, but who knows how I'd react to necrophilia?

Hell, I didn't even know how I'd react. It does seem like the ultimate victimless crime. . .

The terror and chaos of the scene I'd just gone through in the basement of the mortuary was jangling through my mind as I kept the Squareback floorboarded through the dense black night. *Terror. Chaos. Horse trocar.* Goddammit! Why do I always come up with the perfect comeback about ten minutes too late!

I was driving like a madman and coming up on Harper's Hill. I'd have to slow down for the long, steep decline. I had just tapped the brake when the lights behind me loomed much closer, then almost touched my car. They were going to ram me as I was heading down Harper's Hill and run me off the road. How could I stop them from doing just that?

We were halfway down the hill and they had just bumped me, making me accelerate a bit to a speed way too fast for going down the most dangerous hill in the Four Corners area. I was going to crash!

And then, out of the corner of my eye, I saw the truck run-off ramp to the right. Without thinking I yanked the wheel to the right and bowled off the highway into a long stretch of deep sand that slowed me down so fast I banged my face against the wheel. In the rear mirror on the driver's side of my car I saw the two in the cop car behind me, startled by my quick action, start to follow me onto the ramp but they seemed to realize that they'd ram me too hard for *their* safety and tried to continue down Harper's Hill.

They didn't make it. The cop car hit the edge of the road at a 45 degree angle and flipped. I couldn't see it after the first flip but it sounded like it kept flipping all the way down the hill. I was pretty sure I didn't have to worry about those two cops any more.

But could I get out of the sand? The car had died so I started it and tried to back up the ramp through the sand. The ramp was just about level where I was stuck in it and with just a bit of maneuvering I was able to pull the car back up onto the highway and continue down Harper's Hill. I saw the cop car, totally demolished, in a ravine off the right side of the road. It was upside down and there was no way I was going to stop and see what the story was.

I had almost made it down the hill when I saw another set of carlights behind me roaring down the hill. It was the Jaynes' Mortuary hearse.

It was hitting about fifty and I had to make a quick decision: should I try to make it to Farmington and see how my story stood up against the mortician's and the judge's? Or should I do something else?

I was at the turnoff to the La Plata highway and took it, making a big sweeping left turn and heading north. Could my Squareback outrun the hearse? I was going to find out. I kicked it back up to 80 and was staying about 100 yards ahead of the hearse when I saw a big sign ahead saying "Glade Hill Road, 1 mile". It gave me an idea.

The hearse was still on my tail when I got to the junction. I turned right and was on the old road I knew so well that would take me to Chokecherry Canyon. I was surprised to see that instead of being the dirt road it used to be, it was now nicely paved and according to the signs would take me to Sunset Avenue, up by the high school! What the—? I didn't know the Glade Road connected to Sunset. Must be new.

But I saw the dirt road that led to Chokecherry Canyon heading off to the left off the paved highway and took it. If I had to make my stand, I was going to do it on my turf, and thanks to Billy's and my exploration days, I considered Chokecherry Canyon my turf.

The hearse followed me onto the dirt road, about 200 yards back.

Chokecherry Canyon

THE CANYON where the highschoolers had their keg parties was about two miles up the dirt road and I still had a lead on the hearse when I reached it and drove right next to the campfire site and stopped. There was no moon and it was almost pitch black but I knew the area well. I got out of the car and ran across the sooty ground to the edge of the 30-foot high sandstone rock formation. The hearse pulled next to my VW and I heard both doors open. By the dome light I could see that it was Jaynes and Judge Slinger who got out. It looked like the judge had a gun in his hand.

I was thinking that in this darkness there's no way they could see me crouched up against the rock when I saw a flashlight flicker on in Jaynes' hand. Damn! The light angled towards me and I ran farther down the edge of the sandstone and ducked into the crevice that we called Fat Man's Misery. They must have seen me just before I ducked in because I heard Jaynes give a shout and the light settled on the opening of the hole in the cliffside. I knew Fat Man's Misery well and climbed a little farther into it.

The hole in the rock was about the height of a man and it led into a small antechamber that was big enough for two or three people. But as you moved farther the only direction was up. If it had been daylight I could have seen, 25 feet above me, daylight through the opening in the mesa-top. But even though it was pitch dark I was able to climb to a position about fifteen feet above ground level where the internal opening was barely big enough for my torso.

Jaynes made it to the entrance to Fat Man's Misery first and shone his light up into it, revealing my feet on a shelf. Then I heard a wheezing Judge Slinger join him. I moved a few feet higher and the light was no longer on my feet.

"Come on out, Calhoon," I heard Jaynes yell and I kept quiet.

"It'll be easier for all of us if you come down now," the judge added, breathing as if he was on his deathbed.

"There's no way you'll let me walk, knowing all I know," I shouted down the tunnel, thinking that I didn't really know all that much. But they thought I did, I guess.

"What *do* you know?" the judge asked. "Maybe I should tell you everything and then I'll really have a good reason for killing you."

I didn't say anything and then I heard Jaynes stutter, "W-w-what do you mean, 'everything'?"

Slinger ignored him and spoke to me. "You don't think that the story ends with drugs and our little, uh, peccadillo, do you? You think *that* would make me want you to get out of town and never come back? I know who you are and I know what you're after." The judge was shouting into the opening of Fat Man's Misery standing next to Jaynes with the flashlight.

I was ready to ask, "What do you mean?" when I heard Jaynes ask, "What do you mean?"

"Get with the program, Marty, you know what I'm talking about. I'm talking about Calhoon's brother. He was the most beautiful specimen of manflesh I ever saw. I knew I had to have him and I would have too, sooner or later."

"Whaaaat?" Jaynes moaned and the flashlight veered away. "You—and Billy? My best friend?"

"Get real, you little pissant. What do you think turned me away from the living for my needs? The disappointment of not having what I craved more than anything else in the world—"

"You sonofabitch!" I heard the thunk of something metallic hitting against something fleshy and then the gun went off. Three times. The light went out.

I was sweating profusely even though it was a cool night. I waited on my perch inside Fat Man's Misery my mind roiling about these revelations, revelations that I may have suspected, but never knew enough about. Then I heard a huffing from directly inside the tunnel below. The flashlight stayed off.

"I can't see you, but I don't think I need to see you," came the puffing voice of Judge Slinger. He was entering the crevice.

I scuttled up a few more steps, trying to keep to the left where I would be hidden by a slight curve from the vestibule below. A shot rang out and I felt something hot whiz past my face and exit the opening at the top of Fat Man's Misery.

"Are you saying you killed my brother?" I yelled down the shaft, trying to buy some time.

"You know I did," came the wheezing reply from below. "You knew all along, didn't you? That's why you came back to town, isn't it?"

I was slowly moving farther up the tunnel, trying to be quiet about it. I didn't want to give my position away but I had to find out more. "But why?"

"I wanted him but he acted as if he didn't know I did. I used to see him around town and at the mortuary and he simply refused to understand my wants and needs. So I told him that there was a guy up at the Bolack well up on the Bisti that wanted him for a job and drove him up there. I had to kill him; he was driving me crazy."

I could hear him moving around, trying to find a good angle to fire at me once again and I moved several more feet up the shaft, almost to the top. He fired again and this time the bullet missed me by a couple of feet. I quietly slid over the top of the opening atop the mesa and poked my head down and yelled, "I'm stuck, judge, either shoot me or come and get me. I'm at the end of the tunnel." I was hoping that Judge Slinger didn't know anything about Fat Man's Misery.

I figured he only had one bullet left and wanted to make it a good one, and sure enough, I heard him climb up a few feet, trying to get past the curve that kept him from shooting me directly. I had him!

The reason they call the cave Fat Man's Misery is that it's pretty narrow about halfway up the 25-foot shaft. Too narrow for anyone any larger than my 180 pounds. But the miserable part of the shaft is that once you get about ten feet up the thing, it's almost impossible to get back down, not without falling the ten feet onto some really jagged rocks. Anyone of any heft would break both legs and a back trying to jump down.

The only way out—is up. And it's not for a Fat Man.

I stood up on top of the mesa and started trotting to the south along the top of the cliff. I had done this enough with Billy when we were teenagers to know where to step, even in the dark. Five minutes later I was back down to road level and five minutes after that I was back at my car. I could hear the judge yelling inside Fat Man's Misery.

I figured if I waited long enough I would hear the sound of the sixth bullet, but I didn't wait. I drove back down the dirt road and left onto the Glade Road heading to Sunset Avenue. If the bullet didn't end his misery, the varmints would. But then, maybe there would be a high school beer bust this weekend and the judge and the hearse would be found. And Jaynes' body, which I assumed was up by the entrance to the cave.

I didn't care. I drove through town to the Arrowhead Motel, picked up my suitcase and stuff and headed towards Bloomfield. I had three joints to get me to Las Cruces and the relative sanity of the bars. That ought to about do it.

On the way home I thought about Billy. I wasn't coming back to Farmington.

SIEGE ON MAIN STREET

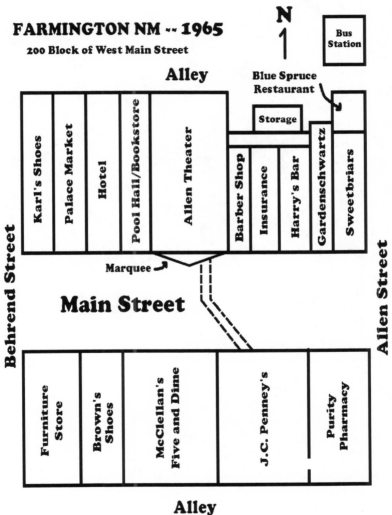

FARMINGTON NM ~ 1965

200 Block of West Main Street

N

Bus Station

Alley

Blue Spruce Restaurant

Storage

Karl's Shoes

Palace Market

Hotel

Pool Hall/Bookstore

Allen Theater

Barber Shop

Insurance

Harry's Bar

Gardenschwartz

Sweetbriars

Behrend Street

Allen Street

Marquee

Main Street

Furniture Store

Brown's Shoes

McClellan's Five and Dime

J.C. Penney's

Purity Pharmacy

Alley

Meeting of the Minds

A SINGLE CANDLE burned in the middle of a cheap wooden table, casting ominous shadows of three hulking figures against the adobe walls of the hogan. Outside, only the burping of hundreds of nascent bullfrogs interrupted the stillness of the desert air. Inside the hogan the three men sat facing each other, eyes wary and squinting. Finally, the man with the tallest shadow, emanating the odor of expensive Cordoba cigars, spoke:

"Dammit, Fantino, between the three of us we own half this town, and the best place you can find for a summit meeting is this crummy hogan?"

Elephantino Cimino, a short, bald man of Sicilian provenance, answered with a gust of garlic-scented breath:

"I'm tellin' ya, Ernie, the Baritone brothers ain't nobody to screw wit'. Both of 'em left Jersey t'ree days ago and dey may be in Farmington right now."

The third man, a swarthy Hispanic who resembled the tall man in facial features, but shorter in stature, blurted:

"Okay, guys, cool it down. We're all on the same side of the boat here. Nobody wants to meet up with the Baritones unprepared. That's why we're here. The question is, what do they want?" Zack Martinez looked at his brother, Ernie, and shrugged.

Fantino Cimino, owner of the Office Bar on East Main in Farmington, New Mexico, explained in his wheezing hack, "Dat's just it, guys. We don't know why they're comin' to town. All I know is dat my uncle from Hoboken called and said the Baritones are comin' wit' an offer we can't refuse."

Ernie, who with his brother owned the El Vasito Bar on West Main Street, scoffed, " 'Offer we can't refuse?' What the hell is that? It sounds like some crapola line from a bad B movie."

The volume of the frogs outside increased as the three men stared at each other in the candlelight. Zack broke the silence in the hogan: "Well, there's nothing we can do now. Let's just wait and see what they want. It may be somethin' as simple as wantin' us to buy our booze through their syndicate. They're syndicate, right?"

"Far as I know," Fantino said. "Hey, I ain't been back to Jersey in t'irty years. My kids all go to Cat'lic school here, fu'chrissakes. I ain't no mob guy."

"Yeah, but with a name like Cimino, every gringo in this town thinks you are," Zack laughed. They all chuckled and sat back in their wooden chairs.

Ernie lit a cigar and said, "Okay, we're settled then. We wait and see what the Baritones want. Now let's get outa here. I just hope I can find my way back to town in the dark. Next time, Fantino, let's meet in town somewhere. This hogan is ridiculous."

The three men exited the Navajo dwelling and got in their cars.

Changing the Marquee

"Gimme an 'F'."

The request came from a tall young man standing on the second highest rung of a 12-foot ladder as he leaned against the brightly lit white marquee of the Allen Theater in the 200 block of downtown Main Street.

Below, a short Hispanic male who looked a lot like a young Sal Mineo shuffled through a stack of red plastic letters then sputtered, "Whaddya mean, an 'F'? There's no 'F' in the movies for tomorrow."

"I was just goofing around, Willie. I figured I would stick an 'F' in place of the 'T" and leave my name up on the marquee for a while." The movie that was ending that night was a re-run from 1955 called *The Tender Trap* with Frank Sinatra and Debbie Reynolds and the two young marquee changers were notorious for temporarily displaying weird, and often obscene, words on the marquee as they changed the titles from the outgoing film to the upcoming film. The double feature for the next night was *The Terror* and *The Blob*, both of which they'd seen years before and had a hard time believing were coming back to the Allen. Steve McQueen, despite his odd style and facial features, was considered quite cool in Hollywood but the star of *The Terror* was a goofy-looking guy named Jack Nicholson, whom they were sure was going nowhere.

Fender, on the ladder, said, "Okay, let's get this show on the road." He looked a little bit like James Dean and the two chums often laughed at the fact that though they looked the part, they weren't at all like the two actors in *Rebel Without a Cause*, one of their favorite films. Willie then started tossing letters up to Fender and Fender tossed other letters down to Willie. Before long, the marquee read "*The Terror* AND *The Blob*". They liked it when the titles were short; it meant less work.

They did the same thing for the other side of the marquee. Unlike the Totah Theater, down the street to the west, the Allen had a double-sided marquee. Then they added "Steve McQueen" and "Jack Nicholson" to the two side panels of the marquee and that part of the job was finished. It was 11 o'clock on a Wednesday night and they were thinking about other things. They still had to staple the 3-foot by 4-foot posters for *The Terror* and *The Blob* over the posters for *The Tender Trap* in the display cases. Most nights after changing the marquee they liked to sit up in the balcony and have a drink and watch the end of the film that was being shown for the last time but there was no way they wanted to see a dog like *The Tender Trap*.

So after stapling up the posters and putting the ladder away in the slot right behind the glass door next to the theater doors they climbed the stairs up to the room where all of the letters were kept. This was their private sanctum, dusty beyond belief and just large enough to have a wall made of 40 or so slots for the letters of the alphabet, numbers and the various ampersands and other characters. If it rained hard, the letters would get cleaned off a bit while on the marquee but if there was a dust storm afterwards, and in March and April there just about always was, they became caked with dust which was then brought up to the letter room. It wasn't Fender and Willie's style to clean the letters.

"I'm up for some cherry brandy. What say you, Willie?"

"Damn, that cherry stuff is too sweet for me. I think I'll go for some mint gin."

"Ghaaak," Fender choked. "You can have all the mint gin you want. In fact, you can have all the gin you want, period. That stuff is nasty."

The two boys had just been graduated from Farmington High School that May and two months earlier they had made the discovery of their lives, two cases of various liqueurs in a small storehouse behind Harry's Bar, two doors down from the Allen Theater.

Willie climbed up the eight steps of a wooden ladder made of two-by-fours to a trapdoor in the ceiling of the room and, reaching under some insulation, pawed around until he found a half-pint of cherry brandy and a half-pint of Piping Rock mint gin. The labels had been half seared off but were still, in most cases, readable.

There had been a fire at Harry's bar a couple of years earlier and the two partly burned cases of booze, each holding 24 half-pint bottles of various brandies, gins and liqueurs, had been stored behind Harry's.

The trapdoor opened up onto the roof of the theater, and from there they could travel, catburglar-style, along the roofs of all of the buildings on that side of the block. The storehouse behind Harry's was easily accessible by jumping down off a catwalk behind the barber shop next door to the Allen into an enclosed alley behind the bar. There were signs in Spanish painted on the walls of the alley indicating that at one time this was *the* back entrance to Harry's. The ends had been sealed off years, maybe decades before, and now it opened only into the small storeroom where they found the two cases.

Ever since they made their discovery they had been enjoying a much classier kind of drunk than their high school compadres, who mainly drank beer that they managed to buy with the help of fake ID cards. During their senior school year they had only drunk on weekends but it was now late summer and they drank pretty much whenever they changed the marquee, two or three times a week.

They each took a swig out of their respective bottles and smacked their lips.

"Let's get outa here," Willie said and the two 18-year-olds, each with a half pint stuffed down the front of their pants, left the dusty room and went down the stairs to Main Street.

Most of their high school friends had cars but neither Fender or Willie did. They enjoyed walking and were able to get to anywhere they wanted in town. It just took them a little bit longer.

As they walked past the doors on Main, the theater, which was about to close, the barbershop, the Allen Insurance agency, Gardenschwartz Sporting Goods and Sweetbriars clothes store, they discussed their plans for the weekend.

"I have to work tomorrow and Friday at Monkey Ward," Willie said, "so I'll probably just stay home tomorrow night. How about Friday at the Vasito?" Willie had a day job working part-time at the Montgomery Ward mail order outlet on the 300 block of West Main next to Foutz's Trading Post.

"Sounds good to me. Nancy Lee and the Wee Three are still in town. I'll meet you at the Totah at nine, Friday." Because of

Fender's job changing the marquees at the theaters, they had a meeting place at both theaters: the letter rooms.

They turned the corner and headed north on Allen Street. As they steadily walked past the Allen Hotel, then turned right on Arrington to cut through the park by the library and across Apache onto Dustin by the Spudnut shop, they took occasional swigs from their bottles. Farmington was a quiet, lazy town, and the cops rarely patrolled that area, so they weren't worried about anything that late at night. Willie was spending the night at Fender's house and they were looking forward to watching some old movies on TV down in the den where there was bed and a couch, sleeping off their buzz till they were awakened by Fender's mother, Maxine, the next morning.

"Have a Tampa?" Willie asked, extending a pack of five cigars to Fender, who took two, giving one back to Willie. Hav-A-Tampas were cheap, sweet cigars that came in packs of five, and were the only things the boys smoked. They rarely finished a cigar, but they liked the wooden tip that each cigar sported, and the mildness of the smoke didn't bother their lungs. They didn't really inhale, anyway.

That summer, they had both registered for the draft and taken their physicals down in Albuquerque, and except for the ominous saber-rattling coming from the White House about some place called Vietnam, life was pretty damn good. Neither of them really had enough money for college, which was the only way for non-rich guys like them to stay out of the military—the National Guard was for the country club set—but the world seemed to lie ahead in all its glory. There was booze and there were girls, which the two had just started to look into seriously, after taking a couple of years to recover from eight years of guilt-riddled indoctrination by the Ursuline nuns at Sacred Heart school. They played in a band, The Torques, and although jobs for their band were few that summer, they had found that nobody really checked IDs at their two favorite bars in town, The Office and the El Vasito, so they could sit in with real, professional bands as often as they could make it down to the bars.

On the radio Bob Dylan wondered "How does it feeeeel?" but Fender and Willie were in a band and had enough booze to last until they got drafted. In 1965 it felt damn good to be 18 years old.

The Second Summit Meeting

"I CAN'T BELIEVE you talked me into coming out to this god-damned hogan again," Ernie Martinez grumbled. "I nearly drove my Lincoln into an arroyo the other night."

"Hey, you think my pickup likes these roads any better?" his brother Zack shot back.

"Wait'll you hear what I got to tell you about the Baritone brothers," wheezed Fantino Cimino. "Dey came to the bar las' night. Two guys. One looks like an ape and the udder looks like a weasel."

"So whadda they want?"

"Well, firs' they act all friendly and interduce me to this bald guy dey said was a brudder of Joe DiMaggio's. Vince, I t'ink his name was. He's a comedian. And wit' him wuz two chink strippers."

" 'Chink strippers?' What's that, guys who work on drywall?" Zack looked quizzical and his brother looked exasperated.

"No, you dum' ass," Fantino retorted, "Chink. You know, Chinese? Chinese babes who take off dere clothes."

"Oh."

"Anyways, we go back inta my office and dese guys, all in suits and ties an' stuff, dey tell me dat dere uncle back in Jersey wants to branch out wit' his strippin' bidness, an' wants me to start hirin' the DiMaggio guy and the strippers six nights a week to do dere t'ing when th' band goes on break."

"Like hell!" Ernie sputtered. "We pay the bands shit and now the mob wants us to start payin' comedians and strippers?"

Zack said, "Y'know, I don't think the mayor and the other Mormons on the town council are gonna go for that one bit."

"Ya tellin' me?" Fantino said. "A'course we don't wanna bring in anyt'ing dat costs more dan what we're payin' for now. But dese guys wuz packing heat, I tell ya. An' by de way, I called 'em 'Mr. Baritone', like t'ree syllables. Bear-it-tone, an' dey hopped all over my shit. It's Bear-it-to-*nee"*, four goddam syllables. Like how's I s'posed ta know? I'm Sicilian, but I been out here in the stinkin' desert most a my life."

"Okay, so these 'Bear-i-to-nee' brothers want you to stock strippers. What'd you say to 'em?" Ernie seemed to be amused as he lit up another of his vile cigars.

"I tole 'em I'd get back to 'em. Whaddya t'ink?"

"Hmmmm. Sounds like you got a problem, Fantino," Ernie mused as he blew out a huge plume of smoke.

Fantino chuckled. "You wish. Dey said dey'd be talkin' to the Martinez brothers nex'."

"Shit," the two Hispanics muttered in harmony.

The three men sat quietly in the smoky circular hogan, looking at each other and the dusty brown walls. Finally, Ernie stood up, threw his half-smoked cigar to the dirt floor and said, "Well, I guess we'll just have to see what the famous Bear-it-to-nee brothers have to say to us. Our customers come in to get drunk and feel up th' waitresses. I don't think havin' a couple of orientals takin' off their clothes would help sell booze at all."

Zack added, "An' I think the Mormons would get their underwear in an uproar. They can live with the dancin' and boozin' as long as it's the Mexis, Navvies and white trash doin' it, but oriental strippers're liable to draw in some a the saints. The cops would be all over us."

"Well, lemme know what happens," Fantino choked.

"An' dammit, Fantino! Ain't you ever heard a the telephone? Next time tell me what you gotta say on the phone. You think the mob has our phones tapped? The Mormons, maybe, but this is New Mexico, not Jersey. I don't ever wanna see this damn hogan again. Ever."

For the second night in a row, three vehicles left dusty tracks in the dirt road, somewhere on the Navajo reservation.

Friday Night at the El Vasito

FENDER AND WILLIE had a quick snort of peach brandy, killing off the half-pint and threw it in the trash can in the letter room on the second floor above the Totah Theater. This room was exactly like the letter room at the Allen, perhaps not quite as dusty, filled with 10-inch red plastic letters and rolled up posters of past shows, to be returned to the distribution company that supplied theaters throughout the west.

It was 9 o'clock on Friday night and the boys were getting restless. Willie had worked all afternoon and was looking for some excitement. Fender had slept most of the day, getting over a hangover from the Everclear he had drunk the night before in the balcony at the Allen while watching *The Terror* and *The Blob*. He got into all shows free—and had since he started the marquee job when he was thirteen—so he pretty much saw everything that came to town, even crummy movies like *The Tender Trap*. He had needed a little bump from the Everclear to get over the weirdness of Jack Nicholson and Boris Karloff hamming their way through the senseless plot of *The Terror*.

"Let's head on out to the Vasito," Fender said and they left the room, saying hello to Carl Ferre who was running the projectors in the room next door to the letter room. Mr. Ferre was one of their favorite high school teachers and he moonlighted as a projectionist, mostly during the summer months. They walked down the stairs, dodging the 12-foot ladder that was kept on the stairway, and strode on out to Main Street, which was abuzz with cars, most of them high school kids dragging Main.

Main Street in Farmington was the main drag, and on weekends and pre-holiday nights there was a constant stream of Mustangs, Chevys, Oldsmobiles, pickups and those weird little new cars called Volkswagens that made the circuit from the Tastee-Freez on the west (next door to the El Vasito) to the A&W on the east.

Fender and Willie knew they could probably hitch a ride to the Tastee-Freez if they walked west on Main but it was such a beautiful, warm Indian summer night they decided to cut a block south and walk out Broadway instead. There was never any traffic on Broadway at night and the dark businesses and homes provided a slightly ominous air as they walked, talking about the Doc Savage or Shell Scott books they had read. They used to talk about pool, but ever since they turned 18, and the pool hall was now legal for them to enter, they rarely played.

There was sort of a "three-year rule" they followed. When they were 12 they were into pinball, because the pinball palace, Don's News Stand on the 100 block of West Main, was considered verboten to anyone under the age of 15. So they became pinball fanatics and spent all their nickels on the superb mechanical games by Gottlieb and Bally. When they turned 15 they put pinball behind them and took up pool, because the Snooker 8, on the 100 block of East Main, beckoned them with its stated age limit of 18. It was a grand place, where customers could cuss at will, and order Pete and Bert, the two rotund managers of the place, to rack their balls for them for a quarter a game. The two boys hoped that even if Man left the earth in spaceships to the moon and the planets, that somehow the Snooker 8 would be caught in a time warp and still be around for centuries.

So they played pool practically every day of their lives during high school and when they turned 18 they tried the El Vasito and the Office Bar, because the drinking age in New Mexico was 21. To their great pleasure, they were never carded at the door of either bar and the two dives became their favorite nighttime haunts.

From time to time they talked about what would happen when they turned 21 and would have to find something else forbidden, and shuddered to think it might be something really sleazy like politics or organized religion. But that was in the future. Tonight was a night for drunken revelry and sittin' in with the band at the Vasito.

Fifteen minutes later they pushed back the double doors of the El Vasito, a squat, one-story adobe-looking building on West Main shaped as if two hexagons had been mashed together at one vertex. The din of the music, the pong of the booze and urine, and the industrial-strength smog of 100 cigarettes hit them like a sack of wet monkey-chow and their eyes watered up, blinding them for a few minutes as they felt their way to their left into the gringo side of the bar.

The El Vasito had been the most infamous dive on the west side of Farmington for decades. Often called "the Bucket of Blood", it had made its peace with the races years back with a pragmatic compromise: the left half of the bar, with the dance floor and bandstand and the Martinez's office, was for gringos. The right side, with its dark atmosphere and long, severe wooden tables and benches, was for Navajos. The Mexicans, by dint of their nebulous swarthiness, could get drunk in either side but were advised to do their most serious debauchery with the whites. It was simply safer that way.

Willie and Fender had been in the bar a dozen times but had never set foot into the Navajo half of the bar.

"Hey, Fender and Willie!" shouted the short, chubby, vivacious woman on the bandstand, thumping a cheap bass guitar as the tall guitar picker on her left, Vern Earnshaw, threw down some James Brown riffs on the George Jones song they were playing. Vern looked a lot like Buddy Holly, but goofier, and knew all the Chuck Berry licks so well he stopped playing them and simply played as if he was backing up James Brown. Somehow, even on the hokiest country and western song, he made it fit.

The bass player was Nancy Lee Jourdan and the band was Nancy Lee and the Wee Three. Nancy's husband Bill played steel guitar and stood at the back of the bandstand on her right looking like a silver-haired model out of Esquire magazine. A dipsomaniac model, to be sure, but in his silver dinner jacket he was by far the most dapper person in the bar. Maybe the whole town. Bill was once voted the fourth best steel man in country music by some magazine, back when he was playing with the Miller Brothers out of Wichita, but to Fender and Willie, he was the *only* steel guitar player in the world. They didn't know much about country and western music, except what they picked up here in the Vasito and at the Office Bar, but if they could ever learn to play the notes Bill did on his steel, they knew they would have it made playing rock & roll.

The two boys pushed their way past the packed dance floor to the bar at the left of the bandstand and ordered a beer each. They nodded to Nancy who was singing the whiney George Jones melody like a truckstop diva, phrasing the song like that straight-arrow Willie Nelson guy who wrote such great songs but had a little trouble sounding like a country & western singer.

All the tables were filled, and the dance floor was too, so Fender and Willie decided to just stand at the bar and listen to the band, nursing their beers. They didn't like beer all that much, but it was the cheapest thing on the menu and they felt they owed it to the bar to spend at least a little money.

Nancy brought the song to a climactic finish and the drummer, Tommy Bee, a disk jockey by day and booze connoisseur by night, announced that they were taking a fifteen-minute break. "Drink up! It's good for ya!" he yelled as the band members put their guitars down and exited the bandstand through a gate in the fence protecting the band from the crowd.

Fender saw Nancy and Bill join Zack and Ernie Martinez by the door to the office, then Vern came over to Willie and started talking about some new songs he had heard down at Everybody's Club the previous Monday, the band's night off. Everybody's was a negro joint on the south side of town which served some great barbeque and had the best jukebox in town, filled with rhythm and blues songs by singers and groups never heard on the city's four country & western radio stations. Not even on KOMA out of

Oklahoma City, which just about everybody in town listened to, could you hear such music. Willie went to Everybody's from time to time but Fender had never had the nerve. Willie's Sal Mineo looks afforded him some protection from the more suspicious denizens of the club, but Fender was so whitebread he wasn't sure he'd ever walk out, if he ever walked in.

Nancy left the conversation with Ernie and Zack and wandered over to the bar and ordered a whiskey straight and said to Fender and Willie, "Hey, young fellers, ya wanna do a couple a tunes?" She knew they did. She had been in the bar business for about ten years, ever since she was a teenage prodigy on the Nashville circuit, and was as jaded as they came. She married Bill because he was the handsomest, hard-drinkingest, best steel player she'd ever heard and they settled down to playing the Ken Gist western circuit, which meant a lot of miles to travel, but low-key, easy clubs to get drunk in.

"You bet, Nancy," Fender piped up, and handed her her drink from the bar. "We haven't done any pickin' since we sat in with you guys last week."

"Okay, give us a couple to settle the place down and we'll get you guys up." Then she and Vern and Bill and Tommy wandered back to the bandstand and started to play the next set.

Fender and Willie stood at the bar and soaked up the notes that Vern was playing on his Stratocaster, wondering when they would ever be able to play like that, and then after a couple of dance tunes Nancy yelled, "Hey, guys, come on up and pick somethin' for us!" The two climbed up on the bandstand through the gate and Fender took the Strat from Vern. Willie strapped on a Gibson ES-335 that Vern kept on the bandstand for playing on some down-home country songs. Nancy then shouted into the microphone, "Hey, let's hear it for a couple a young locals, Fender and Willie!" and about half of the crowd clapped more or less enthusiastically.

Fender murmured something to Bill and Tommy and then started off with the opening lick to "Johnny B. Goode." Willie came in with his favorite rhythm and the race was on. Luckily Tommy the drummer was having none of it and kept the beat fairly steady throughout the song, accompanied by Nancy's solid bass line. Fender and Willie jumped out ahead of the beat and stayed there, their guitars panting to inch out even more of a lead. Bill, on a non-pedal steel, played super-high notes that sounded like young girls screaming out of control. And the dust kicked up by the dancing cowboys and cowgirls and injuns and squaws was sort of like something that might come from a fog machine, if there was such a thing.

Fender played a pretty standard solo and during it he noticed that a couple of odd men sitting at a table near the office—one large, one small, each wearing slick business suits—got up and walked to the office door where they knocked and were soon admitted. No one seemed to notice that Fender's solo meandered more than usual.

Three minutes later the song was mercifully over and someone on the dance floor croaked, "Play the Bird."

Other voices mumbled their agreement and Willie put down his guitar and took the mike off its stand. This was getting to be their standard finale song; it had an easy-to-sing-along-with melody and for some reason the Navajos seemed to find a deep meaning in the words "Pa-pa-ooh-mau-mau."

Willie began with the sputtering a capella intro and the band triumphantly entered at the part that seemed to inspire—or was it enrage?—the Navajos so much. The beat to "Surfin' Bird" was actually the same as Willie's favorite beat so he was able to completely immerse himself in the role as singing Trashman. Just before he began the final sputter of "ba-ba-ba-ba"s that climaxed in the final "pa-pa-ooh-mau-mau" sequence, he threw himself down on the floor of the bandstand, knocking the gate open. From on his back he belted the refrain, and Fender noticed that just before Willie arose for the final babbling, he got a quizzical look on his face, then a hollow, scared look. Veteran entertainer that he was, Willie finished the song with his usual aplomb.

The crowd applauded loudly and Nancy yelled something in the mike as Fender handed the Strat back to Vern, who was laughing at the high weirdness of "Surfin' Bird" being the big song at the El Vasito. But he had an answer for it. He was able to do a spot-on version of the Newbeats' "Bread and Butter" with the annoying falsetto part, backed up by Bill and Nancy on the chorus. The crowd loved it and soon forgot all about "Surfin' Bird." It was just a momentary peak in the adrenaline graph of life at the El Vasito.

Fender and Willie didn't want another drink so they thanked the band with hand signals and headed towards the door. Fender asked, "Hey, what was that all about during the Bird?"

Willie muttered under his breath, which was pretty loud with the band playing, "Not now. See those two guys comin' out of the office?"

"Yeah." It was the two guys in suits.

"Don't look! Let's get outta here."

The two made the door and without looking back shot out into the hot September night. The parking lot was dimly lit by two poles with 100-watt bulbs hanging down but it was easy for them to wend their way through the cars to the south, towards Broadway. One car stood out. A silver and black 1965 Cadillac Coupe de Ville with New Jersey plates.

"Shit!" Willie spat. "That's probably their car. C'mon, let's go."

They were just passing the Caddy when they heard a shout from behind them, near the entrance to the bar. They looked back to see two men, a tall one and a short one, start to run towards them. Fender and Willie hopped a short fence and ran to Broadway, keeping close to the shadows of the houses and businesses on the north side of the street.

They crossed Schwartz Street and as they ducked behind a house they saw the Caddy turn from Main onto Schwartz, its headlights blazing like the fiery eyes of a crazed bull. They ran further into the yard and vaulted over a chain link fence, a dog yapping at them from the back porch. They saw the light of the Caddy veer to the east on Broadway so they headed north through another back yard until they came out on Main Street by the old bowling alley, which had recently been converted into a Western Auto store. They figured the men in the Cadillac would come back to Main so they kept in the shadows as much as possible, passing the Spudnut shop and approaching François Restaurant from the west.

"Quick!" Fender whispered breathlessly. "Behind François." They could hear the screech of the wheels of a big car making fast turns and they just made it behind the west wall of the restaurant as the Caddy screamed by on Main, heading back towards the El Vasito. Behind the restaurant, which was owned by the Kelloff's, old friends of Fender's mother, was a copse of trees and vines. Fender and Georgina, the Kelloff girl who was about his age, had played there when they were kids. The old trails were not so well-defined as they had been a decade before, but they were still there and it was easy, even in the dark, to find their way deep enough inside the thicket that they felt safe from the guys in the car.

"What the hell is going on?" Fender finally gasped and Willie laughed.

"I don't know, but those guys are not from Farmington."

"Why are they chasing us? What did you see?"

"Hold on, lemme get my breath. Did you notice those guys sitting at a table at the Vasito?

"Yeah, I did. Then they went into the office. To see Zack and Ernie, I figured."

"Yeah, well, when I was laying down singing the Bird I happened to look that way just as the door to the office opened a crack. The light was on inside and I saw those two guys in there— and the big one had a gun pointed at Zack!"

"You're shittin' me!"

"No, and that's not the worst part." Willie paused for dramatic effect, something which pissed off Fender regularly. "The other guy, the weaselly one, he looked right at me at the same time. He knows I saw him."

"What kinda gun?"

"Hell if I know! Would it make any difference? We don't know anything about guns."

"You're right. Hmmmm. We got a problem."

From their hideaway in the copse of trees they heard the screech of tires heading east on Broadway, then continue into the distance.

Willie spoke up. "I think that was them. Let's take a dark way back to your house and hope we never see those guys again."

"Yeah. Maybe they don't really know what we look like."

"Right. They only saw us on the bandstand."

Fender wasn't sure if Willie was being sarcastic or not. The two chums found their way out of the trees and shrubbery and cut across Main and took Gladeview up to Comanche, then across to Dustin, Hopi and Monterey. All in all, it had been a pretty good night.

The Hogan Again

THE LONE CANDLE cast shaky shadows as the short, portly Sicilian jiggled the table with his stomach. "So you never want to see dis place again, eh, Ernie?"

Ernie Martinez cursed furiously as he tried to light his cigar. "Goddammit, Zack. Gimme a light!" His brother reached out his lighter and soon the Cuban Claro was making the room brighter with each puff.

"It wasn't funny, Fantino. The big guy pulled a gun on us—in our own club." Zack wasn't used to being the calm, cool brother but Ernie hadn't really recovered from the night before.

"Yah, I know. Dese guys must mean bidness. So, are you gonna go along wit' the stripper program?" The Sicilian seemed resigned.

"Hell, no!" shouted Ernie. "You think we'd be able to stay open past the next town council meeting if we started running Chink strippers every night of the week?"

Zack piped up. "The little guy said it might just be weekends."

"It doesn't matter. The cops would be all over us. Half the Navajos never had an ID in their lives, and you know that if the cops are hangin' around, a lot of the best drinkers in town are gonna move somewhere else."

"Yah, but dey got guns."

"That's right, Fantino, they got guns." Ernie rubbed his chin nervously. "I could tell the police chief, but it's our word against theirs."

"One t'ing for sure," Fantino said, "dey ain't got permits to carry dem concealed in a bar. Not since the big shootout at the Turquoise Bar."

"Yeah," Zack noted, "but they may be too smart to get caught with them. And let's face it, Farmington's Finest ain't the sharpest needles in the haystack."

"Damn I hate this place!" Ernie groaned.

"Yeah, so why'd you call me up an' tell me ta meet you here—" Fantino began.

"Because the goddam *Bear-it-to-nee* brothers are pointin' guns at us and tellin' us we gotta use their strippers. Sometimes a hogan can be the safest place in the world. Nobody but us assholes would ever come here." He groaned again, and as the three men exited the Navajo dwelling, threw his cigar against a wall.

"Goddam place doesn't even have a corner," he muttered.

The three vehicles made their way through the desert back to Farmington.

A Pair of Pants

THE NEXT DAY, Saturday, Fender and Willie woke up late and, since Willie had to put in a few hours at Montgomery Ward, decided to kill some time at the library. They walked to the large new brick building on Orchard, next door to the small rock house where the library of Fender's youth was. There they strolled up and down the aisles looking for titles that promised more than the typical library fare of the day. And of, course not finding anything. They didn't really expect to.

Back in the 50s young Fender was even more curious about anything dealing with sex and had one day spotted a book that appeared to be well-read and intriguing. It had a black taped spine with the title scrawled on it in the white ink apparently reserved for black spined books. SEDUCTION OF THE INNOCENT by a Dr. Frederic Wortham. That looked hot!

And in a way it was. Even at the age of ten Fender knew that there was controversy about sex. Some people, like the nuns, priests, parents and city officials he knew, were against sex. Others, like anyone who had ever written a book, seemed to think sex was some pretty good stuff. Fender was inclined to side with the latter.

But when he opened SEDUCTION OF THE INNOCENT, he found that it was a 200-page rant against comic books—and Fender loved comic books. But the comics mentioned in the book were like none that he'd ever seen. He was partial to Superman, Batman, Plastic Man, Blackhawk, Uncle Scrooge, and for some strange reason he could not put a finger on, Little Lulu. The comics discussed in the book seemed to be of the horror type that he found boring. The text of the book was obviously the kind of preaching he'd had plenty of at St. Thomas' School for four years, so he ignored the text and mainly enjoyed the many pictures found in the book. These were panels from old EC Comics—which Fender had never seen—that showed over-the-top sadism and sexuality that were laughable, even to his ten-year-old sex-hungry brain.

Fender had shown the book to Willie years before and they always got a kick out thumbing through its pages, wondering how an obviously sex-confused hack like Wertham ever got published. But as they learned more about the ways of the world and saw how the forces of censorship and prudery led to Lyndon Johnson and that country over in Asia that was always in the news, Viet Nam, they realized that there was a good chance that the nuns, priests and parents of the world would prevail. Oh well, the thought just made the half pints of booze they were drinking regularly go down easier.

Both of the boys realized that their chortling over the naïvete of the Werthams of the world was a cover-up for what was really bothering them—the two guys with guns that had chased them the night before. They talked it over but they simply didn't have enough information to know what to do, other than be very careful when hanging out at the El Vasito.

Around three in the afternoon Willie needed to leave for Ward's and Fender walked with him downtown. He wanted to buy a pair of Levis and he usually bought them at J.C. Penney, across Main from the Allen Theater. Willie continued down Main and Fender entered the large, well-lit department store, one of the most modern stores in Farmington.

He rarely bought anything except Levis so he knew exactly where to go. After picking up a pair of 30 waist 33 length Levis he took them to a counter with the best looking woman behind it. He took out his wallet to give her a $5 bill and was surprised when she asked, "Are you sure you want those?"

He looked at her quizzically and she said, "The new Levis are available; I thought you might want them instead."

"What are new Levis?" Fender asked. The woman, about 30 with a large beehive hairdo and what appeared to Fender to be 38-inch, C-cup breasts, smiled back at him.

"They're essentially the same, but instead of those buttons on the, uh, fly, they have a zipper."

Fender shuddered a little then stammered, "That sounds dangerous. No, I think I'll stick with the old, regular Levis." The conversation was heading in a direction that made him nervous. He was calm and cool with cocktail waitresses but older women, especially friendly older women, unnerved him, even though he sought them out whenever he could.

The woman laughed. "Sure, Sweetie. That'll be, let's see," — checking a tax table—"four dollars and forty-two cents."

Fender handed her the $5 bill and she wrote up a charge slip and clamped the slip and the bill to a little metal cup attached to a set of taut wires that led up to the second floor balcony. There were wires at every counter in the store, all leading up to the second floor, where the finances were kept. She pulled a lanyard and the small gondola-like cup whizzed up the wire.

"Are you sure you don't need any socks, a shirt, perhaps some underwear?" the woman said, knowing that her breasts were wreaking havoc with Fender's hormones, but enjoying the power.

"Naw, not today," he gulped. "Just the Levis, uh, with the buttons."

She laughed again and wrapped the pants in thin brown wrapping paper, tied it with string and handed it to Fender.

While they were waiting for Fender's change an employee in a business suit walked up and handed the woman a set of keys. He mumbled something to her and walked to the back of the store and the stairs that led up to the accounting department. She slipped the ring, which held about twenty keys, on a nail behind the sales counter.

Just then the gondola came whizzing back down the wire with the receipt and change. She handed them to Fender and said, "You know, you're one of the last customers to get your change from these things. Next week Penney's is switching over to a new, electrical system with cash registers on every pay counter. I kind of hate to see the wires go."

"I know what you mean. One of these days I may not be able to get jeans with buttons."

They smiled at each other wistfully and Fender tucked the package under his arm and left J.C. Penney's. He headed east and was passing by the door of Purity Pharmacy, next door to Penney's and felt a pang of thirst. He turned into the store and checked out the revolving rack of 35 cent paperbacks, mostly Perry Mason and Brett Hallidays, before walking back, past the pharmacist with his wall full of potions, into the soda fountain. He sat in a booth, setting the package beside him, and ordered a strawberry milkshake.

"Stick 'em up!" a voice rasped in his ear and Fender jumped in shock. Then he breathed a big sign of relief as Willie scooted into the booth facing him.

"Damn, Willie, this is not a good time to be kidding about sticking 'em up. What the hell are you doing here?"

"They didn't need me today and I saw you turning in here. Hey, that shake looks good. Think I'll have one." Willie caught the counter girl's eye and mouthed "Chocolate shake."

"So what are we going to do tonight? I don't think the Vasito is a good place. Those assholes in suits may be there." Fender slurped his straw noisily.

"Don't you have to change the marquee tonight?"

"Hey, you're right. Both of 'em. How about we do that then maybe hit the Office late?"

"I don't know if I want to stay out too late. Can I stay at your house again?" Willie's parents knew that on nights when he helped Fender change the marquee he was probably staying at the Tuckers'.

"Sure, but what'll we do till then? *The Flight of the Phoenix* is playing at the Totah but we've seen that a couple of times. I assure you you don't want to see *The Terror.*"

Willie looked thoughtful. "How about we walk on out to the Office now? Kill a little time and have a burger at George & John's then change the marquees and call it a night?"

"Sounds good. But lemme drop these pants off at the Allen. I'll pick 'em up tonight when we change the marquee."

The waitress brought Willie's shake and gave him a big smile. Fender shook his head. Willie sure did play his resemblance to Sal Mineo for all it was worth. But what the hell, it worked.

They finished their shakes and left Purity Pharmacy and crossed the street to the Allen Theater and the letter room. It was a long walk out to the Office Bar but they were 18 and time was endless. And there never has been a more delicious meal than a giant hamburger with green chile from George & John's. For any price.

The Office Bar

THE SUN was going down behind them as they approached the Office Bar. It had a big marquee saying that the Hatch Brothers were appearing and that "cold beer" was available. Fender and Willie knew that the band didn't start until 9 P.M. but they figured they could kill a couple of hours here before changing the marquee at 10.

They entered through the package liquor store in front and said hello to Elephantino Cimino, the owner. He didn't really know their names but he recognized them as the two kids who sang those annoying songs with the bands every now and then. The crowd seemed to like it and they drank as much, if not more, when the boys were singing, so what the hell.

"Hey, guys. You here to see the show?"

"What show?" Fender looked at Willie out of the corner of his eye.

"We're tryin' somethin' new. We got a comedian and some strippers. Dey're gonna do dere t'ing pretty soon—before da band starts. Lemme know what you t'ink."

"Sure thing, Fantino. It sounds, uh, interesting."

Fantino turned to wait on a customer and Fender and Willie strode to the door that led to the dance room behind the liquor store. It was dark and the juke box was playing a Merle Haggard tune pretty loud but the boys had no trouble wending their way to their favorite table, by the door on the west wall, which was the main entrance for the dance hall. It was especially dark in the nook where their table was, but they had a good view of the band-stand.

They each ordered a beer and were getting relaxed in the smoky, thick atmosphere when the door in front of them opened and in walked a huge man and a much smaller man, in shiny, sleek suits, followed by a man with a muskrat on his head and a nymphet on each arm. Fender and Willie instinctively ducked deeper into the shadow and watched warily as the five human beings found a table near the dance floor, twenty feet in front of them.

The table was well lit and once the five ordered their drinks Fender and Willie could observe them in detail. The big man, who looked a bit like a swarthy Tor Johnson, was bald, and had a loud, grating voice that carried all the way to other tables. The small man had a distinct rodent-like air about him, and even though the hiss of his voice cut through the thrum of the room like a razor, one got the impression that no one, including the people he was speaking to, understood a single word. The man with the muskrat on his head, which they finally realized was a toupee, was about six feet tall and appeared uncomfortable to be sitting with Tor and his pet weasel. The two other shapes at the table were more in-scrutable. They seemed to be small, skinny women but the various flowing robes they wore covered everything but their faces, which were billboards for make-up, with every inch covered by something white or black, with maybe a thin line of blood for the lips.

The table the fivesome were sitting at was perfectly placed and unless the two Baritone brothers walked directly towards them, they were safe from discovery. So the boys sat back, ordered another beer and surveyed the Office Bar. They had seen several good bands there, and the Hatch Brothers, out of Las Cruces, were among the best, but they had never dreamed of seeing comedy and strippers in Farmington.

It was 9 P.M. when the juke box was unplugged and a spotlight pointing at the middle of the dance floor came on. Then the guy with the toupee got up and stood in the spotlight with a mike on a cable.

"Thanks for the wonderful introduction, it meant a lot to me. I'm Vince DiMaggio, you might know my brother, Joe. My other brother, Dom, and I used to play a little ball, too, but there's no business like show business, Joe always used to say." His opening set the mood for the rest of the show, which consisted of jokes that might have gone over in the Catskills. But Farmington was not a Catskills kind of town. The crowd was polite, though, and laughed several times, and especially liked his version of the Mexican standard, "El Rancho Grande" which he played quite well on the guitar. Vince's version:

I am el Rancho Grande
I got the gonorrheeee-ah.
   (in a high whistle) "Syph, toooooo!"
I got it from Maria
She gave it to me free-ah
And now I cannot peeeeee-ah.

Ten minutes later the agony was over and the Hatch Brothers filed up to the bandstand. Then Vince walked back onto the dance floor and announced, "Ladies and gentlemen, the Office Bar presents for your voyeuristic pleasures two enchanting jewels of the Orient, two exotic princesses of the rising sun, two intriguing treasures of the Forbidden City: Ming Toy and Jaylo Mein!"

The band kicked in to a rousing rendition of *Woolly Bully* and the two women seated at the table threw off a robe or two and strutted to risers on each side of the bandstand. The bass player and the guitar player had to help the girls onto the risers so the music dropped out a bit but by the first chorus the two Asian products were doing Ed Wood-like dances with strips of thick cloth covering their breasts and loins. Halfway through the song, the strips were cast off and Ming Toy and Jaylo Mein were down to their bikini tops and bottoms, thrusting in vaguely sexual ways at Farmingtonians who thought that some of Conway Twitty's songs "went too far."

The girls did three songs, including a slow number, and everybody seemed to be thankful when it was all over and the band went back to playing dance music for drunks to make time to. The high point came on the third song, Johnny Horton's *Honky-Tonk Hardwood Floor*, when a three-foot long string of beads that Jaylo was twirling around her neck came apart and hundreds of marble-sized beads flew out into the crowd on the dance floor. Until all of the beads were found it was pretty dangerous dancing unless you shuffled your feet more than usual.

By 9:30 Fender and Willie had had enough and exited through the door to the liquor store. The Baritones and their entourage were still at their table near the dance floor.

"So whaddy t'ink?" Fantino wheezed from behind the cash register.

"Uh, I don't like it," Fender said. "The comedian guy was okay but I hope he comes up with some better jokes for his other shows."

"Hah!" Fantino exclaimed. "Dey did t'ree shows last night. Each one he tells the same lousy jokes."

"Damn, Fantino, they must think you got some kinda revolving crowd here," Willie said. "Hell, every time I come here I see the same ol' people."

"Dat's right. Dat's what I tried to tell dese guys. Dey're from back Eas' and dey're puttin' the pressure on me ta turn the Office inta a strip joint."

"So that's what it's all about," Fender murmured. "We saw them out at the Vasito, too."

"Yeah, Zack 'n' Ernie got the same problem. Da main t'ing is, if we got strippers, we gotta have more cops hangin' around." He looked at the two boys shrewdly, and continued. "Dat ain't good for nobody, ain't dat right?"

"You got dat, er, that right," Willie said. "Cops ain't good for anybody."

They said goodbye to the bar owner and left the bar to find a dark, cool evening—and a long walk to downtown where two movie theater marquees beckoned. They saw the Coupe de Ville in the parking lot but this time no one came running out of the bar after them. They decided, anyway, to return to downtown via a southern route, a dirt road that paralleled Main all the way to Vine Street. It was dustier and harder to navigate in the dark than Main Street would have been but they didn't want to chance being seen by the Baritone brothers, without or without their rugged and Asiatic entourage.

Saturday Night Changing Marquees

IT WAS AROUND 10:20 when they made downtown and decided to do the Totah first. The new feature was one that Fender and Willie had been waiting for: *Help!* with the Beatles. Not only was it packed with terrific songs but it was one of the shortest-titled movies ever. The Totah had a set of huge black-painted letters, made out of Masonite and three times the size of the regular red plastic ones, to be used when the title is short enough.

The two marquee changers kept an eye out for the Coup de Ville as they quickly put up the four letters (and the exclamation mark) on the front marquee and added "John" and below it "Paul" to one side panel and "George" and "Ringo" to the other panel. Then they stapled up the new posters and practically ran across the street and down the block to the Allen. No Coup de Ville.

The new feature at the Allen Theater was *The Killers,* a remake of the 1946 film based on an Ernest Hemingway story, this time starring Lee Marvin, Angie Dickinson and Ronald Reagan. The boys were on a roll with the short titles and by midnight the marquee was done and Lee and Angie had made it to the two side panels. They despised Ronald Reagan so they decided to not give him a mention.

While they were working, the final showing of *The Blob* ended and a dozen people streamed out of the theater. A few minutes later, Mary Crawford, the night manager of the theater, locked the lobby doors and said good night to them as she walked to her car, parked in front of Gardenschwartz Sporting Goods. It was typical for Fender and Willie to work past the closing time of the theater.

The boys had done the posters first and Fender was atop the ladder placing the last letter up when Willie spotted an ominous black vehicle coming down Main from the east. He instinctively turned his head away from the car and yelped up to Fender to watch out. Fender was climbing down the ladder as the Coup de Ville drove by, one of the two or three cars that drove by every time the light at the corner of Allen and Main changed. Fender had just closed the ladder and was taking it to the slot in the wall by the glass door that led up to the letter room when they heard a loud shout, "Arresto!" followed by, "Che cosa?" as the Caddy screeched to a halt. It was about thirty yards down Main and just as the passenger door opened and a small, rat-faced man jumped out, Fender and Willie put away the ladder and ran up the stairs to the letter room.

They passed Carl Ferre who was closing the door to the projection room. "I'm locking things up, you two," he said. "You need to get into the lobby again?"

"Naw," said Fender, "go ahead and lock the glass door downstairs. We have some cleaning up to do and I'll lock it with my key when we go."

Ferre nodded his assent and continued down the stairs.

"Quick," Willie whispered and ran into the letter room where he climbed up the ladder to the trapdoor in the roof. Fender threw him the key to the Master padlock and within seconds Willie was on the roof. He ran to the parapet that ran the length of the front of the theater, above the marquee, and cautiously peered down. He saw Mr. Ferre talking to two men in suits, the Baritone brothers. They had parked their Caddy in front of Karl's Shoe Store on the corner of Behrend and Main.

Willie was soon joined by Fender and they strained to hear what was being said below.

"No," Carl Ferre was saying, "the theater is closed for the night."

"Yeah, but what about those two guys? The ones with the ladder?" The large Baritone brother's voice carried up to the roof easily.

Ferre was no fool, and sensing that something was not right about these two, replied, "Oh, those two. They're probably leaving through the rear exit of the theater. The front doors are locked."

He walked off towards his car, which was parked around the corner on Allen by the Blue Spruce Restaurant, and the smaller Baritone took off the other direction, rounding the corner by Karl's, then racing down Behrend to the alley behind the 200 block of Main Street. He ran down the alley to the back door of the theater and tried the door, which was locked.

From above Fender and Willie watched the larger Baritone, whom they assumed was named "Resto" because that's what they heard the weaselly brother yell out to the driver. The smaller brother must be "Chickosa" because that's what Resto answered. Resto paced around in front of the glass door next to the theater, looking around at the deserted block, and peering closely at the odd car that was dragging Main. It was after midnight and the traffic was down to just a few cars.

Soon Chickosa approached from the west. He had walked completely around the block, using the alley. The two boys ducked back as he spoke to Resto. "I don't think they had time to go out the back. I tried the door and it sounds like it's locked on the inside with a chain and a lock. How could they have locked the door if they came out the back?"

"So those punks are still in the theater, eh?"

"I think so.

"So whadda we do?"

"We wait."

"In that case, lemme go back and jam something in the back exit. I'll make it so they *can't* go out the back. You stay here and keep an eye out."

Chickosa once again ran west on Main and turned up to the alley.

"Damn," whispered Fender, "Maybe we should have gone out the back while we could."

"Maybe so, but we have some options, Fender. We know this place better'n anyone." Willie's upper lip curled into an Elvis-like snarl as he said it and Fender knew what he meant. The two had spent the whole previous year exploring the north side of the 200 block of Main Street. Ever since they discovered the trapdoor leading to the roof of the theater, from where they could jump onto the roofs of any of the stores on that block, they had spent many nights figuring out which businesses they could get into and which they couldn't. They weren't interested in any physical goods— except booze—but they enjoyed the power of being able to go to forbidden places.

Fender muddled this around for a few seconds and then said, "Let's go across the street."

Willie smiled, "I thought you'd never ask."

The Siege Begins

ONE NIGHT THAT SPRING, when Fender and Willie were changing the marquee after everyone else had gone home, they had filled up with candy from the snack bar and were lounging in the dark in the back row of the theater, sipping on cokes. "You know, Willie, there's one place in this theater we haven't really checked out yet. What's behind that door right next to the men's room?"

Willie had noticed it before, and had even glanced into the room, seeing it to be a janitor's room of some sort. "Janitor closet, I think," he said.

They finished their candy bars and picked up a big flashlight from behind the ticket booth, then went to the wooden door by the men's room. It wasn't locked.

The light showed it to be a large, dirt-floored room with janitorial equipment along the walls. It was obviously an old room because of the lack of a floor, and was a half-level lower than the main floor of the theater.

Then Fender pointed the flashlight to the far corner of the room and they saw that there was a door-sized opening heading to the south. Willie turned on a light switch by the door they had come in but it was a 40-watter and hardly helped at all. They followed the light of the flashlight and entered the opening. It became a 6-foot tall tunnel with shored-up walls and ceiling and a dirt floor. There were no footprints in the dirt and it appeared by the dust that no one had entered the tunnel for years.

The tunnel extended beyond the power of the light to the south, which would have been under Main Street.

"This is incredible," Fender exclaimed. "It must go across the street to, where, Penney's?"

"Let's see," said Willie.

Feeling like Tom Sawyer and Huck Finn exploring a cave, they continued down the tunnel, which took a small angle to the left about twenty yards into it. "Yep, this looks like it's going to take us underneath Penney's," Fender announced.

Another 20 yards and the tunnel ended in a wooden door. It wasn't locked and the boys cautiously went through it and found themselves in another janitor's closet, this one much better equipped than the one at the Allen Theater. It was after midnight on a week night so they weren't too worried about encountering anyone, but they didn't want anyone to see the light, either.

There was another door on the opposite wall of the janitor's room and it led into the main floor of Penney's. The two explorers had struck gold.

The huge room was mostly dark, with only a couple of low-powered bulbs illuminating it, and from their position at the back of the store they could see the windowed front with the occasional car passing by on Main. Fender started to look around the room some more, checking out the dozens of clothes racks and counters, when the beam of his flashlight hit the front windows just as a cop car drove by.

"Holy shit," he muttered, flipping off the light. The cop drove on but the two boys decided to quit while they were ahead. They went back across the street through the tunnel and decided to explore some more in the future. Since then they had been back a couple of times and knew the layout of the store's back area. There was a large door leading to the loading dock in the alley behind the store, and an iron door on the east wall of the back room that apparently led to the business next door, Purity Pharmacy. It was locked.

Since the two were only interested in music, pool, and booze, and not clothes, they didn't view the discovery of Penney's with the same enthusiasm they did with the motherlode at Harry's Bar. Clothes were something you wore to keep warm and to keep from being nekkid. Other than that, they had no value at all. But booze. . .

So while Chickosa was jamming the back door to the Allen Theater and Resto keeping watch in front, Fender and Willie went down the ladder into the letter room, then into the balcony through the projection room and down into the lobby on the east side, where the men's room was. Even if Resto had been looking through the glass doors into the lobby he couldn't have seen them.

They went through the janitor's closet and into the tunnel. Willie had picked up a flashlight in the letter room so they made good time and were soon in the janitor's room at Penney's.

"We need to figure out a way to get rid of those guys for good," Fender said. "Even if we get out the back of Penney's and make it home okay, we can't be watching our backs every time we go out."

"Damn straight," Willie answered, "but we may be in over our heads. Hell, if Ernie and Zack and Fantino can't handle 'em, how can we?"

"I'd like to know just what they have against us. I mean, so what you saw them pull a gun on Zack and Ernie? Do they think we're gonna testify or something?"

"Maybe it's because they want to get a foothold into the bars here and they can't afford to get accused of armed extortion. You know how the Mormons in this town are."

"Maybe so."

Fender looked around and found a large, dry-cell flashlight on a shelf and picked it up. "Go see if we can get out the back door. I'll keep an eye on Resto." Without turning the flashlight on he crept out into the store, hiding behind counters just in case Resto glanced across the street. Willie went to the back area of the store with his flashlight pointed down.

A few minutes later he returned and whispered loudly to Fender, who was perched behind a counter watching the front of the store, "No luck. The back door is locked. We can't even get to the loading dock."

"Hold it. I got an idea. I know where some keys are. Maybe they'll open the back door."

Fender then got up and slowly made his way into the dimly lit store towards the counter where he had bought his pants that afternoon. He was carrying the big flashlight but he hadn't turned it on. It took him a while to get to the counter because Resto had been joined in front of the Allen Theater by Chickosa and the two mobsters were looking around like sentries in a prison. Fender could only move when they weren't looking across the street.

He finally made it to the counter and ducked behind it, placing the flashlight on the counter as he reached for the set of keys. But as he placed the flashlight down, it suddenly lit up, spraying a bright cone of light straight out the front of Penney's, causing the two heads of the Baritones to jerk up.

"Goddam switch," Fender muttered as he flipped it off and put it on the floor, "it must have been on all the time." He was afraid to stick his head up above the counter but Willie, who saw everything from his perch at the dark back of the store, watched as Resto Baritone strode purposefully across the street and peered intently through the front door of Penney's, shading the view with his hands.

"Stay down!" hissed Willie, who was pretty sure that Resto couldn't hear him through the thick glass. "I'll let you know when it's safe."

"This is a fine mess I've gotten us into," Fender moaned. "I've got the keys. Do you think I can throw them to you?" It was a pretty far distance between them.

"I don't know. It's pretty dark back here. I might not be able to find them if you don't throw them right at me. I can't use my flashlight as long as he's looking."

"Hey, I got an idea. Can you get upstairs without him seeing you?"

"I think so. Why?"

"If you can get up to the accounting department on the second floor, or mezzanine, or whatever they call it, maybe I can send the keys up to you with the gondola thing."

"Worth a try. I'll give you a yell when I'm up there. What the hell is a gondola thing?"

"You'll see. Just get upstairs where the wires all come together."

Fender sat on the floor behind the counter near the front of the room and waited for Willie to get upstairs. He ducked his head around the edge of the counter near the floor a couple of times and saw that Resto was still out in front of the store, but he wasn't peering inside as ambitiously as he was before. Fender heard Resto yell to Chickosa, who was still across the street in front of the Allen, "I coulda sworn I saw a moving light in here. Do you think those little assholes could somehow got inta this store?"

Fender hunkered down even lower. It was dark enough in the back of Penney's to keep Resto from seeing much, but the front part of the store was better lit from the light streaming in from Main Street. His plan depended on Resto's not being able to see something as subtle as the gondola winging its way up the wire to the second floor.

"Lemme know when Resto's not looking," Fender whispered loudly.

A few seconds later, Willie's voice came from the accounting department. "Okay, I'm here. Don't try anything yet. I'll let you know."

"Okay," Fender said, and waited.

Resto backed away from the glass front door and brought his hands down. He was still peering into the store but was also looking around more.

"Now!" stage-yelled Willie, and Fender reached up and quickly grabbed the gondola that was on top of the counter. Then, while keeping his head and shoulders down below the lever of the counter, he placed the keys in the gondola and raised his right hand up and screwed the gondola a half turn, locking it into the upper part of the gondola attached to the wire. He jerked his hand down.

"Is he looking?" Fender asked.

"Hold on. Not now. Not now. Okay, now!"

Fender reached up and grabbed the lanyard and pulled as hard as he could. Immediately the gondola raced up the wire to the accounting department right where Willie was sitting in the dark.

Resto saw something out of the corner of his eye and quickly moved to the windowed door and looked in. Fender and Willie held their breaths.

"I saw somethin'!" Resto bellowed.

"Whassat?" Chickosa yelled from across the street.

"I dunno. It looked like a bat or somethin'."

"Well, stay there and keep an eye out. If either of those two mothers comes outa this theater I'll take care of 'em."

Willie, in the darkness of the second floor, grabbed the gondola and unscrewed it, taking out the set of keys. He then ran downstairs to the back door of Penney's. He tried every key but none of them worked. "Shit!" he moaned, and then decided to see which doors he *could* open. He could get into a few of the offices upstairs but they had no exits. Then he went downstairs and tried the big iron door on the east wall. It worked.

He peered through the door and his flashlight revealed that he was in a storeroom for the soda fountain in the back part of the drug store. He tried the key in the lock on the pharmacy side of the door and it worked. Apparently, Penney's and Purity Pharmacy trusted each other.

But could they escape via Purity Pharmacy? He decided to go back and tell Fender what he had found. He went back to the accounting department and saw that Resto was still looking in the front window. Fender was still trapped.

"Stay where you are. He's still looking," Willie said. "I can't get out the back door but I can get into the drugstore next door. If you can ever get back here, we can probably just hang out until they go away, or until the stores open tomorrow."

"That's doesn't sound good. How the hell are we going to explain what we're doing in here?"

"Well, that may be preferable to explaining anything to Resto and Chickosa."

"You're right. But there's gotta be something we can do. Any ideas?"

There was a long pause and then Willie's voice came down from the second floor darkness, "I got somethin'. Remember Mr. Carlson's chemistry class when we were juniors?"

"Vaguely. I think I got my first and only 'D' in that class."

"Well, I'm thinking about how we can get Resto to go back across the street and how we can take care of both of them."

Then Willie gave a loud cackle, something he always did when he got a great, subversive idea. It made Resto jerk a little and increase his gaze into the store, but Willie didn't care. His idea was so outrageous it didn't matter if Resto grew suspicious.

"So tell me," Fender barked, and after Willie's inevitable dramatic pause, the two young marquee changers worked out the plans of their escape and revenge.

Gunplay on Main Street

ONCE THEY had their plan all worked out to the smallest detail, Fender and Willie put it into action. First, they had to get Resto back over on the north side of the street with Chickosa. Fender was stuck behind the counter as long as the brutish Baritone brother was stationed in front of Penney's.

The plan involved violence. Willie left his perch in the accounting department of Penney's and went downstairs and scampered through the tunnel back to the Allen Theater. Then he went upstairs to the letter room via the balcony and climbed onto the roof. He quickly peered over the parapet and saw Resto across the street, still peering into the store, and Chickosa directly below, pacing around in front of the glass door leading up to the letter room. So far, Chickosa hadn't spent any time directly under the marquee where Willie couldn't see him. That was good. Their plan needed that.

Then Willie left the parapet and jumped off the roof of the theater onto the roof of the barber shop and Harry Allen Insurance to the east of the theater. He crossed that roof and had to climb up onto the next roof, over Gardenschwartz Sporting Goods. There was a skylight into the sporting good store and Willie knew that with a screwdriver, he could flip back half of it and drop into the store. They had done it a couple of times just to see if they could but were leery of leaving any trace of themselves in the store. There wasn't anything they wanted there, but it was full of stuff that other people might want.

He had picked up a screwdriver in the letter room so it was just a matter of a few minutes before Willie had the skylight open. He dropped the eight feet into the dark store onto a table covered with baseball equipment. Willie was 5'7" but he knew that by standing on the table he could get back up through the skylight.

Willie took the flashlight out of his pocket and moved to the rear of the store. He knew it fairly well. There was a huge guncase filled with every caliber of hunting rifle and handgun but that was not what he was looking for. Their plan involved violence but deadly force was not part of it.

Besides, the gun case was well-locked, as it should be. Instead Willie found his way to a smaller, unlocked guncase in a corner and took out a Daisy BB air rifle and a cardboard cylinder of BBs. He walked back to the baseball table and standing on it carefully pushed the BB gun up onto the roof. Then he jumped up and grabbed the edge of the skylight and pulled himself up through the opening. He carefully replaced the skylight and screwed it back into place.

He was now ready to perform the first step of their plan: to get Resto back on this side of the street.

Willie went to the front of the store, overlooking Main Street. There was a big neon sign that stuck up in front of Gardenschwartz and it was easy for him to hide behind it and see what Resto was doing. He was still looking into Penney's half the time and looking around Main Street the other half.

Willie found a wooden box on the roof and set it up about a foot behind the parapet by the neon sign. He sat on it and loaded the BB gun with BBs. It held about 50. Then he placed the barrel of the gun on the parapet and lined up his sights on Resto, whose bald, bullet head glistened in the reflected neon lights of Main Street. Resto's back was to Willie and he had no problem getting a bead on him. Willie wiped the sweat from his face and, waiting until a car whooshed past on its way to who-knows-where, squeezed off a single shot. The sound of the car easily covered the sound of the BB gun and all that was heard was a high pitched yowl from Resto. His right hand flew up to his neck and he turned around and began cursing in Italian.

"What the hell's with you?" Chickosa yelled from across the street.

"Goddam bug or something bit me!"

"There ain't no bugs out here in the stinkin' desert," Chickosa muttered back at him.

"Well, somethin' got me, goddammit." Resto continued to rub the back of his neck and turned back to look inside Penney's again.

Willie sighed and lined up another shot. As soon as another car drove by he pulled the trigger and once again Resto let out a loud wail. This time he began rubbing the top of his head with both hands and cursed even louder than before.

"There's something after me, I tell ya!" He was jumping up and down and getting even madder because Chickosa was starting to giggle.

"Well, there ain't any bugs over here. I don't think there was anything in that store anyway. Come on back over here."

Resto muttered some more to himself and then jaywalked across to join his brother.

"Stage One completed," Willie said quietly. "And now for the tricky part."

He moved the box back where he found it then hopped off the Gardenschwartz roof onto the roof of the radio station and insurance company. Then he climbed up onto the roof of the theater, pushing the BB gun up ahead of him. Entering the trapdoor he took the gun and hid it in the insulation where their stash of liqueurs was, picking up a half-pint of Plum Brandy. He took a swig of it in the letter room then ran through the balcony, down the stairs to the janitor's room and through the tunnel to Penney's. He called out to Fender, who was still hiding behind the counter near the front of the store.

Fender carefully crept back to the darkness at the back of the room, and, after a short side trip to pick up a skein of black knitting wool, joined Willie. "Good job," he said to his amigo, "now let's see if Mr. Carlson was bullshitting us."

The two walked to the iron door leading to Purity Pharmacy and entered the drugstore. Willie still had his flashlight and they quickly found their way to the area where all of the drugs were kept. Willie offered Fender a couple of snorts of the brandy and they began looking for the three ingredients they remembered from their chemistry class. Potassium nitrate, powdered charcoal and sulfur. They found large bottles of each and put them in a bag they found behind the counter.

Once they had the makings for their plan, they went back to Penney's, and were soon back across the street in the letter room. They placed the three bottles of chemicals on the flat board where they assembled the stacks of letters to be taken down to the marquee. There was still about half of the bottle of brandy left so they killed it off.

Then, using a small cardboard box, they mixed together the three ingredients, with about 75% of the mixture being potassium nitrate, 15% powdered charcoal, and 10% sulfur. This they filled the empty brandy bottle with, packing it as tightly as they could.

Once the bottle was filled almost to the top, they took a sheet of paper and folded it into a rectangle about one half inch wide and three inches long.

Willie mused, "I'm glad you remembered that Hav-a-Tampas burn like cigarettes. Otherwise we may have had a problem with a fuse for this thing." He took a cigar from the five-pack he had in his pocket and broke off the wooden stem. Then he broke the cigar in two pieces and took the piece that was about two inches long and wrapped the paper around it, grommetwise, until it was just the right diameter to be shoved into the mouth of the bottle, tightly, with about a half inch of Hav-a-Tampa sticking out and the rest of the cigar extending into the tightly packed powder. Then he took a 15-foot length of the black wool and tied one end of it to the neck of the bottle with a square knot.

"Are you ready?" Willie asked, and Fender nodded.

"Let's show the Baritones how we do things in the stinkin' desert."

An Explosive Climax

THE TWO MOBSTERS were pacing around underneath the side panel of the marquee that read, "Lee Marvin". Every once in a while Resto would rub the back of his neck angrily and Chickosa would grumble that maybe they should just break the glass door and just go in and shoot the little bastards. He lit one cigarette after another, lighting one with the butt of the previous one.

Fender and Willie knew that it was just a matter of time before the Baritones left, or broke into the theater, so they quickly climbed up on the roof and eased their way over to the parapet directly above the gangsters.

It was a crazy idea but it might just be crazy enough to work. Fender held the bottle while Willie took out his Zippo lighter and lit the end of the cigar sticking out. Soon it was burning nicely and the ember was burning down towards the paper grommet.

"This is scary," Fender whispered. "Let's get this thing away from us."

Holding on to the wool, he moved quietly to the parapet and stuck his hand with the smoldering bottle out over the edge about three inches. Then he let the bottle slowly drop, playing out the wool about a foot every few seconds. Willie inched closer to the edge and looked down, seeing that the bottle was descending directly down over the two men pacing below.

Fender kept playing out the wool and the bottle dropped slowly, smoke wafting up from the "fuse".

Resto stopped walking around and leaned his back up against the wall of the theater. "Let's do something. I'm getting tired of waiting around."

"I am too," replied Chickosa. "Pretty soon a cop is gonna get suspicious of us hangin' around here." He flipped his cigarette into the gutter and reached into his pants pocket for his car keys.

"It's funny, though," Resto said.

"What's funny?"

"The smell of your cigarettes. Now that you've stopped smokin', they smell a little bit like cigars."

"What do you mean?"

"Doncha smell that? It smells like some kinda sweet cigar."

It was the last thing either of the Baritone brothers said for a long time.

The Sunday Daily Times

FENDER WOKE UP around ten on Sunday morning. Willie was on the couch and would have slept till noon if Fender hadn't awakened him. They had gotten in the night before around two A.M.

Fender's mother had gotten up a couple of hours earlier and gone to mass and was visiting with some friends so Fender sat down at the kitchen table with a bowl of cereal and the local newspaper. On the front page was a last-minute breaking story.

"Hey, Willie, check this out."

He read:

TWO MEN INJURED IN MAIN STREET EXPLOSION

Dateline Farmington: Two brothers from New Jersey, Luigi and Sylvio Baritone, were severely injured early this morning in front of the Allen Theater in what can only be described as a "freak explosion".

"Luigi? Sylvio? Who the hell are they?" Willie wondered.

Apparently they were standing out in front of the theater when something made of glass exploded near their heads. According to police forensics, the explosion actually occurred slightly above their heads, although nothing else was damaged. Each man received extensive lacerations and although they are expected to survive, will have to remain hospitalized for months to come. They have returned to New Jersey.

Police are looking into the incident and hope to find out what the two men were doing when the explosion occurred.

"Maybe that's the last we'll hear from them," Fender said. "I hope they can't trace anything back to us."

"Yeah, let's hope. I don't relish being on the run for the rest of my life."

"You said it."

Fender took a bite of cereal and thumbed through the rest of the *Farmington Daily Times*. Nothing of interest; a typical Sunday paper.

Then he spotted the mail from Saturday which he hadn't checked. He rifled through it and saw a letter addressed to him from the Selective Service System. "What the . . .?" he spat, then opened it up.

"Greetings from the President of the United States . . ." it began.

"Goddammit!" Fender yelled.

Willie had a similar letter waiting for him when he got home.

The Last Hogan

ZACK, ERNIE AND FANTINO sat around the table smoking and grousing. The hogan was as dirty as ever and the atmosphere was getting close to lethal.

"So are we out of the frying pan yet?" Zack asked.

Ernie flipped his cigar against the wall, sending sparks flying. "Yes, li'l brother, I think we are. Unless the Baritones send some more a' their goons out here."

Fantino wheezed, "I dunno. Dose guys was really messed up. Whoever done it to dem really was vicious. I don't t'ink dey's gonna come back."

"Yeah, it musta been some super-pissed off Mexican who got to 'em. I can't imagine anyone else who could do that." Ernie was fatalistic about his racism.

"So I guess this means we don't have to hide out here at this hogan anymore." Zack looked around hopefully.

"Nope," Ernie said, "but you know what? This place is sorta growin' on me. I mean, out here we don't hafta worry about the mob findin' us. But we also don't hafta worry about the cops findin' us either."

Fantino grunted. "Cops. Who needs 'em? Y'know, I keep t'inkin' 'bout those two young punks dat used ta come inta the club and sing dose crazy songs. I ain't seen 'em since the Baritones got dere's. Dey usedta worry 'bout da cops alla time. I t'ink dey mighta been, whaddyacallit, under-age? I wunner whatever happen ta dem?"

Ernie lit another cigar. "Prolly left town with some band. They didn't drink all that much anyway. I can't see as they ever did anything for us, anyway. Coupla under-age losers. Who needs 'em?"

WEED, WOMEN AND SONG

THE MARQUEE CHANGER

An Adolescent Reminiscence

THERE ONCE was a time when you went to a movie theater because it was the only air-conditioned place in town. There would be two movies which would run one after the other with a newsreel and cartoon between each, and you could stay in the theater as long as you wanted, until they closed the doors at around midnight. Guess what; the world has gotten a lot colder since then.

In Farmington, New Mexico in the 50s and 60s there were two downtown theaters, the Allen and the Totah, and they were my babysitters as a child, just as television is the babysitter of today. My parents were divorced in 1951 when I was four, and when my brothers and I weren't playing baseball or getting knowledge slapped into us by the Ursuline nuns, we were down at the Allen watching B movies.

Admission was 10 cents back then but once my oldest brother Mike started working as a ticket taker, the Tucker boys never paid to get in again. Mike also became the marquee changer for both theaters and when he was graduated from high school, my next brother Bob took over the job. Then when Bob became a projectionist in 1960 I became the marquee changer. We didn't ask the Allens, who owned the theaters; we just considered it a Tucker family job, and passed it on like an inheritance. My little brother, John, became marquee changer when I started my second great job, playing in a band in 1964.

Each theater had a big white marquee, where the titles of the current features were displayed in movable letters. It was my job to change these letters every time new movies came to town. These days, one film may stay at one theater for weeks, but back then the pattern was one movie on Sunday and Monday, a double feature on Tuesday and Wednesday, and another double feature on Thursday, Friday and Saturday.

The most important thing about my job was that it had to be done *after* the last feature of the night had started, which was usually around 10:00 P.M.. So here I was, a thirteen-year-old Huck Finn wannabee, with a job that kept me out on the streets past midnight three nights a week. Can you imagine anything better?

I had a small room where I kept all of the letters. It was incredibly dusty because letters would gather dust while hanging on the marquee for a few days, then I'd bring them in and keep them in their bins, where the dust would fall off on the floor. During the five years I worked as marquee changer I never once considered vacuuming the room. I was a marquee changer, not a custodian, I guess.

I'd walk downtown, which was about a mile from our house, around 8:00 or 9:00 P.M., and either watch some of the movie or go to my room. There I would write down on a sheet of paper what I planned to put on the marquee. Then I would cross off the letters that were already on the marquee from the current movie. No sense in carrying letters that were already up on the marquee. I'd take the new letters I needed downstairs to street level and pile them on the sidewalk where people wouldn't have to step over them. Then I'd whip out my trusty ladder, which was kept in a niche in the wall by the theater.

So there I was, dangling from the top of an eight-foot ladder, moving dusty red plastic letters around, while the teenagers of Farmington drove by in their '57 Chevys and '58 Fairlanes. They were "dragging Main", which meant that they were driving from the A&W on the east of town down Main Street to the Tastee Freeze on the west end of town.

They would shout at me from their cars, and on occasion throw a beer bottle my direction. I was never hit, but the marquee was broken a few times. I learned at an early age that few things are more satisfying than making money while those around you are stumbling around spending it. Later on I *really* learned this lesson when I became a guitar picker and spent my nights making money in bars.

I played games while changing the marquee. Since I'd be leaving some letters on the marquee while I carried others down, the marquee would take on a surrealistic chaos of letters for a short while. I got a kick out of leaving objectionable words on the marquee for the Main-draggers to enjoy. Of course I had plenty of deniability; I didn't really put that four-letter word up there, it just accidentally resulted from changing from one title to another. Hah!

My best friend Geno helped me a lot of the time. He would throw the letters I needed up to me—or I would throw them up to him—and this cut the time needed to do the job down to under an hour. But we never hurried. We didn't care how late we stayed out—we were working.

Another part of the job was to change the posters that advertise the current movies in the front of the theater, and the posters inside the lobby that showed the coming features. I had access to mint condition full-size posters that today would bring thousands of dollars in auctions, but how could I have known? I'd roll them up and send them on to their next destination. If I had only saved a few Marilyn Monroes or Alfred Hitchcocks I'd be a rich man today. Oh well.

I wasn't the only one to benefit from my great job. Since my letter room was upstairs by the projection booth, accessible from a private door, I could get my friends in free at night. We'd sneak past the projectionist and sit in the balcony (which was invariably empty) and enjoy beer and cigarettes while we watched black and white scary movies from Republic Pictures.

The job had other benefits, especially for Bart Simpsons like Geno and me. There was a crate full of Tampax tampons in my room, apparently for a machine in the ladies rest room. Geno and I would take a dozen or so of them and on the way home after changing the marquee, we'd tie them onto the doorknobs of all of the businesses on Main Street. We didn't have to actually see the faces of the businessmen when they opened their stores the next day. Just imagining what they thought was good enough for us—especially when we did it a couple of times a week.

The theater was also a super place to explore at night when everybody had gone and the place was locked up. I had a key since often I would still be working when the place closed. The Allen Theater had a system of tunnels underneath it, which didn't seem to be used for anything. I found some thirty-year old empty bottles of booze down there so at one time, somebody used them as a place to drink.

But the best places to explore were the roofs of that downtown block. My letter room had a trapdoor in the ceiling that led to the roof of the theater. Once on the roof, Geno and I could explore, cat burglar-style, the whole downtown city block. During the winter we would throw snowballs at pedestrians from the roof of Gardenschwartz Sporting Goods store. No one ever thought of looking *up* for the snowballer.

Our biggest score came when we were juniors in high school in early 1964. We found a small storeroom behind Harry's Bar, which was two doors down from the Allen. In this room, which looked like it hadn't been used in the dozen years since there had been a big fire at the bar, we found two cases full of charred half-pint bottles of oddball liqueurs, like Mint Gin, Peach Brandy, Cherry Vodka, etc. Forty-eight half-pints in all. We took them to my letter room and hid them under the insulation in the roof. For the whole summer, while our schoolmates were guzzling cheap beer, we sipped the world's finest liqueurs—and had much classier (and more colorful) hangovers.

We visited the storeroom several times after that but never found anything worthwhile, except a case of tokay. We tried one bottle of that but it was so horrible we gave it to Geno's older brother Robert, who had a hard time giving it away to his friends.

One night around midnight we were in the storeroom and had climbed up on a high shelf when a car stopped outside in the alley behind the bar. It was apparently a police car because he shone his spotlight through the dirty windows of the storeroom. We kept still on the shelf as the spotlight moved around the room. It was just like being in a James Bond movie. The cop, apparently satisfied no one was in the room, drove away.

I remember thinking at the time, "Why is it that whenever I'm in a position of hiding, I *always* have to piss?" I guess it's something you have to get over if you're going to be a criminal or spy. I never have.

Another time we were on the roof and went into an open window in what we thought was an abandoned hotel. All of the rooms were empty except for one which had a blanket on the floor, a can of beer by it, and a book that described how to perform an abortion. We took the beer and thought nothing more about it. We had a vague idea what was going on in that "hotel" but luckily a few years later there was no need for such places. I hope none of the girls I went to school with ever had to visit that hotel. But somebody did.

The job came in handy again when I was seventeen and needed a fake ID card. After everyone had left for the night I'd paw through the Lost & Found to see if any wallets had been lost. I knew I'd never find any money in them because the people that cleaned the theater every night after the last feature had first crack at the cash. But a couple of times I found ID cards that would make me old enough to buy booze and go in the bars. I doubt seriously if I ever fooled anyone in Farmington NM, which borders the Navajo Reservation, but in 1964 I was known as Charles Ben Begay, age 23. "Begay" is such an obvious Navajo name that I can't help but laugh at the idea of a skinny, white boy like me passing for a 23-year-old Navajo Army 2nd Lieutenant. I don't think the liquor store owners back in the 60s cared who you were as long as you had an ID of some sort.

So, other than getting alcohol out of my system at an early age, did I learn anything from this great job? I learned that spelling is important. I cringe at the horrible spelling I see on marquees these days. Don't these people realize that what they put on the marquee is going to be read by hundreds of people, some of whom are literary snobs and actually know how to read and spell? In the five years I was a marquee changer I was called only once to correct a misspelled word. What's the secret? Simple. Read what you've put up before you call the job done. After all, a marquee probably only holds a dozen words.

I also learned responsibility. People depended on the marquees to be accurate, and depended on them to be changed despite the weather. There were times when it was below zero and I was up on that ladder at midnight on a school night. The job came first.

But it had to come to an end. I was in a band by 1964 and it was tough playing until midnight at the teen club or at the high school, then after packing up the equipment, heading down to the theaters for another couple of hours' work. Luckily I had a little brother and he took over for my last year in high school. I even drove by dragging Main a few times as he toiled atop the ladder.

"Proper" methods of childrearing change from decade to decade but I'd have to say that my mother's giving me independence, trust and freedom was the best thing that ever happened to me. I'd hate to hear what the modern nurturers would say about the job she did with her four smart-alecky boys, but I would gladly pit the four Tucker boys in ANY contest against any four "properly-raised" children of the 80s or 90s.

Maybe life is too dangerous in the 90s to allow such freedom, but in Farmington NM in the 60s, Geno and I were Huck and Tom, and I wouldn't trade the memory of those days for anything.

TRAVELS WITH HARRY

A Three-Part Sex Reminiscence

Gail

I HAD HAD a few sex experiences before I met Gail in July of
1964, the summer between my junior and senior years in high
school, but they were mainly just making out in the back seat of a
car. I had touched a few breasts, but never made it beyond the
legendary second base. Once, when I was about 13, Roberta, a
girl from down the block, practically begged me to do it with her
as we lay on a bed in my TV room, but I didn't even kiss her. I
obviously wasn't ready yet.

I grew up in Farmington New Mexico, a small city near the
Four Corners. In 1961 I was given a Spanish guitar by my mother
and later bought a $70 Sears Silvertone guitar and amp. In 1962 I
started playing in bands, the main one being The Torques. By the
end of my junior year, in June of 1964, the Torques were me on
guitar, Harry on guitar, Dwight on bass, and Barry on drums. We
had been playing around Farmington and Durango for about a
year and we thought we were pretty good.

Harry had had his first experience earlier in the year and never
tired of telling me about it, how *The Fugitive,* which was on TV
in the background while he and Bobbie frolicked on the couch at
his home in Bloomfield, would forever be ingrained in his mind
as an aphrodisiac. After a month or so of hearing Harry talk about
sex, I knew it was time I had some too. But how?

It came to pass in July, right after my 17th birthday, that The
Torques had a three-day weekend gig in Durango at Poor Boys, a
3.2 beer joint. Since it served only the low-powered beer, the age
for entry was 18 instead of the usual 21 for bars in Colorado.
Harry, Dwight and Barry *were* 18, and I told the bar owner I was
too. We were looking forward to the job because it was during
the Spanish Trails Fiesta, the Durango equivalent of Mardi Gras,

where all inhibitions were lost—we hoped. Since we were to play Thursday, Friday and Saturday nights, Harry and I decided to stay overnight on both nights, rather than drive the 50 miles back to Farmington.

So Harry and I drove into Durango Thursday day, set up our equipment at Poor Boys, and went looking for a place to stay. One place caught our eye right away: the Central Hotel on Main Street. It was an old, classic hotel from the mining days, but unlike the Strater down the street, which had oodles of rustic class, the Central Hotel was a dump—an old, decrepit four-storey wooden mausoleum in the middle of downtown Durango. Just our style. We checked into a second storey room with one big bed, paid $12 for the three nights, and went off to play our first night's gig.

Harry had made a date with a girl from Bloomfield, where he was from. She showed up at the club that night and she and Harry did a little parking after the club closed while I walked back to the hotel, which was only a few blocks from the club. She mentioned that she had a girlfriend from Durango, Gail, and that she'd fix me up with her for Friday night. Fine with me.

So the next night Harry's girl shows up with Gail, a 16-year-old (who knows, maybe 15) girl, quite cute and with a nifty body. I was impressed and we had a good time talking on the breaks and getting drunk. Very drunk in fact. Dwight's stepfather had come up with Dwight that night from Farmington, and after seeing Gail dance on the tables after our last set had remarked to me that I "shouldn't have any trouble with that one." Little did he know. Or did he?

When we were ready to leave the bar, Gail latched onto me and we stumbled to the car and fell into the back seat. Harry and his girl (whose name I obviously can't remember) got in front and we drove off to the notorious Wildcat Canyon, a make-out place to the west of town. Gail and I started in with some heavy-duty smooching and I was quite pleased when she didn't seem to have any out of bounds bases. We got so steamy, in fact, that Harry and HG got out and took a walk, leaving us up to our devices. I unzipped her Levis and wangled my hand down into her panties and performed my first digital examination. It was much wetter and slicker than I had imagined.

Gail seemed to be getting into it as much as I was but she kept up a drunken patter of "No, you won't respect me," and "Don't," all the while making it easier for my fingers to get into that exquisite wetness. But I should have known things were going *too* smoothly because just when I was getting ready to pull those Levis off and get mine down, she seemed to sort of, well, pass out.

"Gail? Are you there? Gail?" I babbled, half of me wanting her to wake up and get with the program and the other half (slapped into a quagmire of guilt by the good sisters of Sacred Heart School, where I was incarcerated for my first eight years of school) thankful that the "really big sin" had been postponed until a more conscious moment. I figured I could go ahead and do the deed, but compared to Harry's *Fugitive* story, sex with a passed-out girl had much lower ratings, so I didn't. I tried to revive her, with eventual success when Harry and HG returned from their 2 A.M. nature walk.

We drove back to the bar where they picked up HG's car, and made a date with both of them for Saturday night. Then we drove back to the Central. All in all, I thought it was an illuminating night and told Harry about the aborted act, musing that the next night might be different.

And it was.

At the bar on Saturday night we waited for the girls to show up with throbbing expectations. The music that year was surf music, drenched with reverb and fast double-picking, a la Dick Dale and the Deltones. The Durango crowd, thanks to Fort Lewis college, which stood on a big hill overlooking the town, was about three years hipper than any Farmington crowd, and tolerated, if not liked, our music. We had a gimmick that weekend: blinking drums. Barry had installed a momentary on-off switch on his bass drum pedal, with a two-light bulb assembly inside the bass drum, so that with every beat of the bass drum, the drum head would change from blue to red. It was as psychedelic as it got in those days. The only problem was that the red bulb burned out early in the night and the only bulb we could find to replace it was a 100-watt *white* bulb. Talk about lighting the place up! On the fast songs it was like a strobe light and on the slow ones it was blinding to the dancers trying to snuggle on the dance floor. Luckily, the switch broke before too long and we scrapped that idea for good.

Around 10 o'clock Gail walked in and told us that HG couldn't make it that night. She then proceeded to make up for lost time by chugging a few pitchers of beer. By closing time she was as drunk as she had been the night before. I figured I was in for another pass out.

She told us that she lived just outside of town on the Florida road but that she didn't want to go home. So Harry drove up the hill to Fort Lewis with Gail and me in the back seat, making out like monkeys. Halfway up the steep hill, he pulled over to a wide part in the road and parked, keeping his eyes on the road watching for cops or other cars. Meanwhile Gail and I were getting to the unzipped Levis stage. Soon I had hers all the way off and was enjoying her superb butt with both hands as she sprawled on top of me.

Gail seemed to be enjoying it a lot, until she squealed drunkenly, "Hey! I feel more than two hands!" Harry had lost interest in the road, apparently, and was just trying to make sure that Gail didn't fall off of me, injuring herself tragically. I soothed her with soft words, telling her that, no, I would still respect her, even if I allowed someone else to feel her butt. But I was also feeling that it was time I shot or got off the pot, so to speak.

So I managed to pull my Levis down, keeping her on top of me—with Harry's capable help. Meanwhile, without his vigilance, cars were driving by with regularity, washing over the action in our car with brilliant pre-halogen headlights; the action being a big undulating lump in the backseat with a person in the front seat leaning over doing something to the lump with his hands. It may have been a normal scene for late-night Fort Lewis students.

"This is it!" I shouted to myself. "The really big sin!" —(after missing Mass on Sunday or eating meat on Friday, of course). Somehow I managed to insert my eager pego into her dripping apricot-fendu and within a few strokes, I had cast off my virginity forever. Halfway up Fort Lewis hill—as cars drove by.

I was a man at last.

And like a man with limited knowledge (and catholic fear) I pulled out at the last second and came all over my navel. Thereby setting the pattern for what was to become the crustiest night of my life.

Somehow we restored order to Harry's 56 Chevy, got all the right Levis on the right teenage thighs, and pulled a U-turn and headed back to town.

I said, "It's been quite a night, eh, Gail? I guess we need to know where you live so we can take you home."

"I don't wanna go home."

"Well, we gotta take you home cuz we gotta go back to the hotel."

"That's where I wanna go. Take me to the hotel."

Harry looked at Gail as if she were a one-armed man, and I said, "Well, okay, if *you* say so." She was still acting quite drunk.

Out of paranoia we parked a couple of blocks away from the hotel and walked, Gail and I together, and Harry a half-block behind. Harry was showing an unusual amount of common sense in being paranoid about getting caught with an underage girl. I don't remember feeling very many *legal* qualms at all. And by this time my nun-fed guilt trip about sex was expiring on its cross. I was looking forward to a night of wanton *coitus interruptus*.

It was after 3 A.M. and the lobby was thankfully empty. Gail and I walked up to the room, and once inside, I tried to kiss her and her hand accidentally brushed against my eye, curling my eyelashes on that eye under my lid. I was blinded and rubbed at my eye frantically. Oh no! I'm gonna lose my virginity and my eyesight in the same night! Gail was no help at all, mumbling an apology as she stumbled around, and I was just beginning to despair when Harry came in the door. I told him what happened and he looked at my eye up close. He flicked the eyelashes out and I immediately felt relief. Whew! Dodged a bullet that time!

So Harry and I sat on the bed and looked at Gail, standing by the door. There was an awkward moment, and I said, "Boy, I'm pretty tired."

Harry kept up his end of the conversation with, "Yeah, I'm pretty tired too."

And Gail tops us both with, "I'm too tired to fuck. But I have a feelin' that if somebody else idn't too tired to fuck, I'm gonna get fucked!"

With those inspiring words, we all took off our clothes and climbed into the big, wide, bouncy, *squeaky* iron-posted bed. It was dark, but I'd like to think that there was the on-off flashing of a garish neon sign (CENTR L HOTEL or JESUS SAVES) casting its ghastly shadow on our writhing haunches. Maybe there was.

At first Gail and I snuggled as Harry inhabited the far side of the bed. Gail had maneuvered us so that I was in the middle and she on the outside. Before long I had whispered the right words to gain entry into her slick lovepot. This time in a more religiously approved position, so that when I inevitably withdrew and spewed, I did it partly on Gail, and partly on the unfortunate sheets that happened to be protecting that 70-year-old mattress that night. Because the bed squeaked so much, Harry had to stretch full length with his feet against the bedposts at the foot of the bed and his hands on the headposts, pushing the posts apart. It still squeaked, but not nearly so bad.

Harry murmured his approval afterward, saying that he never knew how ridiculous, yet rousing, two people fucking two feet away was. I was in a fairly good mood so I made sure I tumbled off on the outside, placing Gail within arms' reach of anyone who happened to be on the other side of the bed. Soon Gail and I were kissing and rubbing face to face. And once again she felt the unusual *frisson* of three hands fondling her butt at the same time. And only one of them was mine!

She started to complain but I calmed her with soothing words of love, including, "Harry's a good guy. He just wants to touch."

"But you won't like me anymore."

"Yes, I will. I promise. I'll always love you."

"Oh don't say that unless you really mean it."

"Okay. But Harry would really like to, and I don't mind."

Before long, with so many hands, Gail and I were at it again with Harry at his bedpost post. Just as I was getting into a rhythm, we heard footsteps out in the hall. Slow, deliberate footsteps that stopped right outside our door.

"Stop, Fender!" whispered Harry and I did, but Gail was on a roll this time. But she managed to keep quiet enough until the footsteps slowly moved down the hall and into silence. I began my rondo of love again as my fellow Torque acted as sound engineer. Without much ado I reached a third pinnacle of the night, cascading my dwindling, yet still adolescently copious, Niagara on the sheets of cotton—the fabric of our lives.

Before long (in fact, in less than a minute), Harry was plying his case again. "Gail," he murmured. "I sure wanna fuck you too."

"But Fender won't want me to."

I considered my loyalties. "No, it's okay. I'll still like you if you do it with Harry."

"Well, if you say so."

So it came to pass that Gail drifted into Harry's arms. I was blessed with an excellent opportunity to test Harry's "ridiculous yet rousing" theory firsthand. Unfortunately I was pressed into action by the horrific squeaking, which was worse on that side of the bed, apparently. And once again the action was stalled in midstroke by those agonizingly slow footsteps that stopped right outside our thin, 1923 quarter-inch plywood door, secured with a rusty 1909 handsmelted doorlatch. "Stop, Harry!" I whispered shushing out Gail, who was moaning, "Keep going, Harry." My friend, ever the veteran, managed to be perfectly still until the footsteps finally receded, then resumed his artful humping.

After a reasonable amount of time (as far as I knew) Harry withdrew from Gail's font o' plenty and inundated his side of the bed with his own particular brand of DNA (although we didn't call it that back then).

But Gail wasn't ready to quit. In fact, she was just getting warmed up.

Within minutes I was back in the saddle, figuring that if I were to concentrate a bit, I might be able to beat the old slow-stepper out in the hall to the punch. I tried thinking sexy thoughts, conjuring up fantasies such as two guys banging the hell out of a young chick in a sleazy hotel room. And it worked! The steps were still approaching the door when I jettisoned my load on the pitiful percale for the third time, making it even more difficult to find a non-damp spot, which was getting to be a problem. Rejoicing in the afterglow of a race well-run, I shushed Gail, who kept asking for someone to fuck her, as the steps moved down the hall, seeming to say, "Next time, young whippersnappers! I'll get ye next time!"

Now Harry was loath to let Gail's pleas go unanswered, so as he crawled on top of her I sighed and made myself useful with the bedposts. This time Harry found her G-spot (although we didn't call it that back then) and Gail really began to get in stride. She became so spirited that as Harry rode her like a stallion, her hoof, er, hand began caressing my midsection with exquisite sensuality. When Harry would begin to gallop, her hand would dig into the soft folds of my stomach with greater ardor, until after a particularly energetic canter, the ardor began to get a tad painful. "Harder, Harry!" Gail entreated and the willing stud atop her gave her the symbolic whip. "Harder, Harry, harder!"

Meanwhile, in the grandstands, my stomach was being kneaded like an uncooked bagel and the pain was loosening my tongue. "Stop, Harry! Stop!" Her fingernails were digging into the skin of my stomach and I was getting ready to say to hell with the squeaks, my stomach needs me, when I realized that the steps were right outside the door.

Fuck it, I said to myself and grabbed Gail's hand away from my stomach, as the squeaks and Gail's "Harder, Harry!" chant carried them over another sticky finish line. Apparently the steps outside the door lost big, because they faded away, never to come back again. My stomach escaped with second-degree scratches.

We each had another round before drifting off into a well-deserved sleep. By this time lying on cold, clammy, damp sheets seemed like the right thing to do and we didn't wake up until about 9 in the morning.

Gail was dressed and sitting at the dresser, looking rather serious.

Harry and I looked at each other and wondered how this was going to play out. Gail asked, "What happened last night?"

"Well, we all had some really good sex."

"I don't remember anything about it."

"Well, it was no big deal. How about we take you home?"

"Okay."

So we walked out of the hotel, Gail and me together and Harry about a half-block behind, and she directed us to her house in the country. She got out and I said I'd call and she said fine.

As Harry and I drove off in his 56 Chevy, the radio blared into life with that ringing G sustained over D chord that I'll always associate with sex. "It's been a Hard Day's Night!" Harry and I just looked at each other and beat it on back to Durango.

We stopped at the hotel to get our things and ran into the old Spanish lady who ran the hotel. She was gathering the sheets from our room and said we'd have to pay an extra $3 for the girl who stayed in our room. We paid, and got the hell back to Farmington.

The next day we realized we had left a pair of shoes in the room and had to drive back to get them. It was embarrassing asking the old lady for them. Luckily she was no longer there the next time I stayed at the Central, a few years down the road.

Harry and Gail started seeing each other, but a month or so later, Gail got into some trouble with my mother, Barry's mother, and the law, and left town.

Candy

LATER IN 1964 The Torques played a couple of songs at a "Talent Show" at the Allen Theater. We normally would have considered ourselves too sophisticated to play at a talent show (no bucks involved) but since it was at the Allen, where I worked as the marquee changer, I was excited about the whole thing.

We had just learned "Slow Down" by The Beatles so we played it as one of our numbers. Apparently it was way too loud for the old folks in the audience, but the younger set seemed to enjoy it. After playing we sat in the audience to see some of the other acts.

As soon as I sat down, a rather large, swarthy girl of about 16, with thick, black hair sat down next to me and wrapped her arms around my near arm. "Hi, Fender, gosh you guys were great!" Who the hell? I thought.

"I'm Candy and I just love your music."

I looked around furtively and of course the first eyes I saw were my mother's, a few rows away. I tried to act like this was something normal. It was my first inkling of the "groupie" phenomenon.

Harry, sitting on the other side of me, was also eyeing Candy quizzically. I imagined that he, like I, was adding up her pros and cons. We were at that stage of development when it was hard to come up with any cons, other than her being somewhat fat and gross, and those were mere trifles.

As the show ended I managed to extricate myself from Candy and spoke with my mother as she was leaving. "Who is that girl?" she asked.

"I have no idea. See you at home later." Luckily, my mother generally stayed out of my affairs as much as possible.

I went back to Candy and Harry and we left through the rear entrance of the theater to where Harry's car was parked. "Where shall we go?" I asked and Candy said, "Anywhere you want."

Candy and I got in the backseat and Harry drove off, ever the loyal buddy. We drove northwest of town past what would later become Municipal hill, the Elks Club and the jail, to a big water tank. Harry parked the car and turned around to see what was going on. Nothing unusual. Just me under a bare-butted wench.

This time, however, I was feeling no Catholic guilt or fear. That was a thing of the past. The problem this time was that I was having a devil of a time deciding exactly what I wanted to do to this large lagniappe atop me. I finally rolled on top of her, got my Jack Sprat-like legs somehow positioned betwixt her wifely ones, and aimed my lingam at her yawning yoni. Somehow it wasn't the same as it had been with Gail.

After about ten minutes of rocking the car, I began thinking that it was high time I came. And only by thinking about something other than what I was doing was I able reach the point where I could pull out and anoint Harry's Corinthian leather seats with my special brand of myrrh. Old birth control habits die hard.

Oddly, this time Harry didn't volunteer any succor. He just quietly drove us to Candy's house, which, as she directed us, was on East Main Street. On the way, she asked me if I liked my "piece of Candy". Sure thing! We dropped her off and I told her I'd see her at our next dance, maybe.

The next day Candy called me and said to come on over—her dad was out of the house. Harry was over at my house at the time and we decided to check it out. We drove to her house, which was an old, two-story house set back from Main Street 50 yards or so, with a wide dirt driveway. We parked in front of the house, facing Main, and knocked on the door. We were met at the door by Candy and what looked like her clone. Her older sister, it turned out.

We went in and shot the bull for a while, and before long the girls had dragged us into separate rooms. I *think* they were suggesting we do the deed with them right there at their house but Harry and I were a little too nervous about their "father" coming back. They weren't sure when he'd be back either, so they said, "Well, okay, how about this? Come back tonight after 10 and walk around to the back of the house and knock on the second window and we'll come out and we can get drunk and have some fun. Not the first window, but the second."

We said okay and left.

That night by 10 Harry and I were pretty drunk already. In fact I was quite drunk. Along with us was Barry, the drummer in The Torques. We had been driving around trying to decide if we really wanted to try to pick up the girls. Since we were drinking, we of course decided yes.

At this point I'd like to digress somewhat and describe the way The Torques ran that year. For some unfathomable reason, Harry, Barry and I had gotten in the habit of running (when we had occasion to run) in a peculiar, Torque way. The back was held stiff, and leaning back a bit, while the knees were brought high in the air. The arms were swung in an exaggerated fashion, hands into fists, and, most importantly of all, *the thumbs were extended, pointing toward the sky*. It was *our* way to run and we were proud of it.

Back to our story. Harry drove up about half-way to the house, pulled a U and parked, facing Main Street. The house was dark. Harry and Barry waited in the car and I, in a drunken stupor, sneaked up to the house and tiptoed around it to the back. I remember thinking, "Was it the first window—or the second window? And which one is the first window anyway? Counting from which direction?" These were things, in retrospect, I should have determined that afternoon when I was sober.

So I picked a window and began rapping on it, whispering, "Candy, come on out. We're here!" I had been rapping for a minute or so when I detected movement to my right and felt a large fist whistle ineffectually past my ear. "Goddam, fuk'n punk!" the fist wielder blurted, and I can tell by his diction (and the fetid smell of a lifetime of cheap booze) that whoever this was, he was drunker than I was. So I stumbled away from the window and started running around the house towards the car. Behind me I could hear him wheezing and cussing, vowing to get me for violating his girls.

He was no match for the Torque Trot. With center of gravity *behind* me, knees high, and thumbs pointing towards Orion's belt, I raced past the car, rousing Harry and Barry from their alcohol-induced reveries. Harry recognized the Torque maneuver, and immediately started the car and peeled away from my Andy Sipowicz-like pursuer. He picked me up at the street and away we went—never to even *think* about tasting candy from Candy's house ever again. Even when we were desperate.

Judy

THE PATTERN for my love life was becoming concrete: Harry drives me and my paramour around until we do it, then he gives her a try, and finally she drifts off somewhere. And my third romance seemed to began the same way.

Judi was my high school sweetheart, although I wasn't hers. She was a smart, good-looking girl of my age and grade, with straight, shoulder-length brown hair cut in a somewhat Dutch style. In fact I called her my "Dutch girl". I had tried every trick in my arsenal to get her to have sex with me but she was determined to stay a virgin until she graduated. My arsenal mainly consisted of a kiss or two. That was about as far as I'd gotten in two or more years. We were great friends and had snuck out many times at night together but mainly just to do some drinking. No sex.

Until the summer of '65, when we both graduated from high school. She almost immediately lost her virginity to a local brute and I moved into an apartment with Harry—the Huntzinger's apartment house about two blocks from downtown. The Torques were playing pretty regularly around town and in Durango and Harry had a part-time job working mornings at the bus station moving freight around. Somehow we afforded the minimal rent on the apartment, which had a living room with couch and a bedroom with two single beds.

One night at a Torque dance I got linked up with Kathy, a girl who had graduated with me, and we made out a little in the back of Harry's car. She was a very nice girl and I thought that it might blossom into something more.

One day soon after, I was speaking with a guy who had graduated with us, and when I mentioned that I had gone out with Kathy, he asked me if she had told me about her "thing".

"Why, no," I said. "What kind of thing?"

He said, "Oh nothing, it's something that she'll have to tell you herself."

I was left mystified and before long forgot all about this strange "thing".

Well, sure enough, before I had had a chance to go out with Kathy for a second time, Harry had asked her out. Since he had the car (a nifty 56 Chevy) and the Torque prestige, she began going out with him. Ever the fatalist, I just figured it was the way of things and gave them my blessing. I don't remember if I ever mentioned to him the odd conversation I had had about her "thing".

But my heart was always on the prowl for Judi and one momentous summer night Harry and I managed to cajole Kathy and Judi out for a night of drinking and carousing. Apparently neither of them had to go home early because we ended up at the apartment around midnight in a gloriously drunk and good mood. Harry and Kathy retired to the bedroom and Judi and I took the couch in the living room.

She and I made out much more vociferously than ever before, probably because she had confessed to me about the brute. I think she felt that I deserved a good time after all of my patience. I felt the same way.

I'll never forget the wonderful music that accompanied our love-making that night. "Smokestack Lightning" by Manfred Mann. It was the last track on the back side of their album and, as only us oldsters remember, it was played over and over and over again because the record changers of that age, when reaching the end of a 33 album, would lift the arm and go back to the point of what it thought was a 45 record. Which was just before "Smokestack Lightning" began. It is an indication of our dedication to good lovin' that neither Harry nor I considered getting up and changing the record.

So it came to pass that I made love to my childhood sweetheart on a scratchy couch, pulling out at the last moment, creating what afterward we affectionately called "our spot". But not affectionately enough to do it again that summer. Judi and I only had one more experience together, and that was a year later when we spent a night in the Central Hotel, the site of "the crustiest night of my life". Of course we weren't alone—having sex with only one person around was apparently not my style—but this time we were with Mo (a later Torque guitar picker) and a girlfriend of Judi's.

But the story of my first night with Judi is not over. Not by a long shot.

Around three in the morning, not long after we did the deed, I drove Judi to her house in Harry's car, where she snuck in. I went back to the apartment and went to sleep on the couch. Harry and Kathy were still in the bedroom.

Around seven the next morning, Harry got up and went to work at the bus station. I woke up when he left and decided to move to my bed in the bedroom for some more sleep. Kathy was asleep in Harry's bed, which was at right angles to mine.

I was just drifting back into sleep when I realized that there were strange sounds coming from Kathy's side of the room. It—it—it sounded like humping! What in the world? Could she be masturbating over there? With me a few feet away, and probably quite willing to offer my services?

So I sat up in bed and gawked over at Kathy and saw that she was having some sort of fit. Her face was blue and she seemed to be choking. All at once the significance of what her "thing" was hit me like the slap of a wet fist. Epilepsy! She was having a *grande mal* seizure!

Without doing a lot of thinking I jumped up and grabbed her. Her body was bouncing up off the bed with each violent contraction. I reached into her mouth, thinking that she may have swallowed her tongue, and tried to open her airway. It worked but she bit down on my fingers hard, her teeth cutting all the way to the bone. About a pint of yellowish-green bile shot out of her mouth onto the floor. After about a minute of gasping, her convulsions became less forceful and she seemed to be breathing okay. Her eyes never opened and she seemed to be unconscious during the whole thing. She had urinated all over the bed and her pajamas (which were probably Harry's pajamas).

Finally, she seemed to go into a deep sleep, but I kept careful watch to make sure she was still breathing. I called Harry and told him he needed to get back home quick, then I sat on my bed watching her for about a half hour until she woke up. She immediately realized what must have happened, and was embarrassed. But I tried to make her feel comfortable by babbling about how everything was okay and Harry would be there any minute to take her home or whatever she wanted.

Harry showed up and they left. I don't think I ever saw her again and don't remember if Harry ever did, either.

I bandaged my fingers as best I could and the cuts luckily didn't get infected.

That was the end of the summer of '65 and I was soon to go off to college in Las Cruces. Judi went to Fort Lewis in Durango. Harry joined the navy not long after. I don't know what happened to Kathy. I wish the best.

After a couple of semesters of college I dropped out, spent about a year dodging the draft, trying to stay high and get laid. I played for a while in a country & western band at the El Vasito Bar in Farmington and a strip bar in Greeley Colorado, then joined the army in March of 1967, a month before I was due to be drafted.

My travels with Harry were over. We both stayed with music after our brilliant military careers ended and had some more great times in Durango, Farmington and Albuquerque, but in different bands.

DAWN 1979

An Erotic Reminiscence

Note: In the early 90s when I was the editor of a Commodore disk magazine, one of the subscribers who regularly wrote to me was a tattooed woman biker named Patricia. She told me that she made some extra money by writing "letters to the editor" for magazines like Hustler and Penthouse. I was fascinated and she sent me some of her manuscripts, which she said were often real things that she had done, but embellished and eroticized in the proscribed Hustler/Penthouse style. She asked me to send her a story in the same vein, so I wrote up a sexually charged account of an experience I had had back in 1979 when I lived in Las Cruces NM. I wasn't too disappointed when she said that I "didn't quite have the style down"—I wasn't sure if I really wanted to be able to write like the people who wrote to Penthouse. So the following story is true, but tarted up, Hustler-style.

I MET HER where I met all of the women I knew in those days—at the Las Cruces Inn, where I was in the house band. Her blonde hair was about an inch long all over and she was wearing grey overalls. The first thing I thought was that she had just gotten out of prison. I still think that.

She walked into the bar late one night and began fidgeting from table to table as if looking for someone. I was sitting by myself and she asked if she could sit down. She said her name was Dawn and asked me what I did during the day. I said I swam in the pool behind the motel. I asked her what she did and she said she usually swam down by the river but that she was through doing that—because that morning as she was wading she stepped on the bones of what was at least twenty human bodies.

I acted as if I believed her and asked for more information about the bones but she would only answer in meaningless, vague terms. I had to go back to work and she left before the next set was over.

The next day I was in the pool by myself when she walked up to the poolside, wearing jeans and short t-shirt. She asked me if I had a knife and I laughed and said not at this time. She explained that she wanted to cut off the legs of her Levis so she could come swimming with me. She left for a few minutes and came back wearing newly-cutoff jeans. "Uh oh," she said, "I cut one of the legs too high." It was true; she had.

She jumped in and we played around in the water. It was nearly noon so there was no one else at the poolside. As we swam she resumed talking about the bodies in the river and it was obvious she believed her story. I found it very easy to talk to her because I didn't feel any need to make sense or be consistent. I felt like I was a character in someone's novel.

We had been swimming for about an hour when I went underwater with my goggles on and found myself in the perfect position to see past her short cutoffs. In perfect focus I saw the silky blonde pubic hair that almost covered her thin, short slit. As she moved I saw the lips part slightly and a quick ray of coral pink flashed from inside. I felt the cold, tight skin of my scrotum flush with warmth as my cock jerked inside my trunks. It was that moment that I said to myself, "I want to fuck her."

I said we should go over to my house and dry off and we quickly left the motel. The first thing I did at the house was sit in my reclining chair in the living room and lean all the way back. I dropped my sandals on the floor and dangled my bare feet over the footrest, about waist high. Something about the moment made me say, "Hey, come over here," and she walked towards me.

As she moved close to the footrest of the chair I slipped my left foot inside the short side of her cutoffs and caressed her clitoris with my big toe. She stopped and looked down at me as she moved her pelvis against my foot. There were no words spoken as she continued to move in small, rhythmic cycles against my toe. The only sound was her breathing and the exquisite moist whisper of her vulva as my toe slid liquidly from the back of her cunt to the clitoris and back again.

After a while I pulled my foot back and sat up in the chair as she stood in front of me. I put a hand on each buttock, pulled her to me and pressed my face and lips against her bare stomach. Her skin was salty from the chlorinated water and very smooth.

I stood up and we went into the bedroom. I removed her cutoffs and t-shirt and watched her stretch out on the purple comforter on the bed. She lightly pinched her left nipple with her left thumb and forefinger and slowly moved her right hand to her cunt. As the afternoon sun shone on her through the window, I watched her massage her clitoris with her middle finger.

I took off my trunks and joined her on the bed. First we had a few hits on my trusty hash pipe then she crawled on top of me and began kissing me, lightly nipping at my nipples with her lips. She rubbed her moist vulva against my thigh and held my balls in her hand. I began moving in rhythm with her and she moved up and looked me in the eyes before lowering her head and taking my cock into her mouth.

The warmth and wetness of her mouth surprised me as I propped a pillow beneath my head so I could watch my shiny cock slide past her wet lips. The sunlight streamed through the window behind my head, illuminating her face as she licked at the underside of my rigid cock. Her left hand caressed my scrotum with a steady, intense pressure while her right hand grasped the shaft. Her small hand made my dick look much bigger to me than it ordinarily looked.

She had a look on her face that was not serious or frivolous, but some unfathomable emotion in between. She would look at my face as she licked the underside of the head of my cock with her short, broad tongue. I involuntarily thrust my hips forward pushing my cock into her mouth until her lips pressed against her hand. I could feel the hot, wet insides of her mouth press on my dick on all sides with a firm, velvety pressure. I wiggled my hips and she fluttered her tongue on me without loosening her grip.

After a time she raised her head and moved up in the bed until she was straddling my head with her knees. With the window wide open anyone behind the house could see her smooth, white body and small, firm breasts. I didn't care because as I looked up I could see a glistening pearl of pink flesh peeping out between moist, swollen lips. I extended the tip of my tongue till it brushed against her clitoris and she gave a quick jerk.

She lowered her pelvis a little at a time until her vulva was pressed against my open mouth and I tongued the salty slickness of her cunt. She began to moan in earnest and pinched her nipples as she rocked on my face. I grasped her buttocks and slipped my fingers into the cleft and teased her tiny anus. At first she seemed uncomfortable when I pressed a finger on the puckered opening, but soon she pulled away from my tongue, moving her bottom back until the tip of my middle finger entered her anus. I pushed gently with my finger and she moved back onto my mouth with her cunt. She rocked back and forth, impaled on my tongue and my finger at the same time, thrusting each a little deeper into her body with each movement.

I sensed she was about to come so I flicked my tongue against her clit a little faster and harder. She gave a long, low moan and bucked against my mouth in a dozen short, intense jerks. A final contraction of her sphincter pushed my finger out of her as I gave her clitoris a parting lick. She lay down on the bed beside me and kissed my earlobe.

I got up on one elbow and lightly moved my fingernails up and down her body, pushing her until she was lying on her stomach and looking out the window. Every time my fingertips brushed her firm, smooth cheeks her buttocks would twitch and rise a little higher in the air. Pretty soon she had her face and breasts pushed into the silk comforter and I began massaging her upthrust hips and open thighs. I touched her with pliant fingers from her pubic hair to the base of her spine in slow, lingering strokes.

When she started moving her hips from side to side I moved behind her and rubbed her clitoris with my cock. Then I gently pushed into her.

She was swollen from the tonguing and stroking and her cunt felt like a hot, mossy glove. She gasped when I was half in and said, "Slow. I haven't done this in a while." No dick in women's prison, I figured.

I remained still while she moved her hips and slowly pushed her yielding vagina back on my rigid cock. When I felt her clench her cuntlips on the base of my shaft I began to pull back from that exquisite glove. I kept my strokes long, but slow, so she could move her hips and fuck me as much as I was fucking her. We developed a rhythm that put me on the edge of coming for about an hour.

We were both looking out the window as we fucked and saw my grey tabby cat sneak upon some grackles that were drinking from the hose. He was low to the ground and moved at an almost imperceptible speed towards the biggest bird.

I started pumping into silky cunt a little more intently and felt the glow from my cock take the slight edge that signals an impending orgasm. The cat was ready to pounce and I could feel the semen moving to the base of my cock as Dawn clenched her vagina around me.

The cat leapt, the bird squawked, the girl groaned and I came. And came. Her cunt was palpating my jetting cock so strongly that I missed the drama outside. All I knew afterwards was that my balls felt strangely hollow and that my cat was dining on a bird that was black on the outside, but very red on the inside.

Dawn and I got up as the sun went down and I drove her back to the motel. She wasn't staying there—I never knew where she stayed, or where she came from—but she wanted dropped off there anyway. When I came to work that night at the motel lounge, I expected to see her. I wondered how I was going to handle this potentially explosive situation, but I never saw or heard of Dawn again.

Whew! Another bullet dodged.

THE MOTHRA CAPER

A Military Reminiscence

I GUESS the Mothra Caper really began back in October of 1966 in North Hollywood CA when I was 18. I was living there with a friend, Barry, who had invited me out in a letter telling me all about this new kick that was the rage of the coast: *marijuana*. I had just finished with a month-long gig with a country & western band in Greeley CO and since the band was breaking up, I figured what the hell and sold my amp and rode the Greyhound out to LA.

Barry worked during the day so I spent my days watching TV and sampling as much of the new kick as I could afford. Since it was $10 an ounce back then, it was a lot more affordable than booze.

One of the LA TV stations had an afternoon theater which showed the same film ten or so times during the week. This was a new concept to me, and I found that I enjoyed seeing the same movie over and over. One week the film was "Mothra", the classic Japanese monster movie that featured a giant moth controlled by two miniature Japanese girls. I devoured it, and soon Barry and I had added "Mothra" to our vocabularies as a buzzword, meaning anything we wanted. We gave it the Japanese pronunciation, with a long "o".

This being 1966 and my being 18 meant that I was dodging the draft. But the Selective Service System tracked me down and I soon took the physical and found myself rated 1-A, which meant I had a license to be killed. So in March, 1967, I joined the US Army in order to avoid the draft.

Here's the rationale: back then those who were drafted were sent wherever the US Army wanted, which was Vietnam, where the generals needed cannon fodder. Draftees only had to dodge death for two years, though. An enlistee had to eke out three years as a slave to the system. But there was a benefit to joining: you got three pre-enlistment options.

If you signed up for three years you could choose:

(1) The army school you were to go to, or
(2) The country you were to first be sent to, or
(3) To accompany a buddy for a year or so in service.

I figured that if I were to become a technician on the Nike Hercules missile, there would be little chance of being sent to Vietnam, since the Nike Hercules delivered an atomic bomb as its payload. I believed that even the generals wouldn't be so stupid as to escalate Vietnam into an atomic war.

So I enlisted with the guarantee that I would attend the Nike Hercules Guidance System school at Fort Bliss TX. On March 5, 1967 I got off the train in El Paso as a soldier in the US Army. It was around 10 P.M. and there were around 200 of us sitting in a large classroom. We had each been given a pill upon entering the room, ostensibly for "meningitis", but after about an hour I knew that it wasn't for any disease. It was an amphetamine pill to keep us awake all night while we filled out forms and questionnaires. At least the army had some decent dope.

The next morning we were marched to a cafeteria for our very first army meal. We hadn't even gotten haircuts yet. I looked at the food and thought, "Hey, great! Tiny little steaks! Maybe this Army gig won't be so bad after all." Then I took a bite and found for the first time that liver looks a little bit like real meat, but it sure doesn't taste like it. Maybe it was the amphetamine wearing off, or maybe it was the liver, but I knew I was in for a long, painful three years—if I was lucky.

The first six weeks were spent in basic training, a period of pain and degradation. I learned to hate the military mentality and all it stood for. The only thing I liked was the innate inefficiency of the system. For instance, by the third week I figured it was time my basic buddies and I had something to smoke so I wrote to Mo, a band friend who was renting a room at my mother's house in Farmington NM, asking him to find my stash and send it to me.

He did. I expected him to put it in a box or something but noooo. He simply wrapped the baggie with the half ounce of leafy material in one thickness of brown wrapping paper, scribbled my Fort Bliss address on it and mailed it. In 1967 the awareness of drugs was so limited that this cylindrical, crunchy package made it all the way to me, passing through who knows how many hands.

In May 1967 I survived basic training and was assigned to barracks on another part of Fort Bliss to attend the Nike Hercules Guidance school. There I became friends with Klein, Gardner and McGuire, three guys who shared my enjoyment of cannabis. For the next month or so we had a lot of fun dodging the sergeants and those who would try to mold us into militaristic automatons.

At first we struck out while trying to buy weed in Juarez Mexico, just across the border. So we had to make do with what Gardner's girlfriend sent us from San Francisco. What we didn't know was that Gardner was telling her in his letters all about our activities and appreciation.

We found out sometime in July, when the four of us were unceremoniously pulled out of class and told to wait in our cubicle for further orders. After about a day of wondering what was going on we were taken in, one at a time, to be interviewed by the CID, the army's version of the Gestapo. That's when we found out that Gardner's girl had been busted by the SF police, and his letters sent to the army CID at Fort Bliss. All four of us were named, in sentences like, "Fender sure did like the pot and the acid you sent."

The purpose of basic training is to break down the ego so that a recruit will jump into fire at the whim of an officer. Well, our egos were as irrationally strong as ever, but our ambitions were nil. By the time we were jerked out of school, we saw our lives as meaningless and ruined. As long as we were in the army, our bodies were "their" problem, not ours. Our job was to stay as high as possible and to thwart the goals of the "enemy" as long as it didn't require too much labor. The enemy was of course the sergeants and the officers.

We found that all of our cases were to be investtigated by a seedy civilian, McDougal, and that we were his first cases ever. I guess he expected us to confess our sins but we decided to just deny everything and let army nature take its course. I was the first one interviewed and I acted dumb, which we had found to be one of the handiest ways to act while in the army. McDougal told me what they had on us and then ordered me to send in the next suspect, Klein. Before Klein went in, I told him and the other two exactly what the army knew.

Later, McDougal called me in and berated me for squealing, "I thought I told you not to tell!" I acted embarrassed and he seemed mollified. I figured that if this was the caliber of the CID investigators, we just might beat this rap.

So the four of us became "duty-troopers". Every day we were sent to different places around the post to sweep, mop, wax and buff floors, or whatever else was needed. Hmmm. This was quite a bit more interesting than Guidance System school. In fact, the very first place we were sent, two days after getting busted for suspected drug usage, was the US Drug Warehouse at William Beaumont Army Hospital.

There we were, four lowly GIs out looking for new ways to get high, pushing brooms through rows and rows of 15-foot tall racks filled with pills and nostrums. We quickly found that all of the narcotics were locked up, so we had to rely on our encyclopedic knowledge of non-narcotic intoxicants. We tried reserpine, made from rauwolfia, but it only made us sleepy. Then we discovered L-Dopa, which decades later was found to be useful for Parkinson's disease, and also for promoting erections in 90-year-olds. We didn't need the help at the time; we just thought it had a neat name.

It was around this time that I met a beautiful lady at the PX. She worked in the part of the store where cloth insignias were made and sewed onto uniforms. She was a decade older than I was and I doubt if she ever knew that I was seriously flirting with her. She probably thought I was "cute". So, for a lark, I used to stop by and buy insignias from her. Instead of "TUCKER" which was on a patch over the left breast pocket of all of my fatigues, I had a fatigue shirt that read "FENDER". On the shoulder, where the battalion or post patch was supposed to go, I had a specially made peace sign insignia. And above the right breast pocket, where it was supposed to say "US ARMY", mine said "US MOTHRA". This was my favorite off-post shirt.

We had become quite lackadaisical about everything by that fall. Everybody else had to go to class, while we stayed stoned and kept the barracks running. By that time we had been duty-troopers so long we were practically in charge of the whole barracks, if not in an official sense.

We were helped by a discovery we had made in Juarez, a diet pill called Preludin. This was the same pill that the Beatles used to take to stay awake all night in Hamburg Germany before they became the Fab Four. We found that five or ten milligrams of Preludin (which came in five milligram tabs) would keep us running all day or night, as the case may be.

The First Sergeant of the barracks was a particular nemesis to us. He didn't like our attitudes and was always trying to get us to read "The Battle of Dien Bien Phu". He said that book would show us what we were fighting for in Vietnam. I read it and became even more anti-militaristic. How long does it take a bully nation (like France, then the USA) to realize that people who live directly on the earth will die before allowing it to be paved for shopping malls?

But there was almost a connection between the First Sergeant and us. He seemed to know that we were taking pills and smoking dope, and threatened us with the stockade if he caught us, but he never took the simple, but unethical, steps of having us watched by informers. I commend him for that. Then one day when I was cleaning his office, I decided to rifle his desk. There, in his top drawer was a prescription bottle filled with Preludins, in 30-milligram tablets! He was buzzing every day on three times the amount of speed that we were.

This was the US Army in 1967—everyone looking out for himself. If you didn't make waves and call attention to yourself, you could get away with anything. Apparently, we liked the attention.

One night we decided to go to Juarez and perhaps sample some of the prostitutes that the army promoted to its troops. In 1967 it was "smoke 'em if you got 'em" and "a real man takes what he wants from women." Perhaps not in those exact words, but the underlying message was that a soldier had a mission, and women were to be used and not allowed to get in the way. My, how times have changed.

Instead, we got pretty drunk at the Manhattan Club and staggered back across the border around midnight. As always, I hadn't bothered to get an off-base pass. I was also wearing my favorite shirt, with US MOTHRA, the peace sign and FENDER on it.

For the first time ever, the border MPs stopped me and when they determined that I was a GI without a pass, and in a suspicious shirt, they threw me in a paddy wagon and hauled me onto base to the MP station. There the sergeant in charge practically ripped the shirt off my back and made me sit in a corner, awaiting further orders. By this time the booze and pot were wearing off and I was feeling rather sleepy.

I perked up when there was a bustle in the station, with MPs buzzing about an attempted harassment of the poor basic trainee who was guarding the PX. Apparently, a group of hooligans in a truck had thrown beer bottles at the sentry as he was marching around the building. The truck had been stopped later on and the sergeant was trying to organize a line-up to see if the young GI could identify the harassers. He looked at me, shirtless and hung over, and said, "Hey you, get up there and join that line-up!"

So there I was, in line with a half dozen or so guys in civilian dress. As the only one without a shirt I looked guilty as hell...of something. Then I noticed the face of the sentry who was dressed in battle fatigues, complete with M-1 rifle and canteen—it was Mike, a guy one year behind me at Farmington High School! I hadn't seen him in over a year but we had been pretty good friends.

Mike saw me and said, "Hey, Fender," and I gave him a smile and a meek wave. The sergeant caught this and blustered, "Is that the asshole who was throwing bottles at you?"

Mike said, "No, he's just a guy I know," then identified some of the other guys in the line-up. I think the sergeant was quite disappointed at not getting me for two infractions. After the line-up I was sent back to the cell for a few more hours and finally told to get back to my barracks. I was lucky to make it the dozen or so blocks to the barracks without getting picked up for walking around shirtless on an army base.

A few days later I was called in by McDougal. On his desk was my shirt in all its glory. He asked, "Just what is this, 'Mothra'?"

I decided to be truthful. "Well, it's the giant moth that destroyed Tokyo."

He rubbed his chin thoughtfully and said, "Yes, that's true. We contacted the Japanese Liaison Office and 'mothra' does mean 'giant moth'. We also checked with the university administrators where you went to college and they claim to have no knowledge of any subversive groups under that name. Care to explain?"

I decided to act as if it were nothing, which wasn't hard to do, but left enough things unsaid to keep him guessing. I wouldn't be surprised to find that a list of the subversive groups that the FBI and the CIA investigated in those paranoid days contains the group, "US MOTHRA". I had made the big time.

As with all things in the army in 1967, the whole thing blew over. There was no way that the CID could follow up on all of the suspicious things that were happening. Half of the soldiers hated their situation, the other half tolerated it because there was money to be made in war. Only a few officers thought that there was anything noble about the war, and they soon found out differently when they were sent to Nam.

So the Mothra Caper ended when the CID decided to end the whole affair by dropping the investigation in December 1967. The four of us were sent to different bases where we all got reasonably good jobs.

In fact, it was the investigation itself that perhaps saved my life. I went to Redstone Arsenal in Huntsville AL where I became a clerk-typist and chauffeur for an office. This was a group of about ten higher-ranking officers, two sergeants-major (the highest enlisted rank) and a dozen civilian workers, some of them women.

I learned to type and drive a car, (after I had assured the army that I already knew how to do both, but didn't) and was treated quite reasonably by everyone. I spent all of 1968 at Redstone, and became good friends with everyone, particularly the two sergeants-major. It was an irony of military life that the people who were the worst to you were those who were directly above you in rank, the E-6 sergeants and the O-2 lieutenants. Once a person got up to be a colonel or a sergeant-major, they lost some of their lust for power and actually treated the low-ranking slobs as humans.

In November of 1968, there was a big push to "win" in Vietnam. Richard Nixon had just been elected on a "stop-the-war honorably" platform, and of course before long he was secretly bombing Cambodia "back into the stone age", killing hundreds of thousands of women and children whose only crime was that they fed and sheltered their fellow man from the B-52s raining death from above.

It was at this time that I received orders to go to Vietnam. I had one week to get my life in order before flying to Saigon.

It was indicative of the time that the two sergeants-major asked me if I really wanted to go to Vietnam. They surely didn't want to go and they commiserated with any of the poor soldiers who had to go off to a war that was a total debacle. The SGMs were not anti-war demonstrators; these were 30-year veterans of the US Army.

I told them I did *not* want to go and they asked me if I could think of any way I could get out of it. I thought about it for a few minutes and came up with, "Well, when I joined the army I was given a guarantee that I would go to a certain school, the Nike Hercules Guidance System school. Then, because of an investigation which was later deemed groundless by the CID, I was taken out of this school. I think the US Army has the obligation to return me to school."

They looked at each other and agreed that that was a pretty compelling argument. So they changed my orders, sending me to a Nike Hercules Launcher school there in Huntsville. By the time I finished that school, I had less than 10 months left in my three years' duty, so I was too "short" to be sent to Vietnam. I spent the last year back at Fort Bliss, where I was the Operations clerk of a mobile armored battalion.

Thirty years later, people may look back and wonder if some other poor GI was sent to Nam in my place, to die in the jungles. Maybe so, but anyone who was alive and of military age during that dark period of our history will remember the utter divisiveness of the war. I wasn't saved by traitors to the United States; I was saved by career soldiers who had fought in World War II and Korea. They saw Vietnam as the huge mistake it was and they were willing to use "regulations" to keep me from getting killed to further the political ambitions of Richard Nixon and the rest of the war hawks.

The United States was a giant moth in those days, spewing destruction wherever it went. Like Mothra, acting under the control of our two little girls, Nixon and Kissinger, it was righteous, and like every other cause that claims "righteousness", it was dead wrong.

There is no way to explain it to the fifty thousand GIs—many of whom were draftees—who were killed by our country's Mothra Caper.

THE BERTRAND RUSSELL AFFAIR

Another Military Reminiscence

IN THE SUMMER of 1967 I was just out of army boot camp and living in sumptuous barracks at Fort Bliss, Texas, attending a Nike Hercules Missile School by day, getting loaded by night. I was 19 years old and not at all sure I'd survive the next three years.

The sumptuous barracks were three-storey brick buildings with 20-man bays at each end and a dozen or so rooms in between. The building I lived in was one of 20 or more that littered the flatness of Fort Bliss like caskets in the sun. Every morning young GIs would stream out of the barracks like ants on their way to other caskets to study the intricacies of raining death on one's fellow man from a distance of 100 miles. I was one of those ants until I was lucky enough to get investigated for unauthorized drug use.

The whole story is related in *THE MOTHRA CAPER* so I won't go into it here, but by late summer three of my friends and I were firmly entrenched as duty troopers at the casket we called home. That meant we were not students, as everybody else was, but those who spent their days and nights doing whatever needed to be done at the barracks. During the day we would mop and buff the tile floors, and generally look busy, and at night we would man the main desk, answer the phones, and wake everybody up at 5 A.M. Mostly we just tried to stay high and dodge the Captain, the First Sergeant and any other sergeants who were also attending class with the privates. They didn't like the idea of us having the run of the building but what could they do? We had to live somewhere while awaiting the results of the investigation into our suspected drug use.

Technically, we were confined to the building for the duration, but since there was no precedent for permanent duty troopers, the First Sergeant allowed us to go into town on the weekends. However, once he went home for the day around 5:00 we felt free to do whatever we wanted, and often walked into El Paso or across the Rio Grande into Juarez. As long as one of us was around the barracks, they would never know.

One day I woke up and found that a lipoma, a small sebaceous cyst, had popped up on the side of my eye socket, right in front of my temple. Since my body belonged to Uncle Sam, as the sergeants reminded us daily, I wasn't worried. It was their problem. I walked over to the nearest clinic and showed it to a doctor. Typically, he looked at it, told me it was a lipoma, and without asking me what I wanted to do about it, sat me down in his chair, jabbed me with some novacaine (probably cut with water by the doctor himself or one of the GIs that worked at the clinic), and proceeded to remove the bump, which was about as big as a small marble. It was an hour of pain and I ended up with a horrible looking black eye and the ubiquitous Darvons that the army gave for every complaint.

I went back to the barracks and again, typically, no one said anything, even when I started wearing a suave-looking eye patch. I thoroughly enjoyed the double takes that army brass would give me when they drove by and saw one of America's young patriotic soldiers—with an eye patch out of a Van Heusen ad. He looks great, but can he shoot?

The black eye and the patch went away a week or so later and life settled into a routine at the barracks. We'd work around the barracks during the day, dropping off every hour or so to the basement where we'd toke up on the excellent weed that was so cheap in El Paso. The basement was filled with scores of extra lockers, six-foot tall and separate from each other. My buddies and I had arranged the lockers so that by moving a key one near the wall one would enter a labyrinthine corridor made of lockers leading to what we called our "lounge". Here we had smoking and reading materials (William Burroughs' *Naked Lunch* was our favorite), as well as some recording equipment for our late night jam sessions.

At night we'd listen to albums or make recordings. Once we added Hanson, a guy with a Volkswagen, to our coterie, we would drive around El Paso toking up, looking for a place where we could smoke without having to drive. Often we'd end up out in the desert, searching for peyote by flashlight (and never finding any).

One Saturday morning about two weeks after my lipoma caper Hanson and I decided to go into El Paso and check out some bookstores. We spent all day goofing around and when I got back to the barracks I got the news that I was in big trouble. Apparently the Captain had proclaimed a "let's all get together and beautify the barracks" day and he and all of the sergeants mingled with the students until the midafternoon, painting and landscaping the area. Roll had been taken and I was flagrantly missing. AWOL! Perhaps DESERTION! Boy was I gonna get it the next morning when the Captain and First Sergeant showed up.

I assessed my situation and it looked grim. I couldn't claim to have been locked in the basement. They'd discover our lounge. I wasn't in the stockade, although that would have been a damn good alibi. But how about the hospital? It was a crazy idea but it just might be crazy enough to work!

I decided that I needed to go to the hospital and claim to have been there all day. That would be a great excuse for being missing from the barracks. But what illness? It had to be something that I could prove, something more than just a claimed malaise. Then it hit me like the wet fist of an overweight onanist—my lipoma! What if it were to suddenly, and mysteriously, swell back up? I could make it do that.

My first thought, and one that was seconded by buddy Gardner, was to have someone slug me on the scar. It had healed up well but there was still a noticeable scar on the side of my eye socket. Gardner volunteered (rather quickly I must say) and with a few practice swings punched me on my scar. Not hard enough, I told him, and he warmed to the task. His next blow was plenty hard enough but my eye perversely kept its healed look. I needed something more destructive than a 150-pound sadist's fist.

I looked around the room (which was Gardner's) and spied a huge library book: *The Autobiography of Bertrand Russell*. He was a great man; surely his autobiography ought to be hefty enough to cause damage to a young soldier's eye? It was. I started out slowly, with a few tentative whacks, mainly just for practice. Then I applied the *coup de grace* to the stubborn cicatrix. With one mighty blow of the beloved mathematician/philosopher's words, I caused my lipoma scar to double in size and take on the angry red glow of freedom. And I was on my way to the hospital!

I decided the clinic wasn't impressive enough of a medical building for my little drama and walked up to William Beaumont Hospital, a mile or two up Dyer Street. I had it all planned out. I would tell my tale of painful woe to a doctor, get written proof that I had been there, somehow change the time to an earlier hour (if necessary) and walk back to the barracks. In the morning I'd pitifully trudge into the First Sergeant's office, apologize for missing the beautification program, and offer to work all day, even though "the doctor mentioned something about a week off of work."

The plan proceeded nicely. At the hospital I introduced myself to a Spec-4 at the front desk of the emergency ward and asked to see a doctor about an operation that seemed to have gone bad. He had me sign a few forms and within a half hour I was with a doctor. He looked at my eye critically and asked, "It just popped up? Nothing hit it?"

"No sir," I answered respectfully. "It just swole up this morning out of the blue. I've been here all day hoping it would go down, but it hasn't."

"Well," he said, "It doesn't look like anything too bad. Take a Darvon or two and get back to work."

"Yes, sir. I'm on my way as soon as I have a confirmation slip to show my First Sergeant."

He waved me towards the Spec-4 and left. I stopped by the front desk and asked the Spec-4 for something to show that I'd been in to see a doctor. He looked at me condescendingly and said, "You're not going anywhere. You signed an admission slip."

"Yeah, but the doctor said I could go back to my barracks."

"Well, it doesn't matter what the doctor said, you signed an admission slip and that means you gotta be admitted."

I had learned that arguing with a superior officer (or even a Spec-4, who just barely outranked me) was not a good idea in the army, especially when he had paperwork on his side. So I gave myself up to bureaucracy and found myself being led to a hospital ward, where I changed into hospital togs and slipped into a bed that was about 100 times more comfortable than my bed back at the barracks.

When the nurse asked me if there was anything I needed before dinner, I meekly moaned, "How about some Darvs?" She left and soon came back with a cute little pill bottle with a dozen red and gray beauties inside, promising relief from the excruciating pain that somehow I didn't feel all that much. I had struck malingering paydirt!

The next day I expected the doctor to stop by and discharge me but he never came. I read magazines, dropped Darvs and marveled at how much better hospital food was than the swill we got at the barracks dining room. By midafternoon when it looked like the doctor wasn't going to come I called the barracks and spoke to Klein, my buddy who was in charge that day. He wondered what happened to me and thought it was great that I got to stay at the hospital. He said the Captain and the First Sergeant spent a significant part of the day talking about how they were going to throw the book at me once the police or MPs caught me. My buddies, loyal to the core, acted dumb when asked if they knew where I had gone. They figured the hospital would inform the barracks sooner or later. I did too.

That night Klein, Gardner and Hanson stopped by the hospital and brought me some of my books. We sat around the ward for a couple of hours, dropping Darvs, and having a pretty good time. We even went outside and had a smoke or two. At night, the patients were on their own, at least in the ward where I was.

The next day, still no doctor. I asked the nurse what the story was and she said that until the papers for my discharge from the hospital were signed by a doctor, I was staying. I ruefully smiled and said, "Well, I guess the army knows best, but I will probably need some more Darvs." Another dozen, coming right up. The army knows how to take care of its own.

Finally, on the third day the doctor stopped by. The swelling had gone down to practically nothing, but my eye was still red. He looked at me and said, "You look okay, I guess you can go back to your barracks." I thanked him and he went on his way. I asked the nurse on duty how I could go about getting my clothes and she said not until I had discharge papers signed by a doctor. Apparently he forgot to sign the papers for me to leave.

Three more days went by. The gang from the barracks were stopping by every evening on their nightly carousal, so I didn't have to forgo weed whilst I was recovering. In return they enjoyed my Darvons which the US army was kind enough to supply me with to ease my pain. They said that the Captain and First Sergeant had stopped talking about me, probably figuring me for a real deserter, perhaps off to Canada. As far as anyone knew, the hospital had not notified the barracks of my stay.

At last, one week after my fateful meeting with the pacifistic teachings of Bertrand Russell, the doctor came back to the ward and upon seeing me, exclaimed, "What the hell are you doing here? I thought I discharged you days ago!"

I mumbled something about how I needed certain papers and how I missed my barracks and job and wanted so desperately to go back, and he said, "This time you're outta here." Sure enough, in fifteen minutes I was dressed in my khakis and, with discharge papers in hand, on my way back to my beloved barracks. There was no time of admission in the papers, just the date, so I was feeling pretty good. I was a young man, full of piss and propoxyphene, and I had the world by the tail—except of course for that pesky Viet Nam thing that constantly loomed over our heads.

I decided to take advantage of the missing times on the discharge papers. It was morning but who's to say that I wasn't discharged until late afternoon? I wasn't really looking forward to seeing the Captain and First Sergeant. Even though I had the law on my side, there were times in the military life when the law was worthless. After all, if an Officer and Gentleman of the United States Army wanted to bludgeon to death an inferior entrusted to him by the US Constitution, why, surely he had the right?

So I walked down Dyer and decided to check out the Main Post, where the generals hung out. These were slightly more classy 4-storey buildings with offices and auditoriums. I had seen them from the outside but had never been in them. With my papers looking awfully official by my side I went from building to building, respectfully nodding at spiffily dressed generals and colonels—no saluting indoors. The old army adage was right: If you walk around with a clip board, looking like you know what you're doing, no one will bother you.

I went into the largest building and saw that there was some sort of gathering of fellow low-ranking GIs in a huge auditorium. There was a young officer on stage and the audience seemed to be in a good mood. This was unusual. I'd been in several audiences in the six months I'd been in the army, but I'd never seen anyone actually enjoying the experience.

I took a seat in the rear of the auditorium and listened to the officer tell about an assignment for which he was looking for volunteers. He said, "At Fort Detrick we are concerned with chemical weapons, and I'm not talking about bombs. I'm talking about gasses, and drugs, and other kinds of mental warfare. We need people like you to come to Fort Detrick and help us determine which chemicals work and which ones don't." A nervous titter ran through the audience.

"The best thing about duty at Detrick," he continued, "is that there's no duty! No morning musters, no barracks inspections, no guard duty or KP, and get this—no haircuts!" The crowd whooped. "We leave you alone because your work is too important for us to care about military bullshit. You will be testing the army's latest chemical weapons—on yourselves.

"Now, it isn't all fun and games. Some of the volunteers will get the good stuff, LSD, mescaline, and a few goodies that even the hippies out in San Francisco don't know about. Others will do stuff like stick your head into a hole in a wall while some kind of gas is pumped into the small chamber your head is in. You'll be asked to endure the gas as long as you can then tell the supervisors what it feels like.

"No haircuts! No duty! Just drugs and chemical weapons. This is a great opportunity to get high and help out your country at the same time."

I didn't stay long. I had been in the army for less than six months, all of them at Fort Bliss, but I had heard about Fort Detrick. I figured this was an everyday happening in this part of the army. I assumed that everybody knew that the army was using soldiers to test chemical weapons.

But I had been in the army long enough to know that volunteering is generally not a good idea. So even though I probably would have been a model guinea pig for chemical weapons (in the eyes of the brass) I wasn't going to volunteer. Anyway, I wasn't even supposed to be in that crowd.

So I eventually wandered back to the barracks around 5 P.M, just when the Captain and First Sergeant were leaving for home. With hospital papers in hand I strode into the First Sergeant's office and started telling him how good it felt to be back at the barracks. He got up and pulled me into the Captain's office where I repeated my explanation. They studied the papers for a few minutes and with looks of disgust and disappointment on their faces, told me to get out and never come back to this part of the building again.

Good soldier that I was, I did my damnedest to comply. It was the end of a perfectly wonderful affair. I think Bertrand Russell would have approved.

HOW I BECAME A SHARPSHOOTER

Yet Another Military Reminiscence

I WAS ONLY in the army for three years but more weird things happened to me during those three years than in any ten years since. When you're in a rough situation with a bunch of strangers, you make friends fast and ferociously. Wartime is full of ironies, and when your life is on the line, the ironies can become hilarious—and at times, tragic.

In 1967 I was 19 and about to get drafted so, upon the advice of a friend's father, I enlisted for three years, hoping that being an enlistee rather than a draftee, I would have a better chance of staying out of Viet Nam. I was sent to Fort Bliss TX for Basic Training in March of 1967.

I hated it, of course, but found that with the help of the terrific buddies I made, it was doable. We drilled, worked out, crawled through the dirt, stabbed dummies with bayonets shouting "Kill!", and about a month into the 6 week long program we hiked out to the rifle range to learn how to shoot. I had never shot anything more powerful than a Daisy BB Rifle, but I figured it was time I learned.

So we spent a week or so shooting at targets with our M-1 rifles. The M-1 was an obsolete weapon from a war long past, but the word was that there weren't enough M-16 rifles to allow us to train with them. We'd get an M-16 when we went to Viet Nam, they said. Yippee.

I wasn't getting any better at shooting as the time came for us to "qualify" for marksmanship badges, but I figured that if I wasn't good enough I'd get more training. There were three "ranks" of marksmanship: Marksman—the lowest; Sharpshooter—the next best; and Expert—the best shooters. If you couldn't shoot at at least Marksman level, you were "washed out" of Basic Training and either mustered out of the army or had to go through Basic again. Or so they said. I seriously doubt if any-

one were mustered out of the army unless they had some powerful relative or friend behind them.

So it came the big day of the Rifle Qualifications. The company, which consisted of around 200 privates, was called to order
in formation and a sergeant said, "All right, you people, how
many of you pansies have been to college?" I wasn't in the habit
of volunteering anything, but I raised my hand. I had had two semesters of college. "Okay," he bleated, "all you college babies,
go over there."

So about twenty of us congregated away from the rest of the
troops. The lieutenant comes over and says, "Listen up. We figure you college guys are smart enough to follow instructions.
Here they are: No one, repeat, no one in this company shoots less
than Marksman. Got that? No one gets less than a Marksman.
And since you guys are the judges, all of you *will* be Experts.
Repeat, all of you *will* be Experts because you will be judging
each other."

We figured what the hell, the food is bad, the sergeants are sa-
dists and the war is a travesty; the rifle qualifications might as
well be rigged.

So I was a judge and made sure that everybody I judged was at
least a Marksman. Some of those poor guys never even hit a target all day. When it came time for me to judge a fellow judge, he
scored Expert. However, the guy who judged me must not have
been as brilliant in college as I since he gave me a Sharpshooter's
score, rather than an Expert's score. You know what, I didn't
give a damn. I was an atrocious shooter (still am) but after six
weeks in Basic Hell I was ready to get gunned down by whom-
ever Congress said the enemy was.

The story ended happily for me—I studied the Nike Hercules
Guidance System for a few months, got investigated for drug use,
then went to Redstone Arsenal in Alabama where I became a
colonel's chauffeur. I got orders for Viet Nam (as an infantry-
man!) but with the help of some NCOs I had become friends
with, I was able to have the orders rescinded—that's another war
story in itself—and spent my last year as a company clerk back at
Fort Bliss. No Viet Nam for the college boy.

I wonder if the story ended so well for the guys I made into
Experts and Sharpshooters, though. Whenever I'd read about Lee
Harvey Oswald and his Marine training, I'd wonder if his "Ex-
pert" medal was as phony as my "Sharpshooter" medal.

I don't know if this story was repeated at the other Basic Training camps around the country in those days, but I have a feeling that it was. In 1967 it was practically *impossible* to get out of the army once you were in. I had buddies who tried and they were severely punished—then forced to stay longer than their three years. The generals needed fodder; without major losses among the enlisted men, how can the generals claim to have "suffered"?

Oh well. Now that the draft has ended, maybe there's no need for cheating in the new US Army. Maybe everybody actually *is* a Marksman, Sharpshooter or Expert. I just hope that if I'm accused of shooting somebody someday, the prosecution doesn't bring up the fact that, according to my military records, I'm a Sharpshooter.

Could be worse, though. I coulda been an Expert.

HOW I GOT MY MANTRA

The Last Military Reminiscence
(Until the Next One)

THE STORY of how I became a lousy Transcendental Meditator has many beginnings, so I'll start with my first year in the Army—at Fort Bliss TX in 1967. I and my three buddies, Klein, Gardner and McGuire, were on permanent duty-trooper status. We were being investigated for suspected drug use and had been taken out of class—we were in school to become Nike Guidance System repairmen—and as duty-troopers, we spent all our days and nights cleaning up the barracks and doing odd jobs. Most importantly, *unsupervised* odd jobs.

So, for being in the Army, we were living pretty high. We had found a good connection for weed down in Juarez and between us and another couple of guys we had scrounged up enough money, $100, to buy a couple of kilos. But where to keep two large bundles of compacted green leafy material in an Army barracks?

We found the perfect place. At the end of the two-story building was a small 4' x 6' storage room for gardening tools. The door to it was nondescript—it was the only opening on that side of the building—and the roof of the room was tall, maybe 15 feet. There was plenty of room to stock stuff *up* in the room and we found a cozy spot on a high shelf, out of sight unless you climbed up to it on a ladder.

Since we were the only ones who used the room, we felt pretty safe. We'd only visit the stash when we needed to—which of course turned out to be every day.

One day McGuire was waiting in an outer office to talk to the First Sergeant about something when a fellow private, Hahn, walked in. McGuire, making small talk, asked Hahn what he was there for. Hahn says, "Well, I just found the funniest thing. The First Sergeant asked me to dig up some weeds by the mess hall and while I was gettin' the hoe outa that little room, I found a coupla bags of some strange stuff. Like leaves."

McGuire pulled him aside and convinced him it would be better *not* to tell the First Sergeant. McGuire, who was a pacifist, never told us how he did it, but it probably didn't take much convincing. Hahn was a good soldier, and had more in common with us than with the First Sergeant.

When McGuire told us about it, we marveled at our luck and moved the stash. Not long after that our investigation was called off and all of us except Klein were sent to different bases. It was January of 1968 and I was off to Redstone Arsenal in Huntsville AL.

At this time of my life all I knew about Transcendental Meditation was that the Beatles were into it. Alternative to drugs, dream state, peaceful, that sort of thing.

During my year in Alabama I learned more about TM, even reading the book by Maharishi Mahesh Yogi. Today it would be abjectly unreadable to me—I would fall asleep on every page—but back then I could read anything. But my main TM influence was my good buddy Peter Blue. He was heavily into it, meditating twice or more a day, and felt it was well worth doing. It sounded pretty good, but I knew that according to the book, one wasn't supposed to do drugs while meditating. Yeah, right.

But 1968, probably the most eventful year of our lives, gamboled by and 1969 found me transferred back to Fort Bliss, where I was still in a state of stoned non-meditation. I had not met the Yogi.

When I moved back to El Paso, I was a wiser, more crafty soldier. I was a veteran of a foreign war—Alabama was pretty foreign—and I knew much more about the workings of the Army bureaucracy. I knew that if I showed up at my new barracks, orders in hand, sought out the First Sergeant and said I was glad to join the outfit, and when asked, say I was married and had already found quarters off-base, he would never bother checking. He didn't.

I had already found "quarters" and it was not quite worth that much. I moved in with Klein and a philosopher named Olson. We were all Spec-4s and had fairly good jobs. I was the operations clerk, which was a very good job to have since I was the one to schedule things for the sergeants. I could make life tough for them so they did the prudent thing and left me alone. Also, since

I was the only low-ranking guy in my office I was needed at the office at all times and didn't have to stand in formation. I hated standing in formation. I was constantly tempted to raise my right arm and fist and shout "Sieg Heil!" I was lucky and during my 33 months in the service I only had to march in one parade, an event I consider the lowest point of my life. I was scheduled for several but managed to weasel my way out somehow.

The place I moved in was an adobe hovel on Lackland Street, not far from the base. I bought a motorcycle from McGuire, who was back at Bliss too. The hovel rented for $45 a month *utilities paid* so you may be able to picture it. It had three rooms and was a little crowded but Klein was due to be discharged in a month and he'd be taking off.

1969 was even more decadent than 1968 for me. We'd go to the post and do our jobs during the day, then come home at five and get loaded and talk philosophy, watch TV or listen to music. It was quite idyllic for 1969; we had a demeaning workplace, but we had enough money to buy tacos or what would now be called TV dinners and go downtown or to Juarez occasionally. We had a decent connection, every once in a while finding hashish or LSD in addition to our beloved weed. I don't remember being out of pot for any appreciable amount of time, but I guess that's just a function of the human brain: to dampen the bad memories. There were probably lots of times we were out of weed.

One day in the spring of 1969 we read in the local paper that a representative of the Maharishi Mahesh Yogi was going to be in town to initiate people into TM. It was something like $100 but for soldiers or students it was $35. He'd be in town for a week or so.

There were about six of us who regularly hung out together at the house and when we read that we decided that at least one of us ought to give that TM thing a try. Among us we could scrape together the $35. So we had some sort of blind drawing and I won. I was to check out TM and see if it was as good as drugs.

I called the number and was given an appointment at a local motel a few days later. I was to bring an offering of some type of fruit and flower and $35 in cash. I was to be free of drugs.

So I stopped smoking. Nobody else did, of course, but I had decided to give this thing a try.

The night of my appointment I got my fruit and flower and drove over on my motorcycle. I was ushered into an incense-laden motel room and asked for the gifts and the money. I relaxed for a bit then was taken into an adjoining room where there was a decidedly American-looking guy with a crew-cut named Bob. Sitar music wafted throughout the room and, incredibly, there was more incense in this room than the last. He got me to relax in a chair and told me a few things about TM, then gave me my mantra.

Now a mantra is reported to be a powerful thing, highly personal and never to be revealed to unbelievers—or to anyone for that matter. It's the personal sound that, when repeated over and over, will help the *dhong* (or whatever) enter into a state of *satori*. If it's ever revealed, this mighty word will lose its powers and the blessings of *nirvana* will be forever denied to the blasphemer.

My mantra was "I Ying".

Bob started me off saying it slowly and droningly and before I knew it I was in a state I was fond of calling "sleepy". The TMers were right; it does bring on a peaceful feeling. It felt as if I were in a good-smelling, comfortable room, with my eyes closed and an unlimited number of symbolic sheep to be counted. I began to get a greater appreciation for the term "self-hypnosis". It really works.

After about 15 minutes of mantra-ing Bob brought the session to a halt and I rode back to Lackland Street, thinking that there might be something to this TM after all. I felt damn good. I wasn't impressed at all with the presentation, but I liked the meditation.

I told everybody all about it and retreated to my room—to meditate. While outside my room the world went on as before.

A day or two passed. Everyone else continued in their cannabis haze watching me peacefully gliding from room to room, one with the world, enjoying a peach here, helping out a friend there, occasionally drifting into my room for a short "meditational pause". My mantra was always on my lips and love was in my heart.

Then Hahn showed up.

I hadn't seen him in more than a year but he was the same old guy—and he had a very similar song to the one he had a year before. He asked us for advice. "Hey, guys, what would you do if you were out in the desert, just hikin' around an' you saw somethin' wrapped in brown paper, about a foot square, and when you poked at it with a stick, it seemed to have some green, leafy stuff inside?"

"Well," we said, "We'd tell us where this was so we can go see if it's as promising as you say."

So Hahn described the location in detail. It wasn't really out in the desert. It was just behind a trailer at a old movie-town on the highway leading up to Las Cruces. We knew the place. It was a fake western-town with facades instead of buildings. At one time, years before, apparently you could take the kids there and take pictures in front of old western-looking buildings. There was a livery stable, jail, newspaper office, saloon, all the things you'd find in an old west town. They were arranged around a short circle drive. Since its heyday, a few beatup trailers had been moved in among the facades.

We didn't know it, but this was the same type of place Charlie Manson and his Family were living in at the same time in California.

We made a plan. Just in case it was a plant and was being watched, we wanted to be able to get away quickly. I was elected—in those days I was quite popular because of my willingness to do dangerous things—to walk out and grab the package and everyone else was supposed to be in the car which would drive up at the same time. I'd hop in and away we'd go.

The plan went off without a hitch. It was dark and we parked the car about 100 yards away from the trailer. I got out and, in my darkest clothes, sneaked around to the back of the trailer. There didn't seem to anyone around. I had a small flashlight and before long, right where Hahn said it was, I saw a package. I didn't hesitate. I grabbed the package and ran past the trailer to the road, where the car was waiting. I threw the package to the floor of the back seat and we raced off onto the highway.

We took a super-circuitous route home just in case we were followed and checked out the package. Bingo! It looked like a pressed kilo of Mexican weed. We broke it up when we got home and it filled an ammo can to the brim, packed tight. Everyone assured me it was primo stuff.

Transcendental Meditation was in for the fight of its life.

I managed to maintain my stone-less meditation for another couple of days, but the aroma of chemical bliss kept drifting into my *satori*-room. My mantra would stumble as memories of marijuana-misty nights would haunt my *dhong* (or whatever). But I was strong. I was the meditator of the group and it was up to me to keep the experiment pristine and single-blind, if not double-blind.

Then Cramer and Gigi hit town.

Cramer, who in many ways could beat the shit out of the TV Kramer in weirdness, was a buddy from Redstone Arsenal. He had been discharged in early 1968 but had stuck around for a few months. He was much more reckless—he could afford to be since he was no longer under the army's thumb—than the rest of us were and we were a little glad when he had gone back to his native southern California. Mainly we were glad because every time he'd go to California, he'd come back with a hundred or so hits of acid.

Cramer was the world's worst acid dealer. He'd buy 100 hits for $2 apiece and end up taking 60 of them himself, giving away 30, and selling the rest for $1 apiece, trying to impress girls. It sort of worked.

Gigi was a young hippie chick (no words can describe her more succinctly than that) from Las Cruces whom we had met through McGuire. She had regaled us with stories of the sex orgies the teenagers of Cruces used to have, which made us feel a little, well, old. She and Cramer had just driven in from California and they had a couple of hundred hits of orange acid.

They were staying with me and Olson—Klein had been discharged and had gone to school in Albuquerque. There were a few other people around and everybody except me was on acid. I was supposed to be meditating but it was quite a party. Could I stick with my chemical-free regimen?

No. Not a chance. I dropped two hits of acid and rolled a joint the size and shape of a small Louisville Slugger and fired it up. My first weed in about a week. Everyone, including Gigi, took on a familiar glow—the glow of stonedness! Now this was some kinda meditation! The old Yogi and his teachings were being dealt a mighty blow. We had a kilo of free grass and Cramer was in town with acid. I could hear the death throes of my mantra reverberating through my skull—I Ying—I Ying—**I Ying—I Ying.**

It came to pass that just as the acid was taking its supreme effect on my brain that I happened to mention, in the course of normal conversation, that one thing I had never tried while peaking on acid, was sex. No one took particular notice of this pronouncement, since words were only ephemeral wisps of wind blown into the cosmic void by a throbbing, pulsating symbolism, but I noted that Gigi gave me a funny look. I smoked another joint and began climbing into that goldanged void.

And the next thing I knew was that Gigi had taken me by the hand and led me back into my room, scene of all sorts of exciting meditations. She said something like, "Never had sex on acid, huh? We'll see about that." We removed our clothes and soon the void was a lot hotter, sweatier, furrier, moanier, flamier and ec-staticer than anything I'd ever felt. Maybe Henry Miller at his *Tropic of Cancer* peak could come close to describing in words the feeling of peaking on acid and sex *at the exactly the same time* but I'll not try. All I can say is that of all the joyous, lumi-nous, triumphant moments of life, they all pale next to a well-timed blend of LSD and sex. Climbed Everest? Phooey. Flew a space shuttle? Bo-ring. Won the Power-Ball? I spit on the Power-Ball.

Peaking LSD and peaking sex are the best super-sized combo platter on humanity's menu. If it doesn't change your life, you were dead to begin with. It is the most excruciating blackboard scratch of abject pleasure that the human mind can endure.

TM didn't have a chance. I had I'd my last Ying. Oh, I tried it a few times afterwards but it just didn't seem worth the trouble.

Gigi and Cramer took off not long after and I settled down into a blissful existence with that kilo and our nightly smoky rev-elries. I wrote letters about my life on Lackland to a girl I knew back in Huntsville and even though she wasn't all that crazy about me, she was so entranced by my letters that she came out to live with me for my last year in the army. She and I had our own peaks and created our own daughter. We got married right after I got out of the army in January 1970. My daughter, with her admi-rable life, showed just what reactionary dolts Art Linkletter and his crowd are.

Thanks to the war on drugs only teenagers can now get their hands on LSD, and I hear it's quite weak and impure. When I think about the forces (the government, the churches, the media, the business world) that have denied the free-thinking people of the world this most supreme ecstasy, I get what can only be called, "pissed off." Maybe I ought to meditate about it.

BRUSHES WITH DEATH

IT'S BEEN SAID that a man is never more alive than when he is facing death. If that's true, my liveliest moments have been spent behind the wheel of a car, because anytime any of us is driving, we are staring death in the face—whether from a drunk driver, a cell-phone befuddled driver, or worse, a driver who's pissed off at all of the drunk and cell-phone-befuddled drivers all around him.

But for the sake of this reminiscography, I've narrowed my major brushes with death to three—and only one of them involves a car. Well, maybe two.

Brush #1: Death by Shotgun

One night in the summer of 1965, when I was 18 and recently graduated from high school, my friend Barry and I were driving around Farmington, looking for something to do. We were in Barry's mother's car, and eventually decided on driving the 50 miles up to Durango and checking out one of the 3.2 beer bars where bands we knew might be playing. But for that we needed about $10 for gas, cover charge and a few beers. We only had about $5 between us. Where could we come up with $5 quickly?

I had heard from friends that a quick way to get some easy cash was to steal some empty coke bottles and cash them in at a 7-11. A couple of cases ought to get us what we needed. And I knew just where to find a couple of cases of empties: the Encore Motel on Main Street. It was a typical motel, U-shaped, two-story, with a coke machine under the stairwell at the base of the U. So 8 P.M. on that summer night found us pulling into the motel parking lot and parking next to the stairwell.

There was no one around so we casually walked over to the machine and spotted four or five cases of empty bottles next to it. A goldmine! We glanced around again, saw no one, and nonchalantly picked up a case apiece and put them in the back seat of the car. We went back for another two cases and were just putting them in the back seat when we heard a woman yell, "Gramps! There's someone taking our coke bottles!"

We looked up to see a young woman standing outside the office, watching us. Uh oh. She was joined by an old man of about 80 who, upon seeing us, said to the woman, "Go get my gun!" The woman ran into the office.

Without further ado, Barry and I took the cases from the back of the car and put them back beside the machine, all the time being watched by the old man. We were just finishing up when the woman returned with a shotgun and gave it to the old man. He walked to a point about ten feet away from us and with trembling fingers and voice, pointed the gun at us and shouted, "Don't move, you two! Don't make me shoot!"

"Don't worry," we said, "we're not going anywhere. Just stop pointing that gun at us."

"I'm—I'm warnin' you!" he kept babbling, "Don't make me blast you away."

"Okay! Okay! Just don't shoot."

"Martha," the old man said in his trembling voice that kept getting more and more frantic despite our pleas to calm down, "Go call the police."

So for about five minutes we waited, standing beside our car while the man with the quavering shotgun and voice kept telling us to "not make him shoot." After calling the cops the woman joined him in watching us.

There was an eerie feeling of calm that came over me, knowing that my fate was out of my hands—it was all in the trembling fingers of an 80-year-old man who was getting ripped off of $5 worth of empty coke bottles.

"You young punks have been stealing my coke bottles for years and I finally caught you. Don't make me shoot you!" He acted, to us, like he actually wanted us to "make him shoot."

Finally, a police car drove up and when the cop got out and saw the old man with the shotgun pointing at us, his face tightened and he slowly and calmly told the man, "Just lower that gun, sir. Just point it at the ground and take it easy."

The man dropped the gun's barrel and the policeman quickly went to him and grabbed the gun out of his hands. The man began yammering and the cop said, "Let's all calm down here. First, tell me what's going on."

The old man said he had caught the punks who were stealing his empty coke bottles and cackled about it in his tremulous voice. The cop wasn't too impressed, especially when he looked at the scene and saw the cases on the ground next to the coke machine. Within minutes he had ushered the man and woman back into the office and Barry and me into the back seat of his police cruiser. He drove us up to the police station, not saying anything to us on the way.

We were taken to a sergeant's desk and quizzed about what had happened. "We were just stopping by to buy us a coke when the old man accused us of stealing. Thanks for getting us out of there."

The sergeant asked a few more questions, and when he asked us to empty our pockets and saw that we had about $5 in ones and change, he seemed to make up his mind. "You boys are lucky," he said, "and in a way I'm glad you brought this whole thing to a head. That old man has been waving that shotgun around for years and it's time he had it taken away from him. He's going to shoot somebody one of these days."

The policeman had me call my mother to come pick us up and we dropped Barry off at his house. The cops said not to deal with the car until the next day. The next morning Harry came and picked me up and we got Barry and drove down to the motel. Barry's mother's car was chained to an iron railing. We called the police and told them what we had found and by noon, Barry had his mother's car back. We never saw the people at the motel again. I did spent a night at the motel about five years later with a stripper from the Office Bar, which was across the street, but this time without a shotgun screwing up my plans.

As far as I know, nothing more was said or done about the incident. Whew!

Brush #2: The Asthmador Debacle

MY FIRST YEAR in the army has been well-documented as one of chaos, despair and ridiculosity. Most of it I spent as a "duty-trooper" with my buddies, Klein, Gardner, Goggins and McGuire, all of us trying to survive military incarceration by staying high. One day a new guy appeared on the scene, a round-faced GI named Henderson. "Hey," he said, "I'm a Hollywood hippie!" And he was. No matter how decadent we managed to get, he was always a step or two ahead of us. We marveled at his knowledge of drugs and his effervescence when faced with military drudgery. This guy knew dozens of ways to get high.

One day he mentioned something called Asthmador. "It'll fuck ya up."

"Tell us more," we said and he proceeded to describe an over-the-counter asthma medicine called "Dr. Schiffman's Asthmador." It was a powder that an asthmatic was supposed to burn in an ash tray and inhale the fumes. Henderson said that if you take a teaspoonful and swallow it, "It'll fuck ya up."

If only we had been more critical of his inflection and vocabulary. We were thinking that "fuck ya up" sounded pretty enticing.

So one day I happened to be in a drug store and remembered about Dr. Schiffman's Asthmador. They had cans of it! I bought one and took it back to the barracks where we studied it. The active ingredients were "belladonna and stramonium", two substances we knew about but had never tried. Belladonna is from the deadly nightshade mushroom and stramonium is from jimson weed. Let's try it! By this time Henderson had moved on and we were relying on his instructions of taking a teaspoonful.

Ghaaak! It was the worst-tasting stuff we'd ever encountered, a dry, gray-green dusty powder. But we washed it down with cokes and sat around to see what would happen. A couple of us were "ground control" and didn't take the stuff. We were very responsible and prudent drug takers back then. I wasn't one of the prudent ones, of course. About six of us were the experimenters.

In about fifteen minutes we noticed that something strange was coming on. Everything began to get a little "twisty". Voices sounded a mile away, and when we tried to walk, we found that on just about every fourth step, one of our legs would give out and we'd stumble. No matter how hard we tried to concentrate and walk right, we'd stumble. We thought that was pretty funny.

About a half hour of twisted thinking was the extent of my conscious trip. The next thing I remember was waking up in the morning in my bunk. The ground control guys said that we all acted the same way: we could talk, but nothing but gibberish would come out. Just mumbling. But, oddly, the stoned guys talked up a storm with each other, acting as if they understood each other completely. Conversations were going on, all in unintelligible mumbles, all by stumbling guys who wouldn't sit still.

What caused me to swear never to take Asthmador again was ground control's telling me that we all went walking outside the barracks and off-base. When they told me that, I had a horrible memory of going up to a house, knocking on the door, and asking the people at the door for something. Did it happen? It could have. Ground control, who, let's face it, were not thrilled at herding a bunch of bumbling assholes around, told me that at times some of us got away from the pack.

But did that end our relationship with belladonna and stramonium? Of course not. About a month later, when pot was hard to come by because of some chaos at the El Paso-Juarez border, Goggins and McGuire decided to have a little more Asthmador. This time I was ground control—in fact, I was official ground control because I was on "CQ Duty" that night. There was a sergeant who was officially in charge of the barracks over night, but since he had to go to class the next day, he slept and left me to answer the phone, make bed checks, turn off the lights and wake everybody up and get them into formation the next morning.

What a hassle it was keeping an eye on the two mumblers as they staggered around the barracks, running into lockers. Goggins lost control and pissed all down his right leg. One of his cool leather hippie boots (which we all had bought in Juarez) was soaked and he made a horrible squishing sound as he walked. He and McGuire babbled all night to each other, and it seemed to the rest of us that they thought they had solved all of the riddles of the universe. They talked with such logical and reasonable cadence, but they spoke not one intelligible word—at least not to us simple pot-smokers.

I kept waiting for them to come down and go to sleep but they didn't. When 5 A.M. rolled around they were still mumbling and stumbling—and, one eighth of the time, squishing. I got the rest of the barracks up and told the sergeant that everybody was outside on the quadrangle, in formation. I knew they'd have roll call so I *had* to get Goggins and McGuire out there. But they were still too stoned. So I pulled the sergeant over and said, "Sarge, we got a little problem. Goggins and McGuire had the day off today so they went out last night and got pretty drunk. Do you suppose they could be excused from formation? I'll make sure they get written up for missing formation."

The sergeant, who didn't really give a damn, looked at the two pitiful soldiers, who by this time were finally non-ambulatory and relatively silent. He shook his head and said, "I've never seen hangovers like that. Don't let the first sergeant or lieutenant see them."

I didn't, and the whole incident blew over quickly. We all resolved never to go the belladonna/stramonium route again and cursed Henderson in his absence. I have a feeling that if we had taken two teaspoonsful of the stuff, one or more of us wouldn't have lived.

As far as I know, Dr. Schiffman's Asthmador is still sold over-the-counter.

Brush #3: The Wrath of Keown

I SPENT THE YEAR of 1968 in Huntsville Alabama at Redstone Arsenal. It was my second year of the army and I was working in an office as a typist and copy-machine guy. But I was also the driver for the office's car. I had never owned a car before and rarely driven one, but when asked if I could drive, of course I said yes. I figured I could learn on the job—and did.

The office I worked in consisted of about 20 people, most of whom were civilians. The head of the office was a colonel and we were allowed one military vehicle—a 1963 Plymouth—which was mainly for driving the colonel around—with me as chauffeur. But the colonel I worked for had a little sports car, which he preferred over the Plymouth. I think maybe it was his first trip in the back seat with me at the wheel of the Plymouth that convinced him that driving himself around in his sports car was preferable. The Plymouth had a stick-shift and I'm sure he was closer to death with me driving than he had been at any time over the past few years—including his tours of Vietnam.

But in order for our office to merit having an official vehicle, we had to show that it was needed. So, it became my job to hop in the car and drive it around the base and city of Huntsville, racking up enough miles on the odometer to show that we desperately needed this car. I loved the freedom, and spent most of every day parked down by the Tennessee River, reading and smoking pot.

As related in another reminiscence (The Mothra Caper), I had spent my first year in the army at Fort Bliss, under investigation for drug use. At Redstone Arsenal I was given a second chance by the people at my office and we got along just fine. But the day came when I received orders for Vietnam. Thanks to the aid of a couple of high-ranking enlisted men I was able to get those orders rescinded, but in return I had to go to some form of missile school. So in late 1968 I was transferred to the school side of the post for a class on the Nike Hercules launcher system.

But my office didn't want to let me go right away. They wanted me to stay until they could get someone to take my place. And since school was a return to "underling" status with a bunch of GIs who were just out of basic training, I wanted to spend as little time with them as possible. So I played up my importance to the office and used it to get out of as much of the new student life as possible. It was a situation that drives military minds mad: I was a slave with two masters.

So I was still driving the office car as much as possible, while preparing to enter the launcher school.

One of the first things I learned when I entered the school part of the base was that the Commanding Officer of the school was the legendary Colonel Keown (key' ohn). He was considered the biggest asshole on base by his troops. He ruled with an iron fist, and loved to cause as much misery among the soldiers as he could. Get on his wrong side and you were headed for the stockade for the rest of your time in the army. I had been spared his venom because up to the time I became a student I was working for the relatively sane side of the base. Now it was my time to meet Mr. Kurtz and his heart of darkness.

But I was still driving the office's car, and one day I was told to deliver a folder to the school's headquarters. I was still a fairly lousy driver, but I thought I was okay. I drove to the school and parked directly in front of headquarters, where there was plenty of parking space. I delivered the folder to the Spec-4 at the desk and waited for any return confirmation. Ten minutes later I was ready to leave and went back out to the car.

I saw that while I was inside that Colonel Keown's car was parked next to mine. His military car—a Ford—was well-known on base because he used to have himself driven around so he could yell at soldiers who weren't looking as sharp as he liked. In fact the car was parked quite close to mine, even though there was plenty of parking room. Maybe I had parked in the colonel's space?

I got in my car, started it up, and started backing up. I hadn't had all that much experience with parking or backing up because

I mainly drove down to the river, around town, and around base. I rarely went anywhere I had to park. I noticed that I was getting a little close to the colonel's car so I got out and looked. There was about an inch clearance between the two cars. I looked around and didn't see anyone looking at me so I got back in the car and once again tried to back up slowly. The colonel's car seemed closer than before. So I gave the car some gas and backed all the way out, and I think I heard a strange, scraping sound. From behind the wheel I peered at the colonel's car and sure enough, there was a six-foot long gouge in the side of his car, right through the "Colonel Keown – US Artillery".

My heart dropped and I quickly looked around to see if anyone saw me. I saw no one so I sped away, drove to the river and killed off my entire stash of weed. I figured I'd either hear about it— and die—or I'd get away with it.

I was on tenterhooks for the next few days but nothing ever came of it. I purposely didn't keep up with any scuttlebutt coming from the school because I didn't really want to know. If I were to die, I wanted it to be as quick and painless as possible. I never heard anything about it. Eventually I entered the school full-time and quit my association with the office. A month later I finished the school and was transferred back to Fort Bliss where I became a clerk-typist for my last year in the service.

Would Colonel Keown have killed me for gouging his car? Probably not, if there were witnesses around. After all, an officer and a gentleman of the United States Army must kill his subordinates only in proscribed ways, and bludgeoning a bad driver to death is not condoned by the US Code of Military Justice. Ordering poor slobs into hopeless battles is the preferred method.

But I still figure this was a legitimate brush with death. If I had been caught, I would have been sent to the stockade and beaten, which would have pissed me off so much that I would have paid them back somehow, which of course in those days would have escalated into bloodshed on somebody's part—undoubtedly mine.

Colonel Keown will never know how close he came to murder on that day when I had my third and final brush with death.

These days, confronting my mortality when I get out into traffic seems almost like a walk in the park compared to how I felt during those three eventful years when my country wanted me to defend its right to plunder the rest of the world's wealth.

THE JARAMILLO INSCRIPTION

Annotated by

Norbert Tudwallow

THE JARAMILLO INSCRIPTION: THE DEFINITIVE ANNOTATION

NYELLO, NORBERT TUDWALLOW here.

In early 2005 an important document was unearthed, a document that casts new light on just exactly was going on in Farmington New Mexico back in the early 60s. As you know, historians have struggled over this era for decades, many of them going insane because of the lack of concrete data.

One of the most intriguing artifacts from this golden age was an inscription in the high school yearbook of a Fender Tucker by a Geno Jaramillo. We have had the yearbook for years but the inscription was so puzzling that no one actually understood what it was all about.

Until now. Thanks to tireless goading by yours truly, we now have a detailed explanation of the cryptic remarks of Mr. Jaramillo—in the drug-addled words of Fender Tucker himself. And now at last we can truly understand the conflicts and capers listed so diligently in the inscription.

The next few pages are facsimile reproductions of the infamous scribbling, followed by my annotations and the first-person "confessions" of Mr. Tucker. I say "confessions" because oddly enough, most of the things listed may be considered crimes. In fact, there's no way in hell that children of today could do what Jaramillo and Tucker did and be free to walk the streets. They'd be locked in prison with chicken hawks and sadistic guards like the rest of today's unfortunate nonconformists.

But what exactly is the Jaramillo Inscription? As you may know, at the end of each school year yearbooks are passed around for schoolmates to sign and inscribe. Generally these inscriptions are something like "It's been wonderful knowing ya. See ya next year!"

Apparently Tucker wrote something memorable in Jaramillo's yearbook—an inscription that may someday see the light of day—and it inspired Jaramillo to write the masterpiece which is the subject of this book.

The two were seniors at Farmington High School in 1965 when the inscription was written. After graduation, Tucker bummed around for a year or so then was forced into the US Army. Jaramillo joined the US Navy. They lost touch with each other, except for a few short meetings, until 1985 when they met again in Tularosa NM where Geno was house-sitting for a friend. Fender was living in Las Cruces and playing with the Mighty Calhoon Brothers at local bars.

They reminisced a lot and played computer chess, chortling every time they were able to beat Fender's Commodore 64 computer at a high level. They could have played against each other, of course, but they were never competitive that way. They preferred to gang up on helpless software.

Geno later moved back upstate that summer and disappeared in August, last being seen in Bloomfield at a bar. The next spring his body was found in a California ravine, apparently the result of foul play. Nothing more was ever found.

As Fender said, "I lost part of my sense of humor because of Geno's death. There were so many things that were hilarious to us that were no longer funny."

But 1965 was a grand year and the inscription seems to be bubbling with humor. In fact, Fender maintains that 1965 was the best year in all of human history to graduate from high school. Why? Because people who were born in 1946-1947 were able to grow up to the age of 18 without all the brouhaha and wrong information about drugs. They were able to lead normal lives, engaging in alcoholic stupidities and fumbling sex and not have the DEA and other governmental fascists throwing their jackbooted weight around. But just as soon as they escaped the clutches of high school and tasted freedom for the first time, the wonderful drug revolution happened and at the perfect age of 18 or 19 they were able to enjoy the benefits of cannabis and the psychedelics.

Fender maintains that the best way to develop a cozy, nurturing relationship with drugs is to not use them until the right time. If you start too early, or too late, it's doubtful that you will learn to really appreciate the joys of getting loaded on some fine weed. You either go overboard and start shooting speed or you lapse into the neurotic life of the typical drunken insurance salesman. Or worse, you find Jesus and let him do your thinking for you.

Read on, dear reader, and see if the 34 annotated "talking points" in the Jaramillo Inscription offer proof of Fender's thesis. You might be surprised.

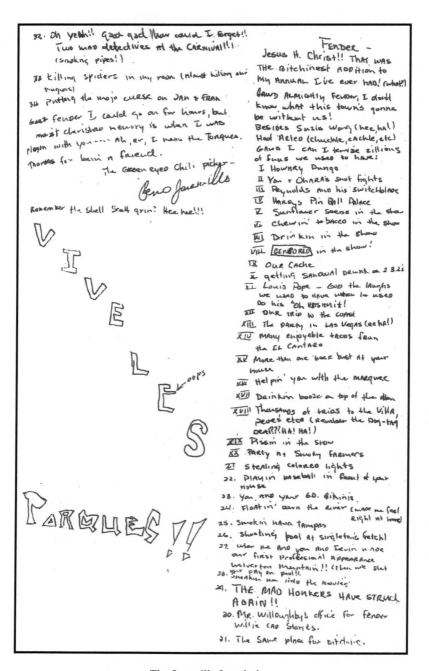

The Jaramillo Inscription

Geno and Fender at Fender's house winter 1966
(pictures by Sherrill Smith)

Geno giving the "fletcho" sign

Geno with his favorite hookah

The Opening Statement

—Fender—

Jesus H. Christ! That was the bitchingest addition to my annual I've ever had! (What?) Gawd Almighty Fender, I don't know what this town's gonna be without us!

Besides Suzie Wong (hee, hah!), Hoof Arted (chuckle, cackle, etc.). Gawd I can itemize zillions of funs we used to have:

One of these days the inscription by Fender will turn up and we will be able to see what inspired Geno to create this document. Until then, this will have to be the definitive annotation of Geno's inscription.

There are two events mentioned above, Suzie Wong and Hoof Arted, both classic capers by the two miscreants.

In 1960 *The World of Suzie Wong,* with William Holden and Nancy Kwan, was released to much fanfare about its controversial subject matter: prostitution. It was so hot that only viewers over 17 were allowed in the Totah theater. At the time Geno and Fender were in the ninth grade and several years under 17.

But Fender and Geno were not about to let a sexy movie slip through their hands so they decided to sneak in to see it. Fender was the marquee changer so he could get in free, and Geno was normally able to get in with him but this film was special and they had to see it surreptitiously.

They managed to sneak into the Totah one night when the theater was packed with adult patrons. They found seats near the right wall of the theater about halfway back and settled in to see some hot sex action—or so they thought. The film was typical boring fare for the time and the only "shocking" thing about it was the young Nancy Kwan claiming to be a "virgin" and using that word.

Now, as you'll find out later in some of the Roman-numeraled tidbits, the boys were great sunflower seed fans and had each ingested several packs. Needless to say, the gastric results began rearing their ugly heads soon after the lights dimmed. Fender's emanations were of the aromatic sort and while no one actually could pinpoint the "feller", grumblings began to erupt around the two lads. Then Geno decided to add his contribution to the attack and to Fender's astonishment let loose a brrrraaaaappp that rico-

cheted off the leatherette theater seat. There was complete silence
in the show. Fender hunched lower in his seat and Geno turned a
shade of red that seemed to have an actual glow in the darkness.
The grumblings gained a decibel or two.

Fender was hapless. He knew it would be dangerous to hold
back on important eructations so his malodorous squeaklets continued. There were two young women sitting directly behind the
two who were having trouble maintaining their composures.

A few minutes later, Geno tilted a bit to one side—toward
Fender, much to his relief—and released another violent, roof-
rattling explosion. The girls were apoplectic and the grumblings
began to take on coherence. "What the fuck?" and "Goddammit!"
were two of them.

The boys sunk even deeper into their seats. Would they be able
to see the rest of the film? Were they to be busted for seeing their
first glimpse of what the Catholic Legion of Decency called a "C"
movie—C for Condemned?

The film progressed and William and Nancy began to spend
quality time on a ferryboat in Hong Kong harbor. Then, just as
Nancy Kwan utters the words that gave the film its salacious reputation, "But I am a, how you say, *virgin,*" Geno let loose with a—

But let's let Fender tell you in his own words.

"I was fearing for my job and wondering how my termination
notice would be worded when Geno cut the final fart. The theater
was in silence anyway because of the shocking word, "virgin" and
Geno's blast reverberated throughout the huge room. The two
girls behind us lost it completely and I was surprised I didn't
hear—or feel—twin driblets on the slanted, sticky floor roll past
us. Then a deep male voice from several rows back of us boomed
out, perhaps for everyone else in the show, saying, 'All right. One
more time like that and we'll see about getting you mothers kicked
out.'

"I was spent. I don't remember anything more about the movie.
Geno and I just huddled deep in our seats and prayed for gastric
continence. We had performed our ultimate blasphemy, and with a
little luck we would survive it. The girls settled down to random
fits of giggling and no one was kicked out that night."

Norbert here again. This is only the introductory paragraph of
the Jaramillo Inscription but it sets the pattern for many of the
following events.

As for "Hoof Arted" this was a crank call that the boys invented. It's been used many times since then but as far as the boys knew, they came up with the idea. They'd call one of the bars in town and say:

"Hello, could you page someone for me?"

"Sure thing!"

"Well, it's a Navajo friend named Hoof."

"Hoof?"

"Yeah, Hoof. His last name is Arted. A-R-T-E-D."

"Okey-doke." Then away from the phone the poor bartender would yell, "Hoof Arted! Hoof Arted!"

Fender and Geno got a big kick out of it, even though they could never maintain well enough to listen to what the bartender had to say to them when he realized what he had yelled. They had to hang up because of laughing so hard.

And now, on to the Roman-numeraled exploits that make up the bulk of The Jaramillo Inscription.

I — Howary Dungo

There were business offices above the entrance to the Totah Theater on Main Street that were accessible via a nondescript door just to the west of the theater. Inside this door was a glass-enclosed marquee showing the room numbers of the half dozen or so businesses upstairs. It was about two feet wide, stuck on the wall and had a lock.

Fender and Geno were the marquee-changers for the Totah and twice a week they would change the letters when the movies would change. They did this at night, after 10 o'clock or when the last feature started.

Perhaps it was because the names and room numbers were made of movable letters—just like the letters on the theater's mar-quee—but Geno and Fender one day decided to see if they could break into the mini-marquee and change the letters, just as they did to the large marquee. They found that a Trim-Trio easily opened the box—as they knew it would. Anything anything can do, a Trim Trio can do better.[6]

---

[6] This was a motto that Fender made up and sent to the Trim Company. He believed it more than they did, apparently, because they never an-

Anyone going to, or leaving the businesses would see them meddling with the marquee so the two lads had to work quick. The first name they saw was "HOWARD A. YOUNG", a local businessman who coincidentally lived just down the block from Fender on Monterey Street. They quickly changed the letters to read "HOWARY DUNGO" and locked the box.

The next time they went to the theater to change the marquee they noticed the name had been changed back. So they switched it again. HOWARY DUNGO was too good a name to forget.

Over the course of a year they change it 20 or 30 times and each time it would be changed back—probably by poor Mr. Young. Tucker's thoughts: "It probably would have been easier for Young to simply change his name to Howary Dungo."

II — You and O'Hara's snot fights

Tucker can't remember anything specific about snot fights but this was not the only secretion that figured in his fights with Pat O'Harrow. When Fender and Geno were in the eighth grade at Sacred heart Catholic School, they were friends with Pat and another ne'er-do-well named Larry Reynolds.

Reynolds started the custom of calling public urination "raring", especially if it involved thrusting the pelvis forward violently to get maximum horizontal range of urine discharge. The boys simply felt that the longer the rare, the classier the urination.

Somehow this custom segued into raring on anyone not paying attention. Any of the young boys could, if not vigilant, experience the ominous warmth of someone else's urine on their pants—from quite a distance in some instances. In fact, one day Pat inundated Fender so maliciously that Fender vowed to get him back. He waited until the perfect moment in Pat's back yard one day and when Pat wasn't looking, he rared valiantly, narrowly missing Pat's shoes. Pat saw what was happening and said what sounded to Fender like "Brrrr!"

---

swered him. A Trim Trio is a small three-bladed knife (with knife, file, fingernail cleaner and bottle cap opener) that Fender cannot live without. The company no longer makes them but luckily he has about a dozen lying around the house.

"What the hell is he brrr-ing about?" Fender said to himself as he rared again, trying for an additional foot or two. Fender didn't know that Pat's familiar name for his 12-year-old sister, Brigitte, was "Brrrr." But then Fender, rarer in hand, looked up to see that they were being watched through the window a few feet away by Brigitte.

Fender's comment, upon being reminded of this debacle, was, "It's so pathetic that the first female to ever glimpse my equipment was the kid sister of a friend. And if I remember correctly, my rare that day was not one of my best."

III — Reynolds and his switchblade

Larry Reynolds showed up in Farmington in 1959 in the seventh grade and quickly became the most unruly student at Sacred Heart. He could fart at will and was willing to do almost anything to shock people. Fender and Geno were glad he came on the scene because compared to Larry, they were regular altar boys—at least in the eyes of the nuns.

Fender can't remember anything about Larry's switchblade but he's bound to have been brandishing it at school or something. What Fender remembers about Reynolds was the day he took finger-popping to its acme of sacrilege.

The boys learned how to make their fingers pop by leaving the forefinger loose and whipping the hand down. The forefinger slaps against the other fingers making a nifty slapping noise. Larry used to finger-pop all the time. In class, in line, walking home, talking to the nuns; he was always popping his fingers. The nuns hated it of course, but they tried to ignore it, praying he'd eventually get cancer of the finger or lose it in an industrial accident.

But one day Larry took it to such extremes that the priest had to officially ban finger-popping on the Sacred Heart schoolgrounds. On his way to the communion rail one day at mass, Larry popped all the way to altar. Everybody in the church was stunned as he approached the rail. That day the practice was condemned by the priests, under pain of mortal sin.

Fender reminisces, "If, instead of banning the practice, the Catholic Church had made finger-popping mandatory as one approached the communion rail, I might actually set foot in a church again." Then, after a few second's reflection, "Nah."

IV — Harry's Pinball Palace

In the middle of the downtown block between Allen and Orchard Streets were two connected businesses: Harry's Pinball Parlor and Don's News Stand. Both were narrow, each consisting of one long room; one was filled with pinball machines, the other with paperback books. The pinball machines were the analog kind, providing five balls for a nickel or a dime, and the books were mainly Gold Medal paperback originals. Can you imagine anything more fantastic?

Geno and Fender would spend most of their after-school hours playing pinball there because technically there was an age limit for the parlor: 15. Once they achieved that age, it was no longer verboten so they moved a block down Main Street to the Snooker 8 Pool Hall where the age limit was technically 18.

Fender reminisces like the old fart he is: "I learned a lotta good stuff playin' pinball. One time Geno and I were there when a bunch of pachucos, a year or two older than us, came in and tilted our machines and told us to get out. We objected and one told us to get out or he'd 'knock the fuck out' of us. I was amazed. I knew the word, of course, but never in that context. If he had said shit, crap, piss or any other bodily fluid, I'd have been okay with that, but what exactly was 'fuck'?

"However, I didn't truly understand the power and flexibility of cussing until one day around this time when Geno and I were standing on a corner of Main Street and Locke. For some reason Geno and Reynolds and Pat and I had gotten in the habit of making horrible retching sounds pretty much just for the hell of it. So I leaned over the gutter and retched violently. There was a cowboy standing a few feet away and he said, 'I wonder what in the bullshit hell is wrong with him?'

"It was an epiphany for us. We suddenly realized that cussing had no formal grammar. You could literally throw cusswords in any way you wanted. After that our cussing flourished in ways you can only imagine."

V — Sunflower seeds in the show

It was inevitable that the boys would soon discover the wonderful expansive properties of sunflower seeds as they digested in the human gut. After all, they were in the habit of eating several packs a day. An added benefit to sunflower seeds were the soggy husks that were left over, to be spat hither and thither one at a time, or even better, released in a glom of spit and shells.

They used to hang out at the theater—having snuck in late at night (see XXVIII)—and sit in the front row at the Allen, spitting their seeds upon the stage. When the gaseous detritus of digestion resulted, the lads would release it gloriously. Usually there were very few people in the theater at the time, thank heavens.

Geno and Fender's greatest sunflower seed experience came one night when they were sitting in the balcony and had filled up a large coke cup full of spit-soggy hulls. Where they got the idea is one of those mysteries that forever cloud history, just like Einstein's theories and the invention of the hula hoop. Somehow they managed to find a piece of black thread, about ten feet long. They punched a small hole in the cup and tied one end of the black thread to the cup. Then they placed the cup on the edge of the balcony wall and dangled the thread down, directly over the aisle below.

They rushed downstairs and sat in the back row of the theater—set back a couple of rows from where the thread dangled down, completely invisible in the darkness of the theater—and waited for their most unfortunate victim to come walking down the aisle. The theater was filled with people.

Well, the first person to come down the aisle was Johnny, Fender's little brother! And he performed like a champ. He walked nonchalantly down the aisle until he got to the place where the thread was. He stopped, looked around confusedly and began making strange motions with his hands around his face. Several of the audience were eyeing him curiously. Johnny then seemed to have found something with his hands and a look of comprehension came over his face. It was a string. But what was a string doing dangling over the aisle? So he did what any red-blooded American would do: he pulled the string.

All of a sudden a cascade of soggy sunflower seed hulls rained down on a wide area of the audience. And most of them knew who the culprit was—the bozo standing in the aisle playing with his face.

Fender remembers, "Geno and I were apoplectic. Our trick had worked better than any trick we'd ever pulled. We were like Cartman when he pulled the buttface gag. But we never tried it again, maybe because we knew it could never work so well a second time. And now, because of the new theater styles, there are no more balconies and the young tads of today must content themselves with unsafe sex and crack. Sad, really."

VI — Chewin' tobacco in the show

Geno and Fender tried to get hooked on cigarettes but never could. If they bought a pack it would go stale before they finished it. So they tried chewing tobacco. That only lasted a couple of days, due to the nausea.

Fender opines, "I vaguely remember trying chewing tobacco. There's no telling what we did with the spit in the show. It's probably best for all humanity that this vice died an early death."

VII — Drinkin' in the show

Whenever Geno and Fender could find some beer to drink, they often had no good place to go to drink it. So they would sneak into the show through the projection booth—which was next to the room where the letters for the marquee were kept—and drink beer in the balcony, which was usually empty. At other times they would drink on top of the Allen's roof, but I believe that is covered in XVII below.

VIII — CENSORED in the show

Apparently Geno was trying to be provocative to readers of his inscription, because there's not much they did in the show that can't be related. Could he be referring to the gaseous expellations?

Fender clarifies, "All I know is that he's not referring to sex because I'm pretty sure we never got any of that in the show. We went to the show to raise hell, not make out."

IX — Our cache

Probably the most successful of Fender and Geno's capers was the acquisition of two cases of half-pint bottles of odd liqueurs and brandies. And a case full of quart bottles of muscatel.

There was a trapdoor to the roof of the Allen Theater in the room where the marquee letters were kept—Fender's room. The boys had explored the roof and found that they pretty much had access to the roofs of all of the businesses on that block. The most intriguing place was a storage room behind Harry's Bar, two doors to the east of the Allen. By swinging down onto a metal catwalk they could then drop down into an enclosed 10-foot long alleyway behind the bar. Apparently this alleyway at one time was open to customers because there were drink prices—in Spanish!—painted on the wall of the old storage room.

The room wasn't locked and one night the two intrepid explorers, trusty flashlights in hand, decided to see what was in this potential trove of forbidden pleasures. They found a room full of dusty junk. The place hadn't been used in years, obviously. They found an old pinball game—which years later Fender unsuccessfully tried to buy from Harry Allen, the owner of the bar. They also found two partly-burnt cases of liqueurs, in half-pint bottles. 24 bottles per case. The labels on many of the bottles were singed but none of them were opened. "Piping Rock" was the brand name of most of the bottles, and there was a wide variety of things like cherry liqueur, peach brandy, mint gin, apricot brandy, etc. The boys were ecstatic. They had struck gold.

There was even a case of 12 quart bottles of muscatel, which seemed to be some sort of wine. So the two explorers, with some degree of difficulty, managed to haul the three cases up to the catwalk, then onto the roof. They stashed the boxes in the insulation just inside the trapdoor, above Fender's letter room.

This must have been in the spring of 1964 because all that summer the two enjoyed drinking with their buddies—except, while everybody else was guzzling beer, they drank only the finest liqueurs, from the bottle, always with their little fingers pointing skyward. The hangovers were atrocious—and colorful—and the party lasted until the 48 bottles were finally exhausted.

They tried the muscatel but couldn't get past the first sip. They ended up giving the case to Geno's older brother, who said he had a hard time giving it away.

As Fender remembers: "Once the booze was gone we kept checking to see if Harry had put some more stuff back in the storeroom, but he never did. One night we were in the storeroom when we saw, through the incredibly filthy windows that opened onto the alley behind the Allen, a cop car stop and a spotlight shine through one of the windows. We quickly turned off our flashlights and climbed up onto a wooden rack, about six feet up on a wall. The cop shined his flashlight through the window all around while we huddled atop the rack, bladders atingle, feeling like James Bonds or the Hardy Boys. Eventually the light withdrew and the cop drove off. It was exciting, but the fact that I always had to piss when hiding from someone kept me from ever dreaming of a career in the CIA."

X — Getting Sandoval drunk on two 3.2s

Fender says he has no memory of this but it's sort of self-explanatory. Andy Sandoval was the drummer in the Torques at the time and apparently the boys brought back a couple of 3.2 percent beers from Colorado for him to drink. Andy later became a lawyer and is now well-known in Albuquerque circles.

As Fender remembers Andy: "He was a real go-getter. He was rebuilding a Model-A roadster when he became a Torque and he knew a jazz drummer who gave us a bunch of tips for playing in a band. Andy was around when I wrote my first song, an instrumental called 'Surf-Buns', and later, in an un-related conversation, once said, 'Don't be so brutal!' I liked the way he said it so much I changed the name of the song to 'The Brutal Surfer' when we played it for the 1963 Scorpion Follies.

XI — Louis Pope—God the laughs we used to have when he used to do his "Oh snit!"

Louis Pope was the first drummer for the Torques, although when he was in the group it was called the Napa 4. It was Fender and Geno's first real band. Louis was a couple of years older than they, and left soon after they played their first gig at the high school. The "oh snit" comes from an anecdote often told by Louis about a friend of his back east who had a cleft palate and would say "oh snit" instead of "oh shit".

Fender provides the origin of the name, the Napa 4. "I was reading an early book about the surfing craze in California and the surfers used the word 'Napa' to mean 'cool', as in, 'It was a real Napa surfboard.' So I thought Napa 4 would be a great name for our band for our first dance, held in the lobby of the high school cafeteria. I even made a big poster with NAPA 4 on it.

"Years later, when I met my future wife, Joyce, in Huntsville Alabama, I told her about the band and she laughed like a loon. She was raised in Vallejo, north of San Francisco, and in those days Napa's main claim to fame was the local asylum, affectionately called the Napa Nuthouse. I still think Napa 4 was a pretty good name, even though we only used it for that one dance. After that we were the Torques."

XII — Our trip to the coast

In 1961 Fender was invited by the Jaramillos to go with them on a trip to Vancouver Canada by car. They stopped in Las Vegas and Berkeley on the way up, and came back through Idaho. Fender remembers these highlights from the trip:

"First was the party and backseat piss debacle in Vegas, but those will be dealt with in XIII below. I distinctly remember that I was reading the recently released paperback edition of CATCH-22 and it seemed to speak to me on the trip.

"In Vancouver Geno and I somehow managed to get away from his parents and found a pool hall. We played a game of snooker on the biggest table we'd ever seen, at least 20% larger than the tables at the Snooker 8. We showed up covered in blue chalk and had to own up to how we spent our time away.

"Then in Boise Idaho, as we drove through the main street, I saw a sign I recognized. It was the same sign that used to stand in front of François Restaurant on West Main Street in Farmington! I knew the Kelloff's, who owned François, well since they were good friends of my mother's. So we stopped and went into the restaurant and sure enough, Mr. Kelloff was there and remembered me. They had left Farmington a few years earlier for the lofty climes of Idaho. We had a great meal, as I remember."

XIII — The party in Las Vegas (ee ha!)

Geno's brother, Robert, was living in an apartment complex at the time and the Jaramillos unwisely allowed Geno and me to stay with him on our night through Vegas. The complex was a singles place, with a central courtyard with pool and apparently nothing but young party animals living in the apartments. Everybody was drinking and swimming and it lasted just about all night long. The only thing I really remember is that Robert said that I needed some "skill" to impress the chicks with and what he came up with was that I could chug a bottle of beer very quickly. I tried, but there were definitely no impressed chicks around me that night.

Fender recalls the next day: "With massive hangovers, we drove back to Henderson to hook up with Geno's parents. It was Robert and Steve Stephens in front and Geno and me in back. Steve was smoking and flipped his cigarette butt out the window as we sped along the highway, which had no speed limit. As Robert explained, 'There's no speed limit between Vegas and Henderson so we are obligated to go as fast as the car will go.' Geno and I thought that sounded reasonable.

"We had gone about ten miles at 95 miles per hour when we started smelling smoke—but it didn't smell like the engine. It smelled like—upholstery! The back seat was on fire!

"So we pulled to the side of the highway and jumped out like a pack of clowns. Steve reached in and somehow pulled the back seat out of the car and we stood and watched it smolder healthily beside the car. There were cars whizzing by us, roiling the smoke that was billowing from the carseat.

" 'We got to put it out. Anybody got any water?' Steve asked. No one did. So Steve unzipped his fly, hauled out his extinguisher and proceeded to attack the most vicious part of the fire. We all followed suit and before long the potential holocaust had been micturated into submission. We congratulated ourselves on having the foresight to inundate ourselves with beer the night before, threw the soggy backseat into the trunk, and continued to Henderson."

XIV — Many enjoyable tacos from the El Cantaro

The El Cantaro—or in Spanish, "the the singer"—was a great Mexican restaurant on the south side of town, owned by Andy Sandoval's family. So after the Torques had finished practicing, or stealing lights (see XXI), or drinking 3.2 beer (see X above), the stalwart band of youths would hie to the back of the restaurant, where they would wait while Andy went in, to come out a few minutes later with a big cardboard box full of tacos. Superb tacos, they were, too!

In the year of our Lord Jesus Christ 1961, the back of the El Cantaro was the site of one of Fender's most important epiphanies. But let's let Fender tell you in his own blasphemous words.

"I had gone to Catholic school for eight years but was finally freed that summer when I was graduated from the eighth grade. I was off to public school! Yet I was still expected to go to mass on Sunday and refrain from eating meat on Friday. For students of the Ursuline nuns of Farmington in that era, breaking those edicts were the two biggest sins a person could commit.

"Then one beautiful summer night Geno, Andy and I ended up behind the El Cantaro and Andy came out with some of the best tacos ever. I was right in the middle of a huge mouthful when it snapped on me that it was Friday. Uh oh. I felt like Huckleberry Finn, deciding whether to turn in Jim and maybe go to heaven or let Jim go, and go to hell. I stood there with cheeks abulge, and—swallowed. 'All right, then, I'll *go* to hell.'

"I immediately felt a wave of relief and was never bothered by papist doubt again. The tacos were delicious, and they still are—especially on Fridays. I must admit that I do feel sorry for the millions of poor Catholics who are eternally roasting in hell right now because they unfortunately chewed on the wrong flesh during the years when the Catholic Church thought that eating meat on Friday was a really big sin. If they'd only had the wisdom to live

until the Ecumenical Council, they'd be sitting on the right hand
of Gawd right now."

XV — More than one beer bust at your house

Whenever Fender's mother was away from the house the young
lads schemed to have a party there. Cars would be parked up and
down the street and noisy music would rumble from the house as
dozens of invited and uninvited guests would show up. The first
occasions were called simply, "parties" but before long a name
had been adopted for them: Mojo Workout. Because Fender's
mother's plans were often sketchy, the word would go out on the
Farmington grapevine, "The Workout is ON!" or, more morosely,
"The Workout is OFF."

As with any teenage party of the period, fights were a big part of
them, probably a bigger part than the illicit sex. One memorable
fight had Roger Shay, a behemoth of a senior, throwing a punch at
some guilty drunk who conveniently passed out just as Roger's
fist swished past his head only to strike mild-mannered, and
slightly insane, David Logan, knocking him cold. It was David's
closest brush with fame as a high school student.

The biggest Mojo Workout occurred during the boys' junior
year when Fender's mother was spending the night at the Smith's
house while they were out of town. Sherrill Smith, a year Fender's
junior, suggested to Mrs. Tucker that she and a friend Shayleen
drive to the Tucker's house and "make sure the dishes were
done." Sherrill and Shayleen found a scene of such debauchery—
for Farmington—that it traumatized them, turning both of the girls
bad for the rest of their lives.

As Fender remembers: "I never got anything at a Workout, other
than a big drunk and hangover. Maybe Sherrill's right and there
was actual debauch going on, but I was always too drunk to join
in, dammit. One thing for sure, if any teenage brats ever tried to
have such a party in my neighborhood I'd be over there in a flash,
telling them to turn the damn music down and stay outa my yard.
Amazingly, the wonderful neighbors we had, the Hobbs', put up
with our noisy crap for the ten years it took the four Tucker boys
to make it through high school."

XVI — Helpin' you with the marquee

The Tucker boys owned the marquee-changing job at the two local downtown theaters, apparently, because once Michael had it in 1955, it was passed down to the rest of the family as it became their time atop the ladder. In other words, changing the marquee became a rite of passage for the Tucker boys. Fender started changing the marquee in the eighth grade and it passed on to Johnny when Fender was a junior and had become involved with the Torques, his rock and roll band.

It was a fantastic job for a young contrarian-in-the-making because it could only be done at night, after ten o'clock when the last feature of the day had started. It generally took an hour or less but it had to be done two or three times a week, no matter what the weather was. Many nights would find Fender and Geno braving icy storms to make sure the marquees had the right letters.

The red, plastic letters for the marquee were kept in dusty rooms above the theater entrances and as Fender and Geno found out, the best way to keep young juvenile delinquents from annoying the hoi polloi in public was to provide the JDs with handy rooms where they could break laws in private, away from the sight of solid citizens. If only Timothy McVeigh and Ted Bundy had had a room o' privacy during their formative years!

The tactics of marquee-changing are described in detail in the first chapter of WEED, WOMEN AND SONG so we will end with a pithy reminiscence from Fender: "Once, in the ninth grade, it was so cold the night I was supposed to change the marquee, I waited until early morning and instead of going to school at Tibbetts, I took the key from the mailbox at the Crawford's—where it was generally kept—and changed the marquee in the morning. Then I went to class around 10 AM, forgetting to replace the key back in the mailbox. SO around noon, Mrs. Crawford called my mother asking about the key, and my mother called the school. I was called out of class and my missing the first couple of periods was discovered. The story of my job came out and the principal, a dolt named Southall, wanted me to quit my job. Fuck that! We finally got it straightened out and I kept the job for another two years.

"These days no one would allow a teenager to roam the streets after midnight, but back then Farmington was relatively peaceful. One night I was walking home after midnight and a big guy in an old car offered me a ride. One of the ugliest guys I'd ever seen. Durango license plates.

" 'Where you been?' he asked.

" 'Went to a movie.'

" 'Did it, uh, get you all teased up?'

" 'Not really. It was a Disney movie.'

" 'How would you like a blow job?'

" 'Uh, no thanks, uh, hey, that's my house right there. I'll get out now.'

" 'It won't hurt.'

" 'No thanks.' And I scampered out of the car a few blocks away from the house. A couple of days later I mentioned to Mickey Miller about the guy and he said excitedly, 'Hey, the same guy picked me up the other night too! I slugged him and got out of the car right away.' I didn't believe Mickey had slugged the guy, who weighed about 250 pounds, but I believed the rest of his story.

"At the time Mickey was a real delinquent in the making and was pals with Eddie Rossen, a big lineman for the football team. One night soon after, Mickey and I were riding around with Eddie in his car when we spotted the old car with the Durango VV license plate. It was Blow Job! So we pulled up next to him and started yelling, 'Hey blow job!' He hunched over the wheel and headed east out of town, towards Durango. We followed him all the way to Aztec, yelling blow job epithets all the way. We never saw him again.

"Another time in the ninth grade I was walking home late at night on Dustin near Tibbetts junior high school and some guys in a maroon VW drove past, obviously drunk, and yelled at me, 'Hey, you! Whose dick you been suckin'?' They made a U-turn and started following me so I ran through a yard to get away. Three of the guys got out of the car and started chasing me. I ran east on Hopi and cut through a small orchard in the middle of the block. I guess I wasn't as fast or smart as I thought because they caught me in the middle of a big empty field on Monterey. They yelled, 'Why you runnin', asshole?' and I said it was because they were chasing me. They were quite drunk and one of them, simply because it seemed the thing to do, slugged me in the eye. Then they got back in the car and drove off.

"The next morning my mother was concerned about my eye and I told her most of the story. We got together with Kent Doak and my two older brothers and they said they'd look around for a maroon VW.

"At school Southall asked me if I'd like to catch the guys who did it to me and I said, sure. He described Lionel Stoabs in detail, practically praying it was Lionel who had done the deed, but I knew Lionel, who was one of the more cool delinquents at the high school and said it wasn't him. So much for Southall's offer of help.

"A few nights later Kent said he spotted four guys in a maroon VW at the Tastee-Freez on West Main and warned them that if they ever did anything like that again they'd pay. They acted guilty, but claimed to have nothing to do with it.

"About a month later I was at the pool hall and saw two of the guys. They acted embarrassed and left soon after. That was the end of that."

XVII — Drinkin' booze on the top of the Allen

Once our stash of liqueurs was drunk Geno and Fender needed another way to get booze, and once again the theater provided an answer. Every night after the shows were over—often while they were still changing the marquee—a cleaning crew would clean the theater, making the floor a little less sticky for the next day's patrons. If they found anything, like a wallet or purse, they'd put it in a big cardboard box behind the ticket booth. Oddly, there was never any money in these wallets or purses, but there were often ID cards. So when Geno and Fender needed identities that would make them 21 or older, they found them in the box. Geno was George Ben Begay for a while and Fender was Sam Chee Arthur.

Once they had their IDs it was pretty easy to visit one of the liquor stores on Main and get a couple of sixpacks, then walk on down to the Allen where they would drink them on the roof of the theater, watching the cars as they dragged Main 30 feet below. As Fender remembers: "It was a great place to guzzle beer and get maudlin. If only Charlie Manson or David Berkowitz had had such a cool place to kick out the jams."

XVIII — Thousands of trips to the Villa, Peve's, etc. (Remember the dog-tag deal? Ha ha!)

Thousands? It was more like five or six times that the lads managed to find a way to get up to Durango and into one of the 3.2 beer joints there. In Farmington the drinking age was 21 but in Durango it was 18 in those enlightened times. Poor Boys—Geno miswrote the name, which should be "PB's"—was one of the places, located right by the river on Main Street in Durango. In 1964 it was where Fender and the Torques were playing when the memorable events of "Travels with Harry"[7] took place.

Surfin' music was big when the boys were doing their Durango thing and the heavy metallic sound exactly matched their drunkenness. The Exotics was their favorite Durango band and Jerry Jimerfield, Tommy Beuten and Sid Levell later became their idols when Fender and Geno got more into guitars.

"The dog tag deal", as Fender remembers it was an occasion when everybody but Geno had an ID. How was he to get in? Amazingly, Geno pulled out a set of dogtags he had around his neck and brayed, "I'm in the goddam army. How can I NOT be old enough to get in this place?" He got in.

XIX — Pissin' in the snow

There has already been too much about urine in this exposé.

XX — Party at Smoky Farmer's

This was the very first big, anarchistic party that the lads were to attend. Smoky was an older, cool guy with a great name and Fender and Geno hardly knew him. But they heard about the party through Geno's brother, Robert, and resolved to be there. Somehow, even though they were a bit young for this party they made it and they even had a drink or two.

Fender remembers, "I have one distinct memory of the whole night—and it's probably wrong. I was sitting on a couch while

---

[7] The salacious details of Fender's deflowering are related in "Travels With Harry" in *WEED, WOMEN AND SONG.*

dozens of older drunkards milled around. The music was loud and brash. Then a smallish blonde woman—who might have been all of a year older than we were—got up on a table and started dancing. Then she took off her blouse and was dancing in her bra. It was more decadent than anything Fender had ever seen, but it was also sort of innocent. There was no sex going on in the open and there was no hint of her revealing more. It was just damn sexy.

"The only problem with this memory is that I distinctly remember the girl to be Lana Lyons, who was later a classmate in high school. She probably would have been too young to be there, and when I asked her about it years later, she denied it vehemently. I consoled her by saying it was an innocent striptease but she still insisted it wasn't her at all. I hesitate to relate this because it might cast doubt on my credibility. Could all of my memories be wrong?"

XXI — Stealing colored lights

Ah, the joys of youthful larceny! Fender and Geno were playing with Andy Sandoval and either Bill Smart or Dwight Babcock in the Torques and of course they needed bright lights to show off the band at a dance. They could go to the hardware store and buy them for $1 apiece or they could go around the town stealing colored floodlights from around motels and other businesses.

Fender attributes his later success to their never getting caught, although, "we did get our fingers burned more than a few times. Stealing cool booze is much easier than stealing hot lights."

XXII — Playin' baseball in front of your house

The Tucker's front yard was grass during the youthful years of the boys. The front of the house was a red brick backstop and Monterey hardly ever had any traffic. It was perfect for whiffleball and other baseball games. Since those halcyon days the grass has been replaced with red rocks and the street is filled with junked cars owned by the low-life neighbors.

As Fender opines, "If I could go back and relive any night of my life, I think one of the nights when we played baseball or kick-the-can with Johnny Harrell, Dwight Babcock, Roberta Young (Howary Dungo's daughter) and other kids on the block would be one I'd choose. Maybe someday Monterey Street will be a haven for kids again, but I doubt it."

XXIII — You and your G.D. bikinis

In 1961 some insane underwear manufacturer decided to make bikini style briefs for men and Fender just happened to buy a pair. They were sheer little things, sort of like today's thongs. Fender and Geno thought they were hilarious and found that while wearing them, a guy was just about forced to strut a bit and ripple a muscle or two like Charles Atlas or Joe Weider. No one would have ever known that Fender had a pair if he hadn't worn them one day at swimming PE at the Lions' pool on Orchard. The class was all ninth-grade boys and after they were all in the pool Fender strutted out of the locker room in his tight, red bikinis, stopping every few feet to strike a he-man pose. The other guys thought it was hilarious and the PE teacher, a coach named Gore, asked Fender if he was embarrassed.

Fender remembers, "I told him I wouldn't have done it if there were girls in the class. He seemed to think it was funny and I never wore them at school again. If Southall had found out I'd probably have been sent to some anti-homosexual reform school. Fuck him."

XXIV — Floatin' down the river (made me feel right at home)

The bikinis have a small part in this particular reminiscence but not when Geno was around. The area around Farmington is known as "Totah" by the Navajos, and it means "three rivers". The Animas comes down from Durango and meets the San Juan around the middle of town. There they flow west as one river until they are joined by the La Plata River on the west side of town. Generally the high school kids would get in the Animas River right before it meets the San Juan and float to the La Plata where there was a car waiting for them. Each person would have an inner tube and a sixpack for the journey. Great fun. The only real hazard was hitting your tailbone on a submerged rock since the river averaged less than two feet in depth.

Geno was on a Hispanic-pride kick when he wrote the inscription and the "made me feel right at home" quip referred to his being a honorary "wetback", even though he was born in Los Alamos NM.

Fender wore his bikinis on a couple of the trips and on one memorable floating down the Animas River up by Bondad CO he and the other guys got out of the water and bought some snacks at the Bondad store. Fender strutted through the place in his tiny red sac-cloth as the owners looked on aghast.

Fender has this to say, "That was the only time I ever wore tight-fitting underwear. Now I prefer boxer shorts made of Thai silk. By the way, I dress to the left."

XXV — Smokin' Havatampas

Havatampas are a sweet-smelling small cigar with a built-in wooden tip. Mild and quite unstinky, as cigars go. The boys tried smoking them when their cigarette smoking habits failed to gel, but they were too expensive. The wooden tips were cool, though.

As Fender remembers it, "I had tried a cigar a few years earlier, when I was about thirteen. It was a big black thing and I thought the idea was to chew on it as much as puff on it. I got righteously sick and vowed to never smoke another cigar again. But Havatampas were so mild I almost got hooked on them. It was mainly Dwight Babcock's influence that kept me away from tobacco. He was a gymnast and didn't like smoking and I went along with him on that. Luckily I changed my mind by 1966 when I met the one true and loyal love of my life, cannabis."

XXVI — Shootin' pool at Singleton's (retch!)

In those days you had to be 18 to get into a pool hall legally. Naturally the boys started hanging out at the Snooker 8 Pool Hall when they were 15, along with some of their more adventurous school chums. But every once in a while there was a crackdown on pool-playing minors and the owners would start being more diligent about checking IDs.

Around 1964 there were three pool halls in the downtown Farmington area. The Snooker 8 on Main Street, the Farmington Pool Hall also on Main right next to the Allen Theater—which later became a damn good bookstore—and Singleton's, a block south of Main on Wall Street. Singleton's was run by a decrepit old man with a lazy eye who didn't give a damn about the law but did care about the quarters that the young kids would bring in. One day, at the urging of Fender and some of his friends he got the idea of turning his pool hall into a "teen club". That way kids as young as 15 could hang out there, spending their quarters.

The San Juan Teens Pool and Snooker Club was formed and officers elected. Fender was president and Ron Ulibarri was veep. For about a week the club was in full swing, packed with kids playing pool, smoking cigarettes—practically a requirement of the club—and making deals to get beer.

Fender laughs, "The beer was the downfall of the SJTPASC. Once some parents found out that their little Susies and Timmies were getting drunk thanks to the pool club they raised hell with Singleton and the city fathers. Singleton was such an obvious pervert that before long the place was shut down and the aspiring delinquents of Farmington had to go back to breaking the law by going to the Snooker 8 or the other place on Main. Funny thing, though, years later my week or two as president of the club was the high point of my résumé. Obviously I had leadership qualities."

XXVII — When me and you and Irvin made our first professional appearance—Wolverton Mountain! (then we shot our pay on pool!!!)

Truly a landmark event in the careers of Fender and Geno was the day they made their professional debut in the alley behind the Snooker 8. They had spent the morning at the grassy park surrounding the Lions Swimming Pool with Lynn Rayburn, a degenerate senior in high school who gave guitar lessons on Saturday mornings. Lynn sort of played in a band with Cecil Irvin, the most notorious guitar player in the school at the time. He knew a few chords and Chuck Berry licks and he charged us $1 each a lesson every Saturday.

Geno and Fender had been joined by Robert Irvin, a friend from Fender's baseball team, and after three or four lessons, knew about as much as Lynn did on the guitar. On the day in question, after the lesson the three lads took their Spanish acoustic guitars and decided to go downtown and see what was happening. They were hanging out behind the Snooker 8 wondering where they could get some pool money when a man poked his head out of an office window next to the pool hall. "Hey, you guys! C'mere!"

Fender remembers it this way. "He said he had some girls in the office who needed serenading and that he'd pay us each a dollar if we'd sing them a song. Would we?! Damn right we would, even though we really didn't know a whole song. So we broke into a three-part rendition of Claude King's 'Wolverton Mountain', emphasizing the corniness of the song. We actually hit some three-part harmony on the 'sweeter than hawney' line.

"The girls thought it was great and my life's work was set in stone at that moment. The guy gave us our three dollars and we had a great time playing pool with it. As a great bar band from Arizona, the Dusty Chaps, later wrote, 'There's somethin' about getting' paid for what I'd be doin' anyway.' Truer words were never written."

XXVIII — Sneakin' into the movies

Fender could walk into the theater anytime free because of his job, but technically his friends were supposed to pay admission. But they went so often they'd have been broke all the time if they'd paid. At the Allen it was easy. They'd just go up to the marquee-changing room then go into the balcony via a small hall that went to the projection room. They only had to dodge the projectionist, who was usually busy. But at the Totah, the only way in was again through the letter room, but there they'd have to go down a staircase and into the lobby through a doorway covered by a Navajo blanket. They had to have perfect timing to get past the girls at the refreshment counter, and especially the ticket taker, who was usually Carl Black or some adult who felt some loyalty to the Allens.

"Still," muses Fender, "there's something about seeing a show for free. Especially if you have a pocketful of sunflower seeds."

XXIX — THE MAD HONKERS HAVE STRUCK AGAIN!!

At the time (1959) there was a spate of terrorism by someone called The Mad Bomber in the national news. So whenever Fender would stay at Geno's house overnight they'd go out after everyone had gone to sleep and roam the neighborhood, looking for cars that weren't locked. Then they'd honk the horn a couple of time and run like demons. They billed themselves as THE MAD HONKERS and even started leaving short notes in the cars for the unwitting and sleep-deprived to find the next day. "THE MAD HONKERS HAVE STRUCK AGAIN!"

"Once again," Fender opines, "the kids of today, not allowed such innocent blowing off of steam, must content themselves with amphetamines, glue and dangerous sex. If only people still left their cars unlocked!"

XXX — Mr. Willoughby's office for Fender Willie Cad stories

This was a turning point in Fender's life, the time he discovered the power of the written word over the demented bastions of prudery that occupied principals' offices in 1964. It all began in study hall when Geno passed Fender a note containing the beginning of a Fender-Willie-cad story. "Willie" was Geno's snooker moniker and "cad" was Craig Alan Daniels, a friend of theirs who played the role of low man on the FWC totem pole.

Fender added to the story and before long "The Mojo Funk Caper"[8] took shape. Basically it's the story of a major annual Mojo Workout to be attended by the FWCs that is infiltrated by an antagonistic Shell Scott. Scott was the white-haired private detective who was a favorite of theirs, created by the great pulp writer Richard S. Prather. Fender's brother Mike had gotten hooked on Shell Scott in college and had passed it on to the boys.

One day in study hall when the story was almost finished the note was intercepted by the study hall teacher. She was shocked by its frankness and immediately turned it over to Mr. H.L. Willoughby, a principal as stunted and stodgy as his name. Fender and Geno were called into his office and received a tongue-

---

[8] The text of "The Mojo Funk Caper" is included in this volume.

lashing of exceptional virulence. Then Fender's mother was summoned to Willoughby's office.

Maxine Tucker had had some dealings with Willoughby when her oldest son Michael had led a raid on the high school one February, putting up a big banner that said, subversively, "Happy Birthday Abe!" It was a major scandal for 1958 and showed that besides not having any sense of proportion, Willoughby was a stupid sack of shit. So she had an inkling of what would happen even before she entered his office.

Willoughby blew any chance he had for a reasonable settlement of the affair by first telling Ms. Tucker that the "story" that had been penned by her son and his accomplice was so vile he couldn't show it to her.

"What the hell?" thought the 55-year-old white-haired matron who had lived through WWII, a marriage to a bald man, and raised four sons with contrarian brains. As she put it later, "I was ready to side with the old fart since they should have been studying instead of writing literature, but when he wouldn't let me even see the evidence I knew he was lying through his teeth, just as he had done years earlier. How could I support him when he wouldn't even let me read the story?"

The episode blew over and Fender and Geno continued their writing. Later that year Fender would read in class a story he had written about one of the better teachers at FHS, Carl Ferre, called "Babes, Bombs, Fender and Company". He credited it to an "obscure author" named Knees Calhoon and it detailed the time that Ferre was trying to sabotage the theater—where he worked as a projectionist—only to have his "fat, fumbly fingers, flabby from filching rolls at hot lunch" thwarted by Fender and his "strong, lithe digits".

"Just what this country needed in 1964," says Fender sarcastically, "more censorship and less anarchistic literature. I blame Willoughby for the Vietnam War and JFK's assassination."

XXXI — The same place for ditchin'

Geno may have ditched more than a couple of times but Fender only remembers doing it once, when the boys, along with Key Club members Louis Pope and Jim Patterson (class of '63, not '65), decided to drive up to Durango and mess around rather than spend a hot Friday in class. They took along a bottle of Everclear and had a wild time, playing on the train that used to be parked alongside Main Street by the river.

They didn't even try to hide the fact they were gone and of course got called in on it the next Monday. It was late in the school year and it soon blew over.

Fender says, "I'm sure just about everybody used to ditch more than we did. It just wasn't our kind of crime. Now that I think back on it I regret every day I spent in school and wish I had ditched more."

XXXII — Oh yeah!! Gad, how could I forget!! Two mad detectives at the carnival!!! (smokin' pipes!)

One night in 1960 or 1961 there was a carnival in town and the two tricksters decided to dress up and see what sort of scandal they could cause. They found the perfect outfits in a pair of beige trench coats and brown fedoras that belonged to Geno's brother Robert and his friend Steve Stephens. With trench coats almost dragging on the ground, fedoras hiding their eyes and Sherlock Holmesian curved Calabash pipes dangling from their lips, the two made quite a pair as they wandered around the carnival grounds, never engaging anyone, but drawing stares from just about everyone there.

Fender remembers it thus: "We didn't have any real plan but we were definitely on the same wavelength for this caper. We learned how to puff the pipes so that a huge cloud of smoke followed us everywhere and we made sure that everyone saw how grim we looked. Obviously we were on a case. A game was afoot!

"The highlight of the night came when Geno and I spotted a couple of uniformed policemen standing near a ride in the middle of the carnival. We purposely kept our eyes straight ahead as we slowly sauntered past them, smoke billowing all around us, hats pulled low. Then, as if planned, about ten feet past them we stopped on a dime, and slowly turned to our left with the precision of an Olympic swim team and gazed back at the cops, pulling the pipes out of our mouths simultaneously. The cops were laughing their heads off.

"We stared at them without a trace of humor, put the pipes back in our mouths then slowly turned to our right and continued walking away from them. I imagine the cops were disappointed that we weren't involved in some sort of murder spree.

"Whenever I think about how we must have looked I can't help but think of Mutt and Jeff. You have to be old to remember who they were but there's something about a tall person and a short person as a team. Geno always made me feel like the big, bumbling doofus of the team, while he was the small, clever trickster. In later years when I was with someone taller than I was, I felt like the trickster. Is this archetypical? Can the taller person be the cleverer one? Of course it's possible, but it doesn't seem right. Maybe it's because of Mutt and Jeff, Martin and Lewis, Laurel and Hardy, Of Mice and Men, et al."

XXXIII — Killing spiders in my room (almost killing our tongues)

Geno and Fender were in the middle of their pipe-smoking period—which lasted about a year —when they found themselves in Geno's room in his house on Camina Entrada in southern Farmington. Bored, and with a full bag of Cherry Blend pipe tobacco, they spied a huge spider crawling across the ceiling. They shut the door and windows tightly then proceeded to puff at bowl after bowl of tobacco, blowing the smoke up towards the spider.

The room soon filled with smoke and they continued to puff away. They decided that either the spider would die—or they would. The spider looked like he might triumph; he continued across the ceiling at a healthy pace. But soon he began to slow and before he made it to a wall, he stopped moving and curled up into a ball, dangling from a gossamer thread.

Fender describes the poignant scene: "Our eyes were smarting from the haze but we were pretty sure we would win. We figured we could blow the smoke directly on the spider if the game got rough and before long we were doing just that. Our tongues felt thick and tarry, and we were definitely getting nauseous when finally the spider fell to the floor, dead from tobacco.

"We made the pronouncement of death then threw open the door, letting a cloud of smoke billow out into the rest of the house. 'What the hell?' Geno's dad, Anselmo, yelled, and we had to explain we were on a humanitarian insect-killing mission. Their

house smelled like Cherry Blend for days after, but it was re-
markably spider-free."

XXXIX — Puttin' the mojo curse on Jan and Fran

Jan and Fran. Jan and Fran. Who could they be? Fender is pretty
sure that Fran is Francene Lagree, a foxy blonde schoolmate of
theirs who lived next door to Geno. Both of the lads had the hots
for her but then, they had the hots for every girl they knew, all of
whom seemed inaccessible. Robert used to tell Geno, "Man, if I
were you, I'd be all over that Francene," but as far as Fender
knew, nothing ever happened. Fender had a great conversation
with her one night when he was spending the night at Geno's but
she moved out of town soon afterward.

Jan may have been Janet Viles, who lived in Farmington for a
while then moved to a nifty home near Cuba NM.

As Fender remembers: "We were always putting the Mojo
Curse on babes in those days. Maybe that was why we never got
anywhere. We got the word 'mojo' from Willie Dixon's 'I Got
My Mojo Workin' ', a song that we learned from the Exotics in
Durango. When I started writing songs in 1961 I resolved to always have the word 'mojo' in every one of them but luckily I
wised up after about four songs."

There was an elaborate mythos about the word "mojo" as can be
evidenced by the inscription in the same yearbook from Fender's
favorite female friend, Judi Vandiver. She called herself a "Mojo
Maid" and Fender and Geno "Mojo Men". Her inscription ends
with the following ominous addendum: "With the rapid progress
of science—by '69' there may be a means of preventing H.F. con-
ditions by the use of M.P."

1969 was the year that those who graduated from high school in
1965 could look forward to graduating from college—if they went
for four years straight. So it was a big year in the future for the
class of '65. As for "H.F." and "M.P." the M probably stands for
"Mojo" but there's no telling what the other letters stand for. It's a
mystery that may never be solved.

Final Paragraph

Geez Fender I could go on for hours, but my most cherished memory is when I played with you....ah, er, I mean the Torques. Thanks for being a friend.

The green-eyed chili picker—

Geno Jaramillo

Remember the Shell Scott grin? Hee hee!!!

Norbert here. Geno played with the Torques up till their senior year when Fender joined with Harry Batchelor[9], Dwight Babcock[10] and Bob Amerman[11] to form the final version of the band.

Both Fender and Geno mastered a certain curling of the upper lip and an squinting of the eyes that would nowadays be called an "shit-eating grin". They used it on the babes whenever they could—with absolutely no success. Even a teenage girl from the 60s knew it was as phony as a cutrate Rolex.

---

[9] See "Travels with Harry" in TALES FROM THE TOWER for some exciting sex adventures aided and abetted by Harry Batchelor, a 1964 graduate of Bloomfield High School. Harry played guitar.

[10] 1963 graduate of Farmington High School who lived across the street from Fender. Dwight played bass.

[11] 1966 graduate of FHS. Bob played drums and died of cancer in 1967.

CHRONOLOGICAL CALHOON

Reminiscences in the Form of Doggerel

BETWEEN THE YEARS 1964 and 1985 I wrote a bunch of songs under my *nom de plume* Knees Calhoon. They just about all began with the words, which resembled poems I had seen in reprints of the *The Pearl* and other erotic magazines from previous centuries. In other words, doggerel. I added music to the doggerel and thanks to my making my living as a guitar picker many of them were actually heard by human ears. In the early 90s, years after I had quit playing professionally, I decided to record them all in my home recording studio.

Here are all of the poems, *sans* music but arranged chronologically, to be read as they were written: doggerel of the worst kind. Each has a short introduction, along with the location where I was when I wrote them. Dialect is proudly used, where applicable. All songs are available on the CD that comes with WEED, WOMEN AND SONG.

HOMICIDE BLUES

Monterey Street, Farmington NM, spring 1964

Knees' first song with lyrics began as a typical blues put-down song but quickly became a life-threatening anthem to domination when the only lyrics that seemed to fit were "ah'mo killya". He loved the fact that the phrase "I am going to" could be whittled down to two simple syllables: ah'mo. He was stuck for a rhyme for the last verse and asked his friend Barry Dunkeson for help. Barry came through with the classic, "Germans will look at you and say 'Nein!'" line and the rest is history.

Well if you ever, an I mean ever,
Ever try to put me down
Well I'll kill ya, yeah ah'mo kill ya
Even though you're the best around
When I get through with ya baby
You'll be the lowest paid hooker in town.

An if you ever, an I mean ever,
Ever try to make me sad
Well I'll kill ya, yeah ah'mo kill ya
Even though you're the best I ever had
When I get through with ya baby
People gonna look at you an feel bad.

So if you ever, an I mean ever,
Ever try to feed me a line
Well I'll kill ya, yeah ah'mo kill ya
Even though you're mighty fine
When I get through with ya baby
German's will look at you an say "Nein!"

THE GIRLS BACK HOME

Huntzinger's Apartments, Farmington NM, summer 1965

This is one of Knees' first songs with lyrics and he obviously didn't spend too much time on them. The song was inspired by a surfin' tune called California Sun *and the guitar lick is a ripoff of Del Shannon's organ solo on* Runaway. *A critic once described the "lie there and moan" line as "so political incorrect that it has to make you smile." In 1965 it was the best most young stud wannabees could hope for.*

I'm goin back where I belong
Where the summer days are twice as long
An the girls I love, love me too.
So keep away don't make me stay
You had your chance you had your way
An now it's time for me to go.

I'm goin back to the girls back home
They don't gimme no lip
They just lie there an moan.

The life back home is for a man
Who doesn't want a Mojo hand
You never gave me the love that I need.
So keep away don't make me stay
You had your chance you had your way
An now it's time for me to go.

I LOVE MY MOJO

Monterey Street, Farmington NM, winter 1964

Another ripoff, this time of Buddy Holly's Not Fade Away. *At least Knees added a chorus in another time signature. This was the first Calhoon tune with a plot, albeit a flaky one. Is there a hidden symbolism to the voodoo doll and bloody pin? Why would a doll bleed? And what kind of do-gooder goes around leaving bloody needles as his calling card? Calhoon never answers these questions. This was Knees' third song with lyrics and he was just still living up to his pledge to include the word "mojo" in all his songs.*

Deep inna jungle way cross the world
A witch doctor say "Hey you needa girl?"
I say "Hey doctor thassa what I need."
He gave me a doll and said "Make it bleed."
I grabbed me a needle an I stuck that doll
A girl comes up to me says "You wanna ball?"
I say "Hey doctor whatcha call this thing?"
He say "It's a Mojo an yo're its king."

I love my Mojo cuz he's my man
My Mojo loves me cuz I'm his hand.
I got my Mojo a-workin on you
An you'll be mine befo he's through.

Well, one of these days you'll come to me
An maybe I'll set my Mojo free.
Or maybe I'll give him to a frien in need
An say "It's a Mojo now make it bleed."
My little Mojo will go on and on
Leavin love wherever he's gone,
An you can tell just where he's been
Cuz you'll always find a bloody pin.

KEEP ME POSTED

White Rocks Dorm, NMSU, Las Cruces NM, fall 1965

Knees' first C&W song. He didn't really like this kind of music in 1965 but figured if he played it, he might as well write it. At the time he had sworn to always have the word "Mojo" in every one of his songs but fortunately, soon after he dropped this particular quirk. Harry Batchelor, the other guitar picker in the Torques, thought the line "doncha get in nobody's car" was deliciously ominous.

Keep me posted baby
On where you goin to
Keep me posted baby
On everything you say and do
No I don't trust yo baby no not one bit
Cuz I happen to know that you're not worth it
So keep me posted baby
An I might keep lovin you.

Keep me posted baby
Let me know just where you are
Keep me posted baby
Doncha get in nobody's car
Well you might fool me baby for a little while
But it won't be long befo I find out chile
So keep me posted baby
An I might forget you're such a liar.

Yeah keep me posted if you want yo man
Yeah keep me posted I want no Mojo hand.

THE SHIT-FUCK

Monterey Street, Farmington NM, circa 1965

Back in 1965 there were a lot of songs introducing new dances and one day when the Torques were rehearsing Knees said, "Guys, we need to come up with a good name for a new dance so we can write a hit record about it." Dwight Babcock the bass player immediately piped up, "The Shit-Fuck!" We shuddered to think about what the dance would be like but this is the song that emerged.

Everybody's doin it, doin it, doin it
Grabbin some ass an screwin it, screwin it
It don't take long sonny if you're strong
Let me show you how so you don't do it wrong.
First you ease it in then in an out, in an out
It hurts so good
It makes you wanna jump 'n' shout
She must have twelve inches
Cuz you're in all the way
Now you know why the cocksmen say

Do the shit-fuck (in an out)
Do the shit-fuck (in an out)
Do the shit-fuck (in an out)
Do the shit-fuck (in an out)
When you feel your balls a-drummin
Sonny then you know you're comin
Do the shit-fuck.

IT'S TRUE

Monterey Street, Farmington NM, spring 1965

Knees wrote this when he was playing with The Torques, and it was one of his few slow songs. The words are pretty insipid but the chords are rather interesting, especially for 1965. Later, in the 70s and 80s in Las Cruces, this was one of the Calhoon Brothers favorite tunes. Mark Coker, the guitar player, said it reminded him of the Beau Brummels.

Though skies are grey my love,
We'll find a way my love
And it's true, I love you

Though leaves may fall my love,
I'll give you all my love
And it's true, I love you.

And you know I need you, it's no mystery
And I'll never leave you but will always be

Right by your side my love,
Not a thing to hide my love
And it's true, I love you.

WHAT CAN YOU DO?

White Rocks Dorm, NMSU, Las Cruces NM, 1965

The White Rocks dorm was a relic of World War II occupation of the campus by excess soldiers from Fort Bliss. The dorm fee was $70 for the fall semester of 1965 for Knees and Dwight Babcock, the Torques bass player, and it was worth every penny. The building was torn down the next semester. Knees wrote this on his bunk, looking out the window at the dust, imagining he was writing a song the Byrds might sing.

Well she don't have much money
But what I want she gets me
When I say let me do something
She don't say no she lets me
But you, what can you do?

Her eyes are so inviting
When she asks me how I feel
Her hands know what they're doin
Her love she can't conceal
But you, what can you do?

You didn't sympathize
Or try to disguise your lies
She lets the world go by
And it's no wonder why she's mine.

BOX LUNCH

NMSU, Las Cruces NM, fall 1965

One day in the late 70s Dwight pulled out his wallet and said, "Knees, I got something here you wrote." It was the lyrics to a song that Knees had written in history class at NMSU in the fall of 1965. Knees had forgotten all about it. Luckily Dwight had kept it in his wallet all that time.

I got hairs in my teeth an blood in my mouth
It's easy to tell I've been down south
Some like to screw an some dry hunch
But I'll always take a juicy box lunch.

When a napkin is handy an the ketchup is flowin
You ask your baby if she might try blowin
She's chewin your cookies
An you're startin to munch
There ain't nothin better than a juicy box lunch.

You're down at the Y an she's startin to function
There's plenty of action
Where her legs make a junction
You got it licked cuz she's startin to hunch
She'll get her rocks from a juicy box lunch.

You keep on goin, it's kicks just to chew
I doubt if she'll kiss you after you're through
You're right in the groove an diggin it a bunch
Who wants to fuck
When you can eat a box lunch?

SYDNEY

North of Durango CO, circa 1965

One day Bob Amerman, Dwight Babcock and Knees went fishing up in Colorado. Knees had his guitar and wanted to write a song at the camp while the other two fished, and when Bob said he'd been wanting to write a love song for Sydney, his girlfriend, Knees volunteered to write the song for him. Unfortunately, the chords were too hard for Bob to play and he never sang it for Sydney. Bob died of cancer a year later.

Oh Sydney,
Our love has lasted,
So let's both look past it
And see what tomorrow will bring.

And don't you see that Sydney,
Our love will grow stronger
Each day will grow longer
Than the day I gave you my ring.

The dreams that we shared will all come true
So never be scared long as I'm here with you.
And don't you see that, Sydney,
The world is our highway
And when things turn out my way
You and I will have our day.

IT WASN'T SIMPLE

White Rocks Dorm, NMSU, Las Cruces NM, 1965

This was inspired by an obscure Bob Dylan song called If You Gotta Go, Go Now. *It wasn't about anyone Knees knew — in 1965 he hadn't had any experience with living with anyone but his family. He had forgotten all about it until the early 90s when he found a copy of the lyrics.*

She didn't try to see me through,
She thought I oughta change my view
It wasn't simple livin with her.
She didn't try to connect at all
She kept the bed away from the wall
No it wasn't simple livin with her.

But my days with her were good for me,
Not only fun but reality
Now fun is cheap but not as real,
Only she can change the way I feel.

She had a way of holdin back
She said our minds were on different tracks
It wasn't simple livin with her.
She blew her mind when things got rough
She held me down but not enough
No it wasn't simple livin with her.

But my days with her were right for me,
Better than they had a right to be
Her leavin me I took in stride,
Now all I got is my pride.

LYSERGIC SONG, DEFINITELY

Gilmore Street, North Hollywood CA, 1966

*Knees was staying with Barry Dunkeson and his band buddy
Norm in North Hollywood when they put this song together.
Norm wrote the chorus and they used to sing it in three-part
harmony in the bathroom (for the reverb) at the top of their
lungs, especially after toking up in the closet. Knees was quite
proud of his many psychedelic references and the backwards guitar solo.*

I met you on a ship
Cosmic laughter made you trip
An excuse a seasoned witch never buys
Thought a girl like you would know,
Lyin's very proud to show
That it's visible to turned on acid eyes.

You filtered out my soul
Left no directions how to hold
Perception's golden revolving doors
I'm offering all I touch
On the altar of too much
The high priestess says she wants much more.

Weave a tapestry of truth
Teaching love to keep its youth
Forgetting all the paths of its frustrations.

Blind man saw me today,
Took a look an walked away
I got a feelin you're tearin down my mind
You got me breathin cellophane,
Watchin shadows made of rain
You want me seein words that say I'm blind.

NOTHIN YOU CAN SAY

Monterey Street, Farmington NM, spring 1966

Actually, a good musician friend of Knees', Mo Moses, wrote most of this song, including the killer guitar lick. Mo was apparently inspired by the Kinks' early songs like You Really Got Me *and* All Day and All of the Night. *Knees sure would like to run into Mo again and pay him the royalties this song has generated.*

You better watch out you better get outa town
If I catch you girl I'm gonna put you down
There ain't no use in you hangin around
I know all about the new love you found
Oh no

Nothin you can say can stop me now,
I'm gonna make you sad somehow.
Nothin you can say can stop me now,
I'm gonna make you sad somehow
Oh no, oh no.

You've been sayin that he treats you right
But I gave you lovin both day an night
One of these days you're gonna see the light
You plead don't hurt me but I just might
Oh no.

GIMME A CHANCE

Monterey Street, Farmington NM, spring 1966

Obviously a blatant ripoff of Bob Dylan's Like a Rolling Stone, *Knees amazed himself by coming up with so many rhymes. It started out as a guitar folksong but ended up as a keyboard tune. The verse about the pill shows that Knees was able to write commercial, politically correct lyrics, even if they didn't exactly agree with his philosophy.*

It takes less than a week
To learn how to speak
So doncha feel cheap
For interruptin my sleep
When you knew I would help you
To get back on your feet
Oh gimme a chance.

You said your life was real
But you never had a thrill
That didn't make you ill
Or crave another pill
When you knew I would help you
An you know I always will
Oh gimme a chance.

You made all kinds of deals
With tramps an their spiels
But you missed a lot of meals
While chasin your bootheels
When you know I would help you
Cuz I know how it feels
Oh gimme a chance.

There once was a time
When I wouldn't lend you a dime
But the change is not mine
An neither is the bind
When you know I would help you

If you don't act too fine
Oh gimme a chance.

When you were on your own
An your mind was blown
But you didn't ask for a loan
So your little pride was shown
When you knew I would help you
Aw you must have known
Oh gimme a chance.

I've taken it all while you were havin a ball
You were feelin so tall
But you were due for a fall
When you knew I would help you
But you didn't give a call
Oh gimme a chance.

HOT POTATO #1

Monterey Street, Farmington NM, spring 1967

Knees was living at home fending off the draft (unsuccessfully) and the other guitar player in The Disciples, Mo Moses, was living there too. Mo liked to play smooth, jazzy chords and this was Knees' stab at using them. The title is a pastiche of the Flying Burrito Brothers' Hot Burrito #1, *which was also a slow song with smooth chords.*

Baby I've left your world behind,
I never wanted to be blind
But you made me feel
Like I was lost in the maze of your mind.

And baby the hold you had on me
Was too real for our love to be
The kind of love
That I could grasp and still be free.

And I hope that you will find
The way to peace of mind
In that world you made so unconsciously
But I doubt you'll ever see
What love can mean when free
The world now turns for me.

SATURDAY BABY

Fort Bliss TX, fall 1967

*Obviously a ripoff of Frank Zappa's Ruben and the Jets' style,
this tune grew out of late night jam sessions in the stairwells at
the barracks, where the reverb was inspiring — and forgiving. It
was the doo-wop song for the five or six guys with guitars and
other noise makers who would gather there. The annoying falsetto wasn't part of it back in the army days; it only was added in
the early 90s when Knees recorded this classic ballad.*

I think of you baby every night,
I want to hold you an kiss you tight
Saturday Baby won't you please be mine?

You are the toughest broad I know,
Whenever you touch me my juices flow
Saturday Baby won't you please be mine?

Saturday night we met at the dance
You looked at me an at my chartreuse pants
Then all at once it was romance,
Oh baby please give me a chance.

JONATHAN CANFIELD

Fort Bliss TX, fall 1967

*It was while Knees was in the army (1967-1969) that he came up
with the brilliant idea of doing a whole album consisting of epi-
taphs. Mercifully, the album ended up consisting of this one song,
which is unusual (for Knees) in that it has a chorus in 5/8 time
and an open guitar tuning.*

He walked kinda funny shufflin along the ground
He talked kinda funny biting off the sound
He died with a footprint on his back.

He lived his life so rightly blinded by his mind
He took his life so lightly left it all behind
His tombstone said his name and nothing else.

Jonathan Canfield, it read
Although he was there in spirit only.

He loved his wife with passion
Till the day he died
She knew it was the fashion
So at his grave she cried
His tombstone fell to dust in thirty days.

1959 PINOCCHIO TIMEX BLUES

Alpine Street, Huntsville AL, fall 1968

Knees was in his second army year at Redstone Arsenal and liv-
ing off-base with Dick O'Murphley and Ron Cramer. He and Pe-
ter Blue, another army buddy, would play some blues on guitar
and harmonica and this was one of them. Knees was inspired by
Bob Dylan's Blonde on Blonde *album and liked the idea of men-*
tioning brand names in a song. He was very proud of the Twis-
taflex line.

I dropped seven pennies onna sidewalk
Reachin in my pocket for a dime
I guess I don't get no hotdog
But at least I got the time.

Some little bastid ran away with all my pennies
Practicin for a life of crime
Now I definitely don't get no hotdog
But at least I got the time.

Cuz I got me a 1959 Pinocchio Timex
I wear it around the upper portion of my leg,
It would cut off my blood flow
But I ain't got none
From the knee on down I just got a peg.

Now I know you got some questions
Like how come I don't wear it on my wrist?
Y'see my Twistaflex's got six inches
An I just got a five inch fist

So why not on my ankle?
Good question I must admit
But y'see I'm kinda myopic
An I can't see my ankle for shit.

NOCTURNAL MISSION

Alpine Street, Huntsville AL, spring 1968

*Knees spent the year 1968 at Redstone Arsenal in Huntsville AL
and at the time he wrote this song was living with some buddies
off-base. It was loosely inspired by the Walter Jenkins affair, a
Johnson-era sex scandal that—as Knees remembers it—involved
gay solicitation in government restrooms with hidden cameras.
Nowadays it would trigger two years of Congressional investigation. Back then it blew over quickly—except for Knees' rap anthem commemorating the incident. It wasn't called "rap" back
then; it was called crummy one-chord crap. Still, it was popular
in the bars.*

Well Ah was sittin inna station
Jus a-waitin fo de bus
When a strange kinda thundah
Cum a-rumblin fum mah guts
Mah eyeballs started rollin
An mah mouf filled fulla spit
Ah knew inna flash
Dat Ah had to take a shit.

Ah hopped upon mah feet
A-lookin fo de loo
Ah saw a coupla signs
But dey was tres ambigue
One of dem said "manager"
Dat didn't sound like me
De other one say Ladies
An dere'd be a ten-cent fee.

Ah stood dere lookin stoopid
Till de thundah cleared mah thoughts
Ah mean whut de hell's de difference
When youse got de screamin trots?
So Ah grabbed me mah las dime
An Ah flung it in de slot
Scampered through de doorway
An took de nearest pot.

Ah hadn't seen no ladies
Or heard no lady shreiks
So Ah was feelin kinda peaceful
Just a-restin on mah cheeks
When Ah hear de door swing open
An some highheels echo in
Dey take de stall right next to mine
Much to mah chagrin.

Ah decided Ah'd wait her out
After a coupla false starts
Ah leaned back on de crapper
An ripped offa coupla farts
Man what a bummer
Ah thought pissed off complete
When Ah feels dis weird scrabblin
On de toppa mah feet.

Ah kinda leaned forward
To get a better view
When Ah saw dis chick's toes
A-diddlin wif mah shoe
Den Ah started wondrin
Jus whut she thinks Ah am
Wif her toes on mah ankle
A-nibblin like a clam
Nibblenibblenibblenibble
Nibblenibblenibblenibble
Nibblenibblenibblenibble
Nibblenibblenibblenibble

Ah figured whut de hell,
De chick she mus be Sapphic
Well shit Ah'll do anything
As long's it's pornographic
When mah door flies open
Dere's a man, big, obese
Badge an gun say CIA
Man say "Yo disturbin mah peace!"

SPACE NEEDLE

Pierce Street, El Paso TX 1969

Knees was inspired by the Velvet Underground's heroin songs and thought he should write one of his own. He worked out an elaborate arrangement for the song based on some oriental melody and recorded it in the living room of the Pierce Street pad. Ray Ott ran the tape deck with its reverb knob that went to 11. Knees uses a kazoo for most of the instrumental solo. The noises he makes at the end were inspired by Shock Theater, *a Friday night horror show on KOB TV out of Albuquerque back in the 50s.*

Woke up this morning,
To the sound of my alarm,
All I felt like doin
Was shootin my arm.
Come to me baby, gimme a fix,
I feel like I'm drowned in that ol river Styx.

Check in my wallet,
Check in my shoes
If I don't find my needle
I'll become one with the blues.
Come to me baby, gimme a fix,
My eyes are like tinfoil,
My teeth feel like bricks.

So tear up my shirtsleeve,
Find me a vein,
In a blink of a second
A strange brain gang bang.
Come to me baby, gimme a fix,
People get naked, expose all your pricks.

BOSTON TRILOGY

Kirtland NM, summer 1970, Monterey Street,
Farmington NM, 1972

This is actually three separate songs blended together. A couple
of them were written in the style of Glen Campbell, who was
popular at the time, and they were all written on the piano.
Oddly, when Knees recorded them in the 90s, he decided to use a
guitar arrangement. The blending almost makes sense.

Boston girl just common people,
But she's been down
On the streets far too long now,
No one wants her around.
She comes to me with tears in her eyes,
Tears she can't cry
Oh what can I tell her
That she doesn't already know.

So if you see her on the road,
Won't you please be kind to her
Try to help her with her load
Cuz she's got such a long way to go
She's all alone but she's comin home.

I'll treat you like a fragile flower
Til you feel like growin,
It's a sadness deep inside to see you fallen.
Like a soothin shade on a summer day,
My love is overflowin,
Your kiss is like the gentle touch of pollen.

Our words are blown away by the eastern wind
And washed into the earth by the rain.
We look up to the sky as the clouds drift by
The grass grows tall around us
Hides us from the train
That's chuggin through the countryside
Headin down to Austin.
It's been a year since we ran away from Boston.

TAKE OFF YOUR CLOTHES

Fort Bliss TX, fall 1969

It must have been a slow day at the warfront when Knees wrote these lyrics. They show that his contrarian spirit was already well in place by 1969. Probably inspired by William Burroughs' Naked Lunch, *it turned into a nifty little anthem to non-conformity.*

You know it's perfectly natural
To pick away at your nose
Yes it's perfectly natural
Take off your clothes.

You know it's perfectly natural
Any way she blows
Yes it's perfectly natural
Take off your clothes.

You know that you got hair
To keep you warm where you need it
You also got a mouth
To make you grow so why not feed it?

You know it's perfectly natural
To lick away at her toes
Yes it's perfectly natural
Take off your clothes.

You know it's perfectly natural
When it flows it flows
Yes it's perfectly natural
Take off your clothes.

THE BALLAD OF SADIE AND JEWEL

Pierce Street, El Paso TX, spring 1969

*Inspired by an actual event in Knees' life, this song has more
salacious double entendres than any other tune in the Calhoon
portfolio. It also has a chord pattern stolen from Blood, Sweat
and Tears'* Spinning Wheel *and a great guitar-driven rhythm.
Sadie's was the name of a notorious brothel/bar in Farmington
in the 50s and although Knees was never fortunate enough to go
there, he wanted to commemorate it in a song. It features promi-
nently in the story,* Jicarilla Mud.

Last Thursday night I was shootin some pool
When my friend Willie say "Hey man!
I do believe I see Sadie and Jewel."
We racked up our balls an we ran.

We knew them girls was just our style
An they knew we was theirs
I'd last seen Sadie at a ten body pile
An Jewel didn't mind splittin hairs

I say "Hi Sadie." Sadie say "Hi."
Willie say "Hey Jewel, come on."
Hopped in my Nash feelin high an dry
Bought us a case an we was gone.

Drinkin an a-drivin Sadie's shiftin my gears
An Jewel's givin Willie the gas
Ain't nothin better than drinkin some beers
An lovin up a nubile lass.

HI HELLO MARY

Highway 666, Southern Colorado, fall 1971

*This song came to Knees as he was driving back from Cortez CO
after playing with Smoky Stover's band at a C&W dive. Loosely
based on Buffalo Springfield's* Mr. Soul *it was always a popular
song in the bars, even though (or maybe because) deep down it's
a paean to pedophilia. Knees always wondered why no one in
R&R ever used the obvious "Mary wanna" pun in a song before.*

Hi hello Mary, creepin up into your teens
Does your momma an your poppa
Know you got such tight little genes?
An does your big sister
Tell you what she do with me?
Does Mary wanna take a chance,
Does Mary wanna set herself free?

Hi hello Mary, you love your loud rock & roll
I can feed you goodies,
All your little mind can hold
An does your big sister
Tell you what she got in her bag?
Does Mary wanna take a chance,
Does Mary wanna take a drag?

Hi hello Mary, livin can be such a ball
Sometimes it's like flyin,
Sometimes it's like havin to crawl
An does your big sister
Tell you bout goin down?
Does Mary wanna take a chance,
Does Mary wanna come around?

ONE HUNDRED YEARS

Monterey Street, Farmington NM, summer 1971

*Knees was out of the army and married to Joyce when he wrote
this song on the piano. He was playing in Durango Colorado and
into Neil Young and his old man songs. Knees wondered if he
ought to sing the song in a Jack Crabb-like croak, but wisely
opted for a more normal voice.*

Brokenhearted dream keeps me movin on
Brokenhearted frame of mind
Will linger when I'm gone
I'm not gonna be the last man in this world
But even though my life was sadness
I lived to see one hundred years.

Brokenhearted love was all I ever won
A brokenhearted life
And now it's almost done
I'm not gonna see the last day of this world
But even though my life was madness
I lived to see one hundred years.

I fought the last century
Livin fast and playin rough
It didn't last long enough
And now it's gettin mighty tough
To even stay alive.
One hundred years old
God have mercy on my soul.

MY BABY'S GONNA LEAVE ME (YESTERDAY)

Monterey Street, Farmington NM, fall 1971

This one started out as a C&W song, written around the corny time-paradox title line, but by the time Knees got around to putting it to music, it acquired a ZZ Toppish shuffle and an Elvis-like All Shook Up *melody on the word "yesterday". With all the overuse and abuse of the word "heart" in modern lyricism, Knees is proud that his only use of the sappy word is in conjunction with the verb, "fibrillatin". He also considers "have my lunch for breakfast" one of his best lines and wonders why Clint Eastwood or Charles Bronson never used it in a movie.*

My baby's gonna do me dirty
She's gonna fill my heart all full of blues
She's gonna make my eyeballs feel like cryin
Yeah my baby's gonna slip me some bad news.

Yeah my baby's gonna sell me down the river
I'll be howlin like a houn dog at bay
An the reason that I know all this will happen
My baby's gonna leave me yesterday.

My baby's gonna have my lunch for breakfast
She's gonna have me babblin like a brook
She's gonna set my heart a-fibrillatin
I'll be squirmin like a catfish on a hook.

Yeah my baby's gonna sell me down the river
I'll be howlin like a houn dog at bay
An the reason that I know all this will happen
My baby's gonna leave me yesterday.

ROCKS

Bayfield Highway, Durango CO, 1972

Knees wrote this on a piano in waltz time in a sort of Floyd Cramer style but he never played it with any of his bands. He heard a late night DJ say something about "having rocks in his head" and Knees thought there might be a pun he could write a song around. When he recorded it in the 90s he decided to use a more upbeat tempo and style.

I met her at a party at my boss' house last night
She was tall an she was pretty
And the moment seemed so right
I looked all around the party,
I was tryin to find my wife
I heard her in the bedroom enjoyin the night life.
So I said "C'mon, pretty girl, come with me." And she smiled.
I said "C'mon pretty girl, you will see."
My heart was goin wild.

Then we went over to my house,
I showed her my king-size bed
I said everything that I knew
But she knew everything that I said
And the only rocks that I got
Were those that were in my head.

We went back to the party,
I wudn't ready to call it a night
Success had played me dirty
But then again there's always my wife
I found her in the bathroom,
She'd been drinkin up a storm
I put my arms around her,
Said "Hmm you sure are warm."

I said "C'mon honey bunch, come with me."
She gave a little shrug.

I said "C'mon honey bunch, you will see.
We'll be snug as a plug in a jug."

Then we went back to our house,
Hopped in our king-size bed
I said "I love you."
"I got a headache," was all she said
An the only rocks that I got
Were those that were in my head.

THE FAVOR

Bayfield Highway, Durango CO, 1972

The big news that year was the "no knock" law that allowed cops to break into your house without knocking if they thought you were doing something they didn't like. Knees gave it a Neil Young flavor and a country accent and liked the fact that his re-venge-crazed protagonist planned to off the seven DEA agents with a knife, instead of a ho-hum gun.

If you guys are interested
I'll tell you why I'm here
So far from my home town
Seven of em came without a knock upon my door
It's amazin how they bring you down.

They tole me all my rights
But they didn't explain my wrongs
I done everything that they said
But if I had known the shape that I'm in now
I'd shot everyone of them dead.

Just about a lid was all that I had
Stuck inside the mattress of my bed
Then they tole me "Kid,
You're gonna wind up bad
This stuff will knock the brains out of your head."

An they tole me they were doin me a favor
But I lost my wife an a year of my life
An I'd give anything for a knife
An a chance to pay them back for their favor.

That's about the size of it
I'll spend a year in jail
There ain't much more to tell
But those seven men for the favor that they done
I'll see them all in hell.

ALL ROADS LEAD TO TUBA

Kirtland NM, 1972

In 1972, Peter and Rockee Blue, army friends of Knees' from 1968, came out to New Mexico for a visit. Along with Knees' wife, Joyce, they went on a two-day trip to the Grand Canyon, finding out that on the southern rim side, you must drive through Tuba City AZ no matter where you go or what you do. The Blues suggested that Knees write a song about "all roads leading to Tuba City".

It's a sad road I'm travelin
Sad because my baby
Tole me that our love is dead
"Go on an beat your head against the wall,"
She said
"I don't think that I can take it any more."

A man tries to make a livin
Doin what he does the best
For as much as he can get
But tell that to a woman
Without lowerin your head
When the life she needs
Is just outside your door.

An the raincloud up ahead is flashin like a sign
Motorcycle nightmare on the Utah line
Do you blame me brothers for changin my mind?
I turn around an head back home.

All roads lead to Tuba
Just like all roads lead to hell
If you're headin for the Canyon
You'll get to know it well.

Well I tried to leave my woman
Somethin I've attempted so many times before
But every time I come on back

A-beggin at the door
I wonder just what I'm tryin to do?

As I ride into Tuba
I get a kinda feelin
That things just ain't the same
Like mebbe someone's changed
All the rules to the game
I wonder if it's me or if it's you.

Then I see the note that's lyin on the bed
Says "Now do you believe that our love is dead?"
Then I start to thinkin
Bout all the things she said
An I go an beat my head against the wall.

WHO CARES AS LONG AS I GET MINE?

Electronics Class, TVI, Albuquerque NM, 1973

One boring day at a vocational school Knees wrote the words to two songs, then went home at noon and wrote the music and recorded them. Death on the Horizon *was the R&R song and this was the C&W tune. The words just seemed to write themselves and Knees was as surprised as anyone when this song turned out to be the world's first bi-sexual country & western song.*

I'm drivin to a pickin job
Bout seventy miles from my home town
An I got my country station blarin
Listenin to the latest sounds
With forty miles down an thirty to go
An country words a-spinnin in my mind
My man my woman my wife, my life!
Sounds like someone's in a bind.

Now a little girl is singin about keepin her man
An warnin her friends to stay away
Or a man is moanin in a mournful voice
About how somebody's gonna hafta pay
You'd think everybody owned someone else
But then only one at a time
My man my woman my wife, my life!
Who cares as long as I get mine?

I'm a man who loves the women,
An my wife sure loves the men
Maybe just the other way around,
Somethin different now an then.
An you know when I find me a woman
My wife usually finds her a man
An if we happen to be together
We lend each other a hand, a hand, a hand.

428

So here I am in another town,
My wife is seventy miles away
An I bet she's with a friend
An they ain't talkin bout the time a day
But tonight when quittin time rolls around
Me an Sally are gonna be feelin fine
My man my woman my wife, big deal!
Who cares as long as I get mine?
My man my woman my life, big deal!
Who cares as long as I get mine?

MY OLD FRIEND, FRED

Motel, Page AZ, summer 1973

Knees and Diane, the singer in the band, obtained some incredible substance that they were told was THC, but probably wasn't. It was a great rubberizer of the body and apparently stimulated the mind because Knees wrote this song in a fitful hour on the stuff one night. It's that most rare of songs, an anti-alcohol song written to be sung in a bar.

Well I know this is a bar an everbody's drinkin
But an ol friend of mine just set me to thinkin
That mebbe we oughta try somethin else.
So if you just settle back an listen a spell
You're liable to hear an educatin tale
About sex, booze and ourselves.

Well I was up in Denver bout two weeks ago
Wudn't doin nothin thought I'd take in a show
So I parked my car an started walkin
The first show I came to was just my style
Triple X-rated called "Everthing's Wild"
A whole buncha sex an not much talkin.

An on the poster I saw the name
Of a guy that I used to know
Ol Fred always said he was gonna make it big
An sure enuf he's the star of the show.

So I paid my admission and went inside
Bought me some popcorn an a three dollar Sprite
Then I saw somethin that stopped me dead
Well remember I tole you a little while ago
About my ol friend who's the star of the show
Well there, the projectionist was Fred.

We must have talked for an hour or two
Bout people and places like ol friends do
Relivin good an bad memories
An I wondered how Fred had sunk so far
When a few years ago he was a big porno star
So I axed him and here's what he tole me.

Put the blame on the whiskey and wine;
They sucked the man outa me
I once had the world spread before my very eyes
But the bottle was all I could see.

So alla you people gathered in here
Guzzlin your whiskey, your wine an your beer
Remember bout my ol friend Fred
Well here was a man who had all he could handle
Till somethin took the wick right outa his candle
An that somethin, here's what Fred said

Put the blame on the whiskey and wine
They sucked the man outa me
I once had the world spread before my very eyes
But the bottle was all I could see.

Well I know this is a bar an everbody's drinkin
But an ol friend of mine just set me to thinkin
That mebbe we oughta try somethin else.

DEATH ON THE HORIZON

Electronics Class, TVI, Albuquerque NM, 1973

Knees was exceptionally bored one day in vocational school and wrote the lyrics to two songs, Death on the Horizon *(a Neil Young-inspired ditty) and* Who Cares As Long As I Get Mine? *(a C&W contrarian song). At noon he decided to take the rest of the day off and went home and wrote the music to both. Obviously, both the lyrics and the music are plagiarisms of what Neil Young was doing at the time with songs like* Down by the River.

Were you down by the river
In the cold last night
Did you see someone lyin on the sand
Did you hear the sound of someone
Cursin black and white
Did you feel the blood on your hands?
Tell the world there's death on the horizon
Murder in the hearts of the people you love
If a song would stain the killer
With the blood of his victim
Would you dare to sing the words
You're thinkin of?
Was he black, was he white?

You never did say if he was a friend
Did you know the other guy too?
Did you get a premonition
Of the coming of the end
Just what the hell are you gonna do?
Tell the world there's death on the horizon
Murder in the hearts of the people you love
If a song would stain the killer
With the blood of his victim
Would you dare to sing the words
You're thinkin of?
Was he wrong, was he right?

THE ROAD

Third Street, Durango CO, 1973

Knees never worked this song out well enough to play it with any of his bands but it seemed like an okay song when he played it at home by himself. Other than having a weird, hard to hit note, stupid lyrics (winning at Keno?), and abject sentimentality, it's one of Knees better obscure tunes.

I grew up in the back of an old Ford
We were drivin too fast to get bored
Daddy kept the radio playin
He said "If you believe in the road
It's just like prayin."

Mama left us as we passed through Reno
For a man who was winnin at Keno
Daddy laughed all the way down to Zion
He said "If you believe in the road..."
Then started cryin.

I spent sixteen years on the road with my pa
Drivin in cars, singin in bars
An those sixteen years were the best I ever saw
Sleepin in cars, followin stars.

We were busted drivin through Albuquerque
Seems the man was lookin out for me
Daddy said "It looks like bad weather
But if you believe in the road we'll be together."

It seems my real father died in San Quentin
So they sent me upstate for detention
Daddy cursed them as they led me away
He said "If you believe in the road..."
He died that day.

MAYBE THIS TIME

Rodeway Inn, Roswell NM 1973

*Knees was playing with the band Country, which was known as
Knees Calhoon in Roswell, when Diane one night wistfully
sighed about a guy she had met at the bar, "Maybe this time he'll
write." It sounded like a good song title so the next night Knees
wrote this song for Diane to sing. She never did but in 1976 Sheri
Williams learned it and sang it with the Calhoon Brothers at the
Las Cruces Inn.*

He's gone, just like all the rest,
I've been more than twice blessed.
It's that same ol sad song again
Only miles apart,
I guess I know that song by heart,
But maybe this time he'll write.

What next, another wakened dream,
I have no mouth and I must scream.
He said someday we would meet again,
Things would be the same
A familiar face, a familiar name,
A friend to share the night.

And a letter won't see me blue,
All it has to say is I'm thinking of you,
Just to reassure me that it was all true.

Uptown, lights are coming on,
People playing until dawn.
And there's something that's up for sale
For every appetite,
Sad songs written every night,
But maybe this time he'll write,
Oh maybe this time he'll write.

OVER THE EDGE

Monterey Street, Farmington NM, 1974

*Our boy was feeling uncreative one day and decided to dash off a
song, just to see if he still could. It was actually more pretentious
than this, with a stupid verse about fish and birds that Knees
wisely left off the final version. No inspiration; just a bunch of
whiny lyrics. Interesting chord pattern, though.*

When a man has been runnin
For as long as I have
He learns it's easier to accept than to refuse
So when I found the perfect lady
An we lived the perfect day
I knew I would someday have to choose
Between my runnin days,
Borrowed nights and you.

When you came into my bedroom
On those cold winter nights
With another man's dust on your skin
I thought about sprinklin
Some salt into your wounds
I was jealous of the places you had been
But it's all back to dust in the end

Why must a man have emotions
It's like havin two brains inside your head
One of them says you want, the other says you need
An neither one can help you when you're dead.

I kept myself from screamin
For as long as I could
Thinkin bout the good things we had done
But then last week's mania
Took us right up to the edge
So I went out an bought myself a gun
With a bullet I could even dark the sun.

435

SAD SAD FEELIN

Monterey Street, Farmington NM, 1974

*Knees was thinking about Diane, the singer in the band Country,
when he wrote this song, but as usual, the plot didn't necessarily
follow real life. If a line rhymed, and had a good sound to it,
Knees would use it even if it suddenly changed the thrust of the
song.*

The last thing on my mind
Was to bring you down with me
What started out as a partnership
Soon had us on our knees
I thought that we would find
A way to make it last
But we were thinkin like we used to
We were livin in the past

Such a sad sad feelin,
To know the one you love
Is the one you got to leave
To be free, to be free, to be free.

There's so much to do
An so little time to live
We thought we'd take the world apart
We had so much to give
So remember me this way
As your partner and your friend
An remember all the times we had
And maybe have again

THE GIRL AND THE MAN

Espina Street, Las Cruces NM, fall 1975

Knees had just started playing with the band at the Las Cruces Inn and liked the way Mark did the Eagles' Lyin Eyes. *So he wrote a song about his daughter, Naomi, that was in the same musical vein. It won a prize in one of the early American Song Festival contests.*

There's a girl in Alabama
She's got golden hair just like her daddy used to
And pictures of his face
Somewhere inside her memory
But she doesn't know him like she really should.

There's a man in Colorado
He's got a burnin dream to live a life worth livin
And to know that the girl
Doesn't feel about her father
The way that he feels about his own.

Baby I'm on my own but I'm missing you
And you're almost grown
I'm a thousand miles away
And I've been four years on the road
But baby I'm through with that
And I think it's time that I made it back
To the girl who's loved by the man.

And the girl in Alabama
Laughs and plays and hardly cries at all
But when she thinks about
The man she calls her daddy
He's not there to brighten up her eyes.

PROGRESS

Near Kayenta AZ, 1975

Knees was driving out to Kayenta on the Navajo Reservation to tune a piano when he spied an article on "Progress" on a newspaper on the seat. It inspired him and as he drove he wrote the lyrics to this song. During the song his car broke down and he had to crawl under the car to fix it, but the irony of it all escaped him and he finished the song before he made Kayenta.

I hear the whine of radial tires
Outside my window late at night
Since the freeway came I don't get much sleep
It used to be so peaceful with a dusty road outside
An with love all around, you and me the only sound
But now I've got eighteen-wheelers screamin through my dreams.

I got a Quesar color TV
With stations round the dial
An we stay up all hours of the night
But I remember evenins when all I had was you
An the words you'd say, I remember to this day
Oh I wish you were here to comfort me and sooth my achin eyes.

But I guess that's progress, can't stand in its way.
Yesterday we were laughin, but I'm cryin today
An they call that progress.

I got a kingsize lectric blanket
To keep me warm at night
An central air the best that money can buy
But I still wake up cold an lonely callin out your name
Ever since you've gone, this house just ain't a home
I'm no good on my own without your love to help me through the
     night.

But I guess that's progress, can't stand in its way.
Yesterday we were laughin, but I'm cryin today
An they call that progress.

NIGHT CALLER

Melendres Street, Las Cruces NM, 1976

A short story by J.D Salinger called Pretty Mouth and Green My
Eyes *inspired this song. In the story a man gets a call from a
frantic buddy who's looking for his wife, who hasn't come home.
The man, who is in bed with a woman, assures him that she'll
return and hangs up. Later, just when we're feeling sure the
woman is the buddy's wife, he calls again and says she just drove
up.*

A telephone rings in a darkened room
And a sleepy voice whispers "Hello."
The clock on the dresser says two A.M.
The chair is covered with clothes
Then a cigarette lights up her face
As she cries into the phone
"Oh Billy I'm so glad you called me here
I'm so lonely and I want to come home."

I can see it all right now
The way that she'll come back to me
But is this the way it'll be?
I think I'll call her now and see.

A telephone rings in a darkened room
And a sleepy voice whispers "Hello."
The clock on the dresser says two A.M.
You can't see the chair for the clothes
Then a cigarette lights up the tears in her eyes
As she cries into the phone
"Oh Billy don't call me here anymore
It's late and I'm not alone."

I can see it all right now
The way that she'll come back to me
But is this the way it'll be?
I think I'll call her now and see.

ALAMO ROSIE

Melendres Street, Las Cruces NM, 1976

Knees heard a line in Viva Max!, *a Peter Ustinov film about the Alamo and someone called "Alamo Rose" and thought it'd make a good song title. There was already a song about Rose from San Antone, but not one about Rose from the Alamo. The words and melody just seem to write themselves.*

There were hard times for us all
Back then in San Antone
But it seemed like we always
Had enough for a drink
An it was right here in this bar
Cross the street from the Alamo
That I first met my Rosie who taught me to think

About the changes that we'd see
As the years rush on by
She said "We can stop them
If you'll just sit here with me.
We'll look out the window at the beautiful Alamo
It never changes and neither will we."

Oh I used to call her my Alamo Rosie
I'll always remember the way that she would say
"I've been here forever and I'll be here tomorrow
Break it to me gently when it all blows away."

I loved her more than was good for a man
But it was love that kept us young
As the years passed like days
I was holding her hand with tears in my eyes
The night she saw the Alamo crumble away.

Oh I used to call her my Alamo Rosie
I'll always remember the way that she would say
"I've been here forever and I'll be here tomorrow
Break it to me gently when it all blows away."
I broke it to her gently when it all blew away.

440

THE GHOST IN THE MIRROR

Jayne Lane, Las Cruces NM, 1977

Knees was getting a little sick of the rehashed ideas and melodies that the C&W world was cranking out and decided he could do just as badly. So he wrote this song, using an exact ripoff of the melody for Heartaches by the Number. *Oddly, the song became a favorite in the Las Cruces area. In the 90s when he recorded it, he decided to sing a harmony to the original melody so it wouldn't be as recognizable as a ripoff.*

By midnight you can find me sittin on this stool
Talkin to my scotch an soda babblin like a fool
Don't think about disturbin me
By askin me to dance
Cuz I'm one shot past bein friendly
An that's two shots past romance.

So I just stare at that ghost in the mirror
A sadder face you'd never want to see
An I wonder why that ghost in the mirror
Seems to be starin at me.

There's a woman sittin down the bar,
I've seen her here before
She takes a drink and sheds a tear
An says she'll have one more
Well I've never been a talker
Or a player of fancy games
An something makes me wonder
If she feels the same.

An now there's two lonely ghosts in the mirror
A sadder pair you'd never want to see
An I wonder why those ghosts in the mirror
Seem to be starin at me.

I'M JUST A MAN

Melendres Street, Las Cruces NM, 1977

Knees was flying high in popularity at the Las Cruces Inn in 1977. The bar was packed every night and he and Mark Coker, the other guitarist/singer, were coming up with new songs every night. In this song Knees put just about every one of the modern C&W clichés he knew. The people at the bar called it that "boy's first kiss" song.

I was a kid for a long time
Livin on the farm there was no need to grow
An sure I love my folks but that ain't enough
When I needed to leave
More than they could know.

Then you came into my life like a whirlwind
An you blew this tumbleweed right offa the farm
Now no matter where we go
I just want you to know
That I love you an lovin you keeps me warm.

Oh I'm just a man, I'll do all I can
But I've never been in love like this before
So try an understand
You're a boy's first kiss
Oh and this boy just can't miss
With a woman like you to take me by the hand
It took a woman like you to show me I'm a man.

SAILOR OF THE CENTURY

Melendres Street, Las Cruces NM, 1977

This is Knees' only foray into post-apocalyptic dystopian song-writing. It began as a catchy phrase, "from the Colorado Islands to the shores of Tennessee" and evolved into a tale about fascism (the teachers), sacrifice and sea-faring adventure. At first it was called Sailor of the Ocean *but something inspired Knees to change the title. It has one of Knees' better chord patterns.*

I've been a sailor for the past seven years
Sailin on the ocean of our country
I've seen the teachers, the preachers of fear
Who kept me from the woman who loved me
In the third year of the flood
We met at Mt Rainier
Where we helped build
The village of the mountain
We lived each other's lives
Through the hunger and the tears
An drank the love that flowed like a fountain.

Now I'm known as the sailor of the century
The man who cheats the forces from above
From the Colorado Islands
To the shores of Tennessee
I'll sail the American Ocean till I find my love

Then the teachers walked among us
And told us of the sea
That lay to the east of the desert
They told us there were places
Where people still were free
Where the teachers had control of the weather

443

She told me there would never
Be another in her life
But she had to see what happened to the east
Before she left we married
In the night of the knife
When I became a killer of the beast.

Now I'm known as the sailor of the century
The man who cheats the forces from above
From the Colorado Islands
To the shores of Tennessee
I'll sail the American Ocean till I find my love

I've been everywhere that there's left to be
And my lady may not want me when I find her
But my life has not been empty
As I sailed across the sea
I'm not just the man she left behind her.

I'M TOO SMART TO BE THIS KIND OF FOOL

Melendres Street, Las Cruces NM, 1977

Knees stole—yes, stole—this title from a woman he met at the Las Cruces Inn. On what was the most traditional, normal date of his life she told him that if she were ever to write a country & western tune, the title would be, "I'm Too Smart to Be This Kind of Fool". He liked it too, and although he never saw her again, he fleshed out the song soon after.

Why do I worry just like a good ol boy?
Why do I treat her like she's my favorite toy?
Jealousy is new to me,
I've always been so fancy free,
But she introduced me to misery
Now I'm learnin that pain's
On the other side of joy.

I'm too smart to be this kind of fool
I know a lot about art
But I don't know what to do.
She tells me things that I never heard in school,
Hell I'm too smart to be this kind of fool.

Why do I need her,
I never needed anyone before
Why do I believe her an keep on askin for more?
As we roll along to the evenin song,
Makin love til the feelin's gone,
An everything I ever knew is wrong
She says "See ya later,"
An leaves me lyin on the floor.

I'm too smart to be this kind of fool
I know a lot about art
But I don't know what to do.
She tells me things that I never heard in school,
Hell I'm too smart to be this kind of fool.

445

MIDNIGHT SUN

Melendres Street, Las Cruces NM 1977

Knees Calhoon was an agreeable contrarian and when the country world was "...getting back to the country..." with "...Willie and Waylon and the boys..." he felt he had to stand up for the inner city. So he dusted off his James Brown chords and wrote what he thought was a sophisticated defense of city living. City living in Dallas *yet!*

This dusty life I'm livin
S'got its own special rhythm
But the city keeps callin my name out loud
Sayin leave it all behind
I got the land I thought I wanted
But I still feel like I'm haunted
By the uptown women in the downtown bars
Dancin cross my mind, cross my mind.

I'm gonna count my blessings, pack my bags
Stash some grass and haul my ass to Dallas
I'll be a city-slicker, sailor
And a salesman all in one
Well I wanna be where
There's always music playin
Where the neon lights me up
Like a midnight son
Midnight son.

So let the suburbs keep on growin,
Let the farmers keep on crowin
Let everybody in their own way
Ride the devil down
I got my mind all made up;
I'm tired of feelin laid up
After I hit every bar in Dallas
Look out Cowtown, Cowtown.

IT'S A SIN TO SAY NO

Melendres Street, Las Cruces NM, 1977

According to Knees' memory, he was inspired to write this as a rebuttal of Nancy Reagan's "Just Say No" garbage, but was that phrase used in 1977? Nancy didn't get elected until 1980. Yet Knees distinctly remembers hating the idea of saying no, and wanting to contradict it in a song. Maybe he didn't write this until the early 80s? In any case the plot and the guitar work are some of Knees' best.

When I was seventeen the world was at war
I delivered groceries to women and old men
And though it happened long ago,
It's never left my mind
What an old grey-haired mailman
Had to say to me then.

One day I rang the bell at a house way downtown
The old mailman was resting on the steps down below
The woman at the door had heartbreak in her eyes
When she asked me, "Please stay a while."
I said I had to go.

She smiled and said, "Some other time,"
As I backed down the stairs
She closed the door and time stood still
For the mailman and me
We stood there without speaking,
Till he looked me in the eyes
He said "You're young and now you own the world
But someday you will see,

That it's a sin to say no
To a woman who's so lonely
She sees the man she loves so much
In a boy of seventeen
It's a sin to say no when a man like me's so lonely
One day you're gonna wake up
And you'll be old as me."

KILLING TIME

Gallagher Street, Las Cruces NM, 1978

The name of this song was inspired by Thomas Berger's book of the same name. In the early 80s Knees sent this song into the American Song Festival, a national songwriting contest, and the next year there were two songs out called Killing Time. *It was a song title whose time had come. Neither song resembled Knees' song.*

You're a killer, time's your victim
He was on our side, still you tricked him
Not so long ago
We had the world on the run
I knew you had friends on all sides of town
We both laughed about the rumors goin round
You never said it
But you made me feel I was the one.

Even though you touched me like nobody else
I'd still have to call it a crime
Cause all the while I was makin love to you
You were only killing time
You were only killing time.

You're a killer, time's your victim
He was all we had, still you tricked him
If I hadn't been so high
I wouldn't have had so far to fall
I don't blame you for takin what I had
But it's all comin back and I feel so bad
You called us lovers
But now you never call at all.

IF THE MUSIC WEREN'T THERE

Gallagher Street, Las Cruces NM, 1978

*Knees played this a couple of times with the Calhoon Brothers at
the Las Cruces Inn but it wasn't particularly danceable, humma-
ble, or memorable. He probably had David Loggins'* Don't Treat
Me Like a Stranger *in mind when he wrote the music. The words
refer to the dance floor at the LCI with its strobe light, a first for
cowboy bars in New Mexico.*

We are gathered here outside the sight of God
To see who we'll join together
Two-by-two twirling in the flashing light
Dancin on the edge of a feather.

We play along but you are the players
Spinning with stars in your eyes
Each woman Carmen, each man Cougie
Each with his own disguise.

So keep on keepin the thrill in sight
As you're waltzing along through the air
I wonder whether she would spend the night
If the music weren't there
If the music weren't there.

When the moves have been made
In this romantic game
We'll pick up the pieces and go
We'll read all about it in the Sunday news
And we'll wait for the next picture show.

MY LADY CRIES WHEN THE TRAIN WHISTLE BLOWS

Gallagher Street, Las Cruces NM, 1980

Knees wrote this for his favorite lady, Jerron Roberts. They spent much of their time in a dreamlike state, letting emotions run wild, and Knees wanted to preserve in song some of her more endearing histrionics.

My lady cries when the train whistle blows
Dreamin bout her past that only she knows
In the night I hold her tighter
To keep her here with me
But as long as that whistle blows she goes
To her railroad days and the girl she used to be.

She rode the rails with her ramblin gamblin man
She kept a cigar in his smile
An a drink in his hand
He kept her for his pleasure
Now the pleasure's all mine
But as long as that whistle blows she goes
To her railroad days and the girl she left behind

She's the finest woman that I've ever known
She's made me a father an given me a home
An I know it all all happened
Such a long long time ago
But my lady still cries
When the train whistle blows.

I SHOULDA BEEN BORN
A THOUSAND YEARS AGO

Gallagher Street, Las Cruces NM, 1980

*Inspired by nothing, this song turned out to have some of Knees'
best lines. He never played it with any of his bands and didn't
really come up with the music until he recorded it back in the
early 90s.*

I shoulda been born a thousand years ago
I'da been a hero of the day
You'd find me on a quest for a damsel in distress
An you peasants woulda cheered me on my way.

I shoulda been born a thousand years ago
Helpin out a lady fair in need
In my suit of armor
I sure woulda been a charmer
Chivalry comes naturally to me.

But I was born in nineteen and sixty-one
A renaissance or two too late
An when I look aroun,
There ain't no treasures to be found
Everything I do is out of date.

So tonight I'll blaze the same ol trail again
Lookin for that same ol grail again
I'm a knight out on the town,
A damsel-huntin clown
Joustin my way back into jail again.

I shoulda been born a thousand years ago
I'm just a man out of time
When I look around today,
Ain't no dragons left to slay
An even if there was it'd be a crime.

SANCTUARY

Gallagher Street, Las Cruces NM, 1980

Knees was thinking of the William Faulkner novel when he wrote this whiney ballad. Too bad he didn't follow the plot better. The song was pretty popular when Knees was playing with Larry Rulmyr, Jerry Phillips, Mike Gregory, Chuck Tidwell, Rex Schafer and Night Flight.

You call on me when you can use me
When you're feelin low you choose me
You count on me
I'm a soft place you can fall

But while you're out gettin lonely
Til it hurts so much you phone me
I'm thinkin someday
I won't be here when you call.

Everybody needs a sanctuary
A place to hide when you're feelin too well known
Everybody needs a sanctuary
I'm somebody and I need one of my own.

I love your mind I've been inside it
But somethin's wrong we're too one-sided
I'm sinkin fast, I can't wait too long

So when your nights begin to bruise you
Let's just hope I don't refuse you
I'm tryin hard but I can only be so strong.

Everybody needs a sanctuary
A place to hide, a friend that you can call
Everybody needs a sanctuary
I'm somebody and I need you most of all.

LET'S JUST PLAY US AS WE LAY

Interstate 40 north of Las Cruces NM, 1980

It started out as a combo golf/cheating song but ended up having nothing to do with golf, except for the "play it as it lays" pun. Knees gave it the first melody that occurred to him—as he did many of his songs—but never played it with his bands. Too bad. It might have been a good bar song.

I had my plans, I had my dreams
I'd sail around the moon, I'd touch everything
I had it all worked out just what I'd do
But one thing I hadn't planned on was you.

We played us cool, we played us smart
We played so well right from the start
An here's my plan for today
Let's forget about tomorrow,
Let's just play us as we lay.

Let's just play us as we lay us together
Let's just play us as we lay us down, down down
Now I'm makin the last plan I'll ever make
Let's forget about tomorrow,
Let's just play us as we lay.

THAT'S HOW SINGERS CRY

Melendres Street, Las Cruces NM 1980

One of Knees' more maudlin numbers, he was trying to write about what he knew. Even as he wrote it he was wondering why anyone would feel sorry for a guy who drifts into town, makes some bucks off the locals, maybe dazzles a cocktail waitress or two, then moseys on. Sounds pretty ideal.

It'll never work out I know it,
There's too many towns gone by.
She wonder why I'm silent,
But that's how singers cry.
She lays her hand upon me, expecting a reply,
I just lie there silently, cuz that's how singers cry.

Seems like I live my life six weeks at a time,
It's better than playing one-night stands,
But it's all the same design.
You can take someone to breakfast,
You can kiss her at her door,
If she comes back the next night,
You can love a little more.

But it'll never work out I know it,
There's too many towns gone by.
She wonder why I'm silent,
But that's how singers cry.
She lays her hand upon me, expecting a reply,
I just lie there silently, cuz that's how singers cry.

There she stands at closing time
Greets me with a smile,
I get to know her just enough
To make it all worthwhile.
But she belongs to her home town
And my show must go on,
I got to be in Tennessee to sing another song.

WHISKEY BEER AND WINE

Gallagher Street, Las Cruces NM, 1981

There used to be a wonderfully rustic bar in Anthony TX called the Anthony Gap. Knees played there quite a bit with Night Flight and got to know the owner well enough to ask her for an old neon Budweiser sign that she wasn't using. He thought it would look great in his living room window at home, but it didn't. It did, however, inspire this song about booze.

There's a neon sign in a smoky little bar
It flashes on and off red and white
And the neon sign it's the story of my life
It tells my tale a thousand times a night.

Whiskey beer and wine
Reads the flashing neon sign
Whiskey beer and wine every night
Whiskey beer and wine
Do you wanna know my sign?
It's whiskey beer and wine.

Once there was a girl, aw but that was long ago
Before I learned to drink my blues away
And once there was a dream,
Oh I wonder where it's gone
Let's drink to it comin back someday.

ON THE SIDE

Gallagher Street, Las Cruces NM, 1981

Knees wracked his brain to come up with an expression of love
that was fresh and meaningful, and this is what he came up with.
You have to admit, very few modern C&W songwriters have ex-
plored the tack on love found here.

Yes it really happened,
That was really you and me
Who spent all that time together,
Lovin so wild and free.
You never said it was forever,
An then one day you were gone
There was a big ol world a-callin
An forever can be so long.

So don't play those halfway games
While your man is out of town
The world has thrown us together
And the sun is goin down.
An don't tell me how you love him now
Cuz I've heard those words too
I know from our times together
You're just too good to be true.

Oh I've loved a few since losin you
But no matter how hard I've tried
I'll never love anyone so much
That I wouldn't want you on the side.

MEAN STANDARD DEVIATE

Gallagher Street, Las Cruces NM, 1984

Knees always liked jokes and stories that had a mathematical basis and decided to write a song about statistics. It preceded "rap" by a few years, and has just about as much profundity as anything else written in that field.

Ah'm yo mean standard deviate
Ah'm half as good as the best but lest yo fo'get
Ah'm half as bad as the wors' an Ah goes firs',
So watchit.

Ah'm yo mean standard deviate
Ah wrap you up inna ball an divide by all
Ah'll be trackin real close, dat ain't no boas',
You bes' watchit.

Ah'm yo mean standard deviate
Almos' made it through school, jus' a li'l bit cruel
An befo' ah'm through Ah'll be jus' like you.
So watchit.

REPETITION

Gallagher Street, Las Cruces NM, 1985

Evolving from disco music, R&R in the 80s was polluting the airwaves with songs that seemed to Knees to be nothing more than a line or two being repeated ad nauseum, as if the listening span of the average teenager had dropped below the five second level. So of course Knees had to write an opus celebrating lyrical and musical laziness. If you don't want to join 'em, then parody 'em, Knees always said.

I don't care if the sun never rises
Long as my music gives me no surprises
An I don't care if the melody's cheap
Long as I can sing it in my sleep.

Repetition, repetition, repetition, repetition.

I don't care if it's June or December
There's just one lick I got to remember
An I don't care if I'm live or dead
Just drive that rhythm right into my head.

Repetition, repetition, repetition, repetition
Repetition, repetition, repetition, repetition
Repetition, repetition, repetition, repetition
Repetition, repetition, repetition, repetition
Repetition, repetition, repetition, repetition
Repetition, repetition, repetition, repetition
Repetition, repetition, repetition, repetition
Repetition, repetition, repetition, repetition.

BAD WEATHER

Southern California Interstate, 1987

Knees was driving back from Riverside CA in a rainstorm when he wrote one of his most normal songs. He had been out to visit Sue Moore, a high school friend, and had chickened out of her challenge for him to tackle California. Knees, not known for his bravery, was an inertia kind of guy and found it difficult to make big changes in his life. Later that year he moved to Shreveport LA to begin his second career as magazine editor.

It's rainin on the freeway
LA's turnin shiny grey.
The people on the freeway
Don't they work so hard to play?
It was rainin the first time we met
We waited it out together
An it may sound funny but you know sometimes
There's somethin good about bad weather.

It was cold livin in Durango
The snow kept us close to home
Now when I'm in Durango
I go out into the cold
An remember all the times that we were snowed in,
I wanted them to last forever.
Cuz when you're with the one you love
There's somethin good about bad weather.

So let the lightnin flash
Let the thunder roar
Let the four winds blow
Let it snow some more.
Mmm, there's somethin good about bad weather.

So we moved out on the Gulf Coast
The most peaceful place we've been
Now we walk out on the Gulf Coast
An watch the waves roll in.
Our love is stronger than a hurricane
It can only blow us closer together
Cuz when you're with the one you love
There's somethin good about bad weather.

So let the lightnin flash
Let the thunder roar
Let the four winds blow
Let it snow some more.
Mmm, there's somethin good about bad weather.

JICARILLA MUD

Gladstone Blvd. Shreveport LA, 2004

Knees had written a short story about Farmington NM in the mid '50s about a peculiar drilling mud that had some interesting properties and since there was a theme song for Jim Weiler's 66 Chevy Nova Blues he figured he should write a haunting love theme for his new story. This is what resulted.

Wild Bill Smith was a man who loved his whiskey
He was greeted with a smile at every bar in town
He knew his guns and how to have his fun
But when the Jicarilla called him—
The deal went down.

Don Tucker was a man with a mission
Livin' every day as lovers do
He knew his mud and he knew his blood
But when the Jicarilla called him—
His aim was true.

Bill Smith was in it for the whiskey and the guns
Tucker was in love with love
Tom Bolack did it for the money and the fame
But only Arky Miley knew—about Jicarilla Mud.

Tom Bolack had a head like a bullet
And he wanted everyone to know his name
He was the man who owned all the land
But when the Jicarilla called him—
He played the game.

Arky Miley was the man with the secrets
And heavy was the price he had to pay
He did it with a smile, laughin all the while
And when the Jicarilla called him—
He led the way.

ANGELUS OF DOOM

Gladstone Blvd. Shreveport LA, 2004

*Knees second short story about the denizens of Farmington NM
circa 1955 involves bowling, dangerous nuns and the same group
of characters who inhabited* Jicarilla Mud. *Knees found it pretty
easy to write songs when the plot has been written earlier.*

It all began at the Snooker Eight
Bottle pool was the game
And it ended at the Navajo Bowl
In Tom Bolack's last frame.

Tucker got the ball rollin'
Takin' Gunter to school
Bill was sacked out in the back seat
Bill Smith was no fool.

But the bells that were ringin'
They were tollin' for you
Sister Mary Edwina
The Angelus of Doom.

Gunter Hedelin packed it in
Recognized the wrong face
He never made it to the finish line
Of the master race.

Tucker knew there was something wrong
'Bout that lyin' nun
An' there ain't nothin' more dangerous
Than a nun with a gun.

But the bells that were ringin'
They were tollin' for you
Sister Mary Edwina
The Angelus of Doom.

First Doodle — 1969

Big Doodle — 1994

THE COMPLEAT CALHOON CD OF MP3s

The CD is not an audio CD. It's a data CD filled with MP3s and can only be played on a computer or a CD/DVD player that supports MP3s.

WEED, WOMEN AND SONG
All of the 60 or so songs written by Fender during his meteoric career as guitar picker. They're in chronological order and the lyrics can be found in the book, THE COMPLEAT CALHOON, and online at www.ramblehouse.com/jookbox

DAINCE WITH THE CALHOONS A collection of hoe-down dance songs, all instrumentals, that Mark Coker, Fender Tucker, Gordon Butler and Steve Roberts recorded in Fender's living room one day in 1986 or so. The Calhoon Brothers played for a couple of dance clubs who wanted a CD of their favorite two-steps and schottisches, and this is the CD.

KATHY DELANEY
   Kathy was a friend of Fender's from Farmington who moved to Las Cruces around the time he did in 1975. She liked to sing and sat in with the Calhoon Brothers a few times. Most of these songs were recorded in Ruidoso at a club where the Bros were playing. Kathy died in the early 2000s.

KICKIN KIN
   A collection of oddball recordings that Fender found on reel-to-reel tapes. There are also a few songs that Fender recorded but didn't fit in the WEED, WOMEN AND SONG category. Many of these recordings were of friends or relatives playing with Fender on guitar.

PEREGRINATIONS
   In the late 90s Fender visited a friend of his in Vermont, Rick Murphy, and one night he bumbled around on a fantastic Kurzweil keyboard that Rick had. Mainly he just dialed in pre-set sounds of

the keyboard (which had hundreds) and adlibbed whatever the wild sound inspired. There are a few "songs" in the bunch but most of this folder is just rambling stuff. Jim Weiler gave each track a title, and in most cases, the title is much better than the song itself.

SHEBANG

These are recordings, mostly instrumental, of Fender's guitar putzing. The songs with vocals are mostly written by Jim Weiler. Fender has several more subversive lyrics by Jim he hopes to put music to someday.

TORQUES

Recorded one night in 1965 at the Boys Club of Farmington NM. The recording techniques were incredibly primitive and it's a wonder the reel-to-reel tape survived. The band was sort of drunk that night but that was typical. Skip Batchelor on guitar; Fender Tucker on guitar; Dwight Babcock on bass; Bob Amerman on drums. Damn, it was fun being a Torque!

UNDEAD

Songs written by Fender and recorded at the Las Cruces Inn by the Calhoon Brothers. These were gleaned from several nights of recording, with different band members, but most were from 1976 - 1980.

RAMBLE HOUSE's

HARRY STEPHEN KEELER WEBWORK MYSTERIES

(RH) indicates the title is available ONLY in the RAMBLE HOUSE edition

The Ace of Spades Murder
The Affair of the Bottled Deuce (RH)
The Amazing Web
The Barking Clock
Behind That Mask
The Book with the Orange Leaves
The Bottle with the Green Wax Seal
The Box from Japan
The Case of the Canny Killer
The Case of the Crazy Corpse (RH)
The Case of the Flying Hands (RH)
The Case of the Ivory Arrow
The Case of the Jeweled Ragpicker
The Case of the Lavender Gripsack
The Case of the Mysterious Moll
The Case of the 16 Beans
The Case of the Transparent Nude (RH)
The Case of the Transposed Legs
The Case of the Two-Headed Idiot (RH)
The Case of the Two Strange Ladies
The Circus Stealers (RH)
Cleopatra's Tears
A Copy of Beowulf (RH)
The Crimson Cube (RH)
The Face of the Man From Saturn
Find the Clock
The Five Silver Buddhas
The 4th King
The Gallows Waits, My Lord! (RH)
The Green Jade Hand
Finger! Finger!
Hangman's Nights (RH)
I, Chameleon (RH)
I Killed Lincoln at 10:13! (RH)
The Iron Ring
The Man Who Changed His Skin (RH)
The Man with the Crimson Box
The Man with the Magic Eardrums
The Man with the Wooden Spectacles
The Marceau Case
The Matilda Hunter Murder
The Monocled Monster

The Murder of London Lew
The Murdered Mathematician
The Mysterious Card (RH)
The Mysterious Ivory Ball of Wong Shing Li (RH)
The Mystery of the Fiddling Cracksman
The Peacock Fan
The Photo of Lady X (RH)
The Portrait of Jirjohn Cobb
Report on Vanessa Hewstone (RH)
Riddle of the Travelling Skull
Riddle of the Wooden Parrakeet (RH)
The Scarlet Mummy (RH)
The Search for X-Y-Z
The Sharkskin Book
Sing Sing Nights
The Six From Nowhere (RH)
The Skull of the Waltzing Clown
The Spectacles of Mr. Cagliostro
Stand By—London Calling!
The Steeltown Strangler
The Stolen Gravestone (RH)
Strange Journey (RH)
The Strange Will
The Straw Hat Murders (RH)
The Street of 1000 Eyes (RH)
Thieves' Nights
Three Novellos (RH)
The Tiger Snake
The Trap (RH)
Vagabond Nights (Defrauded Yeggman)
Vagabond Nights 2 (10 Hours)
The Vanishing Gold Truck
The Voice of the Seven Sparrows
The Washington Square Enigma
When Thief Meets Thief
The White Circle (RH)
The Wonderful Scheme of Mr. Christopher Thorne
X. Jones—of Scotland Yard
Y. Cheung, Business Detective

Keeler Related Works

A To Izzard: A Harry Stephen Keeler Companion by Fender Tucker — Articles and stories about Harry, by Harry, and in his style. Included is a compleat bibliography.

Wild About Harry: Reviews of Keeler Novels — Edited by Richard Polt & Fender Tucker — 22 reviews of works by Harry Stephen Keeler from *Keeler News*. A perfect introduction to the author.

The Keeler Keyhole Collection: Annotated newsletter rants from Harry Stephen Keeler, edited by Francis M. Nevins. Over 400 pages of incredibly personal Keeleriana.

Fakealoo — Pastiches of the style of Harry Stephen Keeler by selected demented members of the HSK Society. Updated every year with the new winner.

Strands of the Web: Short Stories of Harry Stephen Keeler — 29 stories, just about all that Keeler wrote, are edited and introduced by Fred Cleaver.

RAMBLE HOUSE's OTHER LOONS

A Clear Path to Cross — Sharon Knowles short mystery stories by Ed Lynskey.

A Roland Daniel Double: The Signal and The Return of Wu Fang — Classic thrillers from the 30s.

A Shot Rang Out — Three decades of reviews and articles by today's Anthony Boucher, Jon Breen. An essential book for any mystery lover's library.

A Smell of Smoke — A 1951 English countryside thriller by Miles Burton.

A Snark Selection — Lewis Carroll's *The Hunting of the Snark* with two Snarkian chapters by Harry Stephen Keeler — Illustrated by Gavin L. O'Keefe.

A Young Man's Heart — A forgotten early classic by Cornell Woolrich.

Alexander Laing Novels — *The Motives of Nicholas Holtz* and *Dr. Scarlett*, stories of medical mayhem and intrigue from the 30s.

An Angel in the Street — Modern hardboiled noir by Peter Genovese.

Automaton — Brilliant treatise on robotics: 1928-style! By H. Stafford Hatfield.

Beast or Man? — A 1930 novel of racism and horror by Sean M'Guire. Introduced by John Pelan.

Black Hogan Strikes Again — Australia's Peter Renwick pens a tale of the 30s outback.

Black River Falls — Suspense from the master, Ed Gorman.

Blood in a Snap — The *Finnegan's Wake* of the 21st century, by Jim Weiler.

Blood Moon — The first of the Robert Payne series by Ed Gorman.

Chelsea Quinn Yarbro Novels featuring Charlie Moon — *Ogilvie, Tallant and Moon, Music When the Sweet Voice Dies, Poisonous Fruit* and *Dead Mice*. An Ojibwa detective in SF.

Cornucopia of Crime — Francis M. Nevins assembled this huge collection of his writings about crime literature and the people who write it. Essential for any serious mystery library.

Crimson Clown Novels — By Johnston McCulley, author of the Zorro novels, *The Crimson Clown* and *The Crimson Clown Again.*

Dago Red — 22 tales of dark suspense by Bill Pronzini.

David Hume Novels — *Corpses Never Argue, Cemetery First Stop, Make Way for the Mourners, Eternity Here I Come*. 1930s British hardboiled fiction with an attitude.

Dead Man Talks Too Much — Hollywood boozer by Weed Dickenson.

Death Leaves No Card — One of the most unusual murdered-in-the-tub mysteries you'll ever read. By Miles Burton.

Death March of the Dancing Dolls and Other Stories — Volume Three in the Day Keene in the Detective Pulps series. Introduced by Bill Crider.

Deep Space and other Stories — A collection of SF gems by Richard A. Lupoff.

Detective Duff Unravels It — Episodic mysteries by Harvey O'Higgins.

Dime Novels: Ramble House's 10-Cent Books — *Knife in the Dark* by Robert Leslie Bellem, *Hot Lead* and *Song of Death* by Ed Earl Repp, *A Hashish House in New York* by H.H. Kane, and five more.

Don Diablo: Book of a Lost Film — Two-volume treatment of a western by Paul Landres, with diagrams. Intro by Francis M. Nevins.

Dope Tales #1 — Two dope-riddled classics; *Dope Runners* by Gerald Grantham and *Death Takes the Joystick* by Phillip Condé.

Dope Tales #2 — Two more narco-classics; *The Invisible Hand* by Rex Dark and *The Smokers of Hashish* by Norman Berrow.

Dope Tales #3 — Two enchanting novels of opium by the master, Sax Rohmer. *Dope* and *The Yellow Claw.*

Dr. Odin — Douglas Newton's 1933 racial potboiler comes back to life.

Evidence in Blue — 1938 mystery by E. Charles Vivian.

Fatal Accident — Murder by automobile, a 1936 mystery by Cecil M. Wills.

Finger-prints Never Lie — A 1939 classic detective novel by John G. Brandon.

Freaks and Fantasies — Eerie tales by Tod Robbins, collaborator of Tod Browning on the film FREAKS.

Gadsby — A lipogram (a novel without the letter E). Ernest Vincent Wright's last work, published in 1939 right before his death.

Gelett Burgess Novels — *The Master of Mysteries, The White Cat, Two O'Clock Courage, Ladies in Boxes, Find the Woman, The Heart Line, The Picaroons* and *Lady Mechante*. All are introduced by Richard A. Lupoff who is singlehandedly bringing Burgess back to life.

Geronimo — S. M. Barrett's 1905 autobiography of a noble American.

Hake Talbot Novels — *Rim of the Pit, The Hangman's Handyman*. Classic locked room mysteries, with mapback covers by Gavin O'Keefe.

Hollywood Dreams — A novel of Tinsel Town and the Depression by Richard O'Brien.

I Stole $16,000,000 — A true story by cracksman Herbert E. Wilson.

Inclination to Murder — 1966 thriller by New Zealand's Harriet Hunter.

Invaders from the Dark — Classic werewolf tale from Greye La Spina.

Jack Mann Novels — Strange murder in the English countryside. *Gees' First Case, Nightmare Farm, Grey Shapes, The Ninth Life, The Glass Too Many.*

Jake Hardy — A lusty western tale from Wesley Tallant.

Jim Harmon Double Novels — *Vixen Hollow/Celluloid Scandal, The Man Who Made Maniacs/Silent Siren, Ape Rape/Wanton Witch, Sex Burns Like Fire/Twist Session, Sudden Lust/Passion Strip, Sin Unlimited/Harlot Master, Twilight Girls/Sex Institution.* Written in the early 60s and never reprinted until now.

Joel Townsley Rogers Novels and Short Stories — By the author of *The Red Right Hand: Once In a Red Moon, Lady With the Dice, The Stopped Clock, Never Leave My Bed.* Also two short story collections: *Night of Horror* and *Killing Time.*

Joseph Shallit Novels — *The Case of the Billion Dollar Body, Lady Don't Die on My Doorstep, Kiss the Killer, Yell Bloody Murder, Take Your Last Look.* One of America's best 50's authors and a favorite of author, Bill Pronzini.

Keller Memento — 45 short stories of the amazing and weird by Dr. David Keller. Huge!

Killer's Caress — Cary Moran's 1936 hardboiled thriller.

League of the Grateful Dead and Other Stories — Volume One in the Day Keene in the Detective Pulps series. In the introduction John Pelan outlines his plans for republishing all of Day Keene's short stories from the pulps.

Marblehead: A Novel of H.P. Lovecraft — A long-lost masterpiece from Richard A. Lupoff. This is the "director's cut", the long version that has never been published before.

Master of Souls — Mark Hansom's 1937 shocker is introduced by weirdologist John Pelan.

Max Afford Novels — *Owl of Darkness, Death's Mannikins, Blood on His Hands, The Dead Are Blind, The Sheep and the Wolves, Sinners in Paradise* and *Two Locked Room Mysteries and a Ripping Yarn* by one of Australia's finest mystery novelists.

More Secret Adventures of Sherlock Holmes — Gary Lovisi's second collection of tales about the unknown sides of the great detective.

Muddled Mind: Complete Works of Ed Wood, Jr. — David Hayes and Hayden Davis deconstruct the life and works of the mad, but canny, genius.

Murder among the Nudists — A mystery from 1934 by Peter Hunt, featuring a naked Detective-Inspector going undercover in a nudist colony.

Murder in Black and White — 1931 classic tennis whodunit by Evelyn Elder.

Murder in Shawnee — Two novels of the Alleghenies by John Douglas: *Shawnee Alley Fire* and *Haunts.*

Murder in Silk — A 1937 Yellow Peril novel of the silk trade by Ralph Trevor.

My Deadly Angel — 1955 Cold War drama by John Chelton.

My First Time: The One Experience You Never Forget — Michael Birchwood — 64 true first-person narratives of how they lost it.

Mysterious Martin, the Master of Murder — Two versions of a strange 1912 novel by Tod Robbins about a man who writes books that can kill.

Norman Berrow Novels — *The Bishop's Sword, Ghost House, Don't Go Out After Dark, Claws of the Cougar, The Smokers of Hashish, The Secret Dancer, Don't Jump Mr. Boland!, The Footprints of Satan, Fingers for Ransom, The Three Tiers of Fantasy, The Spaniard's Thumb, The Eleventh Plague, Words Have Wings, One Thrilling Night, The Lady's in Danger, It Howls at Night, The Terror in the Fog, Oil Under the Window, Murder in the Melody, The Singing Room.* This is the complete Norman Berrow library of classic locked-room mysteries, several of which are masterpieces.

Old Times' Sake — Short stories by James Reasoner from Mike Shayne Magazine.

Prose Bowl — Futuristic satire of a world where hack writing has replaced football as our national obsession, by Bill Pronzini and Barry N. Malzberg.

Red Light — The history of legal prostitution in Shreveport Louisiana by Eric Brock. Includes wonderful photos of the houses and the ladies.

Researching American-Made Toy Soldiers — A 276-page collection of a lifetime of articles by toy soldier expert Richard O'Brien.

Reunion in Hell — Volume One of the John H. Knox series of weird stories from the pulps. Introduced by horror expert John Pelan.

Ripped from the Headlines! — The Jack the Ripper story as told in the newspaper articles in the *New York* and *London Times.*

Robert Randisi Novels — *No Exit to Brooklyn* and *The Dead of Brooklyn.* The first two Nick Delvecchio novels.

Rough Cut & New, Improved Murder — Ed Gorman's first two novels.

Ruled By Radio — 1925 futuristic novel by Robert L. Hadfield & Frank E. Farncombe.

Rupert Penny Novels — *Policeman's Holiday, Policeman's Evidence, Lucky Policeman, Policeman in Armour, Sealed Room Murder, Sweet Poison, The Talkative Policeman, She had to Have Gas* and *Cut and Run* (by Martin Tanner.) Rupert Penny is the pseudonym of Australian Charles Thornett, a master of the locked room, impossible crime plot.

Sand's Game — Spectacular hard-boiled noir from Ennis Willie, edited by Lynn Myers and Stephen Mertz, with contributions from Max Allan Collins, Bill Crider, Wayne Dundee, Bill Pronzini, Gary Lovisi and James Reasoner.

Satan's Den Exposed — True crime in Truth or Consequences New Mexico — Award-winning journalism by the *Desert Journal*.

Gelett Burgess Novels — *The Master of Mysteries, The White Cat, Two O'Clock Courage, Ladies in Boxes, Find the Woman, The Heart Line, The Picaroons* and *Lady Mechante*. All are edited and introduced by Richard A. Lupoff.

Sam McCain Novels — Ed Gorman's terrific series includes *The Day the Music Died, Wake Up Little Susie* and *Will You Still Love Me Tomorrow?*

Sex Slave — Potboiler of lust in the days of Cleopatra by Dion Leclerq, 1966.

Shadows' Edge — Two early novels by Wade Wright: *Shadows Don't Bleed* and *The Sharp Edge*.

Sideslip — 1968 SF masterpiece by Ted White and Dave Van Arnam.

Slammer Days — Two full-length prison memoirs: *Men into Beasts* (1952) by George Sylvester Viereck and *Home Away From Home* (1962) by Jack Woodford.

Sorcerer's Chessmen — John Pelan introduces this 1939 classic by Mark Hansom.

Stakeout on Millennium Drive — Award-winning Indianapolis Noir by Ian Woollen.

Strands of the Web: Short Stories of Harry Stephen Keeler — Edited and Introduced by Fred Cleaver.

Suzy — A collection of comic strips by Richard O'Brien and Bob Vojtko from 1970.

Tales of the Macabre and Ordinary — Modern twisted horror by Chris Mikul, author of the *Bizarrism* series.

Tenebrae — Ernest G. Henham's 1898 horror tale brought back.

The Amorous Intrigues & Adventures of Aaron Burr — by Anonymous. Hot historical action about the man who almost became Emperor of Mexico.

The Anthony Boucher Chronicles — edited by Francis M. Nevins. Book reviews by Anthony Boucher written for the *San Francisco Chronicle*, 1942 – 1947. Essential and fascinating reading by the best book reviewer there ever was.

The Best of 10-Story Book — edited by Chris Mikul, over 35 stories from the literary magazine Harry Stephen Keeler edited.

The Black Dark Murders — Vintage 50s college murder yarn by Milt Ozaki, writing as Robert O. Saber.

The Book of Time — The classic novel by H.G. Wells is joined by sequels by Wells himself and three timely stories by Richard A. Lupoff. Lavishly illustrated by Gavin L. O'Keefe.

The Case of the Little Green Men — Mack Reynolds wrote this love song to sci-fi fans back in 1951 and it's now back in print.

The Case of the Withered Hand — 1936 potboiler by John G. Brandon.

The Charlie Chaplin Murder Mystery — A 2004 tribute by film scholar, Wes D. Gehring.

The Chinese Jar Mystery — Murder in the manor by John Stephen Strange, 1934.

The Compleat Calhoon — All of Fender Tucker's works: Includes *Totah Six-Pack, Weed, Women and Song* and *Tales from the Tower*, plus a CD of all of his songs.

The Compleat Ova Hamlet — Parodies of SF authors by Richard A. Lupoff. This is a brand new edition with more stories and more illustrations by Trina Robbins.

The Contested Earth and Other SF Stories — A never-before published space opera and seven short stories by Jim Harmon.

The Crimson Query — A 1929 thriller from Arlton Eadie. A perfect way to get introduced.

The Curse of Cantire — A classic 1939 novel of a family curse by Walter S. Masterman.

The Devil Drives — An odd prison and lost treasure novel from 1932 by Virgil Markham.

The Devil's Mistress — A 1915 Scottish gothic tale by J. W. Brodie-Innes, a member of Aleister Crowley's Golden Dawn.

The Dumpling — Political murder from 1907 by Coulson Kernahan.

The End of It All and Other Stories — Ed Gorman selected his favorite short stories for this huge collection.

The Ghost of Gaston Revere — From 1935, a novel of life and beyond by Mark Hansom, introduced by John Pelan.

The Gold Star Line — Seaboard adventure from L.T. Reade and Robert Eustace.

The Golden Dagger — 1951 Scotland Yard yarn by E. R. Punshon.

The Hairbreadth Escapes of Major Mendax — Francis Blake Crofton's 1889 boys' book.

The House of the Vampire — 1907 poetic thriller by George S. Viereck.

The Incredible Adventures of Rowland Hern — Intriguing 1928 impossible crimes by Nicholas Olde.

The Julius Caesar Murder Case — A classic 1935 re-telling of the assassination by Wallace Irwin that's much more fun than the Shakespeare version.

The Koky Comics — A collection of all of the 1978-1981 Sunday and daily comic strips by Richard O'Brien and Mort Gerberg, in two volumes.

The Lady of the Terraces — 1925 missing race adventure by E. Charles Vivian.

The Lord of Terror — 1925 mystery with master-criminal, Fantômas.

The N. R. De Mexico Novels — Robert Bragg, the real N.R. de Mexico, presents *Marijuana Girl, Madman on a Drum, Private Chauffeur* in one volume.

The Night Remembers — A 1991 Jack Walsh mystery from Ed Gorman.

The One After Snelling — Kickass modern noir from Richard O'Brien.

The Organ Reader — A huge compilation of just about everything published in the 1971-1972 radical bay-area newspaper, *THE ORGAN*. A coffee table book that points out the shallowness of the coffee table mindset.

The Poker Club — Three in one! Ed Gorman's ground-breaking novel, the short story it was based upon, and the screenplay of the film made from it.

The Private Journal & Diary of John H. Surratt — The memoirs of the man who conspired to assassinate President Lincoln.

The Secret Adventures of Sherlock Holmes — Three Sherlockian pastiches by the Brooklyn author/publisher, Gary Lovisi.

The Shadow on the House — Mark Hansom's 1934 masterpiece of horror is introduced by John Pelan.

The Sign of the Scorpion — A 1935 Edmund Snell tale of oriental evil.

The Singular Problem of the Stygian House-Boat — Two classic tales by John Kendrick Bangs about the denizens of Hades.

The Stench of Death: An Odoriferous Omnibus by Jack Moskovitz — Two complete novels and two novellas from 60's sleaze author, Jack Moskovitz.

The Time Armada — Fox B. Holden's 1953 SF gem.

The Tongueless Horror and Other Stories — Volume One of the series of short stories from the weird pulps by Wyatt Blassingame.

The Tracer of Lost Persons — From 1906, an episodic novel that became a hit radio series in the 30s. Introduced by Richard A. Lupoff.

The Trail of the Cloven Hoof — Diabolical horror from 1935 by Arlton Eadie. Introduced by John Pelan.

The Triune Man — Mindscrambling science fiction from Richard A. Lupoff.

The Universal Holmes — Richard A. Lupoff's 2007 collection of five Holmesian pastiches and a recipe for giant rat stew.

The Werewolf vs the Vampire Woman — Hard to believe ultraviolence by either Arthur M. Scarm or Arthur M. Scram.

The Whistling Ancestors — A 1936 classic of weirdness by Richard E. Goddard and introduced by John Pelan.

The White Peril in the Far East — Sidney Lewis Gulick's 1905 indictment of the West and assurance that Japan would never attack the U.S.

The Wizard of Berner's Abbey — A 1935 horror gem written by Mark Hansom and introduced by John Pelan.

Wade Wright Novels — *Echo of Fear, Death At Nostalgia Street, It Leads to Murder* and *Shadows' Edge*, a double book featuring *Shadows Don't Bleed* and *The Sharp Edge*.

Through the Looking Glass — Lewis Carroll wrote it; Gavin L. O'Keefe illustrated it.

Time Line — Ramble House artist Gavin O'Keefe selects his most evocative art inspired by the twisted literature he reads and designs.

Tiresias — Psychotic modern horror novel by Jonathan M. Sweet.

Totah Six-Pack — Just Fender Tucker's six tales about Farmington in one sleek volume.

Trail of the Spirit Warrior — Roger Haley's historical saga of life in the Indian Territories.

Ultra-Boiled — 23 gut-wrenching tales by our Man in Brooklyn, Gary Lovisi.

Up Front From Behind — A 2011 satire of Wall Street by James B. Kobak.

Victims & Villains — Intriguing Sherlockiana from Derham Groves.

Walter S. Masterman Novels — *The Green Toad, The Flying Beast, The Yellow Mistletoe, The Wrong Verdict, The Perjured Alibi, The Border Line* and *The Curse of Cantire*. Masterman wrote horror and mystery, some introduced by John Pelan.

We Are the Dead and Other Stories — Volume Two in the Day Keene in the Detective Pulps series, introduced by Ed Gorman. When done, there may be as many as 11 in the series.

West Texas War and Other Western Stories — by Gary Lovisi.

Whip Dodge: Man Hunter — Wesley Tallant's saga of a bounty hunter of the old West.

You'll Die Laughing — Bruce Elliott's 1945 novel of murder at a practical joker's English countryside manor.

RAMBLE HOUSE

Fender Tucker, Prop.   Gavin L. O'Keefe, Graphics
www.ramblehouse.com   fender@ramblehouse.com
228-826-1783   10329 Sheephead Drive, Vancleave MS 39565

Made in the USA
San Bernardino, CA
13 July 2020